AF179836

Studies in the Political Economy of Public Policy

Series Editors
Toby Carroll
Department of Asian and International Studies
City University of Hong Kong
Hong Kong

Paul Cammack
University of Manchester
Manchester, UK

Kelly Gerard
School of Social Sciences
The University of Western Australia
Crawley, Australia

Darryl S. L. Jarvis
Faculty of Liberal Arts and Social Sciences
The Education University of Hong Kong
Hong Kong

Studies in the Political Economy of Public Policy presents cutting edge, innovative research on the origins and impacts of public policy. Going beyond mainstream public policy debates, the series encourages heterodox and heterogeneous studies of sites of contestation, conflict and cooperation that explore policy processes and their consequences at the local, national, regional or global levels. Fundamentally pluralist in nature, the series is designed to provide high quality original research of both a theoretical and empirical nature that supports a global network of scholars exploring the implications of policy on society. The series is supported by a diverse international advisory board drawn from Asia, Europe, Australia, and North America, and welcomes manuscript submissions from scholars in the global South and North that pioneer new understandings of public policy.

International Advisory Board:
Caner Bakir, Koç University, Turkey
Jacqui Baker, Murdoch University, Australia
Shaun Breslin, University of Warwick, UK
Paul Cammack, University of Manchester, UK
Giliberto Capano, Bologna University, Italy
Sydney Calkin, University of Durham, UK
Paul Chambers, Naresuan University, Thailand
Barry Gills, University of Helsinki, Finland
Ruben Gonzalez-Vicente, Leiden University, The Netherlands
Paul K. Gellert, University of Tennessee, USA
Penny Griffin, University of New South Wales, Australia
M. Shamsul Haque, National University of Singapore, Singapore
Pascale Hatcher, University of Canterbury, New Zealand
Heng Yee Kuang, GraSPP, University of Tokyo, Japan
Kevin Hewison, Murdoch University, Australia
Wil Hout, Institute of Social Studies, Erasmus University, The Netherlands
Michael Howlett, Simon Fraser University, Canada
Kanishka Jayasuriya, University of Adelaide, Australia
Lee Jones, Quuen Mary University of London, UK
Zhang Jun, City University of Hong Kong, Hong Kong SAR
Max Lane, Victoria University, Australia
Kun-chin Lin, University of Cambridge, UK
Adrienne Roberts, University of Manchester, UK
Stuart Shields, University of Manchester, UK
Richard Stubbs, McMaster University, Canada
Silke Trommer, University of Manchester, UK
Philippe Zittoun, Science Po, Grenoble, France
All books in the series are subject to Palgrave's rigorous peer review process: https://www.palgrave.com/gb/demystifying-peer-review/792492.

More information about this series at
http://www.palgrave.com/gp/series/14465

Michael Peters

Regulating the Rise of China

Australia's Foray into Middle Power Economics

palgrave
macmillan

Michael Peters
School of Social Sciences
University of New South Wales
Kensington, NSW, Australia

ISSN 2524-7441 ISSN 2524-745X (electronic)
Studies in the Political Economy of Public Policy
ISBN 978-3-030-05465-6 ISBN 978-3-030-05466-3 (eBook)
https://doi.org/10.1007/978-3-030-05466-3

Library of Congress Control Number: 2018963735

© The Editor(s) (if applicable) and The Author(s), under exclusive license to Springer Nature Switzerland AG 2019
This work is subject to copyright. All rights are solely and exclusively licensed by the Publisher, whether the whole or part of the material is concerned, specifically the rights of translation, reprinting, reuse of illustrations, recitation, broadcasting, reproduction on microfilms or in any other physical way, and transmission or information storage and retrieval, electronic adaptation, computer software, or by similar or dissimilar methodology now known or hereafter developed.
The use of general descriptive names, registered names, trademarks, service marks, etc. in this publication does not imply, even in the absence of a specific statement, that such names are exempt from the relevant protective laws and regulations and therefore free for general use.
The publisher, the authors and the editors are safe to assume that the advice and information in this book are believed to be true and accurate at the date of publication. Neither the publisher nor the authors or the editors give a warranty, expressed or implied, with respect to the material contained herein or for any errors or omissions that may have been made. The publisher remains neutral with regard to jurisdictional claims in published maps and institutional affiliations.

Photo credit: Toby Carroll

This Palgrave Macmillan imprint is published by the registered company Springer Nature Switzerland AG
The registered company address is: Gewerbestrasse 11, 6330 Cham, Switzerland

Acknowledgements

My thanks to Elizabeth Thurbon and William Clapton for their wisdom, insights, and patience over the last four years.

Thanks also to the postgraduates of Morvern Brown for their company and to Patrick Richardson who has been an enormous support.

Finally, many thanks to my parents, who have always been enormously supportive of all my endeavours.

CONTENTS

Acronyms

ABARES	Australian Bureau of Agriculture and Resource Economic and Science
ABC	Australian Broadcasting Corporation
ABrA	Australian Broadcasting Authority
ACBC	Australia–China Business Council
ACCC	Australian Consumer and Competition Commission
ACT	Australian Capital Territory
AFIP	Australian Foreign Investment Policy
AIDC	Australian Industry Development Corporation
ANZUS	Australia, New Zealand, United States Security Treaty
APEC	Asia-Pacific Economic Cooperation
APRA	Australian Prudential Regulation Authority
ASEAN	Association of South East Asian Nations
ASEAN+3	Association of South East Asian Nations plus the People's Republic of China, Japan, and Korea
ASIC	Australian Securities and Investment Commission
ATO	Australian Taxation Office
AUSFTA	Australia–United States Free Trade Agreement
AUSTRAC	Australian Transactions Reports and Analysis Centre
CBRC	China Banking Regulation Commission
CCP	China Communist Party
CEO	Chief Executive Officer
Chinalco	Aluminium Corporation of China
CIC	China Investment Corporation
CIRC	China Insurance Regulatory Commission
CISA	China Iron and Steel Association

CNMC	China Nonferrous Metals (Group) Co.
COFT	Committee on Foreign Takeovers
CRA	Consolidated Zinc Corporation or Conzinc Rio Tinto of Australia Ltd.
DFAT	Department of Foreign Affairs and Trade
FATA 1975	*The Foreign Acquisition and Takeovers 1975*
FATR 1989	*Foreign Acquisitions and Takeovers Regulations 1989*
FDI	Foreign Direct Investment
FIC	Foreign Investment Committee
FID	Foreign Investment Division
FIRB	Foreign Investment Review Board
FSF	Financial Stability Forum
FTA 1972	*Companies (Foreign Takeovers) Act 1972*
FTA	Free Trade Agreement
GATT	General Agreement on Tariffs and Trade
GDP	Gross Domestic Product
IAC	Industries Assistance Commission
IMF	International Monetary Fund
MLC	Mutual Life and Citizens Assurance Co. Ltd.
MOFCOM	Ministry of Commerce of the People's Republic of China
MOFERT	Ministry of Foreign Economic Relations and Trade of the People's Republic of China
MOFTEC	Ministry of Foreign Trade and Economic Cooperation of the People's Republic of China
NCC	National Competition Commission
NCSC	National Companies and Securities Commission
NDRC	National Development and Reform Commission of the People's Republic of China
NIAB	National Investment Advisory Board
NSCC	National Security Committee of Cabinet
OECD	Organisation for Economic Cooperation and Development
PB	Financing provided by China's two policy banks: the China Development Bank and the China Export-Import Bank
PJT	Prices Justification Tribunal
PM&C	Department of Prime Minister and Cabinet
SAEC	State Administration of Exchange Control
SAFE	State Administration and Foreign Exchange
SASAC	State Asset Supervision and Administration Commission
SCB	State-Owned Commercial Bank
SGAEC	State General Administration for Exchange Control
SOE	Sovereign Owned Enterprise

SWF	Sovereign Wealth Fund
TPC	Trade Practices Commission
UN	United Nations
US	United States
VDR	Variable Deposit Requirement
WTO	World Trade Organisation

List of Figures

List of Tables

CHAPTER 1

Introduction

On the 31st of January 2008, the largest ever hostile share acquisition in the history of the London Exchange was launched by a Chinese Sovereign-Owned Enterprise (SOE), Aluminium Corp. of China (Chinalco). Valued at $AU15.5 billion, Chinalco's team of brokers at Lehman Brothers acquired 12% of the London-listed Rio Tinto shares—9% of the total listed shares—of the dual-listed Australian–British iron ore producer (Bream et al., 2 February 2008). The funds came from the state-owned and -directed China Development Bank (Uren 2012, 70), with an American aluminium producer, Alcoa, providing 10% of the stake as well. The raid was a response to an offer in November 2007 from BHP-Billiton to merge with Rio Tinto, a proposal to bring the two largest Australian mining companies under one roof. In China, this prospect was not received well. Fearing a situation where a single firm supplied 40% of China's iron ore imports (Uren 2012, 67), He Liangzhou, head of the Foreign Capital Department in the most powerful state economic agency in China, the Development and Reform Commission (NDRC), convened a meeting between himself and the leaders of China's largest coal producer, Shenhua, steel producer, Baosteel, and aluminium producer, Chinalco to discuss "countermeasures" (Uren 2012, 69). The "Dawn Raid" was the result.

Chinalco did not notify the Australian government of their intentions before the coup. Instead, having succeeded in reaching his target by 10 p.m. London time, the President of Chinalco, Xiao Yaqing,

© The Author(s) 2019

M. Peters, *Regulating the Rise of China*, Studies in the Political Economy of Public Policy, https://doi.org/10.1007/978-3-030-05466-3_1

waited seven hours until the Australian market closed and then called the Australian Secretary of the Treasury, Ken Henry, to inform him of the raid and signal Chinalco's intention to submit an investment proposal to the Australian Foreign Investment Review Board (FIRB) (Uren 2012, 70; Leaver and Ungerer 2010, 17). He advised the Australian and British media that the investment was entirely Chinalco's own decision (Roberts and Tschang, 6 February 2008) and that the stake was a "strategic financial instrument" rather than a precursor to a full takeover bid by the Chinese Government, or a manoeuvre aimed at blocking the BHP-Billiton takeover (Freed, 5 February 2008).

Seventeen days after the raid, the Australian Government responded. Treasurer Wayne Swan announced six explicit guidelines for foreign investment proposal reviews (outlined in detail in Chapter 2, Sect. 2.3). Though the government claimed that these did not introduce any changes to the policy but merely clarified it, the "February Guidelines" were nonetheless widely interpreted as signalling a new concern about and scrutiny of SOE investments in light of risks associated with state ownership (Wilson 2011, 287). Contributing to this impression, the Treasurer demanded that ten Chinese investments in the mining sector that had been approved in the three months the government had been in office were resubmitted to the FIRB for approval with extra information pertaining to the role of the Chinese state in their operations (Hewett, 25 April 2008).

In fact, the main effect of the Guidelines was to confuse commentators (Kirchner 2008a, 8; Golding and Bassil 2008, 177–178; ITS Global 2008, 12–13). It was not clear why the Guidelines had been released at all. While the Australian Foreign Direct Investment (FDI) screening regime had been criticised for many years as opaque and inefficient (for example, *Financial Times* 2005), the Guidelines not only failed to respond to these criticisms, but actually added further ambiguities. The first guideline signalled a renewed emphasis of scrutiny on the relationship between a foreign investor and the government of the state from which they originate, but this had been a part of the Policy for at least two decades (Uren 2012, 234). Guidelines two and three—that investors must adhere to the law and that investments would be examined in terms of their competition-hindering effects—were redundant; the second obviously so, and the third already enforced by the Australian Consumer and Competition Commission (ACCC) operating under the *Trade Practices Act 1974*. The fifth guideline—that the government reserves the right to prevent investments that may threaten national security—could reasonably be assumed given similar provisions that exist in every equivalent economy. Finally, the fourth and sixth guidelines—that investments may impact upon Australian Government revenue or the operations of Australian businesses—were so vague as to be virtually meaningless. Any investment is likely to affect the Australian government revenue and is likely to affect the operations or direction of an Australian business. The inclusion of these points provided no basis for a prospective investor to decide whether or not to register a proposal. It could be argued that this ambiguity empowered the Government to conduct investment screening with greater flexibility, but as I will show in Chapter 2, but even then, the institutional arrangements the Rudd Government inherited already afforded the government a remarkably large degree of flexibility. The question remains: why draw the issue on to the public agenda at all?

Once the issue had been placed on the agenda, it was difficult to remove. Whether intended or not, SOE investment came to be one of the defining controversies of the Rudd Government's interaction with its Chinese counterpart, and a number of interest groups and political factions swooped on the issue as a rallying device. On one side of the debate was a loose coalition bemoaning the inadequacy of the Government's efforts to protect Australian interests from sinister foreigners. The coalition drew together the federal Liberal-National Opposition and the federal Green Party—an unusual alliance in Australian politics—as well as the West Australian Premier, Colin Barnett (Wilson 2011, 287; see also the contribution from BHP-Billiton CEO Don Argus in Uren 2012, 95, and Wines 2009). On the other side, a more wonkish coalition of the Australian Business Council, commentators in thinktanks like the Lowy Institute and Centre for Independent Studies (Cook and Thirlwell 2008; Thirlwell and Shearer 2008; ITS Global 2008; Larum 2011), consultants in the "Australia's Open Investment Future" Group (Rae 2008; Makin 2008; Novak 2008), as well as many mining firms and Chinese investors themselves (Wilson 2011, 289) argued that the economic activity was over-regulated, and that Australia and its firms were paying real costs in terms of foregone capital as a result of the inefficient regime (see also Kirchner 2008a, b, 2009a, b, 2012, 2014; Drysdale and Findlay 2009; Drysdale 2011; Berg 2012). Finally, the Chinese ambassador in Canberra published an opinion piece in *The Australian*, insisting that the Chinese investments were not politically motivated, or indeed controlled, by the state (Zhang 2009). In short, the policy, at first glance appears to be an own goal: an unnecessary intervention that was both economically and politically costly.

In this book, I will argue that the changes made to the FDI screening policy by the Rudd Government policy occupied a central position in the Australian Government's engagement with China, and a constituted a central plank in its response to the geopolitical changes occurring in the region as a result of China's rise. The key research questions that guide the study are: first, why did the Australian Government pursue the policy, in spite of widespread criticism and in the face of an orthodox view that the economic costs to the country were high? Alternatively phrased, why did the key policymakers understand Chinese SOE investments as so much of a threat that such costly intervention was deemed necessary? Second, what does the policy imply about the Australian understanding of its relationship with China and its interests in relation to the changes occurring in the region? Third, given the creativity of the Rudd Government in using a tool of economic regulation to pursue foreign policy aims, what does this innovation imply about the trajectory of Australian statecraft? Finally, how can we theorise the problems faced by the Australian Government in light of a deepening integration of the liberal Australian economy and the much larger illiberal Chinese one? My account of the policy suggests that the key policymakers in the Rudd Government understood these problems as having profound importance for Australia's interests, and its position in the world. I analyse and evaluate this claim, and employ Foucauldian governmentality as a theoretical framework to do this.

1.1 The Existing Accounts

There are currently five schools of explanation of the Rudd Government's FDI screening policy. The first account of the policy is the one that the government itself provided. It was claimed the policy changes were not substantive; they were in line with the practices of Australian governments before them (Swan 2008a, b; Rudd 2008a). This is not convincing and an extensive description of the changes that did occur is available in Chapter 3.

The second school of thought holds that the FDI policy was an ad hoc response to an unexpected politicisation of the issue of foreign investment in Australia (Drysdale and Findlay 2009). This line is accompanied by the criticism that the "additions" to the national interest test that appeared in the February Guidelines unnecessarily added uncertainty to the FDI screening regime and policy debate. The most immediate problem with this account is that even if the February Guidelines had been an ad hoc response, there is the subsequent two and a half years of execution of the policy still to be explained. The explanation carries an implied addendum that the government refused to adjust the initial ad hoc settings for the twenty-eight months following February 2008 out of stubbornness. The account is also unconvincingly narrow. Both Kevin Rudd and Wayne Swan spent significant time in China personally; Rudd devoted high-profile speeches to the Australia–China relationship, and invested significant political capital to negotiation rounds of the prospective China–Australia Free Trade Agreement. As I will show in Chapter 5, Rudd had a sophisticated and coherent agenda for Australia's engagement with China. It is not believable that either Rudd or Swan would not appreciate the significance of the issue of foreign investment to the overall relationship, or determine this policy only in relation to domestic concerns.

The third school of thought is that the policy was resource nationalist in character. Wilson (2011, 285) defines resource nationalism as natural resource-endowed states using their legal jurisdiction over resources to achieve national development goals that would not be obtained if the exploitation were left to international market processes. In the crude form of this argument, the screening regime was used as a "mechanism for political intervention in the market for the ownership and control of Australian equity" (Kirchner 2009b; see also Kirchner 2008a). As I show in Chapter 2, Sect. 2.3, there is little evidence of the Australian Government using FDI controls to leverage a greater share of Australian ownership—the regime as a whole was remarkably liberal, and there were no conditions placed in approvals—with one exception—that pursued non-ownership goals; that is, restricting exports or requiring firms to engage in downstream manufacturing activities.

Wilson (2011) provides a compelling case against the account of the FDI policy as resource nationalist, and offers a fourth explanation of the policy: that it was "resource liberal" in nature. That is, that the aims of the Australian Government were limited to "defensively attempting to neutralise the potential for non-commercial behaviour by Chinese SOEs, rather than any broader efforts to restrict their entry into the

Australian mining industry or to distort the operation of international market mechanisms in line with politically mandated national goals" (Wilson 2011, 297). While this is a much more convincing argument than Kirchner's, both accounts are problematically narrow. If the aim was to limit the behaviour of Chinese SOEs to market-conforming behaviour, why use the politically and technically awkward policy tool of the FIRB and at-the-border controls? The policing of market-conforming behaviour could have been left to regulatory institutions better suited to the task, most obviously the ACCC. This would have resulted in less confrontation with the Chinese state, and quite likely significantly more foreign capital flowing to Australia (see ITS Global 2008; Kirchner 2008a, b, 2009a, b, 2012, 2014; Novak 2008; Rae 2008; Makin 2008; Drysdale and Findlay 2009; Drysdale 2011; Larum 2011). Missing from both of these accounts is a relationship from the FDI policy to the government's larger strategy on the China relationship. Missing also is an account of the significance of the firms being Chinese. Without these, the policy cannot appear as anything but illogical: the "problem" of Chinese SOE collaboration can only be the highly improbable potential for an amalgamation of all the Chinese interests into a single "China Inc." firm. Without collaboration, the threat is limited to vertical integration by Chinese steelmakers, which is immediately dispelled first by the difficulty the Chinese firms would have in concealing these practices, and second by the behind-the-border regulatory tools that already existed to deal with such practices. I will argue that neither of these threats capture the problem as Rudd and Swan understood it.

The fifth and final school situates the policy within a geopolitical context. These accounts are rare. One example is Leaver and Ungerer (2010), who bemoan the "underdevelopment" of resource diplomacy as a concept in Australia's strategic posture, and urge policymakers to use "the supply of key commodities as part of a broader set of national instruments to chase export opportunities and to strengthen key strategic relationships" (2010, 3). This is not enormously useful, as the argument is essentially made in the negative: Leaver and Ungerer's implied account of the Rudd government's FDI policy was that it was limited to defensive resource liberalism, as per Wilson's (2011) account but *should* have been otherwise. Nonetheless, again it provides a useful articulation of a more convincing strategy for the FDI policy, should we interpret it as resource nationalist in character. A second work that explicitly connects the FDI screening policy with geopolitical machinations comes from Beeson et al. (2011). They place the issue of ownership of the resource sector, along with taxation, as the two primary impacts of China's rise on Australia's domestic politics (2011, 1374). They argue that China's rise to Australia's most important trade partner has not transformed Australia's strategic orientation, and that Rudd's entire strategy of "Asia engagement" was based on a desire to "contain" China. In this context, the need to pursue and protect "national interests" in the new (global) resource politics is a "potentially zero-sum contest" (2011, 1383) for resource-rich nations like Australia, but in the final analysis, "both ends of this unlikely pairing [China and Australia] have little option other than to make it work" (2011, 1383) and "[i]n the resource politics of the twenty-first century, material forces may trump ideological ones" (2011, 1384). While this usefully provides a geopolitical account of the policy—that targeting Chinese investments was a piece in a larger containment strategy—it is underdeveloped as an argument. The closest the authors come to explaining the direct relationship is to say that the backlash against foreign ownership in Australia forty years ago during the Japanese industrialisation-led resource boom is complicated in this iteration by the resource sector becoming "an even more important part of Australia's overall economic profile" and the fact "that it is 'communist China' rather than the United States or even Japan that is the economic partner driving policy responses" (2011, 1372). Without a clear articulation of why the FDI screening moves advanced any particular geopolitical aim, this account is not convincing. After all, the screening did not stop Chinese SOEs making significant investments in Australia or prevent Australian ore being sold to Chinese steelmakers.

Considered together, the existing accounts of the policy share three shortcomings. First, they understand the problem being solved in overly proximate terms. That is, they fail to articulate a compelling relationship from the policy to the larger engagement with China by Australia. In the accounts where the policy is related to geopolitical aims, there is an oversimplification of Australia's engagement. Based on a narrative of Australia being wedged between its primary security ally, the United States, and its largest economic partner, China, it is deduced that any move that impedes Chinese interests can be understood as strategic balancing or containment. These arguments are not convincing. The FDI screening did not prevent Chinese SOEs making significant investments in Australia or prevent Australian ore being sold to Chinese steelmakers. In fact, implicitly or explicitly, all the accounts that understand the policy as an exercise in the containment of China rest on claims of incompetence on behalf of the policymakers: using FDI screening as a containment strategy would not only be ineffective given the small material cost imposed on the Chinese state from the actions of the policy, but it would also involve significant costs for Australia. First, there would then be the loss of investment capital, both from China and then other sources as global investors repriced the sovereign risk associated with investing in Australia, as well as loss of trade opportunities with China. In addition, there would be costs associated with contravening the OECD guidelines on foreign investment governance (see Rae 2008). In fact, most of these accounts go beyond mere incompetence as their key explanatory cause, and assert that the key policymakers were either illegitimately meddlesome or outright xenophobic. My account removes the necessity of any of these claims: there was a coherent, well-developed logic linking a policy problem with a solution.

The second shortcoming of the existing accounts is their retainment of a liberal image of the world. As I discuss in Sect. 1.1, the liberal understanding of the world takes for granted that the economic realm contains its own self-conditioning and -perpetuating structure and logic. Divisions in the social reality, such as the economic from the political or the geopolitical or the private realm from the public, appear as natural and given. I will argue that as a result of these assumptions, the existing accounts of the policy collectively lack a language to describe the precise threat that Chinese SOE investment posed to the Australian state. Lacking an articulation of any problem that needed solving, these accounts "discover" that the Government's intervention was unnecessary. This does not stem from a positive argument that the problem being solved was not worthwhile, but rather the assumption that it did not exist. To overcome this problem, I will employ Foucault's governmental framework, which takes the criticism of liberal knowledge and arrangement of society as its starting point.

The third shortcoming of the existing accounts, which stems from the first two problems, is the inadequate integration of political, economic, geopolitical, and ideological aspects of the policy. These are treated statically and as if they are unrelated realms. This again undermines the commentators' abilities to access the policy problem as it was defined by the policy's creators. In each of the accounts, the analysts determine for themselves which realm to situate the policy in, and examine the ramifications of the policy in this realm in isolation. As a political stunt, the policy appears as an unforced own goal. As a piece of economic policy, the intervention appears costly and ineffective, not to mention illiberal. As geopolitical posturing, the intervention appears ham-fisted and ineffectual, neither employing Australia's power resources to gain any strategic benefit, nor limiting China's interests in any meaningful way. In my account, the political, economic, geopolitical, and ideological elements of the policy are inextricably intertwined.

1.2 My Account

Instead of trying to work out whether the issue being managed in the FDI screening policy was related to economic regulation or a broader geopolitical strategy, my account holds that the economic, security, and ideological aspects of the policy must be considered in conjunction with one another. The problem posed by the large-scale entry of Chinese SOEs into the Australian economy was that these firms, by dint of their relationship with the Chinese state, had competitive advantages over their rival Australian and international firms. Most importantly, their advantage was access to discounted capital from two Chinese development banks and the Chinese state-run financial system. While the operations of the SOEs were not directed by the Chinese state, they were incentivised financially to pursue investments that were of strategic significance to the Chinese economy. The SOEs were motivated by the generation of profits, and did not collaborate or have any intention to collaborate in the future. Nonetheless, they interacted with their state on a wholly different basis to that of Australian or international firms operating within the Australian economy.

The appearance of a set of firms in the Australian economy that related to the state on a different basis from the liberal Australian and international firms was understood as a threat to the integrity of Australian markets and to the political and economic sovereignty of the Australian Government. These terms—"political sovereignty" and "economic sovereignty"—were produced by Kevin Rudd (2001, 2010) and Wayne Swan (2009) respectively. They referred to the ability of the Australian nation and government to determine the political and economic formations that populated its own society. Most importantly, this threatened the integrity of the relationship from liberal economic governor to liberal economic subject.

To put this in more concrete terms, if a certain set of firms approached the market with a set of advantages, meaning they faced a different set of conditions from all other firms that interacted with the various markets for capital, resources, and labour, this would undermine the empirical and moral bases of the market-based production and distribution systems. It would not be possible to retain the claim that market-based structures of resource allocation were the most efficient. This would undermine the legitimacy of the market, and with it the credibility of the Australian Government, based, as it is in this respect, on the capacity to determine and regulate these economic structures. The outcome of this legitimacy breakdown would be a demand for the Australian government to even the playing field. Either, the Australian state could prevent Chinese SOEs from operating in the Australian economy or it would need to provide Australian firms some form of countervailing discount on capital in order to keep the conditions faced by these firms on par with the Chinese SOEs. The second path was not an inviting prospect. What instrument would best be used? What firms would be eligible for discounted rates? The line between domestic and multinational firms is not always clear. Perhaps most pertinently, what funds would be used to pursue this balancing policy? To enter a bidding match with the Chinese state, the owner of the largest current account surplus and foreign exchange reserves in history, was not a tenable solution. On the other hand, to disallow Chinese SOE investment in Australia entirely would entail foregoing much-needed capital, and entering into protracted and costly political conflicts with both the Chinese state and the Australian mining sector.

In the face of this dilemma, the Rudd Government produced a creative and multifaceted response. It selected FDI screening as a discrete and malleable policy lever that could be used to allow Chinese SOEs entry to the economy, while using these investments to signal to investors and the Chinese state the concerns and interests of the Australian Government. While the SOE investments themselves would be regulated more stringently than any other class, the Prime Minister and Treasurer embarked on a campaign aimed at using Australia's control over vital economic resources to engage China in a conversation on the need to embrace a market-based regional economy. While control over raw resources was the entry point for the Australian Government to place this deep question of the nature of the region on the international agenda, the aim was to convince Chinese state actors and investors of the mutual and long-term benefits of market-based structures. The policy was at once economic, geopolitical, and deeply ideological. These elements cannot be extricated from one another.

1.3 The Argument

My contention in this book is that the relationships between the economic, geopolitical, and ideological aspects of the Rudd Government's FDI screening policy are best understood using Foucault's account of the "governmental" state. Governmentality offers a language and a set of analytical devices that transcend the divides between these realms that exist in liberal political theory. While I generate my explanation of the policy from the statements and logics of the policymakers themselves, I do not contend at all that these actors identified themselves as governmentalists. Rather, I use the framework as a set of second-order constructs that can be used to explain their understanding of the problem being faced and the solution produced.

Foucault's governmental work takes a criticism of liberal knowledge as its starting point. The foundational moves are a rejection of the ontic nature of the state, the economy, and the subjects and objects which constitute the modern political state and society. These are instead treated as produced via historical contests understood as relating at once to knowledge production and power. The foundational aims of liberalism—the set of freedoms afforded to the citizen in a relationship with each other and the state—are reimagined in terms of their technical aspects. Each freedom is considered in terms of its place as an enabling condition of a particular mode of governance. Governmentality is well-placed, I argue, to consider the engagement of the Australian liberal system with the Chinese system, which in important respects is not liberal (though the point is complicated). It does not suffer from the same issues of narrowness that I have criticised the existing accounts (which take liberal beliefs as assumptions) for.

Secondly, beyond providing a set of tools to interrogate and criticise liberal theory and statecraft, governmentality offers a positive alternative account of the state. Foucault understands the state not as a coherent actor, or even institution, but a field of technologies, apparatuses, and dispositifs that are constituted in such a way that they enable a diverse set of actors to pursue a diverse set of strategies of governance. As I have noted above, governmental technologies and apparatuses do not appear within liberal theory. This is due to the clear divide liberalism posits between the state and the realm it oversees. The apparatuses of governmentality sit uncomfortably astride this divide: they are both of the state and of the governed space. Only through the use of such an analytical device is it possible to understand the Rudd Government's claim that the Chinese SOEs' threat to the Australian minerals markets constituted a threat to Australian sovereignty.

Thirdly, governmentality offers an alternative set of questions to ask of a social phenomenon. These can be summarised as an interest primarily in the "how questions" of power and of governance. Instead of taking the objects, subjects, and knowledge that appears within a social phenomenon as more or less given, the approach demands that attention is payed instead to how these came to exist in the forms and constellation that they do. Again, given that the FDI policy in the final account spoke to the constitution of the Australian economy, the nature of the firms that were allowed to operate in it, and the relation from the knowledge elements on which these things rested related to questions of state sovereignty and strategy, governmentality offers a valuable set of tools for pursuing these lines of inquiry.

In relation to the policy directly, governmentality offers a set of concepts that allow me to articulate the threat to the Australian political and economic system as a whole. From a governmental perspective, the market belongs neither to the state nor to its domain. It is a constellation of actors, milieus, and ideas. The relationship between the economic subjects that operate in it and the governors that regulate it is internal to the constellation as a whole, and the capacity of the state to determine the structures of the market—Australia's economic sovereignty—is likewise an internal component of the entire edifice. Understanding the securitised object in terms of this unity, and with a view to the role of knowledge and values such as legitimacy and credibility in the integrity of the whole, allows me to articulate an account of the FDI policy that coherently links a threat to the integrity of Australian market-based structures to the actions taken by the Rudd Government to preserve them, one that does not rest on the irrationality of the policymakers.

My account has two key empirical points of significance. First, as I have noted, it places FDI screening at the heart of the Rudd Government's engagement with China. This is novel in the history of the policy regime itself, and marks a larger divergence in the path of "creative" diplomacy of the Australian state. In Chapter 5, I will place the move within the ambitions of Rudd to return Australian foreign policy to a footing of "creative middle power diplomacy" (Rudd 2008b, c). This entails an activist predisposition and a state aim of constantly seeking out future threats and risks in order to take preventative action before issues arise. Rudd's commitment to middle power diplomacy in the region was deeply held (see Rudd 2001, 2004, 2007; discussed in detail in Chapter 5). The most important initiatives were his stillborn Asia-Pacific Society, the centrality of his role in the response to the Global Financial Crisis in the G20, and the increases in defence funding that occurred under his watch. My account of the foreign investment policy suggests that the ambitions and policy tools the Government was willing to use in the aim of middle power diplomacy were much broader than has so far been recognised. My account suggests that Kevin Rudd and Wayne Swan understood Australia's control over raw resources vital to the comprehensive economic security of major powers in the region afforded them strategic leverage. They used this leverage to initiate a dialogue with China about the nature of the Australia–China relationship, and the rules underpinning the regional economic order. The ramifications of the FDI screening moves at their highest level related to an appreciation that the region was undergoing a major transition and attempted to allow Australia a place to negotiate its future.

Secondly, my account suggests that the FDI screening policy can be used to articulate more precisely the nature of the economic-security nexus in the Australian engagement with China. Where the Australian popular and academic commentary on the significance of the rise of China has been limited to two dominant—unchallengeable even—stories that remain strangely unconnected to each other. On the one hand, it is claimed that the rise of China has offered Australia an extraordinary economic opportunity, a bottomless source of demand for raw resources, as well as education, financial and legal services. On the other, China's rise is treated as a security threat, both directly and as a growing rivalry with the US that destabilises the region. This is unsatisfying. The disconnection between these two beliefs means that every new development in the relationship is met with confusion: there is no possibility of examining with any clarity the interests of Australia as every event is treated as a trade-off between economic benefit and security consternation, and the values of Australia's interest in relation of these to each other are not specified at the marginal level. In the Rudd Government's FDI policy, we can see the relationship between the economic and security aims.

Heightened economic integration was welcomed, but only on the basis that it did not undermine the integrity of Australian economic systems, and the capacity of the Australian Government to determine unilaterally the nature of its own economic system. This latter concern was termed "economic sovereignty" (Swan, 10 December 2009). The security concern is intertwined with the economic one: the securitised object is an economic system and an economic governance arrangement. It rests on the treatment of these objects as based both on an arrangement of forces as well as collectively produced and accepted knowledge. On this basis, I will argue that the security-economic nexus must properly be understood as a triangle of economy-security-ideology. The value of understanding this is that the "problem" of the rise of China, and Australia's interests in relation to it is just as pertinent today as it was in 2007. While the academic community has failed to consider seriously the ambitions of the Rudd Government in terms of actively shaping a new regional economic-security-ideological order, the importance of the task has not faded.

In fact, the significance of the Australian experience has grown even more sharply in recent years as the Chinese move into outward financial projection has increased, and as further liberal countries have responded by securitising the issue in different ways. The United States, for example, in the context of a shift from strategic engagement with China to strategic competition, has recently passed the Foreign Investment Risk Review Modernisation Act. The Act, which received bipartisan support, was "driven by fears of a rising China" and "strengthens the role of the Department of Defense and the intelligence community in deciding who should, or should not, be allowed to invest in the US" (Foroohar 2018). Similar discussions are being had in Canada, the UK, across Europe and in the Asia-Pacific itself. Australia, due to its wealth in resources that were vital for a key and dramatic stage of Chinese industrialisation, serves as a canary in the coal mine for responding to Chinese outward foreign investment. Obviously each of these cases is different, and each state's reaction is shaped by a set of unique interplay of economic, geopolitical, and political interests. What I aim to provide policymakers in other respondent states is not a policy prescription, but rather a language in which to conceptualise and consider these intertwining interests. The Australian response was not "successful" in any straightforward, simplistic sense, but it was deeply considered, I will argue, and understood China's move to outward investment as a substantial change to the global and regional orders.

There are two key theoretical results of the study. It suggests first that governmentality provides accurate insights into the modern liberal state and, second, that the approach offers value in analysing specific policy contests. Governmentality has so far been used primarily to conduct critical studies into relatively abstract components of modern economic and political life, such the centrality of risk (De Geode 2005) and uncertainty (Tellmann 2007) to the ordering of economic rationality, or the role technologies such as statistics (Miller and Rose 1990) or accounting (Rose 1999) in acting as conditions of economic and political actions. In this book, I explore the possibility of using Foucault's framework for analysing more localised phenomena, and for using it to conduct inquiries into state policymaking, in spite of its foundation as an anti-state ideology (Foucault 1978, 89). While there is development of the theory needed, as I discuss in Sect. 1.1 (iv), I argue that both of these uses are possible.

The account is based predominantly on two discourse analyses, the results of which are presented in Chapters 4 (Discourses of Economics) and 5 (Discourses of Security). Using techniques derived from post-structural policy analysis and narrative-based policy analysis, I identify the economic and security logics that the policy rested on. The speeches are drawn primarily from public actors due to the large degree of autonomy that the executive wing of the Australian government had over the policy, but these are supplemented with speeches from commentators outside of government, as per the instruction of Howarth and Griggs (2012; discussed in Sect. 1.2) to take the commentary of a policy as internal to the object being examined and explained. The two discourse analyses are brought together in Chapter 6 to produce a coherent account of the policy that encompasses the logics produced in the two realms, and removes the artificial delineation.

1.4 Outline of the Book

In Chapter 1, I describe governmentality as an alternative theory of the state and as a mode of analytics. I place the framework within Foucault's larger body of work in order to lay the epistemological and ontological foundations of my argument. I examine two issues with using governmentality to do international relations policymaking work: the ambiguous treatments of the domains of the economic and the international. While the framework understands the divisions of these from other domains of the social, the internal workings and nature of both have not been theorised. I conclude that these are problems for the approach, but that governmentality provides the tools necessary to overcome these problems for the purposes of my study. I then describe the steps of Howarth and Griggs' (2012) method for poststructural policy analysis from which I derive the structure of my argument, and the methodological tools taken from postpositivist policymaking studies and narrative-based discourse analysis, which I use in the two discourse analysis chapters that constitute the primary data of the argument. I explain the use of discourse analysis as a method and my selection of texts.

Chapters 2 and 3 compose my initial problematisation of the policy. In Chapter 2, I trace the genealogy of the policy problems that foreign investment screening has been used to resolve in Australia since the practice began at the federal level in the late 1960s. This is done to identify the departure that the Rudd Government made from the existing policy regime in thematic terms. I then describe the institutional, legislative and policy settings that were inherited by the Rudd government and the ways the Rudd Government's actions constituted a departure from these. In Chapter 3, I examine in detail the wave of Chinese SOE investments that the policy departure responded to. I describe the precise relationship between the Chinese state and the SOEs, and the economic significance of the investments for the Chinese and Australian economies. Following the instructions of Howarth and Griggs (2012), as a final step in the problematisation, I re-examine the existing accounts of the policy. As the aim of a poststructural policymaking study involves articulating the conditions of the phenomenon, some of which are ideological, the study is considered inherently imminent. As a result, in Howarth and Griggs' approach, the existing accounts of a policy are reimagined as internal to the phenomena being examined. In an expansion of the comments made above, I identify the liberal foundations of the existing accounts. This is then used as a point of departure for my own examination.

Chapters 4 and 5 are composed of two discourse analyses. In Chapter 4, I examine the statements made by official actors that situate the policy as one of economic regulation. The aim of the chapter is to deconstruct individual speeches using the tools of postpositivist policymaking and narrative-based discourse analysis and then reconstruct a narrative for the policy linking an economic problem with a set of actions taken by the government that resolved it. I argue that the aim of the policy was ensuring all firms were positioned in a competitively neutral way, alongside managing the threat of Chinese SOEs operating according to unified strategies devised by the Chinese State economic agencies. It was deemed necessary to balance, as much as possible, the special privileges of Chinese SOEs born of access to state finances and their positions in relation to the resources needed by the Chinese economy. In the final section, I examine the meaning and significance of a key organisational metaphor that appeared in the speeches in "economic sovereignty."

In Chapter 5, I examine the statements made by official actors that situate the policy in the domain of security. I show that the rise of China was connected by key Australian policymakers to a series of other structural changes, including globalisation and the global financial crisis. The problem these changes caused was first the obsolescence of old policymaking methods of imagining different policy areas to function distinctly, and secondly an undermining of Australian "sovereignty." The solution was an activist, middle power approach to foreign policymaking, an ambition to produce a new regional architecture that brought China and the United States together and dealt with security and economic issues at the same time, and a willingness to use new tools in foreign policymaking, including drawing on the leverage Australia gained over East Asian states by dint of its position as a provider of economically vital raw resources.

In Chapter 6, I bring these two narratives together to produce my own account of the Rudd Government's FDI policy, as it has been described in the section above. I produce my account on a retroductive basis, meaning that the policy can be explained most convincingly were the claims made in Chapters 4 and 5 concerning the logics of economics and security on which the policy was based to hold. I present an account of the policy that assumes that there was a clear understanding of the policy problem being solved—the threat that Chinese SOE investment posed to the capacity of the Australian government to define the structures of Australian resource markets and to govern these—and a policy solution—to convince the Chinese state that it was in its interest to respect the integrity of Australian markets and market discipline. My account does not comment on the efficacy of the policy, but aims merely to produce an account that renders it intelligible.

In Chapter 7, I turn to the questions a more orthodox governmental examination of the policy would seek to answer, as well making some qualified comments on the efficacy of the policy in retrospect. I argue that beyond conforming to the basic tenets of the governmental state, the policy also shows some coherence with Foucault's account of the *neoliberal* governmental state, most importantly that the Australian Government was positioned as a subject of risk in much the way a subject in a neoliberal governmentality is positioned. On the other hand, I argue that the policy shows some divergence from Foucault's neoliberal governmental state in the movement away from the rule of law as the guiding ethos of state intervention. The significance of this point is that as the deep structure of the world in which Australia operates changes, it is likely that the mode of statecraft will need to adjust. In this final chapter, then, I suggest that the FDI screening policy can be interpreted as an early experiment in adapting the governmental state to new conditions. It is important to understand how this experiment worked in order to begin a conversation about the effectiveness of the Australian government's innovations, and the options facing Australia in terms of its strategic positioning in the changing regional and world orders. With regard to its efficacy, I argue that the FDI screening policy was largely ineffective in convincing the Chinese state that conforming to market structures in its interactions with Australian and global economies was in its interests. The key leverage the policy relied on—the belief that the prices for Australian resources being sold to China would remain at very high levels over a very long period—turned out not to be correct. I suggest that the Australian interest would have been better served by investing resources into building coalitions among the many nations around the world facing similar problems with regard to Chinese outward investment. This said, it should be acknowledged that the Rudd Government did make attempts at regional institution building, and as I will show the FDI screening policy should be read as operating in conjunction with efforts to engage China in talks concerning the direction of the region and world orders. It is easy, in retrospect, to say that as these efforts were largely ineffectual and that a different course of action should have been taken. My larger position is that the Rudd Government's understanding of the policy problem itself was astute and remains relevant today.

References

Beeson, M., Soko, M., & Yong, W. (2011). The New Resource Politics: Can Australia and South Africa Accomodate China? *International Affairs, 87*(6), 1365–1384.

Berg, C. (2012, March 15). Foreign Investment and the Whims of Politicians. *The Drum*. Available at http://www.abc.net.au/news/2012-03-13/berg-foreign-investment-and-the-whims-of-politicians/3886786. Accessed 21 Oct 2016.

Bream, R., Burgess, K., Saigol, L., & Dyer, G. (2008, February 2). Dawn Raid for Rio Tinto Stuns BHP. *Financial Times*. Available at https://www.ft.com/content/a51f903e-d09f-11dc-953a-0000779fd2ac. Accessed 20 Oct 2016.

Cook, M., & Thirlwell, M. (2008). *The Changing Global Financial Environment: Implications for Foreign Investment in Australia and China* (Lowy Institute Perspectives, Outcomes Report). Sydney: Lowy Institute for International Policy.

De Goede, M. (2005). *Virtue, Fortune, and Faith: A Genealogy of Finance*. Borderlines (Vol. 24). Minneapolis and London: University of Minnesota Press.

Drysdale, P. (2011). A New Look at Chinese FDI in Australia. *China and World Economy, 19*(4), 54–73.

Drysdale, P., & Findlay, C. (2009). Chinese Foreign Direct Investment in Australia: Policy Issues for the Resource Sector. *China Economic Journal, 2*(2), 133–158.

Financial Times. (2005, February 10). Scrap the Firb. *Financial Times*. Available at http://www.ft.com/intl/cms/s/0/e94b0012-7b0d-11d9-a3ea-00000e2511c8.html#axzz3moMpLVTv. Accessed 21 Oct 2016.

Foroohar, R. (2018, August 12). New Investment Rules Will Squeeze US–China Flows. *Financial Times*. Available at https://www.ft.com/content/607db618-9bbe-11e8-ab77-f854c65a4465. Accessed 3 Mar 2019.

Foucault, M. (1978 [1976]). *The History of Sexuality; Volume I: An Introduction* (R. Hurley, Trans.). New York: Pantheon Books.

Freed, J. (2008, February 5). Rio Just an Investment, Chinalco Says. *Sydney Morning Herald*. Available at http://www.smh.com.au/business/rio-just-an-investment-chinalco-says-20080204-1q25.html. Accessed 21 Oct 2016.

Golding, G., & Bassil, R. (2008). Australian Regulation of Investments by Sovereign Wealth Funds and Sovereign Owned Enterprises. In R. A. Fry, W. J. MicKibbon, & J. O'Brien (Eds.), *Sovereign Wealth: The Role of State Capital in the New Financial Order* (pp. 171–187). London: Imperial College Press.

Hewett, J. (2008, April 25). China Told by Rudd Government to Shelve Mine Deal. *The Australian*. Available at http://www.theaustralian.com.au/business/mining-energy/china-told-to-shelve-mine-deals/story-e6frg9df-1111116159135. Accessed 21 Oct 2016.

Howarth, D., & Griggs, S. (2012). Poststructural Policy Analysis: Discourse, Hegemony, and Critical Explanation. In F. Fischer & H. Gottweis (Eds.), *The Argumentative Turn Revisited* (pp. 305–342). Durham, USA: Duke University Press.

ITS Global. (2008, September 9). *Foreign Direct Investment in Australia—The Increasing Cost of Regulation.* ITS Global, Melbourne, Australia. Available at http://www.itsglobal.net/sites/default/files/itsglobal/Research%20Report%20on%20Foreign%20Direct%20Investment%20and%20the%20Increasing%20Cost%20of%20Regulation%20in%20Australia%20(2008).pdf. Accessed 21 Oct 2016.

Kirchner, S. (2008a). Capital Xenophobia II: FDI in Australia, SWFs, and the Rise of State Capitalism. Centre for Independent Studies. *CIS Policy Monograph, 88.*

Kirchner, S. (2008b, November 27). Foreign Investment Flows Are Damned By Political Bias. *The Centre for Independent Studies.* Available at https://www.cis.org.au/commentary/articles/foreign-investment-flows-are-damned-by-political-bias. Accessed 21 Oct 2016.

Kirchner, S. (2009a, September 30). Canberra's Investment Confusion. *Wall Street Journal.* Available at http://www.wsj.com/articles/SB10001424052748704471504574442281091477054. Accessed 21 Oct 2009.

Kirchner, S. (2009b, August 5). FDI Liberalisation Falls Short. *The Centre for Independent Studies.* Available at https://www.cis.org.au/commentary/articles/fdi-liberalisation-falls-short. Accessed 21 Oct 2016.

Kirchner, S. (2012). The Kingdom and the Quarry: China, Australia, Fear and Greed. *Policy, 28*(2), 58–62 (Review Essay).

Kirchner, S. (2014). *Regulating Foreign Direct Investment in Australia.* Financial Services Institute of Australasia (Finsia). Available at https://www.finsia.com/docs/default-source/industry-reports-foreign-direct-investment/regulating-foreign-direct-investment-in-australia.pdf?sfvrsn=4. Accessed 21 Oct 2016.

Larum, J. (2011). *Chinese Perspectives on Investing in Australia.* Analyses papers series. Sydney: Lowy Institute.

Leaver, R., & Ungerer, C. (2010). *A Natural Power: Challenges for Australia's Resources Diplomacy in Asia.* Canberra, Australia: The Australian Strategic Policy Institute. Available at https://www.aspi.org.au/publications/a-natural-power-challenges-for-australias-resources-diplomacy-in-asia/A_natural_power.pdf. Accessed 21 Oct 2016.

Makin, T. (2008). *Capital Xenophobia and the National Interest.* Australia's Open Investment series paper 8, Institute of Public Affairs. Available at https://www.ipa.org.au/library/publication/1229298839_document_makin.pdf. Accessed 21 Oct 2016.

Miller, P., & Rose, N. (1990). Governing Economic Life. *Economy and Society, 19*(1), 1–31.

Novak, J. (2008). *Australia as a Destination for Foreign Capital.* Australia's Open Investment series paper 1. Institute of Public Affairs. Available at http://www.ipa.org.au/library/publication/1226637929_document_novak_destination_for_foreign_capital.pdf. Accessed 21 Oct 2016.

Rae, J. (2008). *Counting the Cost of Regulation.* Australia's Open Investment series paper 2, Institute of Public Affairs. Available at https://www.ipa.org.au/library/publication/1229298979_document_rae.pdf. Accessed 21 Oct 2016.

Roberts, D., & Tschang, C.-C. (2008, February 6). Why Chinalco's Buying into Rio Tinto. *Bloomberg Associated Press.* Available at http://www.bloomberg.com/news/articles/2008-02-05/why-chinalcos-buying-into-rio-tintobusinessweek-business-news-stock-market-and-financial-advice. Accessed 21 Oct 2016.

Rose, P. (1999). *Powers of Freedom: Reframing Political Thought.* Cambridge, UK: Cambridge University Press.

Rudd, K. (2001). ANZUS and the 21st Century. *Australian Journal of International Affairs, 55*(2), 301–315.

Rudd, K. (2004, October 1). *The Three Pillars: Our Alliance with the US, Our Membership of the UN, and Comprehensive Engagement with Asia.* Foreign Policy Statement by the Australian Labor Party. Parliament of Australia. Available at http://parlinfo.aph.gov.au/parlInfo/search/display/display.w3p;query=Id%3A%22library%2Fpartypol%2FZMZD6%22. Accessed 4 Nov 2016.

Rudd, K. (2007, April 20). *The Rise of China and the Strategic Implications for U.S.–Australia Relations.* Address to the Brookings Institute, Washington, DC. Available at http://www.brookings.edu/~/media/events/2007/4/20china/20070420china.pdf. Accessed 4 Nov 2016.

Rudd, K. (2008a, February 18). Interview with Chris Uhlmann. *AM, ABC Radio.* Available at https://pmtranscripts.dpmc.gov.au/release/transcript-15765. Accessed 21 Oct 2016.

Rudd, K. (2008b, March 26). *Advancing Australia's Global and Regional Economic Interests.* Address to the East Asia Forum in Conjunction with the Australian National University. Department of the Prime Minister and Cabinet. Available at https://pmtranscripts.dpmc.gov.au/release/transcript-15823. Accessed 4 Nov 2016.

Rudd, K. (2008c, April 7). *Australia and the UK—Global Partners in Shaping the Future Global Order.* Address to the London School of Economic, London. Department of the Prime Minister and Cabinet. Available at https://pmtranscripts.dpmc.gov.au/release/transcript-15847. Accessed 4 Nov 2016.

Rudd, K. (2010, May 27). *Prime Minister Speech to the Opening Conference of the National Security College*. Australian National University, Canberra. Department of the Prime Minister and Cabinet. Available at http://pmtranscripts.dpmc.gov.au/release/transcript-17311. Accessed 4 Nov 2016.

Swan, W. (2008a, February 17). *Government Improves Transparency of Foreign Investment Screening Process*. Treasury. Available at http://ministers.treasury.gov.au/DisplayDocs.aspx?doc=pressreleases/2008/009.htm&pageID=003&min=wms&Year=&DocType. Accessed 21 Oct 2016.

Swan, W. (2008b, February 18). *Cth. Parliamentary Debates*. House of Representatives. Available at http://parlinfo.aph.gov.au/parlInfo/search/display/display.w3p;adv=yes;orderBy=customrank;page=0;query=Date%3A18%2F02%2F2008%20QUESTIONS%20WITHOUT%20NOTICE%20Foreign%20Investment;rec=0;resCount=Default. Accessed 21 Oct 2016.

Swan, W. (2009, December 10). *Address to the Global Foundation*. Brisbane, Treasury. Available at http://ministers.treasury.gov.au/DisplayDocs.aspx?doc=speeches/2009/033.htm&pageID=005&min=wms&Year=&DocType=. Accessed 21 Oct 2016.

Tellmann, U. (2007). *The Economy and the Foundation of the Modern Body Politic: Keynes and Malthus as Political Philosophers*. Ph.D. dissertation, presented to Cornell University.

Thirlwell, M., & Shearer, A. (2008). *Is the Foreign Investment Review Board Acting Fairly?* Paper 4 in the Australia's Open Investment Future series. Sydney: Lowy Institute for International Policy.

Uren, D. (2012). *The Kingdom and the Quarry: China, Australia, Fear and Greed*. Collingwood, VIC: Black Inc.

Wilson, J. D. (2011). Resource Nationalism or Resource Liberalism? Explaining Australia's Approach to Chinese Investment in Its Minerals Sector. *Australian Journal of International Affairs, 65* (3), 283–304.

Wines, M. (2009, June 2). Australia, Nourishing China's Economic Engine, Questions Ties. *New York Times*. Available at http://www.nytimes.com/2009/06/03/world/asia/03australia.html. Accessed 2 Nov 2016.

Zhang, J. (2009, April 2). Chinese Seek to Invest, Not to Dominate. *The Australian*. Available at http://www.theaustralian.com.au/story/0,25197,25276296-5017272,00.html. Accessed 21 Oct 2016.

CHAPTER 2

Governmental Policy Analysis

I argued in the introduction that the existing accounts of the policy are unsatisfying. They understand the causes and aims of the policy in too proximate a way and are too wedded to liberal political theory. To overcome these issues, I employ governmentality and poststructural policy analysis. As bodies of theory, these take a criticism of liberal political theory as starting points. They widen the aims of the study by examining the conditions of the phenomena in question, and take this to be a necessary component of an explanation of a policy. Further, they take dramatically different positions on questions of ontology, epistemology, and the nature of power from the liberal schools. In this chapter, I describe the theoretical approach and tools that I have employed to conduct this study.

The value of the governmental approach to my study lies in the tools it provides for examining the "textuality of politics" (Merlingen 2006, 187) in a way that goes beyond the treatment of discourse in poststructuralism. It adds a complex notion of power to the poststructural treatment of discourse and the production of the social world, and provides a set of analytical tropes and methodological tools for examining the technologies and arrangements of governance that appear in the modern state. That is, the framework provides a marriage of macro-level political structures with a set of claims on the execution of government at the micro-level. Where I have criticised the existing accounts of the FDI policy for holding too rigid an account of the features of a liberal society—the autonomy of the market, the separation of the state from the objects and subjects that it governs, a divide between the domestic and international, and another between the state's

© The Author(s) 2019

M. Peters, *Regulating the Rise of China*, Studies in the Political Economy of Public Policy, https://doi.org/10.1007/978-3-030-05466-3_2

aims regarding security and economics—governmentality takes these features as objects of inquiry in the study. First, it demands an account of how these features came to appear in the form that they do, and asks what power effects their forms have. Second, it understands the features as themselves technologies of governance, as well as conditions and products of strategic engagements. The framework is not perfect. As I will show, there are two clear issues that have relevance for my study, in the retention of the economy as a site where values are essentially "unknowable" (Tellmann 2009) and the ambiguous treatment of the ontology of the international realm (Jaeger 2013). These are not fatal, however, and the tools which make governmentality attractive to me—those designed for interrogating the nature of the reality being examined—can be used to overcome them.

In the first section of this chapter, I provide my account of governmentality, situating Foucault's work on it within his by-then established concerns of processes of subjectification and the relation between knowledge and power. I then make some comments on the central category of discourse as it appears in Foucault's work. I indicate how I have adapted the framework for my use in public policymaking analysis, and respond to the two criticisms of the framework that I have mentioned above. In the second section, I describe the stages of my study, which are taken intact from Howarth and Griggs' (2012) method of poststructural policy analysis. In the third section, I describe the tools used in the two discourse analyses that constitute the primary data of this study. These tools were taken from two bodies of work: postpositivist policy studies and narrative-based discourse analysis. Instead of selecting a single framework from within either of these two bodies of work, I produced a toolbox of analytical tropes and possible lines of inquiry, which I used to deconstruct and destabilise the discursive formations that appeared in the subject matter. In the fourth section, I explain my selection of the texts that form the key primary data of the study.

2.1 Governmentality

2.1.1 *Placing Governmentality Within Foucauldianism*

The term governmentality refers to a constellation of cognitive dispositions or discursive arrangements, apparatuses, technologies, and rationalities that form the enabling conditions of "government." At the same time, it refers to the particular analytics that aims to examine these conditions.

I will define the technical terms in this definition in a moment. To situate the theory first, though, it is useful to understand governmentality as Foucault's attempt to connect the methodological and theoretical work of the previous decade[1] with a macro-level analysis of the state. This is achieved by borrowing and altering the concept of the "mentality" from the Annales School, and marrying it with his established interests: the microphysics of power, which is to say the exercise of power at the most intimate level possible; processes of subjectification; the study of the constitutive and power effects of knowledge production; and the relations between "regimes of truth" and "regimes of practice" (Foucault 1980b, 1981a). That is, while the material on governmentality broadens Foucault's ambitions significantly, the guiding themes, methods and theoretical commitments remain constant from his earlier work. We can begin by describing these before turning back to explain how Foucault tweaked the concept of the mentality in order to remain faithful to his established theoretical and methodological commitments, and then define some of the key terms describing discursive formations within governmentality that I use in my work.

The first difference of the governmental approach from liberal political theory is its commitment to an epistemological ontology, common to all poststructuralism, and what I will call a teleological ontology in addition to this. Epistemological ontology refers to the belief that the objects and subjects that appear in social world are constructed via discursive practices. This does not mean that the social world is thought to be in the mind of the beholder, but rather that the formations of the social world are contingent on the stability of the discourses that function by dividing up reality and making it seeable and sayable. The claim to contingency refers to the belief that the forms could possibly have taken a different shape to what they do, no matter how "natural" or objectively "true" they appear to be. In addition to this interest in language games as constitutive of reality, which is common to all poststructuralism, Foucault's own understanding of the processes of knowledge and therefore world creation stresses the power contexts in which they occur, the power involved in enforcing particular contingent discursive paths rather than their alternatives, and the subsequent effects of these discursive formations on conflicts between actors. Knowledge claims are never thought of as merely neutral or functional. My description of Foucault's ontology as teleological reflects the prominence Foucault places on the strategies of subjects as the driving force of knowledge and so world creation. Discursive linkages are formed via strategic interactions. They continue to function insofar as they continue to enable the teleological actions of subjects. This does not mean that discursive formations are "authored" simplistically by actors; formations are produced as a result of strategic interactions as a whole. I also do not mean that Foucault accepts a Hegelian totalising or teleological philosophy of history (Dean 1994, 39). Foucault rejected all progressivist understandings of human knowledge including teleological ones, and held that the paths of events, truths, objects, and subjects, follow no intrinsic logic. Once again, knowledge and things are treated as radically contingent.

The second reflection on Foucault's general approach relates to his treatment of power. Two essential points on power fall immediately from the claims made so far. Firstly, the formations that appear in the social are part of a distinct worldview; they are not "natural." Second, the promotion of a worldview is necessarily at the expense of alternative possible worldviews. This means that power is an ever-present category: having adopted an ontology based on radical contingency, no knowledge element can ever be ever neutral. A sedimented discourse by definition naturalises what it is and depoliticises or marginalises the concerns of those actors that aimed to institutionalise alternate formations. Removing the issue from the initial conflict participants, an epistemological ontology implies that the terrain on which future conflicts are waged is both shaped by power and shapes the allocation and nature of power resources. The alternate position, which Foucault rejects, is that "knowledge can exist only where power relations are suspended" (1977, 27). A second paradigmatic point on the nature of power is Foucault's rejection of "power over" in favour of thinking of power as an essentially enabling property, which he terms "power to." That is, he imagines power as not "essentially repressive" (1980b, 122), but rather as the name given to the constitution of objects and subjects and their positionings in relation to one another that make possible the pursuit of strategic actions. In the first volume of *History of Sexuality*, Foucault (1978, 93) argues that

> [p]ower is everywhere: not because it embraces everything, but because it comes from everywhere... Power is not an institution, not a structure, nor a possession. It is the name we give to a complex strategic situation in a particular society.

This understanding is framed in the governmentality lectures as a rejection of "the model of the Leviathan in the study of power"

(Foucault 1980a, 102). Throughout these three volumes, Foucault aims to decentre the state by rejecting the idea that power emanates downwards from an apex through a hierarchy. It is an extension of the earlier theoretical ambitions to interrogate power at the most microscopic level and to examine the ways knowledge and power are (always) intertwined. The move to thinking of power as an enabling force shifts the aim of analysis from judging the legitimacy of power to examining its technical aspects, which I will discuss below.

The third general theme that continues into the governmentality work is Foucault's treatment of discourse. As with the poststructuralists, Foucault takes his starting point from structural linguistics (most significantly De Saussure 1966), which understands discourse as a contingently structured system of signifiers (Milliken 1999). These signifiers make sense only in relation to one another, via linkages of equivalence and difference. Thus the constitution of meaning is understood as occurring by "temporarily… establishing chains of connotation among different linguistic elements" (Weldes 1996, 98; see Doty 1993). The act of activating such a chain is articulation. Structuring the set of statements are a set of rules that regulate and constitute the formation. An analysis of a discursive formation looks both at the elements within it, on this basis of movements of equivalence and difference, and the logics that regulate it, that render possible the formation and thereby constitute seeable and sayable reality.

Foucault adds a number of claims to this account of discourse. First, discursive formations are always treated as practices rather than objects. Foucault defines discursive practices as "a body of anonymous, historical rules, always determined in time and place that have defined a given period" (Foucault 1972, 117), and it is these systems of rules that is the primary analytical target of the analysis. Second, seeing discourse as a practice, it is always a situated one. The statement is only ever a material, historical event (Foucault 1972, 27) or moment (Laclau and Mouffe 1985, 105). This in turn implies that discursive formations exist only insofar as they are activated, which is to say that there is no such thing as a latently existing statement (Deleuze 1988, 16). Second, discursive linkages are not measured on a basis of truthfulness to gauge their strength. Rather, if there is to be a measure, it can only be the regularity of activations of a discursive link, or to take Georg Simmel's term, its "heaviness" (1900, 106). The relationship to truth is necessarily internal to the discourse, which will have its own regime of truth which shapes claims to accuracy, authority, and other forms of authenticity. Identifying and describing the regime of truth is then a further task that an analysis of discourse takes in this approach, and this relationship from the rules constituting a discursive formation to knowledge once again returns the analysis to a technicalist disposition.

The situatedness of the discursive formation is in relation to time and space, but also in relation to arrangements of power forces. Taking the understanding of power as a strategic arrangement of forces, as above, implies that formations rely on knowledge and truth regimes in order to function, and in turn enforce and regularise that knowledge. The aim when analysing discursive formations/practices is, in Foucault's words, to show "how the coupling of a set of practices and a regime of truth form an apparatus (*dispositif*) of knowledge-power that effectively marks out in reality that which does not exist and legitimately submits to the division between true and false" (2008, 19). As a further implication of the situatedness of discourse, the enforcement of discursive linkages and logics is understood as requiring technologies. Foucault aimed when examining a discourse to turn his attention to the technical aspects of enforcement, as well as the technologies of subversion, displacement, and rejection of discourses. These technologies can be very varied, drawing on ethical, aesthetic, coercive, and other instruments, but all are open to the same lines of inquiry, centring on the technical aspects—the "how questions," to take Mitchell Dean's term (1999, 16–17)—of knowledge production and contestation. As Miller and Rose put it, if a discourse is "a technology of thought," then our analyses must examine "the particular technical devices of writing, listing, numbering, and computing that render a realm into discourse as a knowable, calculable and administrable object" (1990, 5).

The particular discursive formation types that I examine in this study are the dispositif or apparatus, the technology, and the rationality. These are difficult to define clearly in abstract terms and the governmentalists have shown little interest in developing abstract theory on the terms further. Instead, they tend to insist on examining actual instances of the discourse formation types. The dispositif, or apparatus, is the name given to the entire knowledge-power constellation that functions to produce the world-terrain of a given arena, the subjects that populate it, and the modes of thinking that are possible, be they calculative, truth-telling, moralistic, or aesthetic modes of thinking. Giorgio Agamben defines the dispositif as "literally anything that has in some way the capacity to capture, orient, determine, intercept, model, control, or secure the gestures, behaviours, opinions, or discourses of living beings" (2009, 14). In other words, a dispositif is that arrangement of knowledge-power by which governance is made possible. A dispositif functions insofar as it enables strategies of government by a diverse set of actors within it, and continues to exist or is dismantled or adjusted according to the interplay of tactical and strategic interactions within it.

Existing at a level below the dispositif, a technology is a tool of knowledge-power that enables a particular strategy or tactic. If sovereignty as described above is that type of dispositif that situates subjects in relation to an authority and as free citizens with particular sets of rights and obligations, the primary technology of sovereignty is law. The law is available as a technology of domination by the state, as well as resistance to this domination by a whole series of factions other than the state. It is not the exclusive property of any actor or faction. As ever, a technology is studied in terms of its technical aspects and application. The analyst asks how a particular technology functions, what balance of forces enables it to persist, and what transformations have occurred to produce its present form.

Finally, a rationality is the summative term for the mental dispositions that appear within a discursive formation. Again, this is not easily definable in abstract terms. As an approximation, a rationality is the collection for a set of modes of knowing and truth-telling that reflect a particular organisation of reality. To relate it to the terms already introduced, we could say that a rationality is the term given to the larger mental configuration that encompasses and unifies a series of calculative technologies. For example statistics, probability, and risk are the technologies that constitute the population as knowable and subject to intervention. The rationality is the sum of these technologies, but also the name given to the cognitive and other rules governing their use. It both renders these modes of knowing the world and truth-telling coherent and contains further elements that relate to how the technologies can be used. Dean (1999, 17) posits that when confronted with an instance of "ethical governance," we must inquire of its ontology (what the governor seeks to act upon), ascetics (how this substance is governed), deontology (who we are when governed in such a way), and teleology (the end result sought by the act of governance). These are examinations into the mental configurations that appear in a particular type of phenomenon—ethical governance—that intersect technological questions, particularly in Dean's ascetic aspects, but also transcend them in important ways.

2.1.2 The Governmental State

With these points on the general approach made, it is possible to turn to governmentality itself. The first task is to resolve the tension in Foucault's commitment to studying the microphysics of power and the apparently totalising claim of identifying a principle of intelligibility of an entire society in the Annales School's concept of the "mentality." A mentality, for the Annales adherents, referred to the conditions of forms of thought, or the *doxa*, the settled, taken for granted elements in a world. First, it is possibly useful to recognise from the outset that the portmanteau "govern-mentality" was used in a slightly ironic sense for this reason; Dean describes Foucault's use of the Annales School and Braudelian analytical categories as "affectionate" and "playful" (1994, 39–40). Foucault rejects the Annales School's conception of "total history" and Braudel's *longue durée* in his imagination of history composed of "regularity, discontinuity, dependence, transformation" (Dean 1994, 3). Similarly, where a Weberian "total history" aims to identify a governing principle of an epoch which accounts for the coherence of the series of events occurring in the epoch, Foucault's "general history" is "a space of dispersion" (1972, 10).[2] Instead of a generative principle, the examiner seeks regularities in events, but also divisions, disjunctures, discontinuity, and mutations (Foucault 1981b, 68–69). The principle that Foucault produces that both enables the examiner to identify regularities and dispersions but also avoid all reductionist and totalising ambitions is a general preponderance of power technologies towards "government."

Foucault wanted to use the concept of the mentality without moving from his commitment to analysing only microphysics of power and never seeking the "secret" relation from which power emanates on a macro-level. He thus defines government in a minimalist fashion. It refers to practices aimed at shaping or ordering the behaviour of free subjects for some end. The shorthand for this formulation is the "conduct of conduct" (2008, 186). The value of this definition is that it "may be equally valid when we are dealing with phenomena of a completely different scale, such as an economic policy, for example, or the management of a whole social body" (2008, 186). Secondly, it expands government beyond an analysis of the state. That is, conducting conduct can be practiced by many different actors. This is both a point about the object of a governmental study and an empirical claim about the rise of the governmental state through the seventeenth and eighteenth centuries, which experienced a proliferation of agencies, administrators, and other institutions that engaged in practices of government. Government functions for Foucault not as the principle that generates coherence of the whole, but as the rubric through which we interrogate interventions on subjects of power and resistance to this. In order to act on the conduct of a subject, there is necessarily a set of ethical, rational (calculative), and aesthetic conditions, as well as regimes of truth, and interrogating these are the objects of a governmental study. Governmentality, in Dean's terms, is a way of studying the "art of government" (1999, 18), and the mentality aspect of it refers not to a principle of causation, but a space of inquiry where we expect to find experimentation and adaptation with the broad formula of the conduct of conduct.

Using these lines of inquiry, Foucault posits that a new regime of government arose in the mid-to-late-eighteenth century. This is the second use he has for the term governmentality. The governmental state is marked by a move to "security" as the primary mode of intervention by a set of governors and the appearance of a new historical figure, the population, which becomes the necessary object of government. Security is the third in a triptych of power modalities after sovereignty and discipline, which are best described in relation to one another.[3] Sovereignty is that form of government that takes law as its central technology, operates within a territory, and interacts with subjects on an individual basis. Sovereignty creates a binary between the permitted and the prohibited, and imposes a punishment on the subject that transgresses. Discipline, by contrast has no relation to law. It takes an empty space and structures it and the subjects that appear within it rigorously, producing forms in each according to technologies of surveillance and correction. Disciplinary dispositifs appear in Foucault's earlier work on the prison, the school, and the hospital. Discipline, like sovereignty approaches its subjects on an individualised basis, but employs the norm rather than the law as its primary technology, and situates the transgressor in a double position within its code: the transgressor is not disallowed from the system, but is reformed and transformed while remaining within it. Security, in contrast to these, is that form of power which approaches its subject as a population. Thus, a transgression is conceptualised using knowledge of the population: instances of theft are studied using knowledges that construct the world in aleatory, probabilistic terms, and punishment is meted out to thieves according to a logic that optimises resources (Foucault 2007, 5). That is, a particular type and level of punishment can be expected to affect occurrences of theft within the population in a predictable way.

The move to security therefore calls into existence an entire rationality and set of knowledges that do not exist in the other modalities. The population is understood specifically in terms of the milieus of circulation that appear within it. These circulations, which encompass money, labour, goods, and ideas, are understood as a naturally occurring phenomena with intrinsic properties. Governance occurs again using technologies of norms, but unlike in discipline, these technologies aim for optimisation of a property rather than correction. The binary of permitted and prohibited is replaced with an average and a bandwidth of acceptability that must not be exceeded. Two aspects of the rationality underpinning security fall from this. First, the interventions of the governor are imagined as finding their ends within the population: the population is the object of governance, but its optimisation is its end. This means that the basis of evaluation of an intervention is also located internally, and can be stated on technical grounds: the governor is no longer criticised as immoral or illegitimate, but as competent or incompetent. Secondly, it implies that the liberty of the subject, along with a capacity for resistance, is assumed. Indeed, it is a necessary component for the functioning of security.[4] Subjects are both free, including free to resist, and rational, in the sense of responding predictably to interventions when considered en masse. Finally, political economy and statistics emerge as the knowledges by which the population is known and on the basis of which interventions are made.

As I have noted, Foucault places governmentality as the third in the triad after sovereignty and discipline, but I will not follow this move. I would prefer to leave sovereignty–discipline–security as the three abstract modalities of power that are possible within dispositifs aiming to conduct the conduct of people. I do this in order to retain governmentality as the name given to that type of society that rests primarily on security as its mode of intervention, but retains places for apparatuses of sovereignty and discipline as conditions of governance via security. Certainly the law is retained in the governmental state, even as it becomes increasingly subservient to the processes of normalisation that characterise governmentality; eventually in the neoliberal governmental state, the law will be derived from the norm (Foucault 2008, 84). Likewise, the disciplinary institutions of the hospital, school, and prison retain a place in the governmental state, and are necessary conditions of it; the production of workers, for example, and the efficient degree of conformity of citizens to the law, are effects of disciplinary apparatuses. Governmentality refers to the entire dispositif of a society in which a population is taken as both the subject and the object of government, where interventions are made at a distance on the basis of the knowledge of political economy, and with the telos of optimisation.

Governmentality is a type of society, a historically situated project, entailing the expansion of government according to these ratios into all aspects of society, and at the same time the name given to the more or less ordered inquiry into the mentality of particular instances of government, understood as the conduct of conduct.

2.1.3 *Criticisms of Governmentality*

There are two criticisms that have been made of governmentality that pertain to my study and demand comment. The first is that Foucault retained an essentially liberal understanding of the working of the economy, and the second relates to the ambiguous or absent treatment of the international in the framework.

2.1.3.1 The Retention of a Liberal Account of the Economy

Foucault's claim that political economy—as a body of knowledge—is an internal component of governmentality is a significant claim in its own right: the production of knowledge of the milieu of objects and interests within the economy and population can no longer be thought of as politically neutral. However, it does not provide an account of the nature of the economy itself. For Foucault, the birth of political economy, thought of as the establishment of a particular regime of truth, contains a double movement: on the one hand it "… constitutes these practices as a set bound together by an intelligible connection and, on the other hand, legislates and can legislate on these practices in terms of true and false" (2008, 18). The market appears as a technology of truth-telling, but again this is in relation to governmental practice: it is "a site of veridiction… of verification-falsification for governmental practice" (2008, 32). It rests on a set of *produced* freedoms that are necessary to the mode of governance: the freedom "… of the market, to buy and sell, of discussion, of property rights, possible freedom of expression, and so on" (2008, 63). Liberalism must *produce* freedoms, concludes Foucault, and must do so constantly "… but this very act entails the establishment of limitations, controls, forms of coercion, and obligations relying on threats" (2008, 64). Thus, in order to establish and then perpetuate these freedoms, Foucault shows that historically there is an emergence of a set of institutions, practices, and technologies that enable the governor sight and control such that she can ensure that the mechanisms of the economy are working in accordance with their natural or intrinsic properties (2008, 67).

We have then a rejection of the "quasi-ontological difference between the economy and political horizon" and instead "an unbroken plane of governmental strategies and reflections [that] envelops both spheres, taking as its target the regulation of the population" (Tellmann 2011, 287). This is made on the basis that economic phenomena does not function without the enabling conditions put in place by the sovereign. There are three problems with this. First, it reinstates the founding principle of liberal economic governance itself, which is that no actor has—or could ever have—the capacity to access or define the value of economic resources. Tellmann argues that "[d]espite Foucault's critical re-reading of economic discourse, the market ultimately remains for him, as for liberalism itself, a space of invisibility, populated by interested subjects, who are governed in the conditioning of their choices" (2009, 6). The engagement with the forms and relationships that appear in the economy is limited entirely to stipulating the conditions for the appearance and functioning of the economic; there is no inquiry into their internal workings (see Brown 2003). Secondly, it promotes conduct of conduct to the elevated status of *the* understanding of power (Tellmann 2011, 286; see also Collier 2009 on the need to avoid this totalising version of governmentality). This forecloses the possibility of considering how the government of money and things occurs and elides the traditional questions of the role of the material conditions and systems of economic production in the constitution of forms of governance. These moves are unsatisfying first because the state *does* act on money and things, and second because it forecloses the possibility of examining loci outside of the sovereign–subject relationship where the economic is constituted, where it is possible that shaping the conduct of conduct is not the mode of power interaction.

Fortunately, and taking Tellmann's resolution as it stands, Foucault's own work provides the tools to overcome these problems. The starting point of Foucault's work is always to inquire of the type of reality with which we are dealing, and it is possible to use the archaeological and genealogical methodologies to interrogate the formation of economic objects and subjects, for example as Marieke De Goede (2005) does to money and credit, Aitken (2006) does to capital, Foucault himself and then Miller and Rose (1990) do to the economy as a coherent object, and a slew of commentators do to the rational economic subject (Ewald 1991; Brown 2003; Miller and Rose 1990; Spike Peterson 2003; Griffin 2010; De Goede 2005; Best 2007, 2008). The Foucauldian toolbox, Tellmann argues, "is a machine for referring concepts back to the historical record while retaining their conceptual force—rather than being a 'cookie-cutter' that reproduces the same outcomes regardless of the question at hand" (2011, 297).

Nonetheless, there are three ramifications for my study that I can see. First, I take the body of governmental work as a whole, including the work by Tellmann (2009, 2011), De Goede (2005), V. Spike Peterson (2003), and the "cultural economists" (see the edited volume by Best and Paterson 2010), who examine the constitution and government of things as well as interests as analytical forms that can be sought in the phenomena being studied. Second, governmentality cannot be treated as a theory proper on the level of Marxism or liberalism. While, as I will discuss in the next section, the governmentalists have produced a set of claims about the nature and functioning of the state and different institutions in late-modern liberal societies, these are not derived from assumptions about universal objects such as capital or human nature. The program of research within the governmentalist tradition is instead to use the framework as a set of analytical conjectures and questions that can be used to make sense of phenomena on a limited basis. Third, I take Tellmann's precaution not to limit the understanding of power within my study to the conduct of conduct. While my study is for the main part focused on regulatory economic government, and therefore action on interests, I am open to the possibility of the Australian policymakers pursuing strategies on the basis of government of things. To resolve the issue also, if there is a performative delineation between the economic and the political in the governmental state, I would say that it is based on the presence in the economic of a mechanism that verifies value—the market—where in the political realm there are a plethora of verification technologies which do not have the benefit of being anonymous and impersonal. That is, it does not conflict with the claims I have made above to say that there is a structural difference between the realms, insofar as the structure is treated itself as discursively produced and contingent.[5]

2.1.3.2 The Ambiguous Treatment of the Domestic–International Divide

The second criticism concerns the possibility of using governmentality at the international level. The problem that arises is that in the international sphere, the institutional and dispositional arrangements do not necessarily occur the same way they do within the governmental state. There are international elements in Foucault's account of the development of the governmental states. The most explicit aspect of these is the concept of the balance of power, which is presented by Foucault as a "solution" to the problem of empire. Rather than using the term to mean a structure of alliance making, Foucault uses it to refer to a new commitment to maintaining international balance despite the growth of the state, meaning that governmental statecraft contains a requirement to have a knowledge of itself and of other states, and that the functioning of police in each state—the control of all societies—becomes a common good that benefits all members of an international society (Foucault 2008, 60, see Jaeger 2013, 34). Likewise, the globalisation of markets under the Pax Britannica features as a shaping component of the development of the modern liberal governmentality in liberal states in Foucault's account (2008, 55–57). It is clear not only that there is necessarily continuity between the external and internal aspects of a governmentality, for Foucault, but that the two are coterminous (Jaeger 2013, 30).

Solutions to this problem exist and tend to fall into three camps. First, some scholars have attempted to use governmentality to examine instances of governance above the level of the state by "scaling up" the framework, either explicitly or implicitly assuming an "as if" world state (for example Nesadurai 2009). By assuming a world state, I of course do not wish to reify the modern state and imply that where there is governance within a governmental approach it must be by the state. Rather, as I have shown, the security technologies that are the primary tool by which the conduct of conduct occurs within governmentality rely on the existence of institutions such as the market, school, prison, even family. These institutions must conform to the larger governmentality in some sense, and the approach of scaling up governmentality must take as an assumption that the governmentality that is being posited as above the level of the state coheres with these (multiple) substate institutions. I am not convinced yet that this is an assumption that can be made. Foucault's accounts of the liberal governmental states in Britain and France, and then the neoliberal governmentalities of twentieth-century Germany and the United States constantly stress the historical contingency and situatedness of the political and knowledge formations that appear within them. I do not see how it is possible to apply the same theoretical insights in the international context, which is constituted by multiple states that by this logic are constituted by their own unique governmentalities and lower level formations. The second camp tries to pair the insights of governmentality with a more developed macro-political theory. For example, Jonathan Joseph (2010) attempts to embed "the governmentality concept" within a "Marxist-inspired social ontology."[6] These efforts are also not convincing, in my opinion. The ontological commitments Foucault makes which I have described above diverge sharply from Marxist materialism. The task of reconciling the two accounts of the state is a very large one, and I am only aware of superficial attempts to combine the two. I will make some comments in Chapter 8 on the potential for greater engagement between more orthodox international relations theories that my analysis suggests exists, but doing this at the expense of the foundational claims of the approach would rob governmentality of its value.

The third and my preferred solution is drawn from Jaeger (2013), and more or less follows the path of Tellmann (2011) above: the mode of analysis within governmentality is to inquire first of the nature of the reality being examined. In the case of the international, we would ask how the international is constituted within specific temporal, geographic, and power contexts. A governmental account of the international does not deny the divide between the domestic and the international so much as it asks how these two realms are produced in distinction to one another, what tactical and discursive engagements resulted in these productions, what actions the divide enables to what actors, and so on. Again, my primary aim in this study is not to produce an account of how the international and domestic are (co)constituted, but the point that they are so is important to keep in mind. Further, it seems clear that the international and domestic each retains "ontological specificity and irreducibility" (Jaeger 2013, 27) within the governmental approach, insofar as this ontology is a produced according to the theoretical commitments outlined above. I will argue in this book that the Rudd government understood the fundamental problem to be solved as arising from the interaction of the illiberal economic forms of the Chinese economy with the liberal Australian economy. Whether this examination produces insights into the understanding of policymakers within the Australian government of the international generally, rather than only their understanding of China as the other, is open to interpretation. Certainly though, I hope to show that the governmental tools and framework that I have outlined here are very well-suited to the task of analysing this interaction, and thus suitable for use in International Relations work.

As a more practical framing of the same resolution, I have no problem with discussing the interests of states as if they were coherent, unified identities *when these interests are generated by the actors I am examining*. I interpret the FDI policy changes as pertaining to a larger engagement of the Australian state with China, and as Australia's interests are a category used by the policymakers themselves, and other actors within the policy subsystem, it seems reasonable to frame my explanation of their actions in reference to it.[7]

2.1.4 Using Governmentality

Having made these defences, it is now possible to describe precisely how I use governmentality as an approach in this study. Following the point made at the start of this section, I employ governmentality in two senses at once: first as a mode of analytics and second as a set of claims about the constitution of society and the state in late liberal or "governmental" states. I will explain each of these in turn.

The first meaning of the term governmentality that I have described is of a mode of analysing the conditions and constellations of forces that render possible instances of government, understood as the broad formula of the conduct of conduct. That is, there are no given claims about the nature of social subjects or structures that spring from any essentialist or ontic realities; rather a governmental study is one that is shaped by the guiding interests and questions of governmentality. These include, but are not limited to: how did this phenomena come to exist in the way that it does? What power implications exist in the delineation of realms within the given field of reality? What technologies of power exist to render possible instances of government? How do regimes of knowledge and regimes of truth figure in these assemblages of forces that render government possible?

The second meaning of governmentality is as a quasi-theory of the governmental state. In this use of the approach, I am diverging from the program of research as it exists and in doing so making the case to bring governmentality into conversation with alternative approaches. Most obviously, where Foucault intended above all to produce a theory that "cut off the head of the king" (1978, 89), that decentred the state as a more or less coherent and unified whole and as the central locus of power that emanates downwards, I am using the theory to do inherently state-centric work. Instead, in this study, I will treat governmentality as an alternative account of social reality, one with a developed set of claims regarding state institutions, practices, and aims of state governance within a neoliberal governmental state. These are taken from Foucault's work, and from the three waves of governmental work that followed him.[8] That is, it is possible to take the insights into the way political economy (Foucault 2007, 2008), risk analysis (Miller and Rose 1990), or credit ratings (De Goede 2005) as knowledges that constitute and regulate actors and behaviours and as explanations of how political life is ordered. Understanding the methods of governing actors as relating to governmental apparatuses as they are described above opens the analysis to accounts of state actions that diverge dramatically from an account that treats the state as a realm apart from the objects it oversees, such as markets, firms, civil society, and so on. Using the governmental approach, we instead have a language that understands these forms as technologies of governance, not as intrinsically existing objects that present themselves as subject to intervention after taking form.

I use the qualifier "quasi-" in reference to Foucault and his followers' rejection of "theory," taken in the usual sense. The governmentalists insist upon analysing really existing, situated formations, and do not aim to produce claims about general cases. Nonetheless, they have produced an account of the governmental state that can be read as analogous to the liberal and Marxist accounts of the state. Like these grand theories, governmentality posits a central rubric with core ideas through which broad swathes of social phenomena can be rendered intelligible. For liberalism the core ideas are that individuals are rational, creative in some sense, and pursue self-interest. It understands the state as the product of rational individuals coming together to solve collective problems, such as the need for security and the optimisation of a society's resources, as well as the maximisation of individual freedom. For Marxism, the core idea is that all phenomena can be related to the need within a capitalist society to enable the successful realisation of capital: the process by which a bundle of money can go through a series of transformations and emerge with increased value, having actualised itself as capital rather than mere money. It understands the state as a tool that appears as a solution to the problems associated with ensuring the realisation of capital as well as the management of class antagonism. For governmentality, the core claim is that actors are engaged with the problems of the conduct of conduct, and that phenomena at all levels can be understood in terms of the conditions required to enable the conduct of conduct. It understands the state as an amalgamation of tools, technologies, and rationalities that make possible the conduct of conduct. This claim is produced using an ontology that is different to either liberalism or Marxism, but the basic equivalence in the mode of these claims can be acknowledged.

My study, therefore, aims to explain a particular public policy, drawing on assumptions about the nature of the reality being dealt with and the core processes and drives that shape the political and economic realities being examined that are drawn from the body of governmental work that has preceded my own. I do not conduct an archaeological or genealogical study, per Foucault's own work, of the Australian state, but rather take as assumed the results of his and others' genealogical and archaeological studies as the starting points to my own inquiry. At the same time, I do not reject the guiding interests and techniques of governmentality, centred around interrogating divergences and heterogeneity in instances of government, modes of subjectification, and the constitution of objects and subjects that are governable. Rather, I see these as inseparable from my task of explaining the policy in question. My use of the framework, then, sits somewhere between an analytics of government and an exercise in theory-testing. Obviously, the validity of my account does not stem from its coherence with the claims made by Foucault or the other governmentalists, but from how convincing the account is itself, how completely and satisfyingly it explains the actions of the policymakers.

It should be noted at this point that governmentality does not disallow the interests of a number of other political science approaches. For example, my own account of the policy in question includes a substantial examination of the institutional settings that conditioned the policy. As I will argue, the independent status and opaqueness of the Foreign Investment Review Board were crucial factors in affording the executive wing of the Australian Government autonomy over the investment screening policy, and their ability to avoid parliamentary oversight or battles in their changes to the policy. Likewise, in Chapter 3, I devote substantial efforts to tracing the aims of foreign investment screening policy in Australia from the late 1960s to 2007. These components of the argument would very likely appear in an account of the policy based on a historical institutional approach, particularly one that places emphasis on the ideational components of institutions, such as Elizabeth Thurbon's (2016). The difference is that within my approach these factors are considered precisely in terms of their contribution to answering questions relating to the conditions of governability. That is, the institutional conditions that enable or shape the particular ontological, aesthetic, deontological, or teleological conditions, to take Dean's (1999, 17) terms above, of the particular instance of government being examined.

My belief in the superiority of governmentality as an explanatory framework lies in the integration of an account of the possibility of the policy with the account of the policy itself. This, as it turns out in the study, is crucial to the policy being examined, given that the main threat that Chinese SOE investment posed, according to the key Australian policymakers, was to the governability of Australian markets, and the power of the Australian state to unilaterally determine the nature of these constellations. Due to the existing accounts of the policy's commitment to a liberal worldview, they take as assumed the intrinsic, self-creating nature of markets, and the need to secure or preserve these natures does not appear as a possibility. The theoretical intervention of this book on policymaking studies is not that all public policy takes its primary object as the perpetuation of structures of governability, but rather that this is a necessary condition of public policy. This may be a very minor component of the explanation of a policy, say if the governability of the phenomena is very strong and the policymaker has no need to develop, alter or actively retain this capability. Nonetheless, an explanation that pays no attention to the conditions of possibility, thought of specifically in terms of the conditions of governability, is incomplete. Secondly, as analysts, we must be open to the possibility of a public policy taking as one of its substantial aims the construction, alteration, or defence of the conditions and modalities of governability. The failure to leave this possibility open at the start of a study runs the risk of producing explanations of a policy that are incomplete or, as the existing accounts of the Rudd government's FDI screening policy do, provide explanations of the policy that are unconvincing and rest on the ineptitude of the policymakers. The point is not that policymakers are always successful and that our task is to determine exactly what they succeeded at. Rather, it is simply that analyses that do not take into account the need of policymakers to secure the conditions of governability in all sorts of ways or to imagine that these conditions are simple, are likely to "discover" more incompetence than really exists.

As a final point, my approach as a governmentalist shapes not only the type of questions I ask in this study and the final account of the policy I produce, but also the types of critical evaluations of the policy I am empowered to make. Most importantly, the set up of the argument does not provide me an external basis on which to evaluate the policy in the way that a liberal or Marxist study would. That is, there is no basis on which governmentality provides me a way to produce "real" interests of the policymakers, or to evaluate the degree to which their actions furthered their "real" interests. The effectiveness of the study does not hinge on the degree to which policymakers' actions can be said to have furthered or revealed the policymakers' real interests, but rather on the degree to which my account produces a narrative that renders their actions coherent and consistent with the logics and discourses that constituted the arena in which the action occurred. My evaluation of the policy, which I present as an afterthought of the study in Chapter 8, concerns only the aspects of the policy on which governmentality is empowered to make: the degree to which the Australian policymakers' actions enhanced or reduced the capacity of the Australian government to maintain its ability to govern Australian raw resource markets. This is a technical question, not a normative one.

2.2 Poststructural Policy Analysis

Having explained the ontological and epistemological foundations of my approach, it is now possible to turn to a more practical account of how I conduct the study. Despite using a Foucauldian framework, I am not doing genealogical or archaeological work, though I do use the techniques that appear within these two methodologies. The reason for this, as I have noted, is that I set out to complete an un-Foucauldian task: to explain a policy. In order to do this while retaining faith to the claims above, my analysis follows the five steps that Howarth and Griggs (2012; Howarth 2010) stipulate for a poststructural policy analysis. These are not necessarily chronological steps, so could perhaps be called elements of a poststructural policy study. They are listed in Table 2.1. The steps combine a set of poststructural interests—most notably of the conditions for social interaction to occur and the place of specific knowledge constructs in social phenomena—with an aim of providing an account of a policy. The framework is well-suited to my aims in this study.

First, the policy (or practice or regime) in question is problematised, using the method and mode developed by Foucault. This involves inquiring of the way "being gives itself to be, necessarily, thought" (Foucault 1985, 11). That is, one aims to disrupt the naturalness of the objects, knowledges, and identities that appear within the phenomena being examined. This can be done using Foucauldian genealogical excavations, which identify the moment in history when a discursive constellation was settled in order to show its contingency. Alternatively, one can ask what conditions give rise to the phenomena existing at all. Such a question can obviously extend in many different directions, and there are no particular limitations placed on the analyst's production of lines of inquiry. All questions that relate to aspects of the phenomena that seem to require explanation or that relate to the conditions of the phenomena's existence in either material, political, ideological, and articulable senses are valid. Howarth (2010, 324) stresses that this "problematisation is related both to the field of academic questions, and to the social and political issues that confront us in a specific historical conjuncture." This coalesces strongly with the centrality of questions relating regimes of truth to regimes of practice within governmentality, as I have described above. The most salient effect of this last point from Howarth for my argument has actually already appeared in the introductory chapter. I argued that there was no satisfactory explanation of the FDI policy

Table 2.1 Howarth and Griggs' (2012) five steps of a poststructural policy analysis

1. Begin by problemetising a particular policy, practice, or regime. Examine the way "being gives itself to be, necessarily, thought" (Foucault 1985, 11). Relate the problematisation both to the field of practice and the field of academic questions that themselves seek to problematise it
2. The form of explanation of the policy is retroductive, rather than inductive or deductive. A phenomenon is posited as intelligible were a putative explanans to hold
3. The content of the explanation is couched in terms of logics rather than laws, causal mechanisms, or contextual self-interpretations. These logics can be social, political, and fantasmic
4. The putative explanation will comprise a plurality of logics which are linked together to form a particular set of circumstances to render a problematic phenomenon intelligible
5. Posit an internal relation between explanation, critique, and policy evaluation

in the literature, with nearly every explanation resorting to allegations that the key policymakers were either xenophobic, illegitimately meddlesome, or simply incompetent. That is, there was no account of the policy that formed a coherent link from the state actors' aims and interests to their actions. The main reason for this is that all the existing accounts are wedded to a liberal understanding of the world: the state is treated as distinct and separate from the structures and subjects it oversees; and the realms of security and economics are treated as autonomous from one another. The place of liberalism as a mode of knowing the world then appears in my argument in a number of places: as part of a criticism of the existing literature, as a component of the reality in which the policy is situated, and as an end sought by the Australian Government in their interaction with the Chinese firms and state. A second important point is made by Howarth on the particular style of problematisation used here: "in the field of policy studies, the practice of problemetization focuses on the question of problem-definition in a particular field or domain, the various problemetizations of this problemetization, and the efforts of an analyst to problematize these problemetizations" (Howarth 2010, 324–325). As I will show in the next section, the examination of the policy problem, and its link with a solution in the form of a policy narrative, is the guiding theme of my discourse analyses.

The second step is to frame the explanation of the policy in a retroductive, rather than inductive or deductive form. Retroduction occurs when a phenomena is observed and an explanation takes the form of stating that such a phenomena would occur if a hypothesis was true. One infers backwards that as the phenomena did occur, the hypothesis is true. For example, on observing that the lawn is wet in the morning, one might presume that it must have rained overnight. Deduction is disavowed as a result of the ontological commitments that I have outlined above. As I, following Foucault and all the poststructuralists, reject the existence of general laws or principles in the social, it is no longer possible to render instances intelligible by inferring from the general laws. Likewise, induction, meaning the inference from particular cases to the general, is also rendered invalid. In practice, the use of retroduction actually returns us to something quite close to Foucault's own method. Having identified a phenomena that is imagined as anomalous—problematised—there is a movement back and forth between the empirical data and the production of hypotheses until a putative explanation is produced that the analyst is satisfied resolves the confusion and fits the data. In the course of this back and forth, there is likely to be further problematisation, further identification of phenomena in need of resolution, as further inquiry into the nature of a particular field demands it. This practice of oscillating between tasks is what I was referring to above when I noted that the steps are not chronological.

Third, "the *content* of any putative *explanans* in this perspective is couched in terms of logics, rather than laws, causal mechanisms, or contextual self-interpretations" (Howarth 2010, 325, emphases in original). The distinction being made here is that logics are dependent on the meanings produced by the actors. However, logics do not reflect actors' self-interpretations simplistically. They refer to the "rules that govern a meaningful practice" and the "conditions that make the operations of such rules possible" (Howarth 2010, 325, emphases removed). The centrality of logics in the explanation steers the analysis towards meaning-production and meaning effects, according to the framework above. Howarth and Griggs divide up the possible logics into three groupings. Social logics enable one to characterise social practices according to the rules that govern them; political logics enable one to explain and criticise the emergence of social practices or regimes; and fantasmatic logics enable one to explain the way subjects are gripped by discourses (Howarth 2010, 325–326).[9] While there may be some value in these divisions, I do not think they are necessary. The Foucauldian approach intentionally places Howarth and Griggs' "political logics" at the heart of any explanation of a "social logic," so the distinction is not enormously helpful.[10] Likewise, as the key objects and subjects of the phenomena I am examining exist at a level above the individual—states, governments, firms, and so on—and as I follow Epstein (2011) in imagining these as speaking subjects—a category produced entirely discursively as other social identities and not by an intersection of the irreducible realms of language and desire as per a Lacanian individual subject—the value of Howarth and Griggs' "fantasmatic logics" is also of limited value to me. Overall, the original point that the explanation of the policy should be framed in terms of logics stands.

The fourth step is to stress the concept of articulation. The logics that the explanation rests on, the social forms that they produce that render the problematic phenomenon intelligible, necessarily rest on acts of articulation. Articulation, as I have described above, refers to the linking of discursive elements in statements. The significance of this point is that the primary subject matter of a poststructural policy analysis is the discourse that appears in the subject matter, or framed as events: articulations. I will turn in the next section to the techniques I employ to conduct the two discourse analyses that the study is based on.

Finally, one posits an internal relationship between explanation, critique, and policy evaluation (Howarth and Griggs 2012, 324–325). By noting the contingency of social forms, the mode of study necessarily brings to the fore those forms that were excluded and expended in these processes. Likewise, understanding discourse as a practice and the effects of discursive formations not as power-neutral, it is possible to inquire of the elements of domination and silencing that are implicit to the ongoing practices that are necessary for the continued functioning and integrity of specific discursive forms. The point is not to re-found a legitimacy of power—delineating the good uses of power from the bad (Foucault 1997, 27)—rather it is criticism in a technical sense. By destabilising the naturalness of the discursive forms, the analysis necessarily questions existing norms, which "may be accompanied by political challenges to the practices of regime of practices examined" (Howarth 2010, 327). As Howarth (2010, 327–328, emphases removed) neatly summarises:

> … to highlight the political dimension of a practice entails pointing to those aspects of practice which seek to generate, maintain, contain or resolve the public contestation of social norms. Put differently, the political aspects of practice involve attempts to challenge and replace existing social structures, as attempts to neutralize such challenges in a transformist way (Gramsci 1971, 58–59).

These five steps provide the core structure of this book.

2.3 Methods of Discourse Analysis

In this section, I describe the tools I used in conducting my two discourse analyses. These are drawn from postpositivist policymaking studies and narrative-based discourse analysis.

2.3.1 Postpositivist Policymaking Studies

Over the past two decades, a postpositivist challenge to the dominant positivist models of policymaking has appeared.[11] The submissions from Hajer (1993, 1995), Fischer (2003), Fischer and Forester

(1993), Stone (2002), and Kingdon (1995) are unified by positioning discursive conflicts at the centre of their understandings of the policy process, and broadly cohering with the epistemological and ontological positions I have taken above. These approaches reject the aims of prediction and the discovery of universalist laws in the realm of policy-making, instead seek understandings of social action that are grounded in historical contexts and do not have meanings outside of those contexts. They eschew the "rational" model of a policy decision which takes the form of explaining in isolation the policymakers identifying an objective, considering the consequences of possible actions, and selecting the alternative that best achieves the objective (Stone 2002, 11). They hold that social phenomena requires a teleological explanation, meaning that the analysis necessarily "identifies the process of rendering facts *understandable* by interpreting their meanings in the light of relevant social goals and values" (Fischer 2003, 50, emphasis in original). Taking Schattschneider's (1960) insights on political conflict, they tend to place agenda-setting and conflicts over problem definitions as the central dynamics to be explained in policymaking studies. This broadens the subject matter significantly relatively to the positivist approaches, and tends to capture the "messiness" of policymaking more effectively.

Instead of selecting one from among these that I find most persuasive or most conducive to my needs, however, I used this set of theories as an array of tools to be drawn upon as the subject matter required. That is, I took concepts and claims from the theories when setting out to do my two discourse analyses, and drew on them to make sense of the data whenever they seemed valuable. I will describe the concepts from each approach that were used in the study.

Hajer's (1993, 1995) discourse coalitions approach seeks to expand upon Schattschneider's framework by integrating neo-Marxist insights regarding the role of discourse. He focuses on the way in which groups of actors who "share a social construct... an ensemble of ideas, concepts and categories through which meaning is given to phenomena" (1993, 45) form coalitions. The main mechanism presented is unification through a story on a specific problem. Key concepts are "discourse structuration," which occurs when "a discourse starts to dominate the way a society conceptualises the world" and discourse institutionalisation, which refers to the way successful discourses become entrenched in the organisational practices of a society in both formal (that is, institutions) and informal (generally something like "traditional reasoning") ways (1993, 46). While the discourse coalitions approach usefully moves the analysis past "mere reference to interests, analysing how interests are played out in the context of specific discourses and organisational practices" (Hajer 1993, 48), it does leave a large number of unanswered questions, most importantly those relating to why certain discourses or stories shape policy action instead of other ones. For example, are certain stories inherently more compelling than others? Are there certain "discourse entrepreneurs" in the world of policy making, individuals who are more effective at producing and utilising compelling discourses (or trust in themselves)? These are not failings necessarily, if we are happy to answer these questions in relation to specific instances only.

Stone's (2002) narrative-based approach extends on Schattschneider's dynamic of agenda-setting by developing our understanding of the way policy goals, problems, and solutions are defined and how these in turn in divide the set of actors who effect the policy. The link from problem to solution is imagined as a narrative. The approach foregrounds the issues of how one particular problem-definition comes to define a conflict and provides tools to examine the consequences of the event. Stories, containing causal statements, problem, and solution definition, and allocation of subject positions, are one of four main forms of symbolic representation, for Stone. They sit alongside synecdoches—a figure of speech in which a part is used to represent the whole; metaphors—claims of similarity in two apparently unlike figures; and the use of ambiguity—strategic uses of the multiple interpretations that can and do exist for discursive formations—as the primary technologies of the definitional conflict that lie at the centre of the analysis. Stone's insights provided the starting place for the study in the aim of identifying a coherent storyline for the Rudd government's FDI policy, which I felt the existing literature had not supplied.

Kingdon's (1995) "multiple streams" approach, based on Cohen et al.'s (1972) "garbage can" model, holds that there are three relatively independent "streams" that each must be understood to explain policy change. The first is the problem stream, which involves the definition of problems. Problems can come into existence in response to events external to the policymaking arena, can involve framing moves by actors within the arena, or can arise as a result of feedback mechanisms internal to the life of an existing policy. Secondly, there is a policy stream, in which "... proposals, alternatives, and solutions float about, being discussed, revised and discussed again" (Kingdon 1995, 172). These proposals are not formulated in response to policy problems, as per the rational policymaker model, but instead simply exist on their own. Finally, there is a political stream, in which events external to the policy process have relevance to it. It is composed of things like the public mood, pressure group campaigns, election results, partisan or ideological distributions in government, and changes of administration, all of which have important effects on agendas (1995, 168–170).

Policy change occurs when these three streams come together in "policy windows"—opportunities to connect solutions to problems. These usually arise as a result of changes in the political or problem streams (it is rare for a policy innovation to lead to change on the basis of its own volition), but these policy windows are not predictable. First, they exist only in terms of the perception of actors in the policy arena, and secondly, the meaning of a change in the political or problem stream needs to be interpreted by actors, and the ways in which they are interpreted cannot be predicted. Finally, and as a significant point of departure from the punctuated equilibrium model and Advocacy Coalition Framework, Kingdon (1995, 169) argues that while policy does tend to be incremental, as actors deal with complexity and ambiguity in the policy issues, agenda-setting does not. Interest in problems, solutions and even events in the political stream tend to "spike" quickly, and policy windows close soon after opening, meaning that the possibility for sudden change is actually built into the model of policymaking internally, rather than arising only in response to external events as per the dominant mainstream approaches.

The key limitation of the multiple streams approach is an incomplete account of how ideas shape the processes that occur in each stream. Kingdon acknowledges this problem and responds to it by arguing that concentrating on the origins of policy initiatives does not make for a very complete theory as (1) ideas can come from anywhere, (2) tracing origins of ideas tends involves one in an infinite regress, and (3) in the policy arena nobody follows anybody else, meaning that the information network rests on a different set of connections to the formal hierarchies and institutions that give shape to the policy network (Kingdon 1995, 71–76). For my study, this limitation can be ameliorated by using the Kingdon's insights in conjunction with Howarth and Griggs' (2012) poststructural policy analysis, the discourse coalition and narrative-based approaches, and the tools specifically for discourse analysis that I am about to describe.

As a set, the postpositivists reject the "dominant, technocratic, empiricist approach in public policy studies" (Fischer 2003, vii), which they feel "black boxes" a number of important variables, including the place of ideas. The postpositivists are, in turn, criticised for not producing theory proper: testable hypotheses and abstract statements on causality within the policy process (Sabatier 1999). My response to this, taken from Hukkinen et al. (1990, 312), is that my aim in this study has been to start my interrogation with the phenomena itself rather than a set of abstracted assumptions and to ask some set of actors that seem to be involved in the policy for their stories of how the policy came into existence, and then creating a "metastory" that integrates these stories into a more useful object that can be rendered more amenable to understanding. That is, using my terms from the last section, I have shunned deduction and induction as my mode of study. Like Fischer (2003, 51), I hold that "[t]he constructs of social science must inevitably be second-order constructs." One could also say that I have rejected the aim of theorising in policymaking analysis. Instead, I started the study with a catalogue of causal paths that *could* have relevance in this particular case and sought to fit the case study into one or more of these.

2.3.2 Narrative-Based Discourse Analysis

The second group of tools that I used in the study come from narrative-based discourse analysis. Again, the philosophical foundations of the analytical devices cohere with those I have already discussed so I will limit my comments to defining three analytical devices from this literature that I used in the study. As per my treatment of the policymaking literature, I began the study with these concepts as a toolset for understanding discursive structures that could appear in a policy context.

First, I have taken the concept of an "organisational metaphor" from the work of Yanow (1996). Metaphors, for Yanow, are more than literary devices to be used strategically by actors within a policy space. They are taken as an elemental part of language, much as I argued above when noting that linkages of equivalence and difference between discursive elements are taken as the building blocks of all meaning (see Weldes 1996). A metaphor is "the juxtapositioning of two superficially unlike elements in a single context, where the separately understood meanings of both interact to create a new perception of each, and especially of the focus of the metaphor" (Yanow 1996, 132). As a practice of meaning-making, metaphors necessarily direct vision and therefore also obscure aspects of a situation. The significance of metaphors, for Yanow, falls from their capacity to organise action, or in Foucauldian terms, to shape the conduct of conduct. They can reflect and instill tacit knowledge, and thus function in subtle ways. While the identification and analysis of organisational metaphors can be a valuable tool in making sense of a phenomena and for accessing unstated, taken for granted knowledge that exists in a policy space but is not stated explicitly in a discourse set, the aim is not to "remove" metaphors in order to resolve a paradox or simplify the policy problem being solved (Yanow 1996, 135). They are a tool used by the analyst to identify a relationship between thought and action.

Second, I have taken the concept of "basic discourses" from the work of Hansen (2006). Hansen uses the term to refer to a system of signs in which an element exists and is meaningful. Obviously one cannot have only two levels of the discursive "element" and the entirety of language in order to make analytical comments. Foucault uses the terms "discourse" or "knowledge" to refer to a similar mid-level of a particular system of signs that can be analysed within a particular context, such as the knowledge of political economy as the concomitant technology of governance of a population or milieu of circulation. They refer at once to the system of signs in terms both of the content of the system and as a way of knowing a particular reality. For clarity, I will use the term basic discourse when referring to the content of the localised system of signs and knowledge when referring to a predispositional character. It can be expected that multiple basic discourses will appear in the analysis of a complex policy problem. Similarly, a basic discourse encompasses a multiplicity of sets of claims about a subject, as there are multiple schools of political economy each claiming to represent the same reality. This is what Hansen means when she describes a basic discourse as an "ideal type," a construct produced by the analyst rather than discovered by her, and as a "lens through which… a multitude of different representations and policies can be seen as systemically connected" (2006, 46). A basic discourse, then, can be thought of as a more or less widely accepted way in which the reality of a situation is structured, including the division of positions that exist on a given issue. A basic discourse is not tied to any actor or group, but is a collectively produced and accepted construct. Different actors are able to draw on the basic discourse, or elements of it, without sharing an identity or aim, and without subscribing to every statement that appears in the basic discourse as a whole.

Thirdly, I take the narrative as the primary device that structures policy actions. I have already mentioned the role of narratives in the work of the postpositive policy analysts in Hajer (1993), Stone (2002) and Roe (1992). Taking my cue from these, the questions that I asked of the narratives that appeared in the data set were as follows. First, how does a policy narrative link a problem with an action that resolves it? What alternative solutions are foreclosed by the definition of the problem in this way? This can also be stated in the reverse: what problems does the solution suggested foreclose? What claims relating to causality appear in the narrative? What claims relating to accountability for the problem, using the tropes of responsibility and blame, appear in the narrative? Does the concept of crisis appear in the narrative (see 't Hart and Tindall 2009)? How does the narrative predicate subject positions as victims, authorities, subjects of governance, or any other form of interested party? What subject positions do not appear that might have in an alternative narrative? How does one or more narrative come to shape the action of subjects in the policy space at the expense of alternatives? This refers to the mode of authority that resolves the argumentative conflict.

This is not an exhaustive list. It gives an indication of how I examined the texts using the device of the narrative in order to produce lines of inquiry and problematisation of the claims made by different policy actors. Again, the aim was not to identify incoherence or to judge the policy narratives that appeared on any normative grounds. Rather, the idea that a policy must be a story was used as a way of engaging with and then explaining the practices of problem definition and agenda-setting that are taken as a central component of policymaking.

2.4 Operationalisation of the Approach

The two discourse analyses that appear in Chapters 5 and 6 are composed of close readings of key speeches relating to the economic framing of the policy and the security framing of the policy respectively. The purpose of this section is to explain the selection of these texts and the methodology used to examine them.

2.4.1 Text Selection

The mode of text selection is taken largely from Epstein (2008) with a number of changes made to account for the fact that where Epstein aimed to explain a change in whaling discourses, I am using discourse analysis to explain a public policy. The framework for this repurposing is derived from Howarth and Griggs' five steps of a poststructural policy analysis, as outlined above.

To begin the study I collected all the instances where state actors mentioned the FDI screening policy, including formal speeches, parliamentary speeches, policy documents, media appearances, and leaked internal documents. Per Howarth and Griggs' fifth step, I also canvassed the literatures that commented on the policy, both in the academic material discussing the policy and in the media, think tank and policy institute commentaries. From these two bodies of statements—those of policy actors and those of external commentators—I produced the formative nodes of the discursive field on which key policy narratives were founded and the areas of contestation that appeared in relation to it. For example, from this initial examination, I took the divide between the economic and security aspects of the policy as separable and containing their own independent narratives.

From these nodes, I expanded my collection of statements to include speeches made by both state and non-state actors that related FDI screening to larger economic and foreign policy aims and agendas. On the economic side, this meant situating the statements made about the FDI policy in relation to the economic agenda that the Rudd Government came into office with, and then the agenda that the emerged in response to the onset of the Global Financial Crisis. On the security side, it meant situating the statements made about the FDI policy in relation to Australia's engagement with China and the position of Australia in the changing region of East Asia. That is, the narratives of the FDI policy were imagined as nested within larger policy narratives as a way of guiding the expansion of the data set.

The limitations of this expansion of the data set were based on Milliken's (1999) method of researcher interpretation. He writes, "an analysis can be said to be complete (validated) when upon adding new texts and comparing their object spaces, the researcher finds consistently that the theoretical categories she has generated work for those texts" (1999, 234). That is, I ceased seeking new speeches when the predicates that appeared in new speeches ceased adding new elements to my existing understandings of the narratives and nodes of the discursive field.

2.4.2 *Text Analysis*

The aim of a poststructural policy analysis is to posit a policy narrative that retroductively explains a policy (see Sect. 2.2, above). That is to say that the claim to superiority of the given account rests on the degree of fitness to the policy narrative posited with the actions encompassed by the policy. The stress on policy narratives, as outlined above, is my own, rather than Howarth and Griggs', and is derived from the mode of analysis developed by Hajer (1995) and then taken up in relation to policy studies specifically by scholars such as Stone (2002). In Howarth and Griggs' terms, this claim would read that the claim to superiority is the degree of fitness between the logics, social, political, and fantasmic, to the policy actions taken.

The retroductive mode of explanation of the policy has important implications for the mode of analysis of the speeches used as data in the study. Having produced a body of texts, the task of the analysis of these composed of identifying the "powerful narratives" on which the policy was founded. The term "powerful" here is repurposed from Epstein's term "powerful discourse," which she defines as "quite simply, one that makes a difference" (2008, 2). That is, my aim in examining the body of speeches pertaining to the FDI screening policy was to identify narratives and narrative elements that made a difference in the sense of making possible and coherent the policy itself. Thus, the mode of analysis consisted of a back and forth between my own constructions of the powerful policy narratives, and the evidence presented in the texts. As the end products—the policy narratives—are themselves the guide to my analysis of each individual speech, the mode of analysis is to surmise what the powerful narratives are at every point and to revise these in light of the analysis of each individual text. This is further complicated by the fact that policy narratives adapt over time as they are negotiated within a policy subsystem. This means that each text is analysed in view of its location in time, and there is a second interpretation that needs to be made by the analyst as to whether, in light of a new speech, the analysts understanding of the powerful narrative needs to be amended in light of the given speech, or whether the anomalous element in the given speech needs to be understood in light of its role in the development of the final powerful narrative. Once again, this is managed by a constant back and forth between three different objects: the narratives and logics that appear in the speech, the narratives and logics that the analyst understands as being the powerful narratives and logics of the policy, and the development through time of the narratives and logics. How these are brought into cohesion with one another is a matter of interpretation done by the analyst. As per Epstein, the relevance of an element or logic connecting elements in the discursive formation is not based on the "number of occurrences of a locution either in a single text or across a sample of coded texts" (2008, 173), as is the case in other modes of discourse analysis.

Finally, the speeches that are subject to close readings and reported on in Chapters 5 and 6 are not exhaustive of the speeches examined in the study. The texts included in the two chapters are done so on the basis that they add or play substantial roles in sedimentising narrative elements or logics in the development of the powerful discourses. Properly speaking, the chapters should be read as reports on the discourse analyses conducted for the study rather than the complete studies themselves. This is why these chapters include references to texts outside of the ones that are subjected to close readings.

The goodness and replicability of the study rests on the claims that the account of the policy provides a set of logics that render the policy phenomena intelligible, that there is coherence between the claims made regarding the powerful narratives that the policy rested on and the policy actions taken, and that the account of the policy is more convincing than the existing alternatives.[12]

2.5 Conclusion

In this chapter, I have described the theoretical approach and method that I have used to make my argument. In the first section, I argued that Foucault's governmental approach offers the tools to analyse the "how" aspects of governance, paying specific attention to the technologies that are used in knowledge production, contestation, and sedimentation. A focus on power at its most microscopic level, which is the driving ambition of all Foucault's work, is the entry point of his criticism of the Leviathan model of the state, and of an image of power that emanates downwards through a hierarchy. Instead, in the governmental work, Foucault imagines the state as no more or less than the field of technologies, apparatuses, and dispositifs that are constituted in such a way that they enable a diverse set of actors to pursue a diverse set of strategies of governance. Alongside this interest in the technical elements of governance, Foucault adapts the concept of the mentality in order to comment on the unifying elements that appear in a particular type of society. In the governmental state, these are the production of certain freedoms that enable a particular—liberal—mode of governance, and the primary reliance on dispositifs of security as the mechanism by which governors interact with the governed. Security dispositifs are not exclusive in the governmental state, and tend to rest on dispositifs of sovereignty and discipline as enabling conditions. I have argued that governmentality as an approach offers a valuable critique of the liberal understanding of the state based on an ontology based on the constitutive and power-imbued nature of knowledge and truth, a language to discuss objects like apparatuses and dispositifs that cannot exist within a liberal framework due to straddling and producing the divide between the governing state and governed society, and a novel set of questions to ask of a phenomenon of governance that has the potential to produce surprising and valuable results.

I have acknowledged that the governmental framework contains problems for work relating to economics and international relations. First, having disposed of the state as a unified actor in any sense, it seems strange to then employ governmentality in the analysis of the Australian FDI screening policy in which the tropes of "Australian interests" and "Chinese interests" appear so frequently. As a response, I cited Epstein's (2011) treatment of the state as a speaking subject in poststructural International Relations, and argued that the state can function within an explanation of a phenomena in a governmental study insofar as it was produced and used by the actors in question. In this work I do not step into the realm of analysing Australian or Chinese "real" interests; it is beyond the scope of my task. Secondly, I acknowledged that while governmentalists have produced excellent work showing how the economy and the domestic and international are produced as realms and that these divisions of the world should be treated themselves as technologies of governance as a result, there is an ambiguity at the heart of the framework on the internal workings of both the economic and international as realms. My position on these twin problems is that they are unresolved in the literature, but not unresolvable: following the arguments of Tellmann (2009, 2011) and Jaeger (2013), I believe that Foucault's own work provides the tools to overcome these problems. In this study, I leave the question of the "type of reality" being dealt with as one to be examined within the study, rather than producing an answer before the analysis begins.

In the second part of the chapter, I described the tools from policymaking studies and discourse analysis that I have used to structure the study, to select the data on which I base my argument, and with which I conduct the two discourse analyses which sit at its centre. I showed how the five steps of Howarth and Griggs' (2012) poststructural policy analysis cohere with a governmental approach, and resolve tensions that would otherwise appear between the inherent state-centrism of policy analysis and the anti-statism of governmentality. In the final section, I described my use of the post-positivist policymaking theories and narrative-based discourse analysis theories in the two discourse analyses. In both cases, where I might have selected from the existing approaches one that seems convincing and suited to my needs, I instead take from them each a set of analytical devices, which were used to deconstruct the data in the two discourse analyses and to reconstruct the policy in the form of a narrative, the rubric that is common to both bodies.

In the third section, I described the operationalisation of my approach and described my selection of the texts used in the study.

With the theoretical and methodological discussion complete, I now turn to the first of Howarth and Griggs' (2012) steps: the policy problematisation. This is the task of Chapters 3 and 4.

Notes

1. *The Birth of the Clinic* (2003 [1963]), *Madness and Civilisation* (2001 [1965]), and *The Order of Things: An Archaeology of the Human Sciences* (2002 [1966]).
2. The term general history was introduced and described in Foucault's inaugural address at the Collège de France in 1970 (Foucault 1981b).
3. Foucault also places governmentality as one of this triangle, as in sovereignty, discipline, governmentality (2007, 107–108). In order to avoid adding another dimension to the already laden term governmentality, I will use security to refer to the abstracted modality of power and governmentality to refer to the larger dispositifs, or arrangements of forces, that characterise the governmental state.
4. This point contains one etymology of the term security. Foucault inverts Bentham's treatment of liberty as a "branch" of security. For Bentham, freedom and utility are necessarily dependent on the condition of security (*Theory of Legislation* 1911, 96–97). In opposition to this, Foucault holds liberty as an essential feature that makes possible participation within the apparatuses of the governmental state. Stated in reverse this means that

within security, it is necessary for the governor to respect the liberty of the governed such that the natural processes that appear within the population and the milieus of circulation function effectively (see Gordon 1991, 19–20 and Dean 1999, 116–117). There is a second reason for Foucault's use of the term security, which is arguably more important to Foucault himself. This is the biopolitical aspect of governmentality, in which the "naturalness" of the population that is being acted upon and augmented implies that in the shift to governmentality we are "modifying something in the biological destiny of the species" (Foucault 2007, 10). I don't concern myself with the biopolitical aspects of governmentality in this book—insofar as it is possible to leave these aside when doing governmental work—and so for my purposes the inversion of Bentham's formula is the more important derivation.

5. In fact, Foucault muddled the issue by referring to "institutions, political events, economic practices and processes" as "non-discursive" phenomena in *Archaeology of Knowledge* (1972, 163). It is a contentious point, most significantly for Laclau and Mouffe (1985, 107) and the Essex School, who disallow the distinction. Foucault does not mean that these things are not mediated and produced on the basis of discursive practices. Rather, he means that they are non-discursive in the sense that the poststructuralist economist Simmel (1990) meant when he described economic facts as objective in the sense that they appear, from the perspective of the subject, in a manner identical with the objects in the natural world. Prices are not dependent on a subjective position for their formation; they appear for the subject as being characterised within the order of existence, rather than the order of value. Foucault's distinction is not a helpful one, in my opinion, but it is not a debate that impinges on my treatment of the subject matter. Certainly Foucault and Laclau and Mouffe do not differ in their belief that the discursive constitution and mediation of these objects, phenomena and relations are open to examination.
6. Jessop (2007) and Springer (2012) make the same attempt at a marriage of Marxism and governmentality.
7. A defence of this move, taking states as "speaking subjects" as a basis of non-essentialist identity in International Relations can be found in Epstein (2011). Epstein argues that identity above the level of the individual cannot be analysed in terms of subjectivities, as is possible at the individual level, as the identity is not composed in the intersection of desire and language, as per the Althusserian moment of interpellation, but that there is no reason not to treat them as speaking subjects. I am aware that Epstein uses the Lacanian framework as a "corrective to the Foucauldian understanding of the ways in which the subject is created

through subjection to power" (2011, 338). Nonetheless, given my primary use of governmentality is as a framework for understanding the state as an amalgamation of apparatuses rather than an analytics of subjectification, this treatment of state identity is compatible.

8. This is not a recognised account of the history of the school, but at least within the anglosphere, I think there are clear differences between the work of the early governmentalists that knew and worked alongside Foucault; the English writers of the 1990s, most importantly Dean (1994, 1999), Miller and Rose (1990), Lemke (2002), and the edited volume edited by Barry et al. (1996); and the new explosion of governmental work that has appeared from the mid-2000s following the full transcripts of Foucault's three lecture series on governmentality being published in English in 1997, 2007, and 2009.
9. The framework for the treatment of fantasmic relates to Lacanian and then Althusserian interpellation of the subject into discourse and the recognition of the self that occurs in the assumption of identity.
10. Howarth and Griggs, as part of the Essex School, place much greater emphasis on the concept of hegemony, taken from Gramsci and developed by Laclau and Mouffe (most significantly 1985) for use with post-structural discourse analysis. My account of governmentality has not drawn on this category at all, favouring the more anarchical approach of Foucault where the contestations that produce social forms are not so tied to the concepts of historical and hegemonic blocs.
11. The positivist approaches I am referring to are the Advocacy Coalition Framework (Sabatier 1988; Sabatier and Jenkins-Smith 1993), the Punctuated Equilibrium Model (Baumgartner and Jones 1993) and different forms of rational choice new institutionalism (for example Ostrom 1986, 1990; Scharpf 1997).
12. I include within "action" here the symbolic outputs of a policy, meaning those that do not result in "action" narrowly taken, but are still part of the set of phenomena included when referring to the policy.

References

Agamben, G. (2009). What Is an Apparatus? In *What Is an Apparatus? And Other Essays*. Stanford: Stanford University Press.

Aitken, R. (2006). Performativity, Popular Finance and Security in the Global Political Economy. In M. de Goede (Ed.), *International Political Economy and Poststructural Politics* (pp. 77–96). New York: Palgrave Macmillan.

Barry, A., Osborne, T., & Rose, N. (Eds.). (1996). *Foucault and Political Reason: Liberalism, Neoliberalism and Rationalities of Government*. London: UCL Press.

Baumgartner, F. R., & Jones, B. D. (1993). *Agendas and Instability in American Politics*. Chicago: University of Chicago Press.
Best, J. (2007). Why the Economy Is Often the Exception to Politics as Usual. *Theory Culture and Society, 24*(4), 87–109.
Best, J. (2008). Ambiguity, Uncertainty and Risk: Rethinking Indeterminacy. *International Political Sociology, 2*, 355–374.
Best, J., & Paterson, M. (Eds.). (2010). *Cultural Political Economy*. Oxon, UK: Routledge.
Brown, W. (2003). Neo-liberalism and the End of Liberal Democracy. *Theory & Event, 7*(1). Project MUSE. https://doi.org/10.1353/tae.2003.0020.
Cohen, M. D., March, J. G., & Olsen, J. P. (1972). A Garbage Can Model of Organizational Choice. *Administrative Science Quarterly, 17*(1), 1–25.
Collier, S. J. (2009). Topologies of Power: Foucault's Analysis of Political Government Beyond 'Governmentality'. *Theory Culture Society, 26*(6), 78–108.
De Goede, M. (2005). *Virtue, Fortune, and Faith: A Genealogy of Finance, Borderlines* (Vol. 24). Minneapolis and London: University of Minnesota Press.
De Saussure, F. (1966 [1916]). *Course in General Linguistics* (C. Bally, A. Sechehaye, in collaboration with A. Riedlinger, Eds., W. Baskin, Trans.). New York, Toronto, and London: McGraw-Hill Book.
Dean, M. (1994). *Critical and Effective Histories: Foucault's Methods and Historical Sociology*. London and New York: Routledge.
Dean, M. (1999). *Governmentality: Power and Rule in Modern Society*. London: Sage.
Deleuze, G. (1988 [1986]). *Foucault* (S. Hand, Trans.). Minneapolis: University of Minnesota Press.
Doty, R. L. (1993). Foreign Policy as Social Construction: A Post-positivist Analysis of U.S. Counterinsurgency Policy in the Phillipines. *International Studies Quarterly, 37*, 297–320.
Epstein, C. (2008). *The Power of Words in International Relations; The Birth of an Anti-Whaling Discourse*. Cambridge, MA and London: MIT Press.
Epstein, C. (2011). Who Speaks? Discourse, the Subject and the Study of Identity in International Politics. *European Journal of International Affairs, 17*(2), 327–350.
Ewald, F. (1991). Insurance and Risk. In G. Burchell, C. Gordon, & P. Miller (Eds.), *The Foucault Effect: Studies in Governmentality* (pp. 197–210). Chicago: University of Chicago Press.
Fischer, F. (2003). *Reframing Public Policy: Discursive Politics and Deliberative Practices*. Oxford and New York: Oxford University Press.
Fischer, F., and Forester, J. (1993). *The Argumentative Turn in Policy Analysis: Editors' Introduction*. Durham and London: Duke University Press.

Foucault, M. (1972 [1969]). *The Archaeology of Knowledge & the Discourse on Language* (A. Sheridan, Trans.). New York: Pantheon Books.

Foucault, M. (1977 [1975]). *Discipline and Punish: The Birth of the Prison* (A. Sheridan, Trans.). London, UK: Allen Lane-Penguin Books.

Foucault, M. (1978 [1976]). *The History of Sexuality; Volume I: An Introduction* (R. Hurley, Trans.). New York: Pantheon Books.

Foucault, M. (1980a). Two Lectures. In C. Gordon (Ed.), *Power/Knowledge: Selected Interviews and Other Writings 1972–1977* (C. Gordon, L. Marshall, J. Mepham, & K. Soper, Trans., pp. 78–108). New York: Pantheon Books.

Foucault, M. (1980b). Truth and Power. In C. Gordon (Ed.), *Power/Knowledge: Selected Interviews and Other Writings 1972–1977* (C. Gordon, L. Marshall, J. Mepham, & K. Soper, Trans., pp. 109–133). Brighton: Harvester Press.

Foucault, M. (1981a). Questions of Method: An Interview with Michel Foucault. *I & C, 8,* 3–14.

Foucault, M. (1981b). The Order of Discourse. In R. Young (Ed.), *Untying the Text: A Postrstructuralist Reader* (pp. 48–78). Boston: Routledge and Kegan Paul.

Foucault, M. (1985). *History of Sexuality, Vol 2: The Use of Pleasure* (R. Hurley, Trans.). New York: Pantheon.

Foucault, M. (1997). *Society Must be Defended: Lectures at the Collège de France 1975–76* (D. Macey, Trans.). London: Penguin Books.

Foucault, M. (2007). *Security, Territory, Population: Lectures at the Collège de France, 1977–78* (M. Senellart, Ed., G. Burchell, Trans.). New York: Palgrave Macmillan.

Foucault, M. (2008). *The Birth of Biopolitics: Lectures at the Collège de France, 1978–79* (M. Senellart, Ed., G. Burchell, Trans.). New York: Palgrave Macmillan.

Gordon, C. (1991). Governmental Rationality: An Introduction. In G. Burchell, C. Gordon, & P. Miller (Eds.), *The Foucault Effect: Studies in Governmentality* (pp. 1–52). Chicago: The University of Chicago Press.

Gramsci, A. (1971). *Selections from the Prison Notebooks.* London: Laurence and Wishart.

Griffin, P. (2010). Gender, Governance and the Global Political Economy. *Australian Journal of International of International Affairs, 64*(1), 86–104.

Hajer, M. A. (1993). Discourse Coalitions and the Institutionalisation of Practice: The Case of Acid Rain in Britain. In F. Fischer & J. Forester (Eds.), *The Argumentative Turn in Policy Analysis* (pp. 43–76). Durham and London: Duke University Press.

Hajer, M. A. (1995). *Politics of Environmental Discourse: Ecological Modernization and the Policy Process.* Oxford: Clarendon Press.

Hansen, L. (2006). *Security as Practice: Discourse Analysis and the Bosnian War.* London and New York: Routledge.

Howarth, D. (2010). Power, Discourse, and Policy: Articulating a Hegemony Approach to Critical Policy Studies. *Critical Policy Studies, 3*(3–4), 309–335.

Howarth, D., & Griggs, S. (2012). Poststructural Policy Analysis: Discourse, Hegemony, and Critical Explanation. In F. Fischer & H. Gottweis (Eds.), *The Argumentative Turn Revisited* (pp. 305–342). Durham: Duke University Press.
Hukkinen, J., Roe, E., & Rochlin, G. I. (1990). A Salt on the Land: A Narrative Analysis of the Controversy Over Irrigation-Related Salinity and Toxicity in California's San Joaquin Valley. *Policy Sciences, 23*(4), 307–329.
Jaeger, H.-M. (2013). Governmentality's (Missing) International Dimension and the Promiscuity of German Neoliberalism. *Journal of International Relations and Development, 16*(1), 25–54.
Jessop, B. (2007). From Micro-Powers to Governmentality: Foucault's Work on Statehood, State Formation, Statecraft and State Power. *Political Geography, 26*, 34–40.
Joseph, J. (2010). The Limits of Governmentality: Social Theory and the International. *European Journal of International Relations, 16*(2), 223–246.
Kingdon, J. (1995). *Agendas, Alternatives, and Public Policies.* New York: HarperCollins College Publishers.
Laclau, E., & Mouffe, C. (1985). *Hegemony and Socialist Strategy: Towards a Radical Democratic Politics.* London and New York: Verso.
Lemke, T. (2002). Foucault, Governmentality, and Critique. *Rethinking Marxism, 14*(3), 49–64.
Merlingen, M. (2006). Foucault and World Politics: Promises and Challenges of Extending Governmentality Theory to the European and Beyond. *Millenium: Journal of International Studies, 35*(1), 181–196.
Miller, P., & Rose, N. (1990). Governing Economic Life. *Economy and Society, 19*(1), 1–31.
Milliken, J. (1999). The Study of Discourse in International Relations: A Critique of Research and Methods. *European Journal of International Relations, 5*(2), 225–254.
Nesadurai, H. E. S. (2009). Economic Surveillance as a New Mode of Regional Governance: Contested Knowledge and the Politics of Risk Management in East Asia. *Australian Journal of International Affairs, 63*(3), 361–375.
Ostrom, E. (1986). An Agenda for the Study of Institutions. *Public Choice, 48*(1), 3–25.
Ostrom, E. (1990). *Governing the Commons.* Cambridge: Cambridge University Press.
Roe, E. M. (1992). Applied Narrative Analysis: The Tangency of Literary Criticism, Social Science and Policy Analysis. *New Literary History, 22*(3), 555–581.
Sabatier, P. A. (1988). An Advocacy Coalition Framework of Policy Change and the Role of Policy-Oriented Learning Therein. *Policy Sciences, 21*(2), 129–168.

Sabatier, P. A. (1999). Introduction: The Need for Better Theories. In P. A. Sabatier (Ed.), *Theories of the Policy Process* (pp. 3–18). Boulder, CO: Westview Press.

Sabatier, P. A., & Jenkins-Smith, H. C. (1993). *Policy Change and Learning: An Advocacy Coalition Approach*. Boulder, CO: Westview Press.

Scharpf, F. W. (1997). *Games Real Actors Play: Actor-Centered Institutionalism in Policy Research*. Boulder, CO: Westview Press.

Schattschneider, E. E. (1960). *The Semisovereign People: A Realist's View of Democracy in America*. Hinsdale, IL: The Dryden Press.

Simmel, G. (1990 [1900]). *The Philosophy of Money* (T. Bottomore & D. Frisby, Trans.). New York: Routledge.

Spike Peterson, V. (2003). *A Critical Rewriting of Global Political Economy: Integrating Reproductive, Productive and Virtual Economies*. London and New York: Routledge.

Springer, S. (2012). Neoliberalism as Discourse: Between Foucauldian Political Economy and Marxian Poststructuralism. *Critical Discourse Studies, 9*(2), 133–147.

Stone, D. (2002). *The Policy Paradox: The Art of Political Decision Making* (3rd ed.). New York: W. W. Norton.

Tellmann, U. (2009). Foucault and the Invisible Economy. *Foucault Studies, 6*, 5–24.

Tellmann, U. (2011). The Economic Beyond Governmentality: The Limits of Conduct. In U. Bröckling, S. Krausmann, & T. Lemke (Eds.), *Governmentality; Current Issues and Future Challenges* (pp. 285–303). New York and Oxon, UK: Routledge.

't Hart, P., & Tindall, K. (Eds.). (2009). Understanding Crisis Exploitation: Leadership, Rhetoric and Framing Contests in Response to the Economic Meltdown. In *Framing the Global Economic Downturn: Crisis Rhetoric and the Politics of Recession* (pp. 21–42). Canberra: ANU Press.

Thurbon, E. (2016). *Developmental Mindset: The Revival of Financial Activism in South Korea*. Ithaca, NY: Cornell University Press.

Weldes, J. (1996). *Constructing National Interests: The United States and the Cuban Missile Crisis*. Minneapolis and London: University of Minnesota Press.

Yanow, D. (1996). *How Does a Policy Mean? Interpreting Policy and Organisational Actions*. Washington, DC: Georgetown University Press.

CHAPTER 3

The Policy Departure

In this chapter I define the departure of the Rudd government in its FDI screening regime. This, with Chapter 4, constitutes the problematisation section of the book, where I identify surprising phenomena in need of explanation. I do not *define* the government's policy in this chapter. If a policy is a statement of intention on behalf of an authoritative set of decision makers—one that is given in the form of a narrative—then it is logically impossible to define without specifying this aim, and therefore a problem and solution. An orthodox policy analysis might define these things more or less unproblematically at this stage, and then spend the examination considering whether this aim was legitimate on a series of different grounds, and whether the path chosen was optimal, again on a series of different grounds. Given my commitment to the significance of agenda-setting power, and the necessarily political contestation that must precede the definition of the policy problem, beginning the study by defining the object to be explained in terms of a policy aim, problem, and solution is no longer legitimate. Explaining why this understanding of the problem and not some other was settled upon is a major part of the task of the rest of this book. Instead, in this chapter I only specify how the actions of the Rudd government—statements and executive decisions—constituted a departure from the policy settings it inherited.

The chapter proceeds as follows. First, I provide an account of the state of the FDI screening regime that the Rudd government inherited. This is composed of a genealogy of the policy problems that FDI screening has been used to solve in Australia in which I trace changes

© The Author(s) 2019

M. Peters, *Regulating the Rise of China*, Studies in the Political Economy of Public Policy, https://doi.org/10.1007/978-3-030-05466-3_3

in the political, economic, and social logics underpinning successive FDI screening regimes. I then describe the institutional, legislative, and policy settings that were inherited by the Rudd government. In Sect. 3.3, I describe the ways the Rudd government's policy on FDI screening constituted a departure from the existing regime. To do this I describe the changes to the formal policy settings as well as the unofficial changes, meaning the unstated or denied changes to the policy. In the next chapter, I will turn to the catalyst for the Rudd government's policy departure in the wave of large investments from Chinese SOEs into the Australian mining sector.

The legislative and institutional structures inherited by the Rudd Government were remarkably well-suited to its needs. As a result, there was little in the way of substantial changes to these settings. Faced with an apparently difficult task of governing incoming investments from SOEs, FDI screening offered a policy lever over which the government had very tight control of execution, no meaningful oversight, and a very large degree of control over when the issue was on the political agenda. The formal changes that were made amounted to an elaboration on the government's approach to screening investments from SOEs within the bounds of the policy settings of previous governments, and the introduction of an Amendment to the *Foreign Acquisitions and Takeovers Act 1975* (*FATA 1975*). The *Foreign Acquisitions and Takeover Amendment Act 2010* updated the *FATA 1975* to cover new financial products that had not existed in 1975, and maintained the essential intent and operations of the original legislation. Likewise, of the "unofficial" changes, while the government was more active in its examination of state-affiliated investments than any administration before it, no Australian government had ever faced such a large amount of investment from state-owned or -affiliated firms before. The measures introduced to manage the new issue of SOE investment can be understood as cohering with the existing regime, as the Government claimed they did. There is some evidence for the existence of two elements of the policy that were not made official: an aversion to vertical integration in order to enable transfer pricing, and a preference for SOE investments to limit control to fifty per cent for greenfields projects and fifteen per cent for major producers, though these were not strong commitments. There is little evidence that the policy included a concerted effort to dissuade Chinese SOEs from making large-scale investments, as has been suggested (Kirchner 2012; Drysdale 2011; FIRB Executive Member Patrick Colmer, cited in Dorling 2011a, b, c, d).

On the other hand, there were two thematic departures. First, the degree of targeting of a particular investor class—Chinese SOEs—was unprecedented: there was a decision made several months into the term of office that much more scrutiny would be placed on these investments, both individually and as a collective phenomenon. Second, the aim of ensuring that production, pricing, cost-structuring, and marketing decisions were all made on a "market basis" was unprecedented in the history of the policy. I will argue in this book that the key to understanding the Rudd government's FDI screening policy lies in explaining these two thematic departures and the logics that underpin them.

3.1 A Policy Problem Genealogy

In this section I trace the changes in the uses Australian governments have had for FDI screening between 1968, when the practice was first used, and 2007, when the Rudd government came into office. While the uses themselves are important as they reveal a clear set of "legitimate" uses of this form of intervention on the economy and modes of intervention generally, it is possibly more important to note just how many uses screening has had. My genealogy traces twelve distinct aims of the policy and these are listed in Table 3.1. Ten of these are first-order aims—issues in the economy or society that different governments aimed to manage—and two are second-order goals relating to enhancing the capacity of the federal executive to determine and execute the policy. The ease with which successive governments have added to this list of aims speaks to the nature of the policy regime. FDI screening, in Australia, is a policy lever over which the executive government has had almost total discretion and no meaningful oversight. It rests on the catch-all aim of promoting the "national interest". The Foreign Investment Review Board (FIRB) acts formally as an independent advisory body, but it is not a statutory body and has no powers except those delegated to it by the Treasurer. In practice, it functions primarily to shape the place of foreign investment issues on the public agenda according to the needs of the executive core of the government. When the Rudd government came to office in 2007 and was faced with a difficult problem that traversed political, economic, and geopolitical concerns, FDI screening appeared as the perfect tool with which to intervene on its governance object. The ease with which FDI screening could be conscripted into a response to nearly any issue was an important facilitating condition to this.

Table 3.1 Aims of Australian FDI screening regimes prior to December 2007

1. Making up for shortfalls in domestic savings and facilitating economic growth in line with 'natural' potential
2. Limit foreign appropriation of surplus profit from Australian scarce resources; to ensure that returns from Australian production more generally fall to Australian interests
3. Mitigate the negative effects of excessive volatility in the global economy. In practical terms this usually means limiting the risk of capital flight
4. Encourage Australian participation in production (as owners and investors)
5. Manage macroeconomic pressures; use foreign capital flows as a secondary monetary policy lever to manage inflation or balance of payment issues
6. *Second order goal:* mitigate the economic effects of domestic political opposition to foreign investment
7. Attracting foreign capital and organising it into bundles for direct investment; that is, state-led economic development using foreign capital
8. Distribute profits between Australian labour and capital more 'fairly'. In the context of the Whitlam governments this is related to the provision of a social wage
9. Encourage technological development and competition
10. *Second order goal:* enhance the capacity of the federal executive to intervene in the economy in a diverse range of ways
11. Attract large multinational companies
12. Protect Australia's national security

3.1.1 The Need for a Foreign Direct Investment Screening Regime

From its earliest days as a set of British colonies, Australia has relied on foreign investment to make up for inadequate domestic savings (Boehm 1979, 123–155), and FDI has consistently been thought of as a driver of economic development (Faeth 2005, 14; Pokarier 2000, 104; Springell 2012, 155–164). These points have remained as cognitive constants through all Australian FDI regimes, and are listed as problem number one in Table 3.1. Through the 1960s, however, a set of arguments appeared that proposed a much larger role for the federal government in managing inflows of foreign capital. The first reason for this is related to the Australian mining boom of the 1960s. The boom was fostered primarily by the "long growth" of the global economy following the war and the new raw resource needs of the Japanese economy. The structure of a cyclical mining boom sparking public debate and then policy experimentation with the FDI screening was to repeat itself in the 1980s and again in the late 2000s under the Rudd government.

In the context of the 1960s' boom, proponents on both sides of parliament argued that there was a need to curb excessive appropriation of surplus value from Australian workers (Sadleir 2007, 103; problem number two, Table 3.1). A key proponent of the argument was the Labor leader, Gough Whitlam, who used his first press conference as Opposition Leader to politicise the issue:

> There would be no other country with which we compare ourselves in which the national government takes so little responsibility, shows so little initiative… where the natural resources, the things we develop with greatest skill and speed and profit, are passing so rapidly into foreign hands. (quoted in Megalogenis 2012, 12–13)

On the other side of the aisle, the leader of the Country Party and deputy leader of the Holt Coalition government, John McEwan, made a similar point:

> It is not good enough for this country to live by selling a bit of its heritage each year. We do not want to see Australia have its industries unduly in foreign hands, particularly the country's natural resources. (The Australian, July 28, 1965, quoted in Bell 1976, 44)

A second reason proposed for a more activist stance on capital flows that appeared in this debate was to mitigate the effects of an increasingly volatile global financial system (number three in Table 3.1). This increased exposure to volatility was caused by changes in Australia's interactions with the world, as well as a series of structural changes in the world economy and financial system. Through the 1960s there were changes to Australia's key trade partners and sources of capital. Japan took the largest share of Australian exports from 1967 onwards, replacing Britain's primacy, and the United States became the largest source of foreign capital soon after that (Megalogenis 2012, 23). One effect of this was a steady increase in the volume of foreign capital coming into Australia, leading to a peak in 1970 (Whitwell 1986, 196–198), when foreign investment equalled 4.2% of GDP (Bora 1995, 93). The most significant driving force behind the new links to Japan and the United States was the mining boom, followed by fast growth in the agriculture and manufacturing sectors. A second change was Australia's delinking with Great Britain. In 1967 the Holt government made a clear break from the British economy by deciding to maintain the parity of the Australian dollar with the US greenback despite the pound's devaluation against the US dollar. Then, following Nixon's 1971 float, the McMahon government switched the peg to the US dollar. An effect of these decisions was that the Australian dollar remained relatively stable until the end of 1971. Less fortunately, however, Australia's vulnerability to fluctuations in the US economy grew just as the Long Growth of the fifties and sixties came to an end. The result was a temporary end to the period of rising foreign capital flows, with falls starting from the peak in 1970. While Australia had always been a small, open economy with structural vulnerabilities to external volatility, these changes left it open to new risks, the most important being terms of trade fluctuations in relation to Japan and the United States.

A second set of issues are related to structural changes in the global economy, most importantly an increase in financial volatility generally. There was a rise in short-term investment relative to longer-term investment, which is usually attributed to a rise in investment by households into short-term assets (that is, the freeing of previously highly stable capital), and a sharp rise in the number and resources of institutional speculative investors. The latter were often generated by "Euro-" and "petro-dollars," and these new financial institutions produced an early wave of financial securitisation (see Department of Treasury 2000, 12; Pokarier 2000, 119; Schenk 1998, 237; Boughton 2004, 11). The sudden increases in sources of speculative capital then created several bubbles, to which the Australian financial markets were not immune (see Megalogenis 2012, 22 on the 'Poseidon incident' particularly). The most important effects of the increased volatility of the late 1960s for Australia were its destabilising impacts on currencies and primary resources. This is unsurprising as the economy was still dominated by primary industries, often geared towards export.

These changes created a dominant perception of Australia as a small, open economy that was exposed to the ravages of turbulence around the world, a bipartisan consensus that there was a need to increase controls over foreign investment, and a belief that this would be best done at the federal level (Sadleir 2007, 104). These concerns were coalesced in the "MLC affair," an attempt in September 1968 by the British financial group, Sun Alliance, to acquire an Australian insurance company, Mutual Life and Citizens Assurance Co. Ltd. (MLC). The takeover attempt brought to the attention of the Gorton government its inability to control foreign investment. While Prime Minister Gorton was eventually able to block the takeover using legislation specific to the territory in which MLC was located, the affair was a catalyst for the formation of the FDI institutions in the late 1960s (Sadleir and Mahoney 2009, 340).

3.1.2 A Nascent Regime: Promoting Australian Participation and Managing Public Opinion

Before 1968 responsibility for regulating foreign investment flows rested largely with the state governments, with federal restrictions on foreign ownership and participation being limited to restrictions in a few select industries: mainstream banking, civil aviation, and broadcasting (Bell 1976, 46).[1] The reserve bank had some capacity to control *overall flows* of inward investment via its controls over currency in and out of the country (Commonwealth Banking Acts 1924 and 1945 and The Bank Act 1945; see Schedvin 1992). This acted as a secondary monetary policy lever to the setting of interest rates charged by private lenders, which was then determined weekly by the executive of the Government. This is properly thought of as a function of foreign investment governance, and I have included this aim in Table 3.1 at number five. The challenge for the Gorton Government in the face of an incident like the MLC affair, however, was to create a capacity to intervene to block a single investment. In a larger sense, Gorton needed to create a regime that managed all four imperatives identified so far and added a fifth: promoting Australian participation in production.

There were three parts to the regime introduced in December 1969 by the Gorton government. First, a set of "guidelines" provided the government with new powers to prevent foreign takeovers of Australian businesses that were deemed to be "against the national interest." Second, there was a new requirement for foreign interests to gain approval from the Reserve Bank for any borrowings within Australia for investments in which more than 25% of shares were held by non-residents (Sadleir 2007, 109). Third, a new stipulation that foreign interests were allowed to raise new borrowings in Australia in proportion to the equity held in the given enterprises by Australians was introduced (Bell 1976, 46). The three initiatives balanced this bundle of demands well, and it is likely that the regime's efficacy rested on the use of guidelines rather than more rigid statutory law, and the central place for the term "national interest," which was not defined.

The Gorton government's regime remained stable for three years until the McMahon government was forced by public pressure to introduce a legislative basis for the screening regime and establish an institution responsible for executing it. This pressure was partly the result of the new forces of volatility in the global economy, described in the section above, and partly from a more substantial difference of opinion on the role of the state from the Labor Opposition, discussed below. This basis was provided in the *Companies (Foreign Takeovers) Act 1972* (*FTA 1972*). *The Act* expanded the capacity of the Treasurer to reject individual investments and placed the issue of "control" at the centre of the regime. The Treasurer was empowered to prohibit certain interests from acquiring shares in the case of either hostile or invited acquisitions (*FTA 1972*, section 13) or to limit the "beneficial ownership of shares" (section 14). This could be done in the event that an increase of existing holdings in any way that places a foreign person in a "position to exercise effective control of that company; and (ii) the exercise of that control would be contrary to the national interest" (section 14 (b) i and ii).

While the primary aims of investment screening remained stable, the *FTA 1972* introduced a second-order policy aim that warrants inclusion in Table 3.1: the need to manage public opinion on matters relating to foreign investment (aim number six). This was important as public backlash to foreign capital was perceived as raising the risks of mass capital flight (see Sadleir 2007, 115). While managing public opinion could reasonably be said to be a second-order goal of every public policy, in the case of Australian FDI it has a special significance, and the fact that it features in the legislative and policy documents is unorthodox. In the Fraser governments, this element of the policy problem would be refined to mitigating the harmful effects of domestic opposition to foreign investment—harmful effects meaning foregone external capital. In both cases, the effects of the provisions are to enhance the executive capacity of the government, as I will show.

While Fraser's formulation of the public opinion policy problem is much more relevant to the case of the Rudd government, it is worth noting that the second-order goal first appeared in a section of the *FTA 1972* allowing the government to enforce "... adherence to unspecified interim arrangements to assuage 'intense public interest' while the legislation was being drawn up and promulgated" (Sadleir 2007, 117). In both cases the framing of public opinion management as a policy goal places official actors in a strangely anti-democratic position in relation to the electorate that they are ostensibly serving and representing. It implies that an unstated belief of the policy space was that "correct" economic management was a greater priority than adherence to simplistic democratic ideals. The most non-pejorative (at least from a liberal, globalist perspective) way of describing this is to describe the FDI regime as "... a mechanism for managing and defusing nationalist and protectionist sentiment in the community" (Kirchner 2014, 15). The logic amounts to ensuring that the issue was (and is) not used as a political football to the detriment of the economy.

Finally, the anti-democratic nature of this element is complicated again by the following line that appeared in one of the key official documents of the policy regime, the Australian Foreign Investment Policy (AFIP)[2]:

> The Government determines what is 'contrary to the national interest' by having regard to the widely held community concerns of Australians. (FIRB 2007, 68)

As no actor ever stands for "the community" and can authoritatively state what its concerns are, this line amounts to a point of flexibility that an Australian government can draw upon if needed. It positions the government with the electorate, if this is useful, and managing the electorate, if that is useful. The point is not that there is necessarily anything normatively incorrect about these settings; rather, it is that executive power is written into the Australian FDI screening regime and is constantly defended.[3]

3.1.3 Expanding the Remit: Facilitating State-Led Development, Limiting Foreign Appropriation of Profits, and Social Equity

During a short, two-term period in office, the Whitlam government clearly added two new elements to the problem mix, and could be said to have added a third. The two strong additions were an aim to involve the government in production, both indirectly (via market guidance) and directly (by making the bundling of capital for productive investment a task of the state), and promoting social equity (number seven and eight, respectively, in Table 3.1). In both cases, these ambitions centred on the Australian mining sector, which was central to the Whitlam government's FDI regime generally. The third problem element was the protection of "national sovereignty," which I will return to at the end of the section. Overall the Whitlam FDI screening regime had two defining characteristics. First there was a remarkable amount of policy experimentation during the three-year period in the area of FDI. This was largely due to the hostile Senate the government faced during its first term, which forced it to use alternative methods of forwarding its goals from introducing the FDI legislation that they had planned in opposition. Secondly, the list of goals attached to the policy regime was now so crowded that it is difficult to identify single aims of each of the new policy instruments.

Policy instruments that contributed to the already-present policy goals included the introduction of a Variable Deposit Requirement (VDR) scheme, an injection of funds to the Australian Industry Development Corporation (AIDC), and two new advisory bodies charged with enhancing competitiveness in Australian industry: the Industries Assistance Commission (IAC) and Trade Practices Commission (TPC). The VDR scheme is particularly interesting, though mainly in theory, as the economic travails of the mid-1970s forced it to be abandoned. The scheme stipulated that a proportion of all foreign borrowings would need to be held as an interest-free deposit with the Reserve Bank.[4] These funds were held until loan repayments were made, meaning that the effects of the VDR were analogous to a tax on overseas borrowing. It had the potential to help manage volatility effects, in the way a Tobin tax does, and the risk of capital flight, as well as increasing Australian participation in production and ownership. It was intended to provide a stock of funds that the government could use to act as a financier of private enterprises so as to encourage Australian-held equity in major investment projects. It was also imagined that the government would be able to act as a joint venture partner with foreign firms in projects within Australia, with the same aims in mind (see Department of Treasury 1999). In the VDR we can see the ambitious agenda that the Whitlam government envisaged for FDI management. These were small-scale experiments, however, when compared to Whitlam's changes targeted at the mining sector. Given that they were largely unrealised, I have not derived an element for the problem set of this genealogy from them.

With the new mining controls, the Whitlam government aimed to (a) achieve energy independence; (b) extract greater rents from the export of natural resources (Sadleir 2007, 128); and (c) boost Australian participation in the sector (Whitlam 1985, 239, quoted in Sadleir 2007, 126).

The eventual aim was to secure streams of revenue from these involvements that could be used to help fund the provision of a social wage (Whitlam 1985, 238–249; Sadleir 2007, 128). Practically speaking, the government planned to introduce new restrictions on foreign direct investment in the mining sector[5] and controls relating to the sale of resources[6]; advisory committees in mining and other key industries[7]; industry assistance aimed at the development of technological advancement and the fostering of competition; and the creation of government-owned enterprises where market competition was deemed to be ineffective due to the presence of a monopoly (adapted from Johnson 1989, 57, quoted in Table 5.3 of Sadleir 2007, 128).[8] By and large, though, the ambitious minerals program was abandoned when it became clear that the government would not be able to secure financing, despite its best efforts as shown in the Khemlani affair.[9] Finally, when faced with better conditions in the second term, the Whitlam government introduced the *FATA 1975*. The law has been the foundation for every subsequent government's investment screening regime, including Rudd's. I will leave off my discussion of it until the second part of this chapter.

A final point of note on the Whitlam years and the policy goals of foreign investment is Sadleir's suggestion that the administration added the protection of national sovereignty to the aims of the FDI regime. He writes:

> In government the Whitlam cabinet viewed foreign investment as an issue of national sovereignty and a significant contributor to the national economy, not simply an issue of the level of national reserves or the balance of payments as had the preceding Coalition governments. Having placed the well-being of the Australian state above sectional interests (Menadue 2004, 3) the Whitlam government sought to reshape the state and its institutions to better harness national and international economic resources, including capital flows. (Sadleir 2007, 123)

While I think that sovereignty is a crucial discursive element to the Rudd government's actions in relation to FDI, I am not convinced that the distinction Sadleir draws here is analytically valuable. Certainly the Whitlam government operated under an entirely different mode of governance, a form of social economic nationalism, from the Liberal-led governments of the 1950s and 1960s. However, to say that these differences amount to a concern for Australia's sovereignty as a change from the earlier governments is ambiguous. It is also a far cry from the sovereignty-related issues of national *security* that become central to the debate on SOE investments in the mid-2000s, and a long way from the specifically governmental meaning of sovereignty—the integrity of a particular form of governmentality—that I will argue is a necessary analytical device for explaining the Rudd government's actions. For all these reasons, I have omitted Sadleir's suggested problem element from the list in Table 3.1.

3.1.4 Deregulation and Reregulation: Fostering Competition and Empowering the Executive

The rise of competition-fostering as an aim of the FDI regime was accomplished by loosening existing controls over a period of decades while at the same time increasing the state's capacity for economic intervention on a microeconomic level. The move from Whitlam's activist, state-led developmentalism to what is called neoliberal or economic rationalist governance did not entail removing the state from the marketplace. Rather, the new mode of economic rule was founded on a capacity and willingness to intervene in the economy in many places, always according to logics of competition. While I have charted the genealogy from government to government until this point, I will leave this off to describe the rise of competition-fostering as the consistent trend of successive FDI screening regimes from Fraser to Howard.

To begin the description of these changes, there has consistently been liberalisation of the controls that either preceded the early FDI screening regimes or were part of them. The most common form of liberalisation was raising the thresholds below which FDI screening does not occur.[10] The thresholds were raised in 1978, 1981, 1984, 1985, 1986, 1987, 1993, 1999, and 2004 (Sadleir 2007, 194, 258–260, and 315–316). In addition, the Fraser governments partially relaxed the fifty per cent minimum Australian ownership requirement for new enterprises in mining and primary production, and removed the one hundred per cent Australian ownership requirement for new uranium mining projects. In January 1983, Fraser allowed foreign banks to operate in Australia with less than fifty per cent Australian-held equity, on the provisions that they could demonstrate a net economic benefit to Australia by their entry, operated as subsidiaries rather than branches in Australia, and provided an adequately wide range of services (Sadleir 2007, 198–291).

Under Hawke the "two most influential decisions of the 1980s" (Kelly 1992, 76), the floating of the dollar and the deregulation of the financial system generally, should be listed as liberalising moves within the foreign capital governance regime. Measures targeted more directly to FDI under the Hawke governments included an invitation in 1984 for foreign banks to apply for a limited number of licences to operate in Australia, and an amendment to the *FATA 1975* to increase the thresholds for investment proposal screening from ten to fifteen per cent ownership. During the second, third, and fourth Hawke governments, there were further raises of the thresholds for screening, and liberalisation of regulations on non-bank financial institutions, purchases of land intended for development and rural land, new businesses in manufacturing, tourism, and easing of limitations on mining, oil, and gas asset acquisitions (Sadleir 2007, 251–254). Under Keating in 1992, it was announced that no objections to proposals would be raised where the total assets or investment was less than $50 million. Finally, the Howard governments were responsible for removing the special limitations on uranium mining, and the restrictions on foreign takeovers or acquisitions of Australian banks and airlines. In short, over the period there was a consistent and concerted dismantling of controls on investing by foreign interests.

The liberalisation of the FDI controls of the 1960s and 1970s was not entirely one-directional. Tightening of restrictions occurred under all the regimes from Fraser to Howard, though these were often superficial in nature. The most common moves towards restriction occurred in the area of real estate purchases by foreign interests, with instances in 1981, 1982, 1983, 1987, and 1999 (see Sadleir 2007, 194, 258–260, and 315–316). There were high-profile investment proposals refused during Fraser's third term (the Borg-Warner and Bowater proposals), the early stages of Hawke's government (the Dayco, N.W. Ayer Inc. and Sanko Shoji proposals; see Pokarier 2000, 187–188 for details), and the second Howard term (the 2001 Shell proposal).

At the same time as the loosening of controls, there was a proliferation of new governing agencies, each responsible for regulating a relatively constrained domain of economic actions. Understanding the management of foreign capital flows in broad terms, the proliferation was as follows. To the already existing bodies of the AIDC (Australian Industry Development Corporation, established by the Gorton government) and TPC and IAC (Whitlam government), the

Fraser government added the Prices Justification Tribunal (PJT) and the National Companies and Securities Commission (NCSC), and created the FIRB.[11] Under Hawke there were new responsibilities given to the Australian Taxation Office (ATO) and FIRB, as well as number of new agencies created whose operations occasionally crossed those of the FDI screening community: the Australian Transactions Reports and Analysis Centre (AUSTRAC), the Australian Broadcasting Authority (ABrA), AusTrade, the Price Surveillance Authority, and the Industry Commission. Under Keating, the Australian Competition and Consumer Commission (ACCC), the National Investment Advisory Board (NIAB), and the National Competition Commission (NCC) were created. Finally, under Howard the Australian Prudential Regulation Authority (APRA), the Australian Securities and Investment Commission (ASIC), the Takeovers Panel, the Productivity Commission, Invest Australia, and Axis Australia were all commissioned.[12] This comes to nineteen separate bodies, all of which play a role in governing foreign investments or governing an area of economic behaviour that overlaps with the actions of foreign investors. The set of institutions is heterogeneous: some of the bodies are independent from any government, some are quasi-independent, and some operate essentially as public service departments or divisions within departments.[13]

Competition was the coordinating rubric of these bodies just as it came to overlay all economic governance in the context of a shift to neoclassical economics (see Sturgess 1996; Arnold 2000; Sadleir 2007, 217–219) and underpinned the constitutions of the new micro-regulatory agencies. Sadleir (2007, 225) summarises the formula as follows:

> The rational[e] for micro-economic reform was that reforms in trade during the 1980s had "increased the exposure of the internationally traded goods sector to competition… many sectors of the economy… remained sheltered from competition" (ACCC 2000, 19). Thus, micro-economic reform was about increasing competition and efficiency in those sectors by removing existing domestic constraints.

The management of foreign investment flows was naturally a central part of this agenda.

The remarkable proliferation of regulatory and advisory bodies outlined above is important in a second sense; in that, it enhanced the capacity of the executive government to intervene in the economy to a degree greater than the sum of the provisions attached to each of them. Each body had distinct domains of responsibility, but these tended to overlap at the edges. The bodies had different institutional compositions, and different modes and locations of intervention in the economy. This meant that as difficult or novel problems arose, the executive government was able to choose from among its substantial and varied regulatory arsenal, which instrument to respond with. This choice is rarely made explicitly of course, and must be deduced by the analyst. The significance of this point for me is that when the Rudd government encountered a wave of very large direct investments from sovereign-owned enterprises (SOEs), a difficult political problem that required management with very tight control over the political agenda, the FIRB was ideal. Nonetheless, it must be considered as a choice. The choice to use the FIRB still must be thought of as a choice. Indeed, clear alternatives certainly existed: a less intrusive regulatory path might have been to leave the policing of actual anticompetitive behaviour to behind the border institutions designed to deal with just such issues: the ACCC and Australian Securities and Investments Commission (ASIC). These were pointedly ignored by the Rudd government in their response to the Chinese SOE investments, and this should be treated first as a choice and second as one that was made possible by the proliferation of variegated regulatory bodies.

Whether this effect of enhancing capacity for intervention is an effect of all bureaucratic systems, or neoliberal rule, capitalism, or power generally, it seems reasonable to add another second-order goal to Table 3.1: enhancing the capacity of the federal executive to intervene in the economy in a diverse range of ways. Where we could imagine this element as an *effect* of the changes in the style of economic governance, there is also some evidence that protecting the executive wing of government from systems of oversight was intentional. First, in the second reading of the *FATA 1975* in the House of Representatives, a positive reason was given for not providing clear criteria in the Act for the screening of FDI proposals:

> … because criteria must be flexible in their interpretation and application and it has been found that it would be impracticable, consistent with the need for such flexibility, to express the criteria with the precision required by legislative form. (Stewart 1975)

Secondly, decisions made under the *FATA 1975* are specifically exempt from administrative or judicial review according to the *Administrative Decisions (Judicial Review) Act 1977* (paragraph (h); Golding 2010, 222).

3.1.5 *Ensuring High-Profile Multinationals Remain in Australia and National Security*

Two final elements of the policy problem are added by the Howard government: managing reputational damage to the Australian economy and defending national security.

The first of these is easier to discuss after some events—two decisions on FDI proposals—have been explained, as the logic underpinning it is convoluted. The first decision was a refusal to allow the British and Dutch giant, Shell, from acquiring the Australian firm, Woodside Petroleum, in 2001. At the time, the Treasurer (Costello 2001a) justified the decision as follows:

> I have the responsibility to make a decision that must as far as possible withstand circumstances which might change after my decision has been made. Such circumstances can involve changes in the corporate strategies involved in a decision, new or evolving corporate strategies by other companies with respect to the NWS project and changing world demand and supply conditions.

Kirchner (2008a, 13) interprets Costello's decision as reflecting a belief that Shell did not intend to develop the Northwest Shelf, a rich seam of gas in Western Australia. A second interpretation from Harper (2001) was that the rejection had more to do with preventing Shell from engaging in transfer pricing or the "branch office effect." Transfer pricing refers to discounting prices from subsidiaries in foreign countries for a product bought by the home company so as to minimise the tax paid to the foreign government. The branch office effect refers to the loss of employment suffered when Shell reverts positions held by Australians to their own, non-Australian workers, particularly highly skilled positions. Via both channels then the intervention is understood by Harper as being about using microeconomic controls to manage "natural" competition or the downsides of Australia's precarious position as a small, open economy in a global system containing much larger economies. In this sense, it was a return to some of the earliest purposes of FDI screening, but with different economic reasoning.

Harper's reasoning was echoed by Costello's comments made in 2009 on a second decision, made in 2001, which allowed the mining multinational, BHP to list dually with the Australian Billiton with a number of conditions:

> I was determined to ensure that BHP's corporate presence did not disappear from Australia in the same way as CRA [Consolidated Zinc Corporation], so I put conditions on its dual-listed company structure that required the global headquarters to remain in Australia, that this be specified in all public documents, that the majority of board meetings be in Australia, and most importantly, that the chief executive and chief financial officer have their principal residence in Australia. (Costello 2009)

A few paragraphs later, the former Treasurer justified the restrictions slightly paradoxically with reference to a need to represent Australia as open to investment:

> If a country wants to be seen as open to investment it needs to show that there are high profile global companies that operate inside its borders. (Costello 2009)

That is, it is in the country's national interest to be perceived as operating on liberal tenets of openness, meaning freedom from government-imposed interferences. However, it is legitimate to pursue this aim using certain forms of intervention. This point coheres with the Shell decision. The three possible reasons suggested above for Costello's decision to disallow Shell's acquisition of Woodside—preventing the Northwest Shelf asset from being locked out of productive use, preventing transfer pricing, or preventing branch office tax manipulation—all amount to an embrace of a pragmatic mode of economic governance containing elements of a need to engage the reality of Australia being a small, open economy in an environment dominated by much larger markets. This implies a need for strategic engagement with the world on a nationalist basis, and a need for flexibility for the federal executive to shape this engagement in a nuanced way.

My point is not that the orthodox understanding of the Howard governments as essentially defined by neoliberal beliefs and agendas is in need of revision or that Costello's seemingly contradictory logic is illegitimate in any way. Rather, it is that there was a consistent set of beliefs about Australia's place in the world and the role of the federal government in shaping the relationship between the two. This role of shaping a strategic engagement with the world takes the nation as its object, and on a number of occasions understands the aim as not only material (retaining tax revenue streams or productive capacity for the economy in the case of the Shell decision) but ideational. The summary of this policy aim listed in Table 3.1, attracting large MNCs to the Australian economy, is really a proxy for the more general aim of "managing" the Australian economy in the corporate sense of the word: intervening strategically, and balancing the needs of consistency and a clear approach or ideology. The government functions to provide guidance about future actions to market players and defends the material interest of the country.

The final goal of the policy that appears in this genealogy is defending Australia's national security. Michael Wesley (2012) has claimed that throughout the Howard years there was a securitisation of foreign policy, including in Australia's economic relationships. Similarly, a narrative that appears in the literature is that Australia sought autonomy via the fostering of economic interdependence between Australia and its trade partners, and via the strengthening of the strategic alliance with the United States (for a summary see Kalfadellis et al. 2006). Paul Kelly, for example, described a central goal of the Howard governments as the international pursuit of "economic, political and security partnerships creating networks of interdependence as the best means of ensuring Australia's control over its destiny" (2006, 37). Marchick and Slaughter (2008) also link the move to the rise of terrorism, and Thirlwell and Shearer (2008, 9–13) link the rise to the new regionalism, in which security concerns have come to overlay all other interactions. These are all plausible arguments, and I will only note that the element appears in the policy of the Rudd government: on two occasions investments from Chinese SOEs were rejected on the basis of (hard) security concerns.

This concludes the genealogy. It is worth noting first that the twelve aims of FDI governance outlined here appear in the Rudd government's FDI policy. The departures that were made from it did not replace these policy aims. A number of them appear explicitly, and others appear as implicit concerns of the government, or of other actors within the policy space. Secondly, the set of elements affected the contours of the space in which the Rudd government's policy was contested in an important way: the number of precedents and ease with which Australian governments historically have added aims to the practice of screening foreign investments itself provided a degree of flexibility to each new government in shaping its own approach. In short, the Rudd government's departures—the additions made to Table 3.1—were in keeping with the lineage of the policy in that most governments found a new reason to screen FDI, and added it to the existing reasons.

To continue this scene-setting task before describing how the Rudd Government's policy constituted a departure in Sect. 3.3, I will describe the legislative and institutional arrangements that it inherited.

3.2 The FATA 1975, the Policy, and the FIRB

The Australian FDI screening regime rests on the *FATA 1975* (the Act) and the Australian Foreign Investment Policy (AFIP, or the Policy). The Policy does not have legislative force. Nonetheless, on several important points, it is the Policy rather than the Act that guides the government's actions. As a result, the two cannot be understood simply from the text. We must appreciate how they are employed.

3.2.1 The Foreign Acquisition and Takeovers Act (FATA) 1975, the Foreign Acquisition and Takeovers Regulations (FATR) 1989, and the Australian Foreign Investment Policy (AFIP)

The *FATA 1975* replaced the *FTA 1972* and was passed in the final months of the second Whitlam government. It stipulates the types of investment that are subject to at-the-border controls and defines the nature of these controls. The *FATA 1975* empowers the Treasurer to examine investment proposals by foreign interests (a) to acquire a "substantial" shareholding or interest in the assets of an Australian corporation that is valued over a threshold value, or (b) to acquire an interest in Australian urban land. The Treasurer does not "approve" these proposals precisely; rather he or she has the capacity to prohibit a proposal that he or she deems to be against the national interest (sections 18, 19, 20, 21, 21a). Generally speaking, an investment may be deemed against the national interest on grounds relating to the foreign person acquiring a controlling interest in the corporation (section 18), the acquisition altering the corporation's governance and operations, such as board representation or alterations to constituent documents or the management or profit-sharing arrangements (sections 19, 20, 21). Alternatively, the Treasurer can raise no objections to the proposed investment, or subject it to conditions that remove national interest concerns (section 25). In the case of an acquisition that has already been made, the Treasurer is empowered to order the foreign persons to divest shares, assets, or interests in urban land where the acquisition is determined to be contrary to the national interest.

The thresholds that determined when notification to the Treasurer was required in December 2007 were as follows (from FIRB 2008):

- acquisitions of substantial interests in Australian businesses where the gross assets were valued in excess of $100 million;
- proposals to establish new businesses that involve a total investment of $10 million or more;
- takeovers of offshore companies whose Australian subsidiaries or gross assets exceed $200 million and represent less than 50% of global assets.

There are a number of exceptions to these general thresholds. First, there are a number of prescribed sensitive sectors that adjacent legislation imposes foreign investment requirements on. These are (Sanyal [no date] and FIRB 2008):

- the banking sector: foreign ownership must be consistent with the *Banking Act 1959*, the *Financial Sector (Shareholdings) Act 1988*, and the national banking policy;
- airports: the *Airports Act 1996* limits foreign ownership of some airports to 49%; foreign ownership in the Australian airline Qantas is also restricted to 49%, with individual holdings limited to 25% and aggregate ownership by foreign airlines to 35%;
- the shipping industry: the *Shipping Registration Act 1981* requires that ships must be majority Australian-owned if they are to be registered in Australia, unless they are designated as chartered by an Australian operator;
- media: irrespective of size, foreign persons investing in the media sector must seek prior approval; proposals involving shareholdings of 5% or more must also be submitted for examination;
- telecommunications: aggregate foreign ownership of Telstra is limited to 35% and individual foreign investors are only allowed a maximum of 5%.

A second set of exceptions was created in the free trade agreement signed between Australia and the United States in 2005 (AUSFTA). Under pressure to liberalise the screening regime as part of the agreement, the Howard government eventually conceded ground by significantly raising the thresholds as they applied to investors from the United

States. In December 2007, the threshold for US investors was $913 million, significantly higher than that of other investors.[14]

A final exception to the thresholds is that proposals for investment made by foreign governments or their agencies are always required to seek approval from the Treasurer, irrespective of the size of the proposed investment. According to the *FATA 1975* (section 17F),

an entity is a foreign government investor if:

a. the entity is:
   (i) a body politic of a foreign country; or
   (ii) a body politic of part of a foreign country; or
   (iii) a part of a body politic mentioned in subparagraph (i) or (ii); or
b. the entity is controlled by an entity mentioned in paragraph (a); or
c. an entity mentioned in paragraph (a) holds an interest in the entity that satisfies the conditions specified in the regulations.

"The regulations" refers to section 7 of the *Foreign Acquisitions and Takeovers Regulations 1989* (*FATR 1989*). This section provides a second set of asset thresholds that determine when an investment by a foreign government must submit a proposal to the Treasurer for consideration. Section 7 of the *FATR 1989* refers back to section 17C of the *FATA 1975*, which provides room for the government to impose different threshold amounts on different foreign government investors according to the kind of investor it is (for example a sovereign wealth fund (SWF) or an SOE), the kind of corporation concerned, the kind of business concerned, or any other matter (*FATA 1975*, section 17C, parts 3(a), (b), (c), and (d)). To summarise, the issue of foreign government investment is covered in the legislation defining the screening regime. The law centres on the issue of control from the body politic, but (once again) does so in a way that leaves open the task of determining actual reasons for intervening on investments to the Treasurer of the day.

Interestingly, the FDI screening regime that the Rudd government inherited insisted that any direct investment by "foreign governments and their agencies" irrespective of their size required "notification for prior approval." The quotes are from the Policy, which is published by the FIRB as an appendix to the Annual Report (FIRB 2007, 69).[15] The Policy does not have legislative force, but stockholders are urged to consider the appendix "in conjunction with" the *FATA 1975* and the *FATR*

1989 (FIRB 2008, 71, Footnote 1). Seemingly then, the Policy has been understood as overriding the legislation on this point of thresholds for foreign government investments. This is not the only part of the *FATA 1975* that is regularly disregarded.

Once the Treasurer has received notice from a prospective investor (*FATA 1975*, sections 26, 26a), a thirty-day statutory examination period commences. If the Treasurer does not take action (under sections 18, 19, 20, 21, 21a, 22, or 25) within this time, the power to prohibit the proposal or to impose conditions expires. The exception to this occurs when the Treasurer issues an Interim Order (section 22 and subsection 25(3)), which extends the examination period by up to ninety further days. This provision is used in the case of complex or large investment proposals. In the period being examined in this study, Treasurer Swan issued Interim Orders a number of times. Notably, though, he failed to make decisions within the statutory time limits on a number of occasions. The most important of these were the two largest, which were both investments by the Chinese SOE Chinalco in the iron ore giant, Rio Tinto. The first hostile raid was made on the 31st of January 2008, and permission for the transaction to go ahead was not approved until the 24th of August of that year. The second bid increasing the stake in Rio Tinto was made by Chinalco in February 2009 and was awaiting Swan's determination until June 2009. In the end, an official determination was never made as the deal fell apart and Rio Tinto announced a major new collaboration with BHP-Billiton. The significance of this is that it is important to recognise that companies applying to invest in Australia are strongly incentivised to placate the Australian government wherever possible, given that their larger aim is to do business in Australia for a long period of time. The statutory powers do not always define the behaviour of the government, and foreign investors often prefer to accept the government acting outside of its formal limits rather than displease the officials by calling attention to it (Table 3.2).

There is a similar dynamic that prevents prospective investors from criticising the Treasurer's decisions to reject or confer conditions on investments: they would rather keep rejections out of the public's knowledge so as not to lose stock value or position in relation to commercial competitors. The result is that on occasions that the Treasurer or FIRB indicates to an investor that a proposal will be rejected or have conditions placed on it, the firm often chooses to withdraw the application rather than having the rejection made public. It is common

Table 3.2 Applications considered (number of proposals): 2006/2007–2011/2012

Outcome	*2006/07*	*2007/08*	*2008/09*	*2009/10*	*2010/11*	*2011/12*
Total considered	7025	8548	5821	4703	10,865	11,420
Total approved	**6157**	**7841**	**5352**	**4401**	**10,293**	**10,703**
Approved unconditionally	1520	1656	2266	2672	4606	4900
Approved with conditions	4637	6185	3086	1729	5687	5803
Total rejected	**39**	**14**	**3**	**3**	**43**	**13**
Withdrawn	629	521	341	167	390	534
Exempt	200	172	125	132	139	170

Data from Bowman et al. (2014, 6)

practice for the firm to reapply with an amended proposal that deals with the Treasurer's concerns; in other cases, the investment is presumably terminated altogether (see comments made by the Treasurer in Swan 2008c). The reasons for these withdrawals are not recorded publicly, if at all. In addition, approvals that have conditions attached take up a large proportion of approvals, and it is not enormously meaningful to cite these figures as evidence of non-interventionism without any of the details on these conditions. Finally, these figures are mostly composed of decisions on real estate purchases, which are obviously small and numerous. As this examination concerns the Rudd government's policy on productive investments, and particularly investments by SOEs and SWFs, as well as for the first two reasons, I place little store on these figures, and don't refer to them again in this book. Despite these problems Treasurer Swan and FIRB Executive Member Patrick Colmer used these figures in nearly every major speech to defend the claim that the Rudd government favoured a non-interventionist approach, as will be shown in Chapter 6. I include them here only due to the fact that they are cited with such regularity in the debates on the screening regime, and I feel it is necessary to explain why I reject this practice.

Finally, it is important to recognise that the regime functions on a case by case basis, and that there is no obligation under the *FATA 1975* for the Treasurer to provide any justification or explanation for any rejection or condition placed on an investment proposal. These conditions mean that the Treasurer is not compelled to respect precedents in his or her decision-making. The discretion this allows enables the Treasurer to define the point of screening as he or she will, as I have shown in section one. It should also be recognised that this flexibility also extends to more technical aspects of the execution of the policy. For example, a substantial interest (shareholdings) in a corporation is deemed to constitute a controlling interest, unless the Treasurer is satisfied to the contrary in that particular case. However, a shareholding less than a substantial interest could still be regarded as controlling if it is deemed to enable the holder to exert control or material influence over the company (FIRB 2008, 50). This might occur when a person with less than a substantial interest is able to exert a measure of control via representation on the board of the company or when he or she is able to influence the operations or policy of a company by providing technology, finance, or marketing links. Again, shareholdings by multiple foreign holders may constitute a controlling interest if they aggregate to forty per cent or more in an Australian corporation, *unless the Treasurer is satisfied to the contrary.*

3.2.2 The Role of the Foreign Investment Review Board

The final element of the FDI regime, as it was inherited by the Rudd Government, is the FIRB. Ostensibly, the FIRB is an independent advisor to the Treasurer. In practice, the institution occupies a position that is both inside and outside the state, according to the strategic needs of the government. The Rudd government adopted the FIRB in the form they inherited it, using it in much the same way as previous Australian governments: to depoliticise FDI regulation and to deflect criticism of the policy generally and of decisions on individual proposals.

Formally speaking, the core functions of the FIRB are the same as they have been since the organisation's creation in 1976: the provision of independent advice on matters relating to foreign direct investment generally and advice on individual investment proposals awaiting decisions from the Treasurer (FIRB 1977, 1). As a non-statutory body—the *FATA 1975* contains no reference to the FIRB—it has no formal capacity beyond advice-giving, and the executive capacity conferred on it by the Treasurer under the *FATA 1975*. Aside from advice-giving, the FIRB Annual Report of 2005–2006 (the last report signed off by Treasurer Peter Costello) listed the following functions:

- to "foster an awareness and understanding, both in Australia and abroad, of the policy of the Act";
- to "provide guidance to foreign persons and their representatives/agents so that proposals conform with the policy and the Act"; and
- to "monitor and ensure compliance with the policy and the Act" (FIRB 2007, 3).

In a number of senses, then, the FIRB is internal to the government. Firstly, monitoring compliance with the policy is certainly a practice of the state, and could only be done with the authority conferred upon the institution by the state. Secondly, alongside the neutral tasks of providing guidance to foreign persons on the policy and fostering awareness and understanding of the policy, the FIRB is also often tasked with defending the policy settings as well as advertising Australia as an investment destination to foreign capital. While one might have expected the FIRB to perform a critical function, given its positioning as an independent, advisory body to the government, there is little evidence of this in public. If the various boards have made criticisms, either of the regime, or the policy of a particular government, these have been in private. In this sense, too, the FIRB is internal to the state.

On the point of board members advertising Australia as an investment destination, this practice is again as old as the institution itself. The board was created in a context of the continuing turmoil of the stagflation crisis and a shortfall of capital in the economy, and the first members appointed to the board, Sir Bede Callahagn and Tim Besley, were tasked with explaining to the world that Australia welcomed capital, and that the rules put in place regulating it were sensible and equitable. This involved speaking at events in the United States, Canada, the United Kingdom, Germany, France, and Japan (Sadleir 2007, 172–173). As the regime was populated with parallel bodies as noted above, this task was brought more clearly within the operations of the government under AusTrade, the Australian Trade Commission established by the *Australian Trade Commission Act 1985*. The bodies within AusTrade responsible for this were the NIAB, Axis Australia, and then Invest Australia. However, FIRB board members continue to include spruiking Australia as an investment destination and a component of all major speeches, and attending investment fairs as part of their role (for example, see Di Giorgio 2011).[16]

The executive member of the board is also the formal representative of Australia at certain international forums. For example, he or she is the Australian National Contact Point for the OECD Guidelines for Multinational Enterprises and related corporate social responsibility issues. The role is to ensure the effective promotion and implementation of the OECD Guidelines in Australia (FIRB 2009, 55). This is a perfectly logical decision: the executive member is an official of the Treasury, and the Foreign Investment and Trade Policy Division, which provides the secretarial staff to the FIRB, has a central place in negotiating positions on international investment issues. The position is clearly internal to the state, however, and the executive member of the board should not be thought of as "independent" in his or her role of advising the Treasurer in any way that a regular public servant is not.

Beyond these roles, there are reasons relating to makeup of the institution which imply that the board is more accurately imagined as internal to the state. As noted above, the Board's secretarial staff is composed of treasury officials from the Foreign Investment Division (FID), previously the Foreign Investment Review Branch. In its initial form, the board was composed of two persons, one with a business background and one senior Treasury official. As the number of board members gradually grew, the new additions have all been from outside of government, but the position of executive member has remained an appointment from the FID. The effect of this structure, in Sadleir's words, is that "the FIRB could be seen as operating at arm's length from the political and policy core of the national government, while operating sufficiently close to the core to ensure a high degree of access to government decisionmaking" (2007, 198). In practice, the routine decisions (generally speaking real estate purchases and small and standard investments in productive enterprises) are delegated to the secretarial staff, which is to say the Treasury staff. The larger decisions are obviously made by the Treasurer himself or herself (Di Giorgio, quoted in Rural and Regional Affairs and Transport 2013, chapter five, paragraph 5, page 47). The role of the actual members of the board, then, appears to be to amalgamate advice from a series of state bodies, the ACCC and the ATO, the predominant among them, and present these in a coherent way with a recommendation for the Treasurer. My point is not that the board is inconsequential; it is difficult to say how influential their recommendations are on the decisions made by the Treasurer, either generally or in particular cases. Finally, even if the board members do function with a high degree of independence from the government, as is claimed, the fact that the board's advice is not public mean that its independence does not result in meaningful oversight of the execution of the policy. Institutionally speaking, the board is highly integrated with bodies that are internal to the state.

On the other hand, the FIRB can be thought of as external to the state in one way, and this has an important political effect. The board is external to the state in that it is outside of the democratic controls of the political system. This means that the task delegated to it—the initial assessment of investment proposals and the gathering of advice from the range of stakeholder institutions that the state is made up of—are outside of the public political realm. The effect of this, combined with the control the Treasurer has over the actual decision-making, is that the government has an increased capacity to remove a particularly contentious decision from the political agenda, or at least to dilute its attention. If agenda-setting power is as significant in policymaking as I have claimed (see Chapter 2, Sect. 2.3; see also Schattschneider 1960; Bachrach and Baratz 1962), then the ability to delay a decision on a proposal until attention has dissipated is an important one.[17] This is a very standard tactic from Australian governments, which have consistently refused to comment on matters that are before the board. The FIRB is thus usefully positioned outside of the government by holding its independence up as something that must be respected. This tactic was used a number of times by the Rudd government, with the most important examples being the two proposals by the Chinese SOE, Chinalco, to obtain stakes in Rio Tinto. This is discussed in Chapter 6. Overall, it is clear that the institutional and legislative arrangements of the foreign investment screening regime were highly conducive to the needs of the Rudd Government. Just as past Australian governments had done, the Rudd Administration found that the architecture of the FIRB, *FATA 1975*, and the Policy allowed them to execute their screening policy with little meaningful oversight and remarkable control over the appearance of foreign investment screening on the public agenda.

3.3 How the Rudd Government's Actions Constitute a Departure

Up until this point, the chapter has outlined the state of the Australian FDI screening regime as it was when the Rudd government came to office. In this section, I describe the actions of the Rudd government that constitute changes to the formal aspects of the policy and changes in the executions of the policy. The purpose of my study is to explain these changes.

As listed in Table 3.3, there were six clear changes to the formal settings of the policy, and three changes made to the informal aspects of the policy. The official changes number two, three, four, and six do not relate to this study. Number two was an easing of a regulatory setting relating to vacant commercial land. The move was coherent with the Rudd government's overarching narrative of moving to free bottlenecks in the economy that were adding to the strong inflationary pressures. Number three was a liberalising move. It was explained as cutting unnecessary red tape, was in line with the recommendations of the 2006 Banks Taskforce (Bowen 2008a), and contributed to the efforts to add liquidity and stimulus to the economy in the darkest months of the Global Financial Crisis. Number four was a liberalisation of thresholds, much in the vein and trend of the liberalising moves of the preceding governments (see Sect. 3.1, part three above). Finally, number six responded to growing complaints that foreign investors were saturating housing markets in large cities, and that this was keeping house prices and rents unfairly high. All these changes were (relatively) uncontroversial and do not feature in the phenomena being explained here.

Instead, I aim to explain why the Rudd government intervened the way it did on investment proposals from Chinese sovereign-owned enterprises. This involves explaining the official changes to the policy settings numbers one and five, and the three unofficial or speculated changes, as well as the changes in the execution of the policy that can be extrapolated from looking at the decisions made by Treasurer Swan on individual investment proposals. In both cases, the departure from the Howard government's policy lies in a new interventionism and a targeting of this intervention to a very specific class of incoming investments. In the first part of this section, I describe the departures that existed in changes to the policy settings and in the second part I will describe the departures that existed in the changes to the execution of the screening policy.

3.3.1 Changes to the Policy Settings

The "February Guidelines" released by the Australian government were in response to a huge hostile bid on the London Stock Exchange by the Chinese SOE Chinalco for Rio Tinto shares. This was not officially the case however (Swan 2008b; Rudd 2008); the stated aim was "improving the transparency of the foreign investment screening process" (Swan 2008a). As outlined above, the regime already treated

Table 3.3 Changes made by the Rudd government to the settings of the FDI screening regime

Official changes to the policy settings made by the first Rudd government
1. 17 February 2008: Announces six 'Guidelines' for the screening of investment proposals made by foreign governments and their agencies (Swan 2008a). These are listed in Table 3.4, below
2. 23 April 2008: Extended the timeframe for the development of vacant commercial land from twelve months to five years. This removed an unnecessary constraint and struck "…the right balance between encouraging competition while preventing foreign investors from land-banking and speculating" (Bowen 2008a)
3. 18 December 2008: Eight changes introduced to streamline the screening arrangements for acquisitions of residential real estate by foreign persons (Bowen 2008b); all amount to easing of restrictions
4. 4 August 2009: (a) Amended the *Foreign Acquisitions and Takeovers Regulations 1989* to replace the four lower business thresholds with one higher threshold of 15% or more of a business valued at $219 million or more. (b) Index the new unified threshold on 1 January each year against the GDP price deflator. (c) Abolish the requirements that foreign private investors notify the Government when establishing a new business in Australia valued above $10 million (Swan 2009a)
5. 12 February 2010: Passed the *Foreign Acquisitions and Takeover Amendment Act 2010.* This applied retrospectively starting from the 12th of February 2009 and ensured that the provisions of the *FATA 1975* applied to transactions with complex financing arrangements, that had come into use since the original legislation was written
6. 24 April 2010: Announced that all temporary residents seeking to purchase an existing property in Australia must submit a proposal to the FIRB for screening; introduced a civil penalties regime to complement the existing criminal penalties regime that had constituted the compliance mechanism; introduced a new compliance monitoring regime, with a national data bank and a 1-800 community hotline (Sherry 2010)
Unofficial changes to the policy settings made by the first Rudd government
1. The 'seventh guideline'. This refers to the government's aim of preventing vertical integration—that is, having consumers of a product able to affect or take control of decisions regarding the production and pricing of that resource (see Thirlwell and Shearer 2008; Murphy 2009)
2. The 'Colmer Doctrine'. Announced by FIRB Executive Member Patrick Colmer on 24 September 2009 in a speech later released following a freedom of information request. It referred to the government's preference for foreign investments into the resource sector to be limited to a 49.9% controlling share in new projects and a 14.99% share in existing projects (see Kirchner 2010). The existence of this rule was always denied by the government, and there were several decisions made that do not accord to it, such as Ansteel's acquisition of Gindalbie Metals shares in May 2009
3. 'Pose disincentives for larger scale Chinese investments' (words from Wikileaks release of report by US Embassy in Australia officers; Dorling 2011a, b, c, d; Berg 2012). Not publicly revealed until after Rudd's axing as prime minister; always denied by government officials

government-affiliated investors differently from private investors, and thus there was already an implication that there were "additional factors that must also be examined" (Swan 2008a). Swan explained that this was because:

> ... investors with links to foreign governments may not operate solely in accordance with normal commercial considerations and may instead pursue broader political or strategic objectives that could be contrary to Australia's national interest. (Swan 2008a)

He then "clarified" the government's policy on sovereign investments with the six guidelines, which are listed in Table 3.4.

However, far from improving transparency, the announcement was widely criticised as fostering further unnecessary uncertainty about the government's intentions (Kirchner 2008b; Drysdale and Findlay 2009; Drysdale 2011, 57). Certainly the announcement did little to eliminate the aspects of the regime that had been criticised for producing ambiguity: the central but undefined term "national interest," the role of the FIRB, and the lack of oversight of the government on the policy's execution. Further, the guidelines themselves offered little new

Table 3.4 February 2008 guidelines for screening foreign investment proposals

1. An investor's operations are independent from the relevant foreign government. In considering issues relating to independence, the Government will focus on the extent to which the prospective foreign investor operates at arm's length from the relevant government
2. An investor is subject to and adheres to the law and observes common standards of business behaviour
3. An investment may hinder competition or lead to undue concentration or control in the industry or sectors concerned
4. An investment may impact on Australian Government revenue or other policies. For example, investments by foreign government entities must be taxed on the same basis as operations by other commercial entities. They must also be consistent with the Government's objectives in relation to matters such as the environment
5. An investment may impact on Australia's national security. The Government would consider the extent to which investments might affect Australia's ability to protect its strategic and security interests
6. An investment may impact on the operations and directions of an Australian business, as well as its contribution to the Australian economy and broader community

From Swan (2008a)

information about the government's practices, which invited the question: why release the guidelines at all? The first guideline signalled a renewed emphasis of scrutiny on the relationship between a foreign investor and the government of the state from which they originate, but this had been a part of the Policy for at least two decades (Uren 2012, 234). Guidelines two and three were technically redundant, as they were already enforced by the ACCC operating under the *Trade Practices Act 1974*. The fifth point—that the government reserves the right to prevent investments that may threaten national security—could reasonably be assumed given similar provisions that exist in every equivalent economy. The fourth and final guidelines were so vague as to be virtually meaningless. Any investment is likely to affect the Australian government revenue and is likely to affect the operations or direction of an Australian business. The inclusion of these points provided no basis for a prospective investor to decide whether or not to register a proposal. They instead provided grounds for the Australian government to reject or place conditions on a proposed investment, so could be said to provide space for the government to execute the policy. Even this cynical reading is unsatisfying however, as this space had already existed.

A seventh, un-stated guideline was also rumoured to have existed from the time of the February Guidelines (see Thirlwell and Shearer 2008, 4). This was an aversion to vertical integration and transfer pricing. The clearest indication of the criteria was given in a speech from the Executive Director of the Treasury's Markets Group, Jim Murphy, to the Australia–China Investment Forum twenty months later on 4 November 2009:

> When considering a proposed investment, we are particularly attentive to, and carefully consider, any case in which a proposed investor in a resource is also a buyer in that resource.

These comments were echoed by Treasurer Swan on 10 December 2009(i):

> … 'we carefully consider cases where a proposed investor is also a buyer of the resource–in particular, where the proposal involves potential control over pricing and production…

The criteria could reasonably be considered as an elaboration of the second and third criteria, but in the context of the tumultuous iron ore contract pricing negotiations of 2007–2010 (see Chapter 4, Sect. 4.2), the seventh guideline could also (if it existed) be interpreted as the Australian government wading into the iron ore pricing wars. In any case, the government was not opposed to vertical integration in all its forms: as David Uren has pointed out (2012, 81 and 106), the Australian aluminium industry was and is highly vertically integrated, and no bids were made by the Rudd government to change this. Likewise, and even more pointedly, the iron ore industry itself had elements of vertical integration, with Japanese steel-producing firms holding minority shareholdings in several joint-venture projects run by BHP and Rio Tinto (Wilson 2011, 332).

A second "unofficial" change to the policy settings was the so-called Colmer Doctrine. The Colmer Doctrine refers to comments made by the executive member of the FIRB board, Patrick Colmer, to the Australia China Business Council (ACBC) on 24 September 2009. Specifically, Colmer stated:

> In the resource industries and where there is significant government ownership, our Government has expressed a preference for projects which are joint projects in various forms, and in particular we are much more comfortable when we see investments which are below 50% for greenfields projects and around 15% for major producers. However, as I have said, we do look at all investment proposals on a case by case basis and there are examples where we accepted quite readily different arrangements to that.

The comments were reported in China as a new Australian FDI policy (Uren 2012, 104), and in Australia as a far more explicit statement of the existing policy than Swan had ever given, most notably by *The Australian's* Matthew Stevens, who coined the phrase "Colmer Doctrine" (Stevens 2009). The speech was made on the same day that the FIRB refused an investment proposal from China Non-ferrous Metals for 51.6% of the Australian rare earths producer Lynas Corp.

Following its delivery, the speech was not placed on the FIRB's website and requests for copies of it were "ignored or denied", only to be accessed after a freedom of information request by Centre for Independent Studies blogger Stephen Kirchner (2010). The existence of any "hard and fast rules" was then denied in speeches by both Jim Murphy (2009) and by Treasurer Swan on 10 December 2009, who both emphasised the architecture of the screening regime as being centred on "case by case" system. The specific comments from Swan denying the existence of the Doctrine were:

> Of course, if you were concerned solely about predictability, it could be very simple to fix. You would set hard and fast rules, with capped shareholdings, and no discretion. You could publish them on a website, and simply tell non-compliant proposals not to bother.
>
> But no-one with a real interest in Australia's economy would seriously suggest this… and I have approved applications above and below the various 'caps' the Government has been said to have. (Swan 2009f)

Given that all of the decisions that the Colmer Doctrine was applied to were investments from Chinese SOEs, the case that the Doctrine existed is arguably given weight by a Wikileaks' release. The file released was a cable from the US Embassy in Australia reporting on a confidential discussion between Colmer and US Embassy officials in September 2009 (the same month as Colmer's ACBC speech). It was not released until 2011. The Embassy's report, titled "New Foreign Investment guidelines target China" included the following:

> FIRB general manager Patrick Colmer confirmed to Econoff [economic officers] the new guidelines are mainly due to growing concerns about Chinese investments in the strategic resources sector. (US Embassy staff, quoted in Dorling 2011a, b, c, d, clarification by Dorling)

The cable also linked the "new guidelines" to changes in the thresholds for screening and the issue of complex investment schemes, "which sought to circumvent existing FIRB rules" (quoted in Dorling 2011a, b, c, d) and that the *FATA Amendment Act 2010* sought to defend against (see below). The cable reports the existence of "a stricter policy aimed squarely at China's growing influence in Australia's resources sector" and "[posing] new disincentives for larger-scale Chinese investments" (quoted in Dorling 2011a, b, c, d). This is, of course, a different claim to the fifteen per cent, fifty per cent rule, and for this reason "posing new disincentives for larger scale Chinese investments" is listed as a third unofficial change to the policy's settings.

The final policy setting change was the passing of the *FATA Amendment Act 2010*. The Amendment was a response to the second

Chinalco bid for Rio Tinto shares. The bid needs to be understood in context, and will be explained at greater length in Chapter 5. For now, it is sufficient to say that Rio Tinto was under threat of being taken over by its largest Australian rival, BHP-Billiton, throughout 2008. In order to dissuade BHP-Billiton's advances, it took on significant debts, the most significant of which was a $40 billion purchase in the aluminium producer, Alcan in early 2008. In February 2009 it had avoided a second takeover bid from BHP-Billiton, but was in need of financing to cover its outstanding debts. In February 2009, the chief executive of Rio Tinto, Tom Albanese, announced a plan for a second Chinalco acquisition in Rio Tinto in which it would inject a further $19.5 billion through a convertible note issue ($7.2 billion) in conjunction with a series of joint ventures worth $12.3 billion. The plan was designed to get maximum cash into Rio while preserving a public shareholding structure that it was thought the FIRB would accept: Chinalco's shareholdings would rise from 9 to 18% of the group (3% above the 14.99% maximum allowed by the government's approval of the January 2008 raid) and non-controlling stakes in several core assets. The use of convertible notes would also mean that the Chinalco investment would rank ahead of ordinary shareholders in the event of Rio collapsing. Notably also, the deal would mean that Chinalco would gain access to information concerning marketing operations of iron ore.

An hour before the deal was announced, FIRB executive member Colmer called the Chinalco team in Australia and advised them that the Government was about to make an announcement, which included the line: "[i]n light of the growing use of more complex investment structures, the government intends to clarify the operation of the foreign investment screening regime" (Swan 2009a). Swan announced the government's intention to introduce legislation that would become the *Amendment Act 2010*, outlined above, to make sure complex transactions, including convertible notes, would be covered by the FIRB screening regime, and apply retrospectively starting in February 2009. While the *Amendment* was clearly in response to the Chinalco bid, the FIRB's annual report of that year described it as clarifying the operation of the *FATA 1975* to ensure that it applied equally to all foreign investments irrespective of the way they were structured, and intended to capture complex investment structures which may have provided avenues of control beyond that provided through traditional shares or voting power (FIRB 2011, 40).

Albanese's plan eventually unravelled in June 2009 with the Australian Government never having ruled on the investment proposal, despite once again having exceeded its statutory time limit. The FIRB had indicated in meetings in April 2009 that it believed it would be anti-competitive for Chinalco to take equity stakes in Rio Tinto's aluminium assets on the grounds that Chinalco was already China's biggest aluminium producer (Uren 2012, 106). This was despite a ruling by the ACCC issued on the 25th of March that the transaction posed no significant issues relating to competition (ACCC 2009). Chinalco offered to reduce its stake in the Pilbara joint venture from 15 to 7.5% among other alterations, but in the final meeting, held on April 2009, the FIRB stated that deal was "too big and too complex" (Uren 2012, 106). The plan was finally cancelled by Rio Tinto's large investors in London. These investors feared that the deal gave Chinalco a bigger real stake than the proposed 19% and in any case felt that with a swift turnaround in the iron ore market prices during the period of negotiation with the FIRB, Rio Tinto no longer needed the capital injection to resist the BHP-Billiton takeover. That is to say, while the Australian Government did not make a decision, its prevarication was certainly a factor in the dissolution of the deal. In addition, on the day that the second Chinalco acquisition of Rio Tinto shares had failed, Rio announced the successful conclusion of negotiations with BHP for the merging of iron ore production operations in the Pilbara, though with operations relating to the selling of product remaining separate. The *Amendment Act 2010* was passed in February 2010 nonetheless, and can be understood as a successful bid by the Australian government to prevent Chinalco from increasing its stake in the Australian iron ore giant.

3.3.2 Changes in the Execution of the Policy

The final task in defining the Rudd government's policy departure is to summarise the changes that can be deduced by examining the decisions of the government in executing the policy. Once again, only a portion of the executive actions relate to the policy examined here, as most of the matters processed by the FIRB are for residential and commercial property investments and do not relate to this question. The nature of the wave of investments is summarised in the next chapter, where I examine the catalyst of the policy departures.

The executive decisions that do relate to this question are listed in Table 3.5, which provides all the decisions on Chinese SOE investments into the Australian mining sector that Wayne Swan issued a statement on. Statements are only issued very occasionally for "particularly high profile proposal[s]" and when there are no issues of "commercial sensitivity" (spokesman for Wayne Swan's office discussing the China Uranium Development purchase of Energy Metals, quoted in the *Australian Financial Review* 2010). In practice this means that relatively few decisions receive this treatment, and I have included a list of all the successful investments by Chinese SOEs in the period that did not receive statements from the Treasurer in Table 3.6 to show this. Of these investments, any conditions imposed on the firm are unknown, as are the details of earlier iterations of the investments that the FIRB indicated would not be approved. Any proposals that were not successful, but were withdrawn before being officially rejected are also omitted.

From this set of decisions, we can deduce a set of preferences of the government and verify the statements in the last section in which the government defined its policy. The first point of note is that the conditions placed on these investments are relatively harsh. The final decision of Swan (under Prime Minister Rudd), Yanzhou's purchase of Felix Resources was an approval for a complete acquisition, but nonetheless required the creation of an Australian branch of the Chinese company, stipulated that many of the executive positions be filled by persons whose primary place of residence was Australia, insisted that at least one director be "independent" from Yanzhou, and that the majority of board meetings be held in Australia. In any case, a further requirement was that the newly created Australian affiliate of Yanzhou would be listed publicly on the Australian Securities Exchange by the end of 2012. At this time, Yanzhou's holdings would be required to not exceed 70% of the Australian affiliate, and to not exceed 50% of the assets of Felix Resources. These conditions are reminiscent of those that Peter Costello placed on his approval of the joint listing between BHP and Billiton in 2001 (see Sect. 3.1, part iv above, and Costello 2001b). However, that decision referred to a merger while Yanzhou's purchase of Felix Resources was an acquisition. The conditions of divestment of a large part of the company in the course of three years and three months were also much more invasive than any condition in the BHP-Billiton decision. Throughout the two-and-a-half year period in question, there was an increased willingness to impose harsh conditions on foreign

Table 3.5 Decisions on foreign investment proposals where the details are publicly known

Date of decision	*Investor*	*Level of state ownership (%)*	*Target*	*Value ($AUm)*	*Decision*
2 January 2008	Sinosteel	100	Midwest	1200	Approval of 100% Acquisition[a]
24 August 2008	Chinalco	100	Rio Tinto plt.	15,500	Approval of up to 14.99% stake (amounting to 11% of Rio Tinto Ltd)
21 September 2008	Sinosteel	100	Murchison Metals	[unknown]	Approval, conditional upon controlling no more than 49.9%. Had earlier issued an Interim Order for an application to acquire 100%[b]
24 June 2009	Chinalco	100	Rio Tinto Ltd.	19,500–27,900 (est.)	No decision made except the issuing of an Interim Order. Plan eventually falls apart on 24 June 2009
27 March 2009	Minmetals Nonferrous Metals	90	OZ Metals	1200	Approval of 100% with conditions.[c] Interim Order issued March 23, 2009 and it was indicated that the initial application would be rejected
31 March 2009	Hunan Valin Iron and Steel	100[d]	Fortescue Metals	650	Approval to acquire up to 17.55% with conditions[e]
8 May 2009	Ansteel		Gindalbie Metals	200 (in addition to 530 committed previously to the Karara project)	Approval to increase holdings of up to 36.28% with conditions[f]
23 September 2009	Wuhan Iron and Steel		Western Plains Resources	40	Application for 50-50 venture rejected due to proximity with Woomera missile testing range[g]

(continued)

Table 3.5 (continued)

Date of decision	*Investor*	*Level of state ownership (%)*	*Target*	*Value ($AUm)*	*Decision*
24 September 2009	China Nonferrous Metals		Lynas Corp.	505	Rejection of application to recapitalise the rare earths producer by acquiring 51.6% of the company[h]
23 October 2009	Yanzhou Mining	52.86	Felix Resources	3500	Approval for complete acquisition with conditions[i]

From Swan (2008d, e; Swan 2009b, c, d, e), Sherry (2009), *Sydney Morning Herald* (2009), Lynas Corporation (2009)

[a]The approval notice included the line: "Sinosteel has recently acquired more than 97% of Midwest Corporation Limited (Midwest) which has iron ore deposits adjacent to Murchison's. Midwest and Murchison have previously sought to merge their operations by takeover proposals that did not proceed"

[b]Further information supplied by Wilson (2011, 298). The notice is no longer available on the Treasury website

[c]Any person nominated by Hunan Valin to Fortescue's Board will comply with the Director's Code of Conduct maintained by Fortescue

- Any person nominated by Hunan Valin to Fortescue's Board will submit a standing notice under the Corporations Act of their potential conflict of interest relating to Fortescue's marketing, sales, customer profiles, price setting, and cost structures for pricing and shipping
- Hunan Valin and any person nominated by it to Fortescue's Board will comply with the information segregation arrangements agreed between Fortescue and Hunan Valin

[d]Hunan Valin Iron and Steel was 100% owned by the Hunan provincial government, and is thus an SOE. Its acquisition of Fortescue was facilitated by the China Investment Corporation (CIC), an extremely large SWF. The conditions placed on the transaction

[e]must operate mines as separate business with commercial objectives

- must operate mines via companies with headquarters in Australia
- prices set by sales teams headquartered in Australia and with reference to "international observable benchmarks and in line with market practice"
- maintain or increase production at a bunch of places ("subject to economic conditions") in order to "protect Australian jobs"; it was also stipulated that the level of employment of indigenous persons must be maintained or increased
- rejects Prominent Hill site as it is within the Woomera Prohibited ground. OZ Minerals intends to continue and further develop the mine though
- OZ Minerals assets to be run as a "separate business unit according to commercial objectives, including the maximisation of product prices and long term profitability and value"

[f]Statement recognises that Ansteel is also a 50% partner with Gindalbie in the large $1.8 billion Karara iron ore project, which was agreed to in September 2007 before the Rudd government came into office. An attachment to the Must not alter 50:50 ownership of processing plant in China

- must support development of Oakajee port and use it when it is constructed
- Ansteel is required to maintain certain levels of Australian participation in a pellet plant in China

[g]Decision announcement unavailable, but details were released publicly (see *Sydney Morning Herald* 2009)

[h]Deal was initially approved by the FIRB, but this was overridden by Treasurer Swan. “Conditions” were suggested for China Nonferrous Metals to reapply—the stake to be limited to 49.9% and less than half of the company’s board to be Chinese—but no reapplication was ever made. Details acquired from a transaction update from Lynas Corporation (2009)

[i]operate its Australian mines through a company, Yancoal Australia Proprietary Limited (Yancoal Australia), that is incorporated and headquartered in Australia and is managed in Australia using a predominately Australian management and sales team

- ensure Yancoal Australia, and any of its operating subsidiaries, have at least two directors whose principal place of residence is in Australia, one of whom will be independent of Yanzhou and its related entities
- ensure that the Chief Executive Officer and Chief Financial Officer of Yancoal Australia have their principal place of residence in Australia
- hold the majority of Yancoal Australia’s board meetings in Australia in any calendar year
- list Yancoal Australia on the Australian Securities Exchange by the end of 2012 and, by that time, reduce Yanzhou’s ownership of Yancoal Australia to less than a 70% holding and Felix Resources Limited’s existing assets to no more than 50 per cent and from then on to not exceed 50%
- market coal produced at all of its Australian mines on arms-length terms with reference to international benchmarks and in line with market practices
- continue to all four of the Felix mining operations, including completing the development of the Moolarben mine, which was not then online

Table 3.6 Chinese SOE investments into the Australian resource sector that did not receive statements when approved by the treasurer

Date of investment	*Investor*	*Target*	*Equity acquired (%)*	*Value ($AUm)*	*Source of financing*
2007–9	SOE Consortium	Yilgarn Resources	50	250	PB
2007–9	CITIC Pacific	MacArthur Coal	20	1000	SWF
2007–8	Rockcheck	Aurox	12	15	SCB
2007–10	Tonghua I&S	Cairn Hill	10	14	SCB
2008	Wugang	Eyre Iron	60	260	PB
2008	Wugang	Centrex	15	10	PB
2008	Shougang	Balmoral South	18	58	PB
2008	Jiangsu Shagang	Grange Resources	45	NA	Private, state grant
2008	Shougang	Mt. Gibson	40	NA	SCB
2008	CMG	Cape Lambert	100	400	SCB
2008	Hunan Valin	Golden West	11	27	SCB
2008	CITIC Pacific	SinoIron	100	560	SWF
2008	Xinwen Mining	Coal Exploration Permits	100	1500	SCB
2008	China Western Mining	FerrAus	10	21	SCB
2009	Baotou	Bungalow	50	40	SCB
2009	China Metalurgical Investment Company	Beyondie	50	200	SCB
2009	Chongqing Minerals Development	Extension Hill	60	NA	Local government
2009	China Railway Materials Corporation	FerrAus	12	13	SCB
2009	Jinchuan Group	Fox Resources	11	18	SCB
2009	Baosteel	Aquila Resources	15	240	SCB

(continued)

Table 3.6 (continued)

Date of investment	*Investor*	*Target*	*Equity acquired (%)*	*Value ($AUm)*	*Source of financing*
2010	Sichuan Taifeng	IMX	20	47	Private
2010	Huaxi	Lincoln	13	8	Private
2010	Shenhua	Centennial	10	200	SCB
2010 (1)	China Uranium Development	Energy Metals		–	

Adapted from Wilson (2011), 292–294

PB: financing provided by China's two policy banks: the China Development Bank and the China Export-Import Bank

SWF: Sovereign Wealth Fund

SCB: State-owned commercial banks

No statement was released by the Treasurer due to issues of "commercial sensitivity," though Swan made the following comments to the media: "FIRB approval does not give foreign investors the right to mine or export uranium. It doesn't do that at all… We have a whole regime that deals with that and that was put in place by the Minister for Resources… This government proudly applies a national interest test, and we proudly apply that particularly in circumstances where state-own enterprises are involved" (Australian Financial Review 2010)

investments, relative to the administrations that preceded the Rudd government. This was never stated as a policy aim or intention of the Rudd government, but is a characteristic of their execution of the policy that is uncontested in the literature.

A second point of note is that the government's willingness to intervene and impose harsh conditions did not change enormously over the period. There is, surprisingly, no discernible change in the execution of the policy before and after September 2008 when Lehman Brothers collapsed and the economic agenda of the Australian government was drastically altered. As will be shown in Chapter 6, the aims of the government from its time in opposition through to September 2008 centred on a narrative of managing multiple inflationary pressures, before turning abruptly to providing liquidity and stimulus to the economy. The FDI policy is an exception to this change.

Thirdly, it is clear that the Colmer Doctrine—a preference for investments in greenfields projects to not exceed fifty per cent ownership and investments in major producers not to exceed 15%—was precisely a guideline. There are instances in both Table 3.5 and 3.6 that violate both parts of the doctrine. Likewise, the "seventh guideline"—an aversion to vertical integration—appears to have been applied in a flexible manner. Conditions relating to pricing appear in the conditions of many of the approvals listed in Table 3.5, but the government's concerns were not sufficient to prevent these investments occurring altogether.

Finally, it is clear that the impact of the new interventionism in this area fell almost exclusively on investors from China, and that the major investments that troubled the Australian government so much were exclusively from SOEs. This is not to say that the changes to the policy were designed to disrupt investments from China on that basis, or designed to target state-affiliated institutional investors on that basis. The wave of SOE investments was unprecedented in Australia's history, as will be shown in Chapter 5. It is nonetheless the case that the majority of interventions by the Australian government were on the transactions involving Chinese SOEs. This much is not contested in the literature. Nor is the fundamental point that the increased scrutiny that the Rudd government insisted on giving to state-owned investors was itself a departure. In fact, this has always been contested by officials from the Rudd government (see Chapter 6). However this has never been taken seriously by any commentators following the politically charged nature of the government's actions in the first months of office. First, there was high public consideration of the first Chinalco bid for Rio Tinto. Second, there was the government's unprecedented move to pressure ten Chinese companies to withdraw the applications they had lodged with the FIRB in order to resubmit them at a later date with further information relating to their ownership structures (Hewett, 25 April 2008).[18]

Thematically, it is possible to make the following deductions from the government's interventions. First, the government was sensitive to national security issues. The evidence for this exists in the Minmetals Non-ferrous Metals-OZ Minerals acquisition and the Wuhan Iron and Steel-Western Plains Resources acquisition, both of which were rejected due to proximity to Australian defence facilities. The motivations for these rejections have been questioned (see Chapter 7 and Uren 2012, 102–104), but taking these decisions at face value, it is possible to say that there is coherence in these national security issues with the government's stated policy in the February guidelines.

Second, the government aimed to maximise Australian participation in decision-making wherever possible. This included stipulating that (a) companies' boards had representation by Australian residents (for example, the Yanzhou-Felix acquisition); (b) when using secondary companies, that their headquarters were in Australia (Hunan Valin-Fortescue); (c) setting limits on the proportion of ownership (most approvals with conditions); (d) and, most invasively, stipulating a degree of Australian participation in a processing plant in China (Ansteel-Gindalbie).

Third, the government considered the market structure of the resource in which the investment was made, and aimed to "maintain diversity of ownership" (Swan 2008e) within that market. The phrase is taken from Swan's eventual approval for Sinosteel to take shares in Murchison Metals. The initial proposal followed soon after Sinosteel acquisition of 97% of a second Western Australian firm, Midwest Corporation Limited, which had iron ore deposits adjacent to those of Murchison. In Swan's statement, the principles he cited were a need for "diversity of ownership within the Mid-West region" and that the development of "significant new resource areas should occur through arrangements that are open to multiple investors" (Swan 2008e). This is a convoluted argument. First, "diversity of ownership" is a slightly different aim to a resource being "open to multiple investors," the first implying a positive preference where the latter does not. Second, if the concern related to anti-competitive practices, it seems an economically inefficient governing method to police potential for such practices, rather than leaving such regulation to better-suited behind the border regulatory institutions like the ACCC, as I have noted above. The counter example of this was the government's reticence on all three occasions to allow Chinalco to take or increase its ownership in Rio Tinto. It is perhaps more accurate to say that the government considered the market structure of the resource in which an investment was made and sought a number of ends. In some cases, this was the competitive functioning of the market. In some cases it was that the Australian mining industry's development was supported; for example the Ansteel–Gindalbie conditions which required Ansteel to support the construction of the Oakajee port and then use it when it came online. Sometimes the end sought was that important assets in the Australian mining industry remained Australian-owned (the Chinalco–Rio Tinto decisions and nondecision). These concerns were balanced against a desire to allow investments into the economy, as evidenced by the creative solution to the Yanzhou–Felix acquisitions, which was to require the creation of an Australian subsidiary, Yancoal, and require divestment of majority control in the newly created firm within three years.

Fourth, the government was interested in keeping production and pricing decisions within the market. Conditions aimed at this included insisting that, "prices set by sales teams headquartered in Australia" with made with reference to "international observable benchmarks and in line with market practice," as well as insisting that any conflicts of interest in relation to pricing, marketing, or cost-structures were declared by any persons nominated to the board (Swan 2009c). It also included enterprises run in Australia but owned by the foreign entity be operated as if it were an Australian firm: OZ Minerals assets were required to be run by China Minmetals as a "separate business unit according to commercial objectives, including the maximisation of product prices and long term profitability and value" (Swan 2009d). Nearly all of the statements released by the Treasurer, or the Deputy-Treasurers on specific decisions, as well as all of the major speeches made on the policy (see Chapter 5) emphasised this concern.

In summary, there is strong coherence between the stated policy of the government in relation to its screening of foreign government-affiliated investments, most notably in the February Guidelines, and the government's execution of the policy. There is limited evidence for the existence of the Colmer Doctrine thought of as a hard rule. However, the majority of decisions conform to the 15–50% preferences, and it is conceivable that the Doctrine existed as a soft guideline that was (usually) not published. There is no strong evidence that the execution of the policy targeted Chinese investors on the basis of their nationality, as all of the only SOE investments screened during the period were from China. On the other hand, it seems coherent with the government's concern about market structures that the investments were considered in light of other holdings from Chinese state-affiliated firms. The government appears to have pursued a number of social and developmental goals simultaneously with its screening and use of conditions, much as previous Australian governments had.

There are two clear departures in the government's execution of its policy from its precedents, however. First, the Rudd government was much more enthusiastic in its use of screening and conditions than previous governments, first in the frequency with which it intervened, and second in the degree of imposition it was willing to press on the investors. There was a marked increase in the attentiveness of the government to incoming investments, and this can be seen most clearly in the change of approach that occurred from February through to April 2008, when the government clearly decided on a much more activist path. Second, the active and dogged task of ensuring that production and pricing decisions conformed to market logics was a task that had not appeared in the history of Australian FDI screening, and was not listed in Table 3.1. It is these departures precisely that constitute the phenomena that must be explained.

3.4 Conclusion

The purpose of this chapter has been to define the departure of the Rudd government in its FDI screening policy. I have avoided discussing the policy announcements and actions in the usual language of policy-making studies so as to avoid falling into the trap of assuming aspects of the policy problem and solution appeared unproblematically. Given the claims made in Chapter 2, this is illegitimate. Instead, I have tried to merely describe how the Rudd government's actions were different to those of the governments that came before it, and identify anomalous aspects of the phenomena.

The legislative and institutional structures that the Rudd government inherited were very well-suited to the government's needs. The policy instrument of FDI screening offered a way to accept capital from the wave of Chinese SOE investments, but also manage the issues it posed. It allowed the government to control the public debate on its response by removing decisions from the public realm to the "independent" FIRB by refusing to comment on proposals being processed. Due to the nature of the FIRB, an advisory body staffed by treasury officials and with a senior treasury official as the executive member, the government (meaning specifically Treasurer Swan) was able to continue to exercise control over the processing of matters, and retained total control over the execution of the policy. Two substantial changes were made to the policy settings, in the release of the February Guidelines and passing the *FATA Amendment Act 2010*. The latter was clearly a direct response to the second Chinalco bid for Rio shares, and it is one of the tasks of this book to explain why the February Guidelines were released.

In addition to the formal changes to the policy settings, there were a number of unstated changes. These included the introduction of the Colmer Doctrine, an aversion to vertical integration and, it has been argued, an ambition to pose disincentives for larger scale Chinese SOE investments. With regard to the last of these, it is clear that special attention was given to this class of investor, and that the government's stance was highly interventionist and imposing. While it is reasonable to assume that this did dissuade some investments being made—this has been argued by most commentators on the policy, as will be shown in the next chapter—it does not follow necessarily that this was an aim of the government.

With regard to the execution of the policy, many of the policy goals that FDI screening had been used for by previous governments—the aims listed in Table 3.1—reappeared in the Rudd government's execution. There were two clear departures, however. First, the degree of targeting of such a specific class of investor, Chinese sovereign-owned or affiliated enterprises, was unprecedented. All proposals made by these investors given much more scrutiny than any other, which would have been a component of the FDI policies of all Australian governments before that of Rudd. Instead the departure lies in how often rejections and conditions were imposed. It is not possible to quantify this precisely, as many of the rejections were never made public due to the proposal being withdrawn before the formal rejection was issued, and many of the decisions to approve did not have the details of the approval published. However, from the proposals and decisions that are on public record, listed in Tables 3.5 and 3.6, it is clear that the Rudd government was much more willing to intervene using the policy instrument than any government before it. Secondly, there was a thematic departure. The aim of ensuring that production, pricing, cost-structuring, and marketing decisions remained on a "market-basis" was unprecedented in the history of the policy regime. I will argue in this book that this is the key to understanding the novelty of the problem of Chinese SOE investment as Kevin Rudd and Wayne Swan understood it.

Notes

1. The federal government also stipulated a number restrictions on mining licenses and exports of certain minerals from the Northern Territory at this time.
2. The relationship of 'the Policy' to the legislation in the FDI screening regime is discussed in the next section.
3. See Kirchner (2012, 60) on the role of the FIRB in allowing the Australian government to defuse political sentiment in favour of a more interventionist policy. The point he makes is that the institution "serves to normalise rather than contain political interference" (2012, 60).

4. The proportion changed over time, meaning that the scheme functioned as a secondary exchange control for the central bank, hence 'Variable'. It was generally between 25 and 33%, and was moved to five and then finally zero percent in 1974 (Department of Treasury 1999, 49) as the inflation-inducing oversupply of capital soon reversed.
5. A soft fifty percent foreign ownership ceiling on mining enterprises and bans in uranium and oil exploration by foreign actors were implemented.
6. Coal and iron ore were both subject to price controls, determined by the Minister for Minerals and Energy and enforced via levers relating to exports (Sadleir 2007, 130, citing Smith 1979, 242).
7. This was realised in the IAC and TPC, mentioned above.
8. The point about technology and competition development is that it constitutes a new element in the policy problem genealogy. I will add it formally in the next section on the Fraser governments.
9. The 'Khemlani' or 'loans' affair refers to a series of meetings between the Minerals and Resources Minister, Rex Connors, and a London-based commodities trader, Tirath Khemlani. In December 1974, Connor was given permission by the federal executive Loan Council to secure $US4 billion for the purpose of developing Australian minerals and energy resources in a way that ensured Australian interests retained control over them. The approval was revoked in early January and then reinstated again in late January with a limit of $US2 billion. However, Khemlani failed to secure funds for the venture and when it became public, it resulted in the resignation of Connors, the removal of Jim Cairns, the Treasurer and Deputy Prime Minister, from the front bench, and contributed to the Fraser Opposition's decision to refuse the supply of government and thus the dissolution of the Whitlam government (see Megalogenis 2012, 65–70 and the National Archives of Australia [date unknown]).
10. The mechanism is explained in the next section which outlines the *FATA 1975*.
11. I could include the two bodies commissioned by the Whitlam government here to manage FDI screening: the Foreign Investment Committee (FIC) and the Committee on Foreign Takeovers (COFT). They are replaced by the single institution of the FIRB (see next section) and so have not been listed.
12. Arguably this list could include all the parliamentary and policy guidance and coordination bodies created within the executive, for example Howard's International Economic Policy Coordinating Group, which was composed of deputy secretaries of the Departments of the Treasury, Foreign Affairs and Trade (DFAT), and Prime Minister and Cabinet (PM&C). These are also part of the institutional fora responsible for

regulating the actions of foreign investors. I have excluded them on the basis that they are a step removed from actual intervention in the economy, and also because I have no evidence that such bodies did not exist just as much before the period of 1975–2007 as during it.

13. The most important institution for FDI screening, the FIRB, can arguably be placed in all three categories as I will show in the next section.
14. Similar provisions have since been included in free trade deals with New Zealand, Japan, South Korea, Chile, and now China.
15. The wording from this report is as it appeared in the last statement of the policy published by Treasurer Costello and is thus the version that Treasurer Swan departed from with the February 2008 guidelines. The 2006/2007 Annual Report (FIRB 2008) was released in February 2008 and the appendix contains the changes announced that month.
16. Public statements of this length by members of the board are relatively rare. Mr. Di Giorgio's is the only such speech published on the FIRB's website. I include it here as the clearest example of this part of his role being uncontroversial. Other speeches by FIRB board members are available elsewhere and are discussed in later chapters of this book. Advertising Australia as an investment destination is common to the majority of them.
17. This point obviously only refers to investment proposals that the public know about. Many investment proposals are not made public for the reasons discussed earlier in the section.
18. The firms are believed to have resubmitted applications but with smaller proposed investments in iron ore companies in Western Australia (Hewett, 25 April 2008).

References

ACCC. (2000). *Submission to the Productivity Commission Review of the Prices Surveillance Act 1983.* ACCC (Australian Competition and Consumer Commission). Available at http://www.pc.gov.au/inquiries/completed/prices-surveillance-act/submissions/sub010/sub010.pdf. Accessed 28 Oct 2016.

ACCC. (2009). *Chinalco (Aluminium Corporation of China)—Proposed Acquisition of Interests in Rio Tinto Ltd.* Public Competition Assessment by ACCC. 25 March 2009. Available at http://registers.accc.gov.au/content/index.phtml/itemId/866064/fromItemId/751043. Accessed 30 Oct 2016.

Arnold, D. (2000, November 2). *Labour's Economic Policy and the Competition State: A Social Democratic Critique of the Political Economy of the Third Way.* Paper presented at A Third Way and Beyond Conference, University of Sussex.

Australian Financial Review. (2010, February 23). Fed: Swan Says Approved Energy Metals Takeover by China Entity. *Australian Financial Review*. Available at http://www.afr.com/news/politics/fedswan-says-approved-energy-metals-takeover-by-china-entity-20100223-ivzbi. Accessed 30 Oct 2016.

Bachrach, P., & Baratz, S. M. (1962). Two faces of power. *American Political Science Review, 56*(4), 947–952.

Bell, H. F. (1976). Australian Government Policy in Relation to Foreign Investment. *The Australian Quarterly, 48*(1), 44–58.

Berg, C. (2012, March 15). Foreign Investment and the Whims of Politicians. *The Drum*. Available at http://www.abc.net.au/news/2012-03-13/berg-foreign-investment-and-the-whims-of-politicians/3886786. Accessed 21 Oct 2016.

Boehm, E. A. (1979). *Twentieth Century Economic Development in Australia*. Melbourne: Longman Cheshire.

Bora, B. (1995). The Implications of Globalisation for Australian Foreign Investment Policy. In *Globalisation: Issues for Australia*. Canberra: Economic Planning Advisory Council, Australian Government Publishing Services.

Boughton, J. M. (2004). *The IMF and the Force of History: Ten Events and Ten Ideas That Have Shaped the Institution* (IMF Working Paper). Washington, DC.

Bowen, C. (2008a, April 23). *Government looks to Increase Competition Across the Economy with Changes to Foreign Investment Rules*. Treasury. Available at http://ministers.treasury.gov.au/DisplayDocs.aspx?doc=pressreleases/2008/025.htm&pageID=003&min=ceb&Year=2008&DocType=0. Accessed 29 Oct 2016.

Bowen, C. (2008b, December 18). *Rudd Government Moves to Make Administrative Changes to Foreign Investment Review Process*. Treasury. Available at http://ministers.treasury.gov.au/DisplayDocs.aspx?doc=pressreleases/2008/107.htm&pageID=003&min=ceb&Year=2008&DocType=0. Accessed 29 Oct 2016.

Bowman, M., Gilligan, G., and O'Brien, J. (2014, February 13). *Foreign Investment Law and Policy in Australia: A Critical Analysis*. Paper presented at Centre for Law, Markets and Regulation, CIFR Symposium: Financial Market Development Stream, University of New South Wales School of Law.

Costello, P. (2001a, April 23). *Foreign Investment Proposal—Shell Australia Investments Limited (Shell) Acquisition of Woodside Petroleum Limited (Woodside), Australian Government*. The Treasury, Media Release 25. Available at http://ministers.treasury.gov.au/DisplayDocs.aspx?doc=pressreleases/2001/025.htm&pageID=003&min=phc&Year=&DocType=0. Accessed 28 Oct 2016.

Costello, P. (2001b, June 4). *Foreign Investment Approval of BHP Limited-Billiton Plc Merger*. Treasury. Available at http://ministers.treasury.gov.au/DisplayDocs.aspx?doc=pressreleases/2001/040.htm&pageID=003&min=phc&Year=2001&DocType=0. Accessed 30 Oct 2016.

Costello, P. (2009, February 18). Rio Feathers Should Stay in Our Nest. *Sydney Morning Herald*. Available at http://www.smh.com.au/federal-politics/rio-feathers-should-stay-in-our-nest-20090217-8a9a.html. Accessed 28 Oct 2016.

Department of Treasury. (1999, July 20). *Australia's Experience with the Variable Deposit Requirement*. Treasury Economic Roundup, Australian Government, The Treasury. Available at http://archive.treasury.gov.au/contentitem.asp?ContentID=193. Accessed 28 Oct 2016.

Department of Treasury. (2000). *Implication of the Globalisation of Financial Markets*. Submission to the House of Representatives, Standing Committee on Economics, Finance and Public Administration: Inquiry into the implications of the globalisation of international financial markets for macroeconomic policy and the operation of financial markets. Commonwealth of Australia, Canberra.

Di Giorgio, F. (2011, November 9). *Speech to the 3rd China Overseas Investment Fair*. China World Trade Centre. Foreign Investment Review Board. Available at http://firb.gov.au/about/news-media/Publications/pressreleases/2011/001.asp. Accessed 13 Sept 2015.

Dorling, P. (2011a, February 15). How BHP Boss Derailed Rio's $23.9b deal. *Sydney Morning Herald*. Available at http://www.smh.com.au/business/how-bhp-boss-derailed-rios-239b-deal-20110214-1atpp.html. Accessed 25 Oct 2016.

Dorling, P. (2011b, March 3). Labor's Secret Curb on China. *The Age*. Available at http://www.smh.com.au/national/labors-secret-curb-on-china-20110302-1bex9.html. Accessed 25 Oct 2016.

Dorling, P. (2011c, March 3). Laws 'Aimed to Limit' Chinese Investments. *Sydney Morning Herald*. Available at http://www.smh.com.au/business/laws-aimed-to-limit-chinese-investments-20110302-1bexm.html. Accessed 25 Oct 2016.

Dorling, P. (2011d, March 3). Australia Worried China Buying Up Resources. *Asia Sentinel*. Available at http://www.asiasentinel.com/econ-business/australia-worried-china-buying-up-resources/#frameId=appnext_widget&height=64. Accessed 25 Oct 2016.

Drysdale, P. (2011). A New Look at Chinese FDI in Australia. *China and World Economy, 19*(4), 54–73.

Drysdale, P., & Findlay, C. (2009). Chinese Foreign Direct Investment in Australia: Policy Issues for the Resource Sector. *China Economic Journal, 2*(2), 133–158.

Faeth, I. (2005). *Foreign Direct Investment in Australia: Determinants and Consequences*. Ph.D. thesis, submitted to the University of Melbourne.

FIRB. (1977). *Report 1977*. Canberra: Australian Government Publishing Services.

FIRB. (2007). *Annual Report 2005–2006*. Australian Government, Foreign Investment Review Board. Available at http://firb.gov.au/about/publication/annual-report-2005-2006/. Accessed 28 Oct 2016.

FIRB. (2008). *Annual Report 2006–2007*. Australian Government, Foreign Investment Review Board. Available at http://firb.gov.au/about/publication/annual-report-2006-2007/. Accessed 29 Oct 2016.

FIRB. (2009). *Annual Report 2007–2008*. Australian Government, Foreign Investment Review Board. Available at http://firb.gov.au/about/publication/annual-report-2007-2008/. Accessed 29 Oct 2016.

FIRB. (2011). *Annual Report 2009–2010*. Australian Government, Foreign Investment Review Board. Available at http://firb.gov.au/about/publication/annual-report-2009-2010/. Accessed 30 Oct 2016.

Golding, G. (2010). *Australian Regulation of Foreign Direct Investment by Sovereign Wealth Funds and State-Owned Enterprises: Are Our Rules Right?* Thompson Reuters (Professional) Ltd. Australia. Available at http://sitesdev.thomsonreuters.com.au/journals/files/2010/09/ABLR38.4_Golding_article.pdf. Accessed 28 Oct 2016.

Harper, I. (2001). In the National Interest. *Policy, 17*(1), 59–67.

Hewett, J. (2008, April 25). China Told by Rudd Government to Shelve Mine Deal. *The Australian*. Available at http://www.theaustralian.com.au/business/mining-energy/china-told-to-shelve-mine-deals/story-e6frg9df-1111116159135. Accessed 21 Oct 2016.

Johnson, C. (1989). *The Labor Legacy: Curtin, Chifley, Whitlam, Hawke*. Sydney: Allen and Unwin.

Kalfadellis, P., Gray, J., & Freeman, S. (2006). *The 'National Interest' and the Screening of Foreign Direct Investment in Australia* (Working Paper 14/06). Department of Management Working Paper Series ISSN1327-5216. Australia: Monash University.

Kelly, P. (1992). *The End of Certainty*. Sydney: Allen and Unwin.

Kelly, P. (2006). *Howard's Decade: An Australian Foreign Policy Reappraisal*. Sydney: Lowy Institute for International Policy.

Kirchner, S. (2008a). Capital Xenophobia II: FDI in Australia, SWFs, and the Rise of State Capitalism. Centre for Independent Studies. *CIS Policy Monograph, 88*.

Kirchner, S. (2008b, November 27). Foreign Investment Flows Are Damned By Political Bias. *The Centre for Independent Studies*. Available at https://www.cis.org.au/commentary/articles/foreign-investment-flows-are-damned-by-political-bias. Accessed 21 Oct 2016.

Kirchner, S. (2010, February 19). More Inscrutable Than the Chinese. *The Australian*. Available at http://www.theaustralian.com.au/opinion/more-inscrutable-than-the-chinese/story-e6frg6zo-1225831954203. Accessed 21 Oct 2016.

Kirchner, S. (2012). The Kingdom and the Quarry: China, Australia, Fear and Greed. *Policy, 28*(2), 58–62 (Review Essay).
Kirchner, S. (2014). *Regulating Foreign Direct Investment in Australia*. Financial Services Institute of Australasia (Finsia). Available at https://www.finsia.com/docs/default-source/industry-reports-foreign-direct-investment/regulating-foreign-direct-investment-in-australia.pdf?sfvrsn=4. Accessed 21 Oct 2016.
Lynas Corporation. (2009, September 24). *CNMC Transaction Update*. Lynas Corporation Ltd. Available at http://www.asx.com.au/asxpdf/20090924/pdf/31kxjlh82hdnh3.pdf. Accessed 3 Nov 2016.
Marchick, D. M., & Slaughter, M. J. (2008). *Global FDI Policy: Correcting a Protectionist Drift* (CSR No. 34). Council on Foreign Relations. Available at http://www.cfr.org/foreign-direct-investment/global-fdi-policy/p16503. Accessed 28 Oct 2016.
Megalogenis, G. (2012). *The Australian Moment*. Camberwell, VA: Viking Australia.
Menadue, J. (2004). *Speaker's Notes, 1974 Whitlam Cabinet Release*. Canberra: National Archives of Australia.
Murphy, J. (2009, November 4). *Speech to the Australia–China Investment Forum*. China World Trade Centre, Treasury. Available at http://archive.treasury.gov.au/contentitem.asp?ContentID=1656. Accessed 29 Oct 2016.
Pokarier, C. J. (2000). *Politics of Foreign Direct Investment in Australia, 1960–96*. Ph.D. thesis, submitted to the Australian National University.
Rudd, K. (2008, February 18). Interview with Chris Uhlmann. *AM, ABC Radio*. Available at https://pmtranscripts.dpmc.gov.au/release/transcript-15765. Accessed 21 Oct 2016.
Sadleir, C. (2007). *On the Frontier: Australia's Policy Approach to Foreign Direct Investment 1968–2004 as a Case Study in Globalisation, National Public Policy and Public Administration*. Ph.D. thesis, submitted to the University of Canberra.
Sadleir, C., & Mahoney, G. (2009). Institutional Challenges and Response in Regulating Foreign Direct Investment to Australia. *Economic Society of Australia Economic Papers Series, 28*(4), 337–345.
Schattschneider, E. E. (1960). *The Semisovereign People: A Realist's View of Democracy in America*. Hinsdale, IL: The Dryden Press.
Schedvin, C. (1992). *In Reserve: Central Banking in Australia, 1945–75*. Sydney: Macmillan.
Schenk, C. R. (1998). The Origins of the Eurodollar Market in London: 1955–1963. *Explorations in Economic History, 35*(2), 221–238.
Sherry, N. (2009, October 23). *Foreign Investment Decision—Felix Resources (Yanzhou to Acquire Felix Resources)*. Treasury. Available at http://ministers.treasury.gov.au/DisplayDocs.aspx?doc=pressreleases/2009/081.

htm&pageID=003&min=njsa&Year=2009&DocType=0. Accessed 30 Oct 2016.

Sherry, N. (2010, April 24). *Government Tightens Foreign Investment Rules for Residential Housing*. Treasury. Available at http://ministers.treasury.gov.au/DisplayDocs.aspx?doc=pressreleases/2010/074.htm&pageID=003&min=njsa&Year=&DocType=0. Accessed 29 Oct 2016.

Smith, G. (1979). Minerals and Energy. In A. Patience & B. Head (Eds.), *From Whitlam to Fraser: Reform and Reaction in Australian Politics* (pp. 233–250). Melbourne: Oxford University Press.

Springell, S. (2012). *The Theory of Policy Alignment: An Ideational Explanation for Change*. Ph.D. thesis, submitted to UNSW.

Stevens, M. (2009, October 2). Political, Not Skin, Pigment Is the Issue. *The Australian*. Available at http://www.theaustralian.com.au/archive/business/political-not-skin-pigment-is-the-issue/story-e6frg9lx-1225781834339. Accessed 30 Oct 2016.

Stewart, F. (1975, May 22). *Cth. Parliamentary Debates, 'Foreign Takeovers Bill 1975 Second Reading'*. House of Representatives. Available at http://parlinfo.aph.gov.au/parlInfo/genpdf/hansard80/hansardr80/1975-05-22/0134/hansard_frag.pdf;fileType=application%2Fpdf. Accessed 28 Oct 2016.

Sturgess, G. (1996). Virtual Government: What Will Remain Inside the Public Sector? *Australian Journal of Public Administration, 55*(3), 59–73.

Swan, W. (2008a, February 17). *Government Improves Transparency of Foreign Investment Screening Process*. Treasury. Available at http://ministers.treasury.gov.au/DisplayDocs.aspx?doc=pressreleases/2008/009.htm&pageID=003&min=wms&Year=&DocType. Accessed 21 Oct 2016.

Swan, W. (2008b, February 17). *Press Conference: Waterfront Palace*. Brisbane, Treasury. Available at http://ministers.treasury.gov.au/DisplayDocs.aspx?doc=transcripts/2008/028.htm&pageID=011&min=wms&Year=2008&DocType=2. Accessed 30 Oct 2016.

Swan, W. (2008c, July 4). *Australia, China, and This Asian Century*. Speech to the Australia–China Business Council, Melbourne, Treasury. Available at http://ministers.treasury.gov.au/DisplayDocs.aspx?doc=speeches/2008/021.htm&pageID=010&min=wms&Year=2008&DocType=1. Accessed 3 Nov 2016.

Swan. W. (2008d, August 24). *Chinalco's Acquisition of Shares in Rio Tinto*. Treasury. Available at http://ministers.treasury.gov.au/DisplayDocs.aspx?doc=pressreleases/2008/094.htm&pageID=003&min=wms&Year=2008&DocType=0. Accessed 30 Oct 2016.

Swan, W. (2008e, September 21). *Foreign Investment Approval: Sinosteel's Interests in Murchison Metals Ltd*. Treasury. Available at http://ministers.treasury.gov.au/DisplayDocs.aspx?doc=pressreleases/2008/100.htm&pageID=003&min=wms&Year=&DocType=0. Accessed 30 Oct 2016.

Swan, W. (2009a, February 12). *Amendments to Foreign Acquisitions and Takeovers Act.* Treasury. Available at http://ministers.treasury.gov.au/DisplayDocs.aspx?doc=pressreleases/2009/017.htm&pageID=003&min=wms&Year=&DocType=0. Accessed 29 Oct 2016.

Swan, W. (2009b, March 27). *Foreign Investment (Rejection of China Minmetals Application to Acquire OZ Metals).* Treasury. Available at http://ministers.treasury.gov.au/DisplayDocs.aspx?doc=pressreleases/2009/029.htm&pageID=003&min=wms&Year=2009&DocType=0. Accessed 30 Oct 2016.

Swan, W. (2009c, March 31). *Foreign Investment Decision (Hunan Valin Iron and Steel Group to Acquire Shareholding in Fortescue Metals).* Treasury. Available at http://ministers.treasury.gov.au/DisplayDocs.aspx?doc=pressreleases/2009/032.htm&pageID=003&min=wms&Year=2009&DocType=0. Accessed 30 Oct 2016.

Swan, W. (2009d, April 23). *Foreign Investment Decision (China Minmetals to Acquire Assets of OZ Minerals).* Available at http://ministers.treasury.gov.au/DisplayDocs.aspx?doc=pressreleases/2009/043.htm&pageID=003&min=wms&Year=&DocType=0. Accessed 30 Oct 2016.

Swan, W. (2009e, May 8). *Foreign Investment Decision (Ansteel to Acquire Gindalbie Metals).* Treasury. Available at http://ministers.treasury.gov.au/DisplayDocs.aspx?doc=pressreleases/2009/045.htm&pageID=003&min=wms&Year=2009&DocType=0. Accessed 30 Oct 2016.

Swan, W. (2009f, December 10). *Address to the Global Foundation.* Brisbane, Treasury. Available at http://ministers.treasury.gov.au/DisplayDocs.aspx?doc=speeches/2009/033.htm&pageID=005&min=wms&Year=&DocType=. Accessed 21 Oct 2016.

Sydney Morning Herald. (2009, September 24). China Fails in Another Bid for Resources Firm. *Sydney Morning Herald.* Available at http://www.smh.com.au/business/china-fails-in-another-bid-for-resources-firm-20090924-g4l7.html. Accessed 30 Oct 2016.

Thirlwell, M., & Shearer, A. (2008). *Is the Foreign Investment Review Board Acting Fairly?* Paper 4 in the Australia's Open Investment Future Series. Sydney: Lowy Institute for International Policy.

Uren, D. (2012). *The Kingdom and the Quarry: China, Australia, Fear and Greed.* Collingwood, VIC: Black Inc.

Wesley, M. (2012). Australia's Foreign Policy Machinery. In J. Cotton & J. Ravenhill (Eds.), *Middle Power Dreaming: Australia in World Affair: 2006–2010* (pp. 261–272). Melbourne: Oxford University Press.

Whitlam, G. (1985). *The Whitlam Government 1972–1975.* Melbourne: Penguin.

Whitwell, G. (1986). *The Treasury Line.* Sydney: Allen and Unwin.

Wilson, J. D. (2011). Resource Nationalism or Resource Liberalism? Explaining Australia's Approach to Chinese Investment in Its Minerals Sector. *Australian Journal of International Affairs, 65*(3), 283–304.

CHAPTER 4

The Policy Problematisation

In this chapter I describe the immediate catalyst for the Rudd government's experimentations with the FDI screening policy and canvass the existing accounts of why the government responded the way it did.

In the first section I describe the causes of the sudden wave of large-scale investments in the Chinese "Go Out" and Iron and Steel Industry Development policies, as well as a series of changes to the structures of interaction between Chinese firms and the state institutions governing them. The relationship of the Chinese state to its SOEs is important to describe because a number of the accounts of the Australian FDI policy rest on different assessments of the Chinese state's capacity for interfering in the commercial decisions of these firms. My position is that while the Chinese state governing bodies were not able to direct operational decisions of SOEs, their capacity for shaping the actions of the firms was significant, and certainly greater than the capacity of a liberal government. Importantly, I also argue that the incentives offered to SOEs by the Chinese state—discounted borrowing rates in the nationalised financial sector and from China's two large development banks—allowed the SOEs to operate at a significant advantage to their Australian and international rivals.

In the second section I comment on the material significance of the Chinese investments for the Australian economy. In the last chapter I noted that the FDI screening policy was remarkably unchanged by the onset of the Global Financial Crisis (GFC) and the dramatically altered needs of the economy. In this chapter I show that China rose to be the

© The Author(s) 2019

M. Peters, *Regulating the Rise of China*, Studies in the Political Economy of Public Policy, https://doi.org/10.1007/978-3-030-05466-3_4

most significant trade and investment partner of the Australian state. While this would usually imply a power imbalance between the two states in favour of the much larger economic power, this was tempered by a belief within the Australian government that China's consumption of iron ore would remain strong enough to underpin historically high prices and volumes of iron ore demanded into the long term. This is important to remember, I will argue later in the book, as the Australian government understood its control over access to strategically important raw resources as a point of leverage over states buying these resources. The belief that this leverage would not be temporary was an important feature of the Australian government's strategic engagement with China.

In the final section of the problematisation stage of the policy, I re-examine the five existing accounts of the policy, and show that they share liberal foundations. The existing accounts are reimagined as internal to the subject matter being examined, as per the instructions of Howarth and Griggs (2012) for a poststructural policy analysis (see Chapter 2, Sect. 2.2). My account of the policy, which appears in Chapter 7, holds that the Australian policymakers believed that the Chinese state-company relationships did not respect foundational assumptions of the liberal world order. Their rise as an economically significant component of the global economy was understood by Kevin Rudd and Wayne Swan as a potentially tectonic shift in global politics, and one that was severely to the detriment of the liberal West's interests. The policy problem was simultaneously an economic, geopolitical, and ideological one, and this nexus cannot be articulated within liberal economic or geopolitical language. This account rests on the understanding of the Australian state as a governmental one, in which liberalism appears: it is the rationality that encompasses the political and economic conditions, beliefs and arrangements of the particular freedoms that enable the use of technologies of security (see Chapter 2, Sect. 2.1). Given my approach, my explanation of the policy is necessarily a critique of the existing liberal accounts of the policy, which must be concomitant with the rationality of liberalism and the functioning of the governmental dispositifs being examined. Such a critique is what Howarth and Griggs (2012) are referring to in the fifth component of a poststructural policy analysis, which is the positing of an internal relationship between explanation, critique, and policy evaluation (2012, 324–325).

4.1 China's Go Out Policies

The "Go Out" or "Go Global" policy was an effort from the Chinese state from the early 2000s onwards to encourage the internationalisation of Chinese enterprises via the creation of overseas affiliates.[1] The program functioned by providing financial incentives and administrative support to SOEs and private firms to invest abroad. The aims of Going Out were to strengthen the competitive advantages of the internationalising firms, and recursively to enhance China's domestic economic restructuring and development. It was also used as a tool, alongside diplomatic efforts and strategic aid-giving, for the state to ensure that the Chinese economy had access to raw resources considered vital to its functioning and industrial transformation. The policy is best understood as a step in a trajectory of moves integrating China back into the global economy, starting with Deng's reforms of the late 1970s. In this section I will briefly describe the Go Out policy and this trajectory as a way of explaining the precise relationship between the Chinese state and the SOEs that invested in Australia in the late 2000s.

In the mid-1990s, the reform program begun by Deng Xiaoping in 1978 quickened pace and moved towards establishing market-based structures. China's economic policy regimes moved from the "command" structures of direct intervention by the state over business decisions to regimes based on arms-length rules applied by a wide set of administrative bodies (Bach et al. 2006). The regime administering outward foreign direct investment from China followed this pattern closely.

The period between 1978 and 1991 was characterised by timid experimentation with allowing outward FDI. The "open door" policy was, from its inception, intended to facilitate the entry of foreign multinationals into China as well as the internationalisation of Chinese firms (Voss et al. 2009, 146). The aims of allowing and even encouraging outward investment were established very early in the period: securing access to domestically scarce natural resources; accessing and transferring technology to China; enhancing export possibilities for Chinese firms; and improving the management skill and knowledge of Chinese enterprises. Nonetheless, there was very little in the way of actual outward flows, largely as a result of the institutional ambiguities of the early regime, and the strength of the political factions that feared the negative impacts of outward foreign investment on domestic investment and economic development. The ambiguities arose from the number of administrative bodies that shared responsibilities for governing outward FDI, the most important of which were the powerful Ministry of Commerce (MOFCOM),[2] the National Development and Reform Commission (NDRC), the State Administration and Foreign Exchange (SAFE)[3] and the State Council, the legislative body responsible for setting economic policy and managing China's economic development.

The responsibilities were as follows. The State Council selected a set of state-owned and state-coordinated enterprises to establish foreign affiliates. Having been selected, the enterprises could apply to the SAFE for foreign exchange use approval. The SAFE's approval was made on the basis of the proposed project's concordance with the national foreign exchange plan, which was produced by MOFCOM, the Ministry of Finance, SAFE, the Bank of China, the State Planning Commission, and the State Council. The investment proposal would then need to be approved by either MOFCOM, if the investment was less the $US10 million, or the NDRC, if the investment was more than $US10 million. Alongside the approval from SAFE for the use of foreign exchange, the approval by MOFCOM or the NDRC would require a statement from the Chinese embassy in the target country, an investment recovery plan, and documentation on the legal environment of the target country (adapted from Voss et al. 2009, 146–147). As a result of the effort required to produce such an approval and the uncertainties around whose authority was required at each stage of the application, the costs to the Chinese firms of outward investment were high, and little investment occurred.

Between the late 1980s and late 1990s, there was a period of refining this administrative environment, and a movement towards actively encouraging outward investment, rather than the more ambiguous policy of supporting outward investment but retaining tight controls over it. The transition was led by the highest echelon of the state: in 1992 Deng Xiaoping travelled to the south of China to show his support for economic reforms and the establishment of market structures there. This provided strength to the liberalising factions within the China Communist Party (CCP) and the economic administration bodies. Soon after, in the early 1990s, *promoting* outward FDI from China became an official component of the national economic development plan (Voss et al. 2009, 149). This move was endorsed by Jiang Zemin (Zhang 2003, 69), then the chairman of the CCP, who would, as president of China, announce the Go Out policy in 1998 (Cai 2006, 624).

Following these moves by the national tier of government, local and provincial authorities in the late 1990s began encouraging companies under their supervision to establish affiliates abroad. The reasons listed above for promoting outward FDI noted above remained stable, but Tan (1999) suggests a new motivation appeared at this point and became dominant: circumventing trade discriminations imposed by the host countries of investment and trade projects.

There was a period of tightening following the Asian Financial Crisis, which was compounded by moves by MOFCOM unrelated to the crisis, to tighten outward FDI controls in order to stymie the defalcation of state assets via international ventures. This involved consolidating the approval process, with the effects of increasing the monitoring and enforcement of regulations on outward investment projects. Nonetheless, the broad trend continued to be towards greater encouragement of internationalisation. At the same time as its consolidations, MOFCOM introduced financial and administrative measures to encourage light industry firms to internationalise, selected thirty-three SOEs to receive priority state assistance to invest abroad as an initial trial, and moved to establish assembly plants overseas to support the export activities of Chinese firms (Voss et al. 2009, 151).

Thus, the announcement of the Go Out policy at the end of the 1990s was entirely in keeping with the trajectory of the administration of outward FDI since 1978. It retained the same goals as the moves to allow outward investment in 1978, broadly speaking: to encourage Chinese firms to internationalise using financial incentives and administrative support in order to strengthen the competitive advantage of Chinese firms and aid in the economic development of the Chinese economy. It reflected both the belief that China had developed economically sufficiently to take its place in the global economy, and the renewed urgency of upgrading the productivity of Chinese firms that faced new international competitors as a result of the new allowances related to China's accession to the World Trade Organisation (WTO) in 2001.

There were a number of measures included in the policy package. First, the government simplified and then abolished the feasibility study required as part of the documentation for investment approval applications, preferring to rely on market forces and the managerial capacities of the investing enterprises (Voss et al. 2009, 152). This was followed in 2002 and 2003 with the removal of the foreign exchange risk assessment and exchange rate risk analysis requirements. Twenty-six further requirements of a similar nature previously imposed by the SAFE's application procedures were removed over 2002 and 2003 (Voss et al. 2009, 152). Second, controls on international capital movement were eased, with a follow-up removal in 2006 of the foreign exchange cap available to domestic enterprises for outbound investments, also previously imposed by the SAFE. Thirdly, the requirement for investing firms to place a security with the SAFE for the duration of the project was abolished. Fourthly, firms were allowed to raise money for their foreign investments on the global finance markets (Voss et al. 2009, 152). Fifthly, there was a decentralisation of the regulation of outward foreign direct investment. Six coastal provinces were selected in 2002 to allow outward FDI approved by the local SAFE branch as a trial, and this was then nationalised in 2005 (Voss et al. 2009, 152). MOFCOM approvals were likewise delegated to the regional MOFCOM offices, with the exception of all investments going to seven designated countries (Voss et al. 2009, 153).[4] As the approval process was decentralised, the number of administrative bodies involved in approving outward investment proposals increased. The key bodies of the State Council, SAFE, MOFCOM, and NDRC all remained, but regulations on outward FDI were added at the national, and more often local level, by the State Asset Supervision and Administration Commission (SASAC), the ministries of Finance and Foreign Affairs, the China Insurance Regulatory Commission (CIRC) and the China Banking Regulation Commission (CBRC) (Voss et al. 2009, 153). Finally, the thresholds designating responsibility for approval of outward FDI applications were changed. Resource-seeking investments exceeding $US30 million in value and non-resource-seeking investments exceeding $US10 million required approval from the NDRC. Resource-seeking investments above $US200 million and non-resource-seeking investments above $US50 million required approval by the State (Voss et al. 2009, 153). Other investments were approved by the provincial MOFCOM offices.

In addition to these changes, the Go Out policy also provided positive incentives to encourage Chinese firms to invest abroad. These generally came in the form of tax concessions and preferential access to finance using the state-owned commercial banks and development banks, the China Development Bank and the China Export-Import Bank. A number of loans were also made available from China's SWFs (see Table 3.6 for an indication of how prevalent concessional finance was used by private Chinese firms investing in Australia between 2007 and 2010).

An important event in escalating this part of the program was the co-decision in November 2004 of the NDRC and Export-Import Bank of China to "provide credit support to the key overseas investment projects encouraged by the state" (Murphy 2008, 3). Large-scale outward FDIs from China grew rapidly after this point, as did the overall flows of outward FDI (Ministry of Commerce 2011, 81). The management of the positive incentive programs, which were implemented by a diverse set of financial, administrative and regulatory bodies, as noted above, was made possible by the "Outbound Catalogue". First published by the MOFCOM and NDRC in 2004, the Outbound Catalogue listed the Chinese government's preferred destinations for outbound investments and its preferred industries. It followed on Premier Wen Jiabao's announcement in March 2004 that the state would evolve the Go Out policy to more tightly coordinate the investments of Chinese firms (OECD 2008, 83). It guided the allocation of monies from an "acquisition fund," which not only provided a highly valuable competitive advantage to Chinese firms in the global economy, but also allowed MOFCOM and SAFE offices, both at the provincial and federal level, to influence investment decisions of Chinese firms and to continue influencing the business decisions of both state and non-state owned enterprises. Annual appraisals by MOFCOM and SAFE of the performance of overseas affiliates of Chinese firms would determine whether subsequent approvals of outbound investment and the expatriation of staff were granted (Voss et al. 2009, 154, see Ministry of Commerce 2004). Salidjanova (2011, 4) also claims that the various state authorities had the additional capacity to appoint executives to the state-owned firms. In this way Chinese firms can truly be said to have had autonomy over their own pricing, production and distribution decisions, but the involvement that administrative bodies were able to retain should not be understated.

Finally, through the 2000s, the Chinese government came to use foreign policy and aid-giving more strategically to enhance the investment prospects for Chinese firms, and this is often understood as a component of the Go Out policy. High-profile state visits were often used to smooth the way for Chinese companies to enter host countries. Australia was included in this practice, with visits from Premier Wen Jiabao to Western Australia in 2006 and President Hu Jintao to the same mineral-rich state in 2007. Likewise, bilateral investment and trade agreements signed with other nations have facilitated Chinese firms' investments. China's official development aid-giving was generally conditional on the receiving country awarding Chinese companies construction and other large-scale contracts (see Wilson 2011, 286 on China's "energy diplomacy" in Africa and Latin America).

As a slight aside, Elizabeth C. Economy, writing in *Foreign Affairs* in late 2010, argued that this new use of geopolitical capacities by the Chinese state marked a development in the policy, and seems to imply that the new elements of this activism should be thought of as a second "wave" of Going Out (2010, 147). Going Out 2.0 was marked by the addition to the acquisition of raw resources of "remaking global norms and institutions," an aim that amounts to "transforming the world as it transforms itself" (Economy 2010, 142). This obviously conflicts with my account of the (single) Go Out policy to this point. For my purposes, it is sufficient to say that the uses of state capacities for signing agreements with other states and aid-giving were commensurable with the stated aims of the policy. The divergence Economy refers to is important, but it did not occur until the onset of the GFC, which is to say after the major changes to the Australian FDI policy had occurred.

The purpose of explaining the Go Out policy in this depth has been to clarify the relationship between China's policy goals and the wave of investments by Chinese state- and non-state-owned enterprises that was the catalyst for the Rudd government's FDI screening changes. The relationship between Chinese firms and their state is closer than the equivalent in liberal states, but this does not imply that the firms were acting on the direct instructions from officials in the Chinese state bodies. Rather, the relationship between the Chinese state and the investing firms was complexified by a number of factors. First, the sheer number of administrative bodies involved in governing outward FDI by the mid-2000s made understanding a clear relationship between a single entity of the state and a given firm difficult. Indeed, the complexity of the institutional environment was a hindrance to the Chinese firms themselves (Voss et al. 2009, 144). Second, the Go Out policy is better understood as a loosening of controls over outward foreign investment, rather than a sudden decision to use the build-up of foreign reserves by China as a strategic weapon of statecraft. Thirdly, while the management of Chinese firms by the administrative bodies would not be called liberal in Western terms, the controls did not extend to the state officials being able to make the enterprises' business decisions for them. Rather, the governance occurred via a system of positive and negative incentives stretching into the future, in a manner that is sometimes called "parental" governance (Ring et al. 2005). Finally, the real advantages of Chinese firms relative to their competitors, either domestic firms in the host countries of Chinese outward FDI, or non-Chinese multinationals, should not be understated.

4.2 Chinese Foreign Investment and the Australian Policy Problem

This section describes the significance of the wave of Chinese investments that occurred as a result of the Go Out Policy to the Australian economy. While the investments were not of enormous material significant when considered alone, when understood as a new component of Australia's economic interaction with the global economy in the future, and as a component in a rapidly changing regional iron ore market, their importance for Australian interests appears to be much greater.

The significance of Chinese FDI flows to Australia can be confusing. On the one hand, the wave of investments that began in September 2006 and continued through the period of the Rudd government's term of office and beyond came from a very low base, with an average of $AU180 million capital flowing from China to Australia in the decade leading up to the change (Drysdale 2011, 59). Compared with this, the figures listed in Tables 4.1 and 4.2 signify a remarkable rate of growth.[5] Naturally then, China continued through the period in question to hold markedly less FDI stocks in the Australian economy than other, more established countries, such as the United States, Britain, and Japan. The Australian treasurer, Wayne Swan, drew on this point in a number of speeches, pointing out that at the end of 2008, the total stock of Chinese investment amounted to "one fifth of one percent of foreign direct investment in Australia" (Swan 2008c). Three years later, the FIRB executive member, Frank Di Giorgio (2011), was able to point out in a speech to the China Overseas Investment Fair that Chinese investment stock still did not constitute a single percent of the total and that China was ranked twelfth among Australia's largest investors.

These figures belie the significance of Chinese investments over the period in two ways, however. First, while China became Australia's key trading partner and a significant source of capital flows very quickly, there were good reasons to believe that these new conditions would remain in place for a long way into the future. Thus, the government's response to the wave of investments was anticipatory and responded

Table 4.1 China's outward FDI flows and stocks, 2004–2010 (millions of US dollars)

Destination	*2004*	*2005*	*2006*	*2007*	*2008*	*2009*	*2010*
TOTAL (flows)	5497.99	12,261.17	17,633.97	26,505.09	55,907.17	56,528.99	68,811.31
Australia (flows)	124.95	193.07	87.60	531.59	1892.15	2436.43	1701.70
TOTAL (stock)	44,777.26	57,205.62	75,025.55	117,910.50	183,970.71	245,755.38	317,210.59
Australia (stock)	494.58	587.46	794.35	1444.01	3355.29	5863.10	7867.75

Adapted from Ministry of Commerce (2011, 82–93)

Table 4.2 FIRB approvals by country of investor, China as proportion of total

	From China ($AUm)	*Total ($AUm)*	*China as proportion of total (%)*	*From China into minerals sector ($AUm)*	*Total into minerals sector ($AUm)*	*China as proportion of total (%)*
2004–2005	264	119,473	0.22	39	33,501	0.12
2005–2006	7259	85,751	8.46	6758	19,749	34.22
2006–2007	2640	156,387	1.69	1203	32,279	3.73
2007–2008	7479	191,879	3.90	5311	64,275	8.27
2008–2009	26,599	166,709	15.96	26,254	90,622	28.97
2009–2010	16,282	139,503	11.67	12,186	80,922	15.06

Adapted from (FIRB 2006, 29; 2007, 37; 2008, 39; 2009, 41; 2010, 37; 2011, 35). (In 2005–2006, two approvals in the mining sector combined to a value in excess of $6 billion, taking up the lions share of the $7.3 billion from China to Australia in FDI that financial year [FIRB 2007, 35]. It is not clear what these investments were.)

to the symbolic concerns with Chinese SOE investments, rather than any short-term and immediate material ones. In fact, the 2007/2008 budget predicted that it would take at least ten years for iron ore prices to decline by 20%, and this view was maintained throughout the period in question, with the 2011/2012 budget stretching the figure to twenty years (see Uren 2012, 3). Second, the investments were heavily focused in the Australian mining sector, and came to constitute a significant proportion of the capital coming into the traditionally foreign-capital heavy sector (on the role of foreign capital in Australian resources and mining see Drysdale 2011, 61; on the proportion that Chinese investment made up of the total over 2004–2005 to 2009–2010, see Table 4.2).

Secondly, the significance of Chinese investments as a policy problem requires an understanding of the changes occurring in the East Asian iron ore markets over the 2000s as a result of the rise of China. These changes created a conflict of interests between the Australian producers of iron ore and the Chinese consumers. The Chinese government's responses to this conflict were a key factor in the Rudd government's changes to the FDI policy.

The changes in the East Asian iron ore markets over the decade of the 2000s were driven by the rise of China as the world's preeminent producer of steel, and thus consumer of iron ore. The growth in China's demand for iron ore (as well as coking coal, copper, aluminium and a

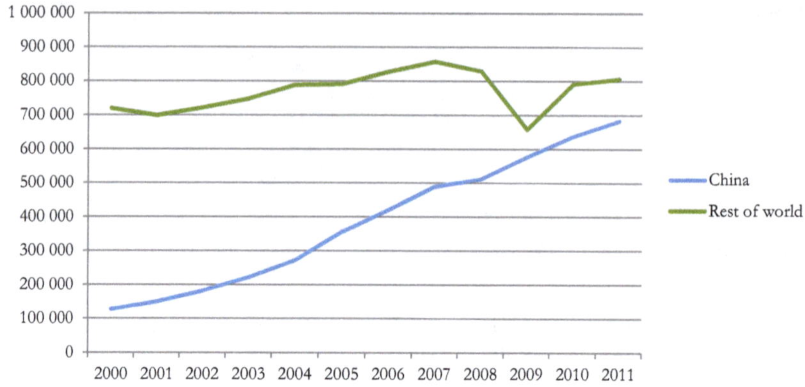

Fig. 4.1 Annual steel production 2000–2012 (million tonnes per annum): China and the rest of the world From Solberg (2012, 49), information from the World Steel Association annual crude steel production statistics

Table 4.3 World iron ore imports by steelmakers 2000–2009 (million tonnes per annum)

	Japan	*Korea*	*China*	*Rest of World*	*World Total*
2000	131.7	39.0	70.0	238.0	478.7
2001	126.3	45.9	92.3	213.9	478.4
2002	129.1	43.3	111.5	230.5	514.4
2003	132.1	43.1	148.1	287.2	610.5
2004	134.9	44.2	208.1	248.4	635.6
2005	132.3	43.5	275.2	246.0	697.0
2006	134.3	43.9	326.3	250.2	754.7
2007	138.9	46.2	382.8	253.4	821.3
2008	140.4	49.5	443.4	240.3	873.6
2009	105.5	42.1	627.8	148.2	923.6

From Wilson (2012, 332), data from UN Comtrade Database

host of other minerals) from the early 2000s caused global prices and volumes traded to rise dramatically. Figure 4.1 shows the growth of Chinese steel production over the decade and Table 4.3 shows the resulting growth of Chinese iron ore imports. Both also contrast the growth in Chinese steel production and iron ore importation with that of the rest of the world. Chinese consumption of the ore swiftly displaced the existing structures of the regional and global markets, with

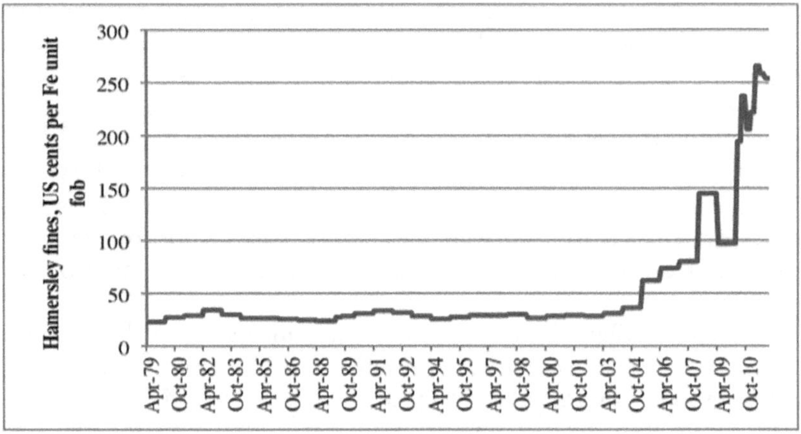

Fig. 4.2 Asia-Pacific benchmark iron ore prices 1979–2011 (From Wilson [2012, 332]; data from UNCTAD Database)

two important effects. First, the increase in demand led to sharp price increases in the benchmark iron ore prices. This can be seen clearly in Fig. 4.2, and contrasts with the remarkable price stability that had characterised the market in the decades preceding 2005. Secondly, the rise of Chinese steel production displaced the dominance of Japanese steelmakers that had constituted the main group of iron ore buyers, and also the de facto leaders in the annual benchmark price-setting negotiations.

Historically, a very high proportion of iron ore sales have occurred under the structure of long-term contracts, usually of five to ten-year lives (Wilson 2012, 332). This practice dates back to the mining boom of the late 1960s and provided steelmakers and iron ore producers with much-needed stability. For the steelmakers, the costs of stopping production are very high (Uren 2012, 154). Thus they have been willing historically to pay significant premiums to secure stability in supplies of the required inputs of iron ore and coking coal. For the iron ore producers, the high costs of exploration and early project development has meant that stability of income has been valuable in facilitating the assembly of capital and borrowings necessary to production. As well as the use of long-term contracts, the East Asian iron ore market has benefitted since the 1970s from the existence of annual benchmark pricing. Prior to 2005, the benchmark prices were produced annually by a series of negotiations between the oligopolistic suppliers of ore, and the oligopsonistic buyers, two informal cartels more or less balancing out the market power that would result from either structure in a more standard market. In practice, the negotiations would be held between a "champion" firm from either side of the market, most often the Australian producer Rio Tinto and the Japanese buyer Nippon Steel (Wilson 2012, 332). Other firms would then set their contracts in line with the prices determined by this negotiation. Spot markets for iron ore fines and lumps existed, but these accounted for a small proportion of sales historically.

The rise of China as a steel-producing giant displaced the price-setting system. While the increase in demand could itself be expected to put significant upward pressure on prices, the changes from 2005 were made more stark by the shift in power in the market (see Fig. 4.2). The Chinese steel mills were less concentrated than their Japanese and Korean counterparts: the Japanese industry was dominated by five large firms and the Korean by one, while the top ten Chinese firms in the early 2000s accounted for only half of China's production (Uren 2012, 155). As a result, the Chinese firms, led by Baosteel, were unable to organise sufficiently to present the cartel-style front in negotiations that the Japanese traditionally had. After a small price rise in 2004, the benchmark prices rose 71% in April 2005. The 2006 and 2007 negotiations resulted in smaller increases, largely as Vale tried to increase its market share in China despite the extra costs of shipping ore from Brazil amounting to $60 per tonne of ore relative to from Australia (Uren 2012, 157). By 2008, however, Rio Tinto was sufficiently empowered to refuse the 71% benchmark price increase that Vale had already secured in negotiations, and successfully demanded nearly double the 2007 price.[6] Vale later demanded a "catch up" price increase of 12%, but aborted the bid after the collapse of Lehman Brothers (Uren 2012, 161).

The Chinese state institutions appreciated the dilemma for steelmakers early in the decade, but were relatively unsuccessful in responding to it. There were two official initiatives announced in the NDRC's 2005 Iron and Steel Industry Development Policy: the sponsoring of new iron ore suppliers (Article 30) and the creation of a Chinese importers' cartel (Article 39). The first was a boost to the Go Out policy described in the last section, with the detail that steel-producing firms themselves were encouraged to invest overseas in iron ore projects.[7] As per the existing Go Out policy the main mechanism consisted of preferential access to finance from the state-owned banking system and the two development banks. An explicit objective of the policy was to develop "captive mines" controlled by the Chinese steelmakers, emulating the vertical integration that Japanese steel producers had achieved in Australian iron ore producing firms as early as the late 1960s (Solberg 2012, 69). The second initiative entailed promoting coordination among the Chinese steel firms for annual price-bargaining purposes, and the general secretary of the China Iron and Steel Association (CISA), Shan Shanghua, was delegated responsibility for the program. Shan was empowered via control over the distribution of iron ore import licenses, and from 2009 by CISA itself leading the annual negotiations with Vale, BHP-Billiton and Rio Tinto. While these negotiations resulted in significant cuts in the benchmark prices, the negotiations were drawn out months further the usual period, and the 2010 negotiations resulted in the end of the benchmarking system altogether. Instead, the market (following a deal not involving the Chinese at all) adopted a quarterly price, based on the spot prices of the preceding three months. The first of these prices was almost double the 2009 annual benchmark.

More pointedly on the subject of the catalyst for the Australian FDI policy changes starting in February 2008, Shan also initiated a boycott by Chinese steel mills of ore from the two Australian giants, BHP-Billiton and Rio Tinto. This was in response to Rio failing to fulfil its long-term contract by as much as 46% and directing large volumes on to the lucrative spot markets instead (Steel Guru, 16 May 2008). Rumours of the boycott began in January and February of 2008 and the boycott was declared publicly in May (Steel Guru, 16 May 2008). The boycott was not successful as a negotiating tactic, and soon began to disintegrate, as the Chinese steelmakers proved incapable of being organised. While CISA was able to proclaim China's willingness to slash steel production by 10% in order to enforce the boycott (Steel Guru, 16 May 2008), Shan was undermined by the high costs of halting the production process for the steelmakers and CISA's inability to track import consignments across the complex network of the Chinese steel industry (Uren 2012, 162). Most significantly, the boycott attempts are almost certain to have cemented in the Australian imagination the idea that the Chinese steel producers, the predominantly state-owned investors into Australia, and the Chinese government were in meaningful collusion in a strategy to undermine the market conditions that were so lucrative for Australian ore producers (see Uren 2012, 94–100 on this view being held by leaders from BHP-Billiton, the Opposition Liberal and National Parties, the Australian Workers Union, and the Green party). It was this collusion, rather than any material significance, that catalysed the Australian policy changes.

4.3 The Liberal Foundations of the Existing Accounts of the Policy

Thus far the problematisation part of the policy analysis has been composed of defining how the Rudd Government's actions constituted a departure from the FDI screening policy it inherited and describing the immediate catalyst for this departure. In this final section I canvass the five existing schools of thought on why the Rudd Government acted the way it did. These schools situate their accounts of the policy in relation to domestic Australian politics, international economic ideologies, and geopolitical considerations. Despite the oddly dispersive character of the set, I will argue in this section, the existing accounts share three faults. First, they understand the problem being solved in overly proximate terms. This point refers least to the geopolitical accounts, but even in these, which locate the policy changes within a wider engagement with a rising China, there is a failure to articulate a convincing strategy that is furthered by the Australian government's decision to impose additional screening requirements on Chinese SOE investment proposals. My argument in this book is that the FDI policy was shaped by Kevin Rudd and Wayne Swan's ambitions relating to the coming world order and the integration of China into a world order amenable to the interests of the existing liberal powers. Second, the existing explanations are limited by a liberal language of politics, whether it is domestic, economic, or international politics. As I will show, without any language to discuss the "assemblages" of economic and political beliefs, actors, and objects that enable and underpin liberal governmentality, it was not possible for any of these accounts to articulate the threat that the Chinese SOEs actually posed to the Australian state. Finally, there is an inadequate integration of political, economic, geopolitical, and ideological aspects of the policy. These are treated statically and as if they are unrelated realms. This is a product of the first two errors, and undermine the commentators' ability to access the policy problem *as it was defined by the policy's creators.*

The first school of thought, the account the government itself provided, is that the policy changes were not substantive. This was the line that Swan and Rudd took personally in relation to the February Guidelines (Swan 2008b; Rudd 2008): the Guidelines "clarified" or "improved the transparency" of the existing rules only (Swan 2008a). It was also the way the government framed the introduction of the *FATA Amendment Bill 2010* (see Chapter 3, Sect. 3.3, part i). This account can be easily rejected as a tactic in agenda management. An extensive description of the changes that did occur is available in Chapter 3, along with an argument that the government was markedly more interventionist than previous Australian governments had been. The interventions were targeted almost exclusively on large-scale investments by SOEs, all of which happened to come from China.

The second school of thought holds that the FDI policy was an ad hoc response to an unexpected politicisation of the issue of foreign investment in Australia. Drysdale and Findlay (2009) suggest in their conclusion that the rapid rise of China caught many in Australia by surprise and that two high-profile investments—Sinosteel's application to take over Midwest (approved in November 2007 by the Rudd government immediately upon assuming office) and Chinalco's raid on Rio Tinto in early 2008—introduced political confusion and uncertainty into Australia's foreign investment regime (Drysdale and Findlay 2009, 153). In 2011, Drysdale (2011, 57) expands this thesis to argue that the Australian government was "initially caught off guard by the speed and scale of the surge in Chinese investment in the resource sector". He then argues that the release of the February Guidelines "might have seemed [politically expedient] at the time"—in the face of an Opposition calls to block the Chinalco bid on Rio Tinto (2011, 57) and widespread community resistance to foreign ownership generally (2011, 56)—but the "additions" to the national interest test unnecessarily added uncertainty to the FDI screening regime and policy debate.

This thesis is unconvincing for a number of reasons. First, it does not seem reasonable to say that the possibility of large-scale investments from China caught the government off-guard. David Uren has reported that, in the month leading up to the Chinalco raid on Rio Tinto,

> ... Rudd had been asking Treasury for a position paper outlining how to deal with a takeover bid for a major resource company coming from a Chinese government-owned company. Not only had none been

> forthcoming, but the government's impression was that Treasury didn't see the point. It believed that Treasury was taking a classic liberal view that foreign investment was good for the country and only extreme circumstances would require government intervention under the *Foreign Acquisitions and Takeovers Act*. (Uren 2012, 66)

Rudd, by contrast, "[h]ad been worrying about the issue since before Christmas" (Uren 2012, 66) and "was very clear that China's desire for Australia's natural resources raised issues of national security" (2012, 67).

Secondly, even if the February Guidelines had been an ad hoc response, there is the subsequent two and a half years of execution of the policy still to be explained. As I have noted in Chapter 3, the Rudd government issued Interim Orders in a number of cases, adding a further ninety days to the thirty allowed to it statutorily to object to an investment proposal, and then failed to comply with this extended limit on a number of occasions. An important example of this, given Drysdale and Findlay's claim, was the initial Chinalco bid for a stake in Rio Tinto: the government did not issue an approval notice until the 24th of August 2008, nearly seven months after the dawn raid of January 31. In addition to this point, the execution of the policy appears to have been remarkably consistent throughout the government's term of office. As I have noted, there was very little, if any, easing of the policy in the months following September 2008. This is remarkable, given the shortfall of liquidity in the Australian and world economies in the immediate onslaught of the GFC.[8] Drysdale and Findlay's claim carries an implied addendum that the government refused to adjust the initial ad hoc settings for the twenty-eight months following February 2008 out of stubbornness.

Thirdly, the thesis is too narrowly conceived. To suggest that Kevin Rudd and Wayne Swan decided on one of the most important aspects of the Australia–China relationship during their period in office predominantly on the basis of managing public opinion and limiting the Opposition's capacity to capitalise on community fears is not convincing. Rudd gave a high priority to the China relationship. Both he and Wayne Swan spent significant time in China personally; he devoted high-profile speeches to the Australia–China relationship and invested significant political capital to negotiation rounds of the prospective China–Australia Free Trade Agreement (FTA). As I will show in Chapter 6, Rudd had a sophisticated and coherent agenda in Australia's engagement with China. It is not believable that either Rudd or Swan would not appreciate the significance of the issue of foreign investment to the overall relationship, or determine this policy predominantly in relation to domestic concerns.

The third school of thought is that the policy was resource nationalist in character. In the crude form of this argument, the screening regime was used as a "mechanism for political intervention in the market for the ownership and control of Australian equity" (Kirchner 2009b). Kirchner goes on to argue that the conditions attached to foreign investment approvals were "explicitly protectionist in intent, with the Treasurer stating that they are aimed at protecting local jobs" (Kirchner 2009b). In a later work, he called the policy "mercantilist" and reflective of a "central planning mindset" of the Australian politicians (Kirchner 2012, 58) on the basis that it had "effectively become an arm of Australian domestic industry and employment policy" (2012, 60; see also Kirchner 2014, 19).

The more sophisticated form of the argument situates the Australian policy change within a wider global turn towards resource nationalism and understands the aims of the policy as maintaining the Australian iron ore producers' oligopolistic power in the regional iron ore market. Wilson (2011, 285) defines resource nationalism as natural resource-endowed states using their legal jurisdiction over resources to achieve national development goals that would not be obtained if the exploitation were left to international market processes. There are three main techniques to this: enlarging profits by mandating increases in traded prices for commodities through export controls or participation in cartels; capturing profits via minimum local ownership requirements; and establishing downstream manufacturing activities by requiring the local processing of resources by multinational corporations (Wilson 2011, 285). The rise of Chinese "energy diplomacy" is a central feature in this turn towards resource nationalism globally (Wilson 2011, 286): in developing countries, predominantly in Africa and South America, China has "exchanged" aid monies, investment funds, and infrastructure and technology boosts for exclusive access to the produce of designated raw resource projects.

While China's use of these tactics are important for the Australian case, the accounts that hold the FDI policies as resource nationalist have understood Australia's interests as defending *from* predatory interventions from the Chinese state, rather than embracing resource nationalist practices itself. The argument for resource nationalism, it should be noted, has more often been articulated by critics of the strategy and the Australian government's interventionism and used as a foil to promote the virtues of a more laissez faire approach. That said, there were clearly vocal proponents of a screening policy of targeting Chinese SOEs according to resource nationalist principles. The Nationals, led by Barnaby Joyce, ran a campaign lobbying against Chinese investments entitled "Keeping Australia Australian." When given support for this agenda by the Greens (an unlikely alliance in normal Australian politics), the Nationals were able to force the government to convene a Senate Inquiry into the issue in 2009. Again, in a confidential submission opposing the second Chinalco bid for Rio Tinto shares, BHP argued that the transaction "will have the clear effect, and is intended to have the effect of substantially reducing the prices paid by the Chinese steel mills for iron ore, particularly that produced in Australia" (quoted in Uren 2012, 95). It went on to argue that the transaction would

> ... result in effective control over Rio Tinto passing to Chinalco and, as a State Owned Enterprise, to the Chinese Government. Rio Tinto would likely be the foundation of a powerful China Mining Company.

Both of these arguments amount to resource nationalist interventionism according to Wilson's definition. Neither were made by the government, which always explicitly rejected the charge of resource nationalism (for example, Swan in an interview with David Uren in Uren 2012, 90). The findings of the Senate Economics Committee report (the Senate inquiry) were that the government's settings were appropriate and did not need changing to manage the Chinese investments (Senate Economics Committee 2009) and the government did not *explicitly* rule on the second Chinalco bid (see Sect. 4.3, in this chapter, part i). However, the effective practice of holding Chinese SOE investment proposals to additional scrutiny on the basis of different principles and more stringent control thresholds (the Colmer doctrine, see Sect. 4.3, in this chapter, part i) could be argued to cohere with both the Nationals/Greens' call for boosting Australian control of resource production and BHP's warnings of Chinese state-strategising.

Wilson's 2011 article provides a compelling case against the account of the FDI policy as resource nationalism, and offers a fourth explanation of the policy: that it was "resource liberal" in nature. He argues that the execution of the Australian government's policy were limited to "defensively attempting to neutralise the potential for non-commercial behaviour by Chinese SOEs, rather than any broader efforts to restrict their entry into the Australian mining industry or to distort the operation of international market mechanisms in line with politically mandated national goals" (Wilson 2011, 297). There is little evidence of using FDI controls to leverage a greater share of Australian ownership. Nor is there evidence of using FDI controls to pursue "non-ownership" goals—restricting exports or requiring firms to engage in downstream manufacturing activities.[9] Wilson's conclusion from this is that the policy is better understood as liberal in character, rather than economic nationalist.

I agree with Wilson's reasoning, but would again add that both the resource nationalist account and Wilson's resource liberal account are problematically narrow. Wilson does well in dismantling the idea that Rudd and Swan had positive ambitions for the Australian resource industry, but his liberal resource account fails to provide satisfactory explanations to the policy nonetheless. If the aim was to limit the behaviour of Chinese SOEs to market-conforming behaviour, why use the politically and technically awkward policy tool of the FIRB and at the border controls in the first place? The policing of market-conforming behaviour could have been left to more to regulatory institutions better suited to the task, most obviously the ACCC and ASIC. This would have resulted in less confrontation with the Chinese state, and quite likely significantly more foreign capital flowing to Australia (see ITS Global 2008; Kirchner 2008a, b, 2009a, b, 2012, 2014; Novak 2008; Rae 2008; Makin 2008; Drysdale and Findlay 2009; Drysdale 2011; Larum 2011). What is missing from both of these accounts is a relationship of the FDI policy to the government's larger strategy on the China relationship, at a level above the iron ore industry and even resource sector. Secondly, the language of these accounts is itself limiting: they take as assumptions the liberal forms of and relations between firms and states. Thus, the threat of Chinese SOE collaboration is limited to the highly improbable "China Inc" or, in Don Argus' (the CEO of BHP) term, a "China Mining Company" outcome.[10] Without collaboration, the threat is limited to vertical integration by Chinese steelmakers, which is immediately dispelled by the difficulty of concealing these practices, and the Australian legal right to then intervene to prevent it within the Australian jurisdiction. I will argue that neither of these threats capture the problem as Rudd and Swan understood it, which was that the advantages bestowed on Chinese firms by the Chinese state and the state-run financial system undermined the principles on which liberal economic governance rested.

The fifth and final existing account of the policy situates it within a geopolitical context. There are three variants of the account. First, Donna Weeks' 2011 article examines the possibility of an East Asian security community. She suggests that "natural resources procurement [could] become the strategic (resource) culture, a source of power and security, underpinning the region's cognition of its shared interests" (2011, 77). The article does not examine the Australian FDI policy explicitly, but the implication is that utilising its control over assets vital to Japanese, Chinese and other states' "comprehensive security" (in the sense of the Japanese security debates of the 1980s; see Ravenhill 2013 for an account of the rise of resource nationalism in conjunction with the doctrine of comprehensive security) could facilitate Australia's entry into the regional community. She notes that Rudd sent Richard Woolcott on visits to twenty-one states as Special Envoy for the Asia-Pacific Community in the first twelve months of his period in office. Rudd tasked Woolcott with an almost identical goal to the one Bob Hawke had given the diplomat in the late 1980s when he had been instrumental in facilitating the birth of the Asia Pacific Economic Cooperation. If we are to understand the FDI policy in relation to Rudd's Asia Pacific Community initiative, then the role of FDI screening, by implication, was to establish Australia as an active player in the strategic machinations of regional resource geopolitics. This is not an argument made by Weeks, but I include it as a coherent account of how the FDI policy could be fit into a wider geopolitical story.

Leaver and Ungerer's 2010 paper, using a similar logic, calls for a framework for thinking about and then using the leverage born of being a supplier of vital resources. They bemoan the "underdevelopment" of resource diplomacy as a concept in Australia's strategic posture, and urge Australia to use "the supply of key commodities as part of a broader set of national instruments to chase export opportunities and to strengthen key strategic relationships" (2010, 3). They cite the origin of a link between the trade, security and environment concerns of Australia to Foreign Affairs Minister Alexander Downer's August 2004 visit to Beijing. In this meeting Downer committed the Howard Cabinet to beginning talks about a FTA, advised China that Australia's strategic position was not pre-committed to Washington's ends, and returned to Australia with the secret knowledge that China wished to buy uranium from Australia for an expanding civil nuclear program (2010, 6–7). While the Rudd government maintained this trade-security-environment link, they argue, there was a failure to pursue an active strategy using resource diplomacy beyond the traditional commitment to free-market principles. Again, this argument is made in the negative: Leaver and Ungerer's implied account of the Rudd government's FDI policy was limited to defensive resource liberalism (as per Wilson's 2011 account) but *should* have been otherwise. Nonetheless, again it provides a useful articulation of a more convincing strategy for the FDI policy, should we interpret it as a resource nationalist in character.

Finally, Beeson et al. (2011) make an argument that explicitly connects the FDI screening policy with geopolitical machinations. They place the issue of ownership of the resource sector, along with taxation, as the two primary impacts of China's rise on Australia's domestic politics (2011, 1374). They argue that China's rise to Australia's most important trade partner had not transformed Australia's strategic orientation, and that Rudd's entire strategy of "Asia engagement" was based on a desire to "contain" China. In this context, the need to pursue and protect "national interests" in the new (global) resource politics was a "potentially zero-sum contest" (2011, 1383) for resource-rich nations like Australia, but in the final analysis, "both ends of this unlikely pairing [China and Australia] have little option other than to make it work" (2011, 1383) and "[i]n the resource politics of the twenty-first century, material forces may trump ideological ones" (2011, 1384). While this usefully provides a third logic on which to build a geopolitical account of the FDI policy—namely that targeting Chinese investments was a piece in a larger containment strategy—it is undeveloped as an argument. As close as the authors come to explaining the direct relationship is to say that the backlash against foreign ownership in Australia forty years ago during the Japanese industrialisation-led resource boom is complicated in this iteration by the resource sector becoming "an even more important part of Australia's overall economic profile" and the fact "that it is 'communist China' rather than the US or even Japan that is the economic partner driving policy responses" (2011, 1372).

The three arguments listed above do not provide accounts of the FDI screening policy that place it within a wider Australian geopolitical strategy precisely, with the exception of the Beeson, Soko and Yong paper. I have outlined them as a provision of the sorts of arguments that are implied by the accounts that cast aspersion on the policy by suggesting that it rests on "xenophobia" (Kirchner 2008a; Makin 2008; Berg 2012; Golding 2014)[11] or accounts that similarly make the vague insinuations that the Australian government was targeting Chinese investments for non-economic reasons from the media (Berg 2012; Dorling 2011a, b, c, and d[12]; Wines 2009) or politicians (West Australian Premier Colin Barnett such as in his interview with Tony Eastley [Eastley 2013]; comments from opposition and independent senators in the debate on the *FATA Amendment Bill 2010* [see Joyce 2010; Xenaphon 2010; and Ludlum 2010]; or the debates on foreign ownership in Australian agricultural land which followed from the initial concern over investments into the mining sector [for example Liberal-National Coalition 2012[13]]). My point is that there was a widespread deployment of arguments that rested on an implied link between FDI screening and Australian geopolitical aims or concerns. These arguments very often did not specify what this link was precisely, so I have included three accounts that do articulate what such a link might actually be.

The first criticism of these accounts is of course that the link from FDI screening to geopolitical aims is poorly articulated. This is partially due to the fact that many of the sources I have annotated are not defending the thesis, but either criticising it, or suggesting it as an option in the case of Leaver and Ungerer. It is also partially due to the fact that many of the sources are either media commentators or politicians, who take the simplistic narrative of Australia being wedged between its primary security ally, the United States, and its largest economic partner, China, and deduce that any move that impedes Chinese interests can be understood as strategic balancing or containment. Without a clear articulation of why the FDI screening moves advanced any particular geopolitical aim, this account is not convincing. After all, the screening did not stop Chinese SOEs making significant investments in Australia or prevent Australian ore being sold to Chinese steelmakers. Certainly the aim was not to strengthen the economic or security relationship with China, as Leaver and Ungerer bemoan, and there is no clear evidence that it was used as leverage to insert Australia substantially into regional architecture-building processes in the way that Weeks suggests it might have been.

Secondly, and more substantively, there is an oversimplification of Australia's engagement with China in these accounts. In the geopolitical language used, Australia's strategies are limited to hedging (containing) and bandwagoning. Using FDI in such a way would not only be highly ineffective materially, but would also involve significant costs for Australia, not least of all the consequences of contravening the OECD guidelines on foreign investment governance (see Rae 2008).

There would then be the loss of investment capital, both from China and then other sources as global investors repriced the sovereign risk associated with investing in Australia, as well as loss of trade opportunities with its main economic partner in China. In short, these accounts almost require very poor strategic thinking from the Australian government, which, indeed, is the point being made by many of the critics of the Rudd government's interventionism.

These points made, my own position is that geopolitics is very important in explaining the policy. However, much as the economic accounts, the language of geopolitics used in all the existing explanations is not sufficient to capture the policy problem or aim. Two of the above accounts allude to complicating factors to the geopolitical story: Leaver and Ungerer's (2010) claim is based on a trade, security, environment *nexus* (which they do not develop beyond noting that it exists) and acknowledge that there is an "ideological" aspect to the engagement that they believe will be trumped by material considerations. Similarly, Beeson et al. (2011) assert that the fact that China is a communist nation is a complicating factor, but do not specify what complications arise from this. As I will show in Chapters 6 and 7, Rudd's highest level geopolitical ambitions related to the future character of the world order. The engagement with China from the West, in Rudd's vision, hinged precisely on questions of rule-making and -taking in the international sphere and the need to induce China to be both. I will argue in this book that an accurate articulation of the policy problem posed by SOEs involves understanding the significance of the new role of sovereign capital in the global financial system as its capacity to undermine the foundations of liberal economic governance. This problem is thus simultaneously one of geopolitics, economics, and ideology. To understand and describe it, we need a language that can describe this nexus. Foucauldian governmentality provides such a language. Specifically, the language of technologies of governance provides a way to articulate why Chinese SOE investments constituted a threat to the existing governance apparatuses in Australia.

4.4 Conclusion

This chapter and the preceding one constitute the problematisation of the policy changes. In this chapter, I have described the immediate catalyst of the changes to FDI screening introduced by the Rudd government in the wave of large-scale investments into the Australian mining sector from Chinese SOEs. This wave was caused by China's Go Out and Iron and Steel Industry Policies. I have described in detail the relationship between the Chinese state bodies and the SOEs. While the state institutions like the NDRC, MOFCOM and SAFE were not empowered to make operational decisions of the Chinese firms, they were able to shape the behaviour of these companies by affecting hiring decisions and shaping the firms' access to capital from the state-run financial system and development banks. I have shown that Chinese SOEs were given special incentives and conditions to invest in overseas raw resource ventures in order to further state-mandated interests for China, and that it is reasonable to say that they were given advantages not afforded to equivalent non-Chinese firms in the Australian and world economies. I have shown that the material significance of these investments, and China's consumption of iron ore with them, was very high, and I have established that the Australian government expected this consumption to remain at historically high levels a long way into the future. While this has not happened, it is nonetheless an important point to note, as ownership over vital raw resources features in a number of the existing accounts', as well as my own, as a point of strategic leverage for the Australian government vis-a-vis other states in the region.

Finally, I have canvassed the existing accounts of the policy. The four broad schools of thought, leaving aside the government's own non-account, understand the problem and aim of the FDI screening changes as relating to domestic politics, international economics, and geopolitics. While there are some accounts that try to draw links between these areas, for the most part each account has tended to pick one of these three realms in which to situate the policy. I have argued first that the existing accounts understand the problem and aim of the policy too locally; they look to overly proximate strategic conflicts in which to understand the government's actions. I have also argued that the existing accounts are limited by the liberal language and assumptions that they use. We simply do not have a language in liberal politics that enables us to link the economic, geopolitical, (domestic) political and ideological elements of this policy problem in a satisfying way. In the remainder of the book I will employ Foucauldian governmentality to articulate the shape of this nexus and to explain the policy problem as it was conceived by Kevin Rudd and Wayne Swan and why they responded as they did. In order to do this, I trace the narratives and articulations produced by these policymakers, which constituted the policy. This is the task of Chapters 5 and 6.

Notes

1. The precise origin of the Go Out policy is contested, with different accounts dating its adoption by China between 1998 and 2003. See Voss et al. (2009, 160, Footnote 3) on this point. They provide examples of four different positions on the matter and explain the discrepancies as deriving from access to original sources in Chinese and to different authors referring to the policy being mentioned or actually being implemented.
2. More precisely, the responsibility lay with the administrative body that would become the MOFCOM after two evolutions. During this first period of opening up, the body was the Ministry of Foreign Economic Relations and Trade (MOFERT). In 1993, the MOFERT was replaced by the Ministry of Foreign Trade and Economic Cooperation (MOFTEC), which was itself replaced by the MOFCOM in 2003. At the last change responsibility for domestic trade, foreign economic coordination, and the coordination of international trade in industrial products and raw material were added (Voss et al. 2009, 159, Footnote 2). As a result MOFCOM played a central role in the implementation of the Go Out policy through the 2000s.
3. Like MOFCOM, SAFE is the modern iteration of earlier bodies, in this case the State General Administration for Exchange Control (SGAEC), which was replaced in 1982 by the State Administration of Exchange Control (SAEC), which was in turn replaced by the SAFE in 1994.
4. The seven designated countries included the United States, Japan, and Iraq. The power to approve investments to these countries remained exclusively with the national MOFCOM office.
5. The figures in Tables 4.1 and 4.2 do not correlate precisely. This is because accessing reliable data on Chinese investment is extremely difficult. For a comprehensive discussion, see Hendrischke and Li (2013). The main two reasons they give are that the statistical bureaus of recipient countries do not collect or publish detailed breakdowns of investment flows from China, and that the information provided by the Chinese statistical bureaus are heavily distorted towards tax havens as a first destination for capital movements and often do not indicate their final destinations (Hendrischke and Li 2013, 2).
6. Precisely, Rio Tinto received a 79% rise for iron ore fines (lower quality ore) and a 96.5% rise for lump (higher quality ore) working out to an average rise of 85% for Rio Tinto and a little less for BHP (due to lump taking up a relatively high proportion of Rio's exports compared with BHP) (Garnaut, 26 July 2008).

7. The policy also listed five other minerals that would receive outward investments subsidies.
8. There was an easing under Prime Minister Gillard, though this falls outside of the scope of this study.
9. A single, minor exception to this (not acknowledged by Wilson) was the Ansteel decision (Swan 2009), which required the Chinese firm to maintain certain levels of Australian participation in a pellet plant in China.
10. This appeared in a private submission from BHP to the Australian Government. It is quoted at length in Uren (2012, 95–97).
11. The charge of actual xenophobia can be dismissed immediately. There is no evidence that the Australian government were anti-Chinese for reasons simply of race, and any references to this from the authors are rhetorical.
12. Dorling's four 2011 articles are not commentaries; he is reporting on the Wikileaks release of a US Embassy cable reporting on discussions with FIRB Executive Member Patrick Colmer in which Colmer described the Australian government's intentions as "to pose new disincentives for larger-scale Chinese investments".
13. This is a discussion paper published in 2012. It was the product of an inquiry by the Australian Bureau of Agriculture and Resource Economic and Science (ABARES), commission by the Gillard Government in November 2010.

References

Australian Liberal and National Party Coalition. (2012). *Foreign Investment in Australian Agricultural Land and Agribusiness.* Discussion paper by Australian Liberal and National Party Coalition. Available at http://shared.liberal.org.au/Share/Foreign_investment_discussion_paper.pdf. Accessed 2 Nov 2016.

Bach, D., Newman, A. L., & Weber, S. (2006). The International Implications of China's Fledgling Regulatory State: From Product Maker to Rule Maker. *Political Economy, 11*(4), 499–518.

Beeson, M., Soko, M., & Yong, W. (2011). The New Resource Politics: Can Australia and South Africa Accomodate China? *International Affairs, 87*(6), 1365–1384.

Berg, C. (2012, March 15). Foreign Investment and the Whims of Politicians. *The Drum.* Available at http://www.abc.net.au/news/2012-03-13/berg-foreign-investment-and-the-whims-of-politicians/3886786. Accessed 21 Oct 2016.

Cai, C. (2006). Outward Foreign Investment Protection and the Effectiveness of Chinese BIT Practice. *Journal of World Investment and Trade, 7*(5), 621–652.

Di Giorgio, F. (2011, November 9). *Speech to the 3rd China Overseas Investment Fair*. China World Trade Centre. Foreign Investment Review Board. Available at http://firb.gov.au/about/news-media/Publications/pressreleases/2011/001.asp. Accessed 13 Sept 2015.

Dorling, P. (2011a, February 15). How BHP boss derailed Rio's $23.9b deal. *Sydney Morning Herald*. Available at http://www.smh.com.au/business/how-bhp-boss-derailed-rios-239b-deal-20110214-1atpp.html. Accessed 25 Oct 2016.

Dorling, P. (2011b, March 3). Labor's Secret Curb on China. *The Age*. Available at http://www.smh.com.au/national/labors-secret-curb-on-china-20110302-1bex9.html. Accessed 25 Oct 2016.

Dorling, P. (2011c, March 3). Laws 'Aimed to Limit' Chinese Investments. *Sydney Morning Herald*. Available at http://www.smh.com.au/business/laws-aimed-to-limit-chinese-investments-20110302-1bexm.html. Accessed 25 Oct 2016.

Dorling, P. (2011d, March 3). Australia Worried China Buying Up Resources. *Asia Sentinel*. Available at http://www.asiasentinel.com/econ-business/australia-worried-china-buying-up-resources/#frameId=appnext_widget&height=64. Accessed 25 Oct 2016.

Drysdale, P. (2011). A New Look at Chinese FDI in Australia. *China and World Economy, 19*(4), 54–73.

Drysdale, P., & Findlay, C. (2009). Chinese Foreign Direct Investment in Australia: Policy Issues for the Resource Sector. *China Economic Journal, 2*(2), 133–158.

Eastley, T. (2013, June 5). Foreign Investment Rules Discriminate Against China: Colin Barnett. *ABC*, AM with Tony Eastley. http://www.abc.net.au/am/content/2013/s3774719.htm. Accessed 2 Nov 2016.

Economics Reference Committee. (2009). *Foreign Investment by State-Owned Entities*. The Senate of the Australian Federal Parliament. Australia: Commonwealth of Australia.

Economy, E. C. (2010). The Game Changer: Coping With China's Foreign Policy Revolution. *Foreign Affairs, 89*(6), 142–152.

FIRB. (2006). *Annual Report 2004–2005*. Australian Government, Foreign Investment Review Board. Available at http://firb.gov.au/about/publication/annual-report-2004-2005/. Accessed 1 Nov 2016.

FIRB. (2007). *Annual Report 2005–2006*. Australian Government, Foreign Investment Review Board. Available at http://firb.gov.au/about/publication/annual-report-2005-2006/. Accessed 28 Oct 2016.

FIRB. (2008). *Annual Report 2006–2007*. Australian Government, Foreign Investment Review Board. Available at http://firb.gov.au/about/publication/annual-report-2006-2007/. Accessed 29 Oct 2016.

FIRB. (2009). *Annual Report 2007–2008*. Australian Government, Foreign Investment Review Board. Available at http://firb.gov.au/about/publication/annual-report-2007-2008/. Accessed 29 Oct 2016.

FIRB. (2010). *Annual Report 2008–2009*. Australian Government, Foreign Investment Review Board. Available at http://firb.gov.au/about/publication/annual-report-2008-2009/. Accessed 1 Nov 2016.

FIRB. (2011). *Annual Report 2009–2010*. Australian Government, Foreign Investment Review Board. Available at http://firb.gov.au/about/publication/annual-report-2009-2010/. Accessed 30 Oct 2016.

Garnaut, J. (2008, July 26). To the Brink of War. *Sydney Morning Herald*. Available at http://www.smh.com.au/business/to-the-brink-of-war-20080725-3l0e.html. Accessed 1 Nov 2016.

Golding, G. (2014). Australia's Experience with FDI by State Controlled Entities: A Move Towards Xenophobia or Greater Openness? *Seattle University Law Review, 37*, 533–580.

Hendrischke, H., & Li, W. (2013, September 27). *Chinese Direct Investment in Australia—Characteristics and Integration*. Paper presented at 7th China Goes Global Conference, Bremen Germany. Available at http://www.chinagoesglobal.org/wp-content/uploads/2013/08/Hendrischke_and_Li_CHINESE_OUTBOUND_DIRECT_INVESTMENT_IN_AUSTRALIA.pdf. Accessed 1 Nov 2016.

Howarth, D., & Griggs, S. (2012). Poststructural Policy Analysis: Discourse, Hegemony, and Critical Explanation. In F. Fischer & H. Gottweis (Eds.), *The Argumentative Turn Revisited* (pp. 305–342). Durham, USA: Duke University Press.

ITS Global. (2008, September 9). *Foreign Direct Investment in Australia—The Increasing Cost of Regulation*. ITS Global, Melbourne, Australia. Available at http://www.itsglobal.net/sites/default/files/itsglobal/Research%20Report%20on%20Foreign%20Direct%20Investment%20and%20the%20Increasing%20Cost%20of%20Regulation%20in%20Australia%20(2008).pdf. Accessed 21 Oct 2016.

Joyce, B. (2010, February 2). *Cth. Parliamentary Debates, 'Foreign Acquisition and Takeovers Amendment Bill 2009 Second Reading'*. Senate. Available at http://parlinfo.aph.gov.au/parlInfo/search/display/display.w3p;db=CHAMBER;id=chamber%2Fhansards%2F2010-02-02%2F0125;query=Id%3A%22chamber%2Fhansards%2F2010-02-02%2F0000%22. Accessed 2 Nov 2016.

Kirchner, S. (2008a). Capital Xenophobia II: FDI in Australia, SWFs, and the Rise of State Capitalism. Centre for Independent Studies. *CIS Policy Monograph, 88*.

Kirchner, S. (2008b, November 27). Foreign Investment Flows Are Damned By Political Bias. *The Centre for Independent Studies*. Available at https://www.cis.org.au/commentary/articles/foreign-investment-flows-are-damned-by-political-bias. Accessed 21 Oct 2016.

Kirchner, S. (2009a, September 30). Canberra's Investment Confusion. *Wall Street Journal*. Available at http://www.wsj.com/articles/SB10001424052748704471504574442281091477054. Accessed 21 Oct 2009.

Kirchner, S. (2009b, August 5). FDI Liberalisation Falls Short. *The Centre for Independent Studies*. Available at https://www.cis.org.au/commentary/articles/fdi-liberalisation-falls-short. Accessed 21 Oct 2016.

Kirchner, S. (2012). The Kingdom and the Quarry: China, Australia, Fear and Greed. *Policy, 28*(2), 58–62 (Review Essay).

Kirchner, S. (2014). *Regulating Foreign Direct Investment in Australia*. Financial Services Institute of Australasia (Finsia). Available at https://www.finsia.com/docs/default-source/industry-reports-foreign-direct-investment/regulating-foreign-direct-investment-in-australia.pdf?sfvrsn=4. Accessed 21 Oct 2016.

Larum, J. (2011). *Chinese Perspectives on Investing in Australia*. Analyses papers series. Sydney: Lowy Institute.

Leaver, R., & Ungerer, C. (2010). *A Natural Power: Challenges for Australia's Resources Diplomacy in Asia*. Canberra, Australia: The Australian Strategic Policy Institute. Available at https://www.aspi.org.au/publications/a-natural-power-challenges-for-australias-resources-diplomacy-in-asia/A_natural_power.pdf. Accessed 21 Oct 2016.

Ludlum, S. (2010, February 2). *Cth. Parliamentary Debates, 'Foreign Acquisition and Takeovers Amendment Bill 2009 Second Reading'*. Senate. Available at http://parlinfo.aph.gov.au/parlInfo/search/display/display.w3p;db=CHAMBER;id=chamber%2Fhansards%2F2010-02-02%2F0127;query=Id%3A%22chamber%2Fhansards%2F2010-02-02%2F0000%22. Accessed 2 Nov 2016.

Makin, T. (2008). *Capital Xenophobia and the National Interest*. Australia's Open Investment series paper 8, Institute of Public Affairs. Available at https://www.ipa.org.au/library/publication/1229298839_document_makin.pdf. Accessed 21 Oct 2016.

Ministry of Commerce (MOFCOM). (2004, October 1). Provisions on the Examination and Approval of Investment to Run Enterprises Abroad. *Order of the Ministry of Commerce of the People's Republic of China No. 16*. Ministry of Commerce, People's Republic of China. Available at http://en.pkulaw.cn/Display.aspx?LookType=3&Lib=law&Cgid=55499&Id=3726&SearchKeyword=&SearchCKeyword=&paycode=. Accessed 1 Nov 2016.

Ministry of Commerce (MOFCOM). (2011, September 16). *2010 Statistical Bulletin of China's Outward Foreign Direct Investment*. Ministry of Commerce, People's Republic of China. Available at http://english.mofcom.gov.cn/article/statistic/foreigninvestment/201109/20110907742320.shtml. Accessed 1 Nov 2016.

Murphy, M. (2008, May 27). *Issues in Focus: China's "Going Out" Investment Policy*. Freeman Briefing, Center for Strategic and International Studies. Available at https://csis-prod.s3.amazonaws.com/s3fs-public/legacy_files/files/publication/080527_freeman_briefing.pdf. Accessed 1 Nov 2016.

Novak, J. (2008). *Australia as a Destination for Foreign Capital*. Australia's Open Investment series paper 1. Institute of Public Affairs. Available at http://www.ipa.org.au/library/publication/1226637929_document_novak_destination_for_foreign_capital.pdf. Accessed 21 Oct 2016.

OECD. (2008). *OECD Investment Policy Reviews: China 2008*. Organisation for Economic Cooperation and Development. Available at http://www.oecd.org/investment/investmentfordevelopment/41734421.pdf. Accessed 1 Nov 2016.

Rae, J. (2008). *Counting the Cost of Regulation*. Australia's Open Investment series paper 2, Institute of Public Affairs. Available at https://www.ipa.org.au/library/publication/1229298979_document_rae.pdf. Accessed 21 Oct 2016.

Ravenhill, J. (2013). Resource Insecurity and International Institutions in the Asia-Pacific Region. *The Pacific Review, 26*(1), 39–64.

Ring, P. S., Bigley, G. A., D'Aunno, T., & Khanna, T. (2005). Perspectives on How Governments Matter. *Academy of Management Review, 30*(2), 306–320.

Rudd, K. (2008, February 18). Interview with Chris Uhlmann. *AM, ABC Radio*. Available at https://pmtranscripts.dpmc.gov.au/release/transcript-15765. Accessed 21 Oct 2016.

Salidjanova, N. (2011, March 30). *Going Out: An Overview of China's Outward Foreign Direct Investment* (USCC Research Report). U.S.-China Economic and Security Review Commission. Available at http://www.uscc.gov/sites/default/files/Research/GoingOut.pdf. Accessed 1 Nov 2016.

Steel Guru. (2008, May 16). *Iron Ore Price Negotiations—CISA to Boycott Spot Sale by Rio*. Steel Guru. Available at http://steelguru.com/steel/iron-ore-price-negotiations-8211-cisa-to-boycott-spot-sale-by-rio-/45654#tag. Accessed 1 Nov 2016.

Solberg, T. (2012). *Mine Your Own Business! Economic Interdependence and Sino-Australian Relations in the 2000s*. Masters thesis, submitted to Department of Political Science, Oslo University, 6 June 2012. Available at https://www.duo.uio.no/handle/10852/36979. Accessed 1 Nov 2016.

Swan, W. (2008a, February 17). *Government Improves Transparency of Foreign Investment Screening Process*. Treasury. Available at http://ministers.treasury.gov.au/DisplayDocs.aspx?doc=pressreleases/2008/009.htm&pageID=003&min=wms&Year=&DocType. Accessed 21 Oct 2016.

Swan, W. (2008b, February 17). *Press Conference: Waterfront Palace*. Brisbane, Treasury. Available at http://ministers.treasury.gov.au/DisplayDocs.aspx?doc=transcripts/2008/028.htm&pageID=011&min=wms&Year=2008&DocType=2. Accessed 30 Oct 2016.

Swan, W. (2008c, June 11). *A Modern Relationship with China*. Speech to the Central Party School, Communist Party of China. Treasury. Available at http://ministers.treasury.gov.au/DisplayDocs.aspx?doc=speeches/2008/019.htm&pageID=010&min=wms&Year=2008&DocType=1. Accessed 1 Nov 2016.

Swan, W. (2009, May 8). *Foreign Investment Decision (Ansteel to Acquire Gindalbie Metals)*. Treasury. Available at http://ministers.treasury.gov.au/DisplayDocs.aspx?doc=pressreleases/2009/045.htm&pageID=003&min=wms&Year=2009&DocType=0. Accessed 30 Oct 2016.

Tan, R. (1999). *Foreign Direct Investments Flows to and From China* (PASCN Discussion Paper No. 99–21). Makati: PASCN.

Uren, D. (2012). *The Kingdom and the Quarry: China, Australia, Fear and Greed*. Collingwood, VIC: Black Inc.

Voss, H., Buckley, P. J., & Cross, A. R. (2009). An Assessment of the Effects of Institutional Change on Chinese Outward Direct Investment Activity. In A. Alon, J. Chang, M. Fetscherin, C. Letterman, & J. R. McIntyre (Eds.), *China Rules: Globalisation and Political Transformation* (pp. 135–165). Houndmills, Basingstoke, and Hampshire, UK: Palgrave Macmillan.

Wilson, J. D. (2011). Resource Nationalism or Resource Liberalism? Explaining Australia's Approach to Chinese Investment in Its Minerals Sector. *Australian Journal of International Affairs, 65* (3), 283–304.

Wilson, J. D. (2012). Chinese Resource Security Policies and the Restructuring of the Asia-Pacific Iron Ore Market. *Resources Policy, 37*(3), 331–339.

Wines, M. (2009, June 2). Australia, Nourishing China's Economic Engine, Questions Ties. *New York Times*. Available at http://www.nytimes.com/2009/06/03/world/asia/03australia.html. Accessed 2 Nov 2016.

Xenaphon, N. (2010, February 2). *Cth. Parliamentary Debates, 'Foreign Acquisition and Takeovers Amendment Bill 2009 Second Reading'*. Senate. Available at http://parlinfo.aph.gov.au/parlInfo/search/display/display.w3p;db=CHAMBER;id=chamber%2Fhansards%2F2010-02-02%2F0126;query=Id%3A%22chamber%2Fhansards%2F2010-02-02%2F0000%22. Accessed 2 Nov 2016.

Zhang, Y. (2003). *China's Emerging Global Business: Political Economy and Institutional Investigations*. Basingstoke, UK: Palgrave Macmillan.

CHAPTER 5

Official Discourses of Economics

This chapter traces the narratives and articulations that, along with a set of executive actions, constituted the FDI policy of the Rudd Government. Using close readings of key speeches from Australian state officials, I show that while the key policy change was made in a moment of "institutional ambiguity" or crisis, this was downplayed by the officials, who chose to frame the policy as a continuity of the FDI screening regime that they had inherited. This was done to sediment the presupposed knowledge of the policy: that market disciplines were preferable for the constitution of firms and for shaping price and production decisions in the Australian resource sector. While much of the policy actions aimed at constituting a special position for the Australian Government in relation to firms, sectional interests, public opinion, and the Chinese State for tactical reasons, the logics underpinning these tactics are instructive. Most importantly, they rest on the appearance of the market as a site of truth (and its constitution within the policy) and liberal economic governance as in the interests of all actors involved. These points may seem innocuous, but this is belied by the constant effort from Australian state officials to defend them.

My methodology for the discourse analysis has been described in Chapter 2. In the first section, I situate the policy within the larger economic agenda of the Rudd Government, and the chapter is composed of a series of close readings of key speeches from state actors, and then a set of "displacements" where I treat the speeches as a set. In the close readings, I draw on analytical devices from postpositivist policy studies

© The Author(s) 2019

M. Peters, *Regulating the Rise of China*, Studies in the Political Economy of Public Policy, https://doi.org/10.1007/978-3-030-05466-3_5

and narrative-based discourse analysis methods, and try to find instances of discourse structuration (Hajer 1993, 1995), synecdoches, metaphors, and strategic ambiguities (Stone 2002), policy windows (Kingdon 1995), and "organisational metaphors" (Yanow 1996). From these I try to construct an economic policy narrative, linking a problem with a solution and assigning subject positions (Stone 2002). In the displacement section, I examine the ways the policy narrative changed over time, noting actually that it was surprisingly unchanged by the onset of the global financial crisis; how the articulations that appear in the speeches have constitutive effects; and how the official discourse differed from dominant themes in the articulations of non-state actors on the policy.

The key findings from the close readings are that a primary aim of the policy was ensuring all firms were positioned in a competitively neutral way, alongside managing the threat of Chinese SOEs operating according to unified strategies devised by the Chinese State economic agencies. It was deemed necessary to balance, as much as possible, the special privileges of Chinese SOEs born of access to state finances and provided on the basis of their positions in relation to resources needed by the Chinese economy. A key organisational metaphor that appeared was "economic sovereignty." This term was used only once, by Treasurer Wayne Swan late in the period being examined, but contains significant explanatory value. Economic sovereignty refers to the Australian Government's ability to unilaterally define the forms of actors and structures that appeared in the Australian economy in ways that make them amenable to liberal governance. The term is the nexus between economic and security issues that made up the Rudd Government's understanding of the challenges of the rise of China, and should be understood as the primary aim of the policy. It is this logic that explains the Government's willingness to forego material interests in much-needed foreign capital injections into the Australian economy, and to wear the constant criticism of the policy from a host of domestic and international actors.

5.1 Context and Crisis

The broad economic narrative that the Rudd government had employed in the 2007 election campaign, which continued to frame decision-making through the first part of their term of office, was that the Australian economy faced "positive" problems in the context of "a sustained period of economic growth" (Swan 2007a) in Australia, and needed an active and responsible government to manage these problems. The problems were articulated and linked as follows (Swan 2007a):

> The combination of strengthening wage growth and continuing weak productivity growth implies nominal unit labour costs are increasing. This provides further evidence of capacity constraints such as skilled labour shortages and infrastructure bottlenecks...
>
> That's why I say that inflationary pressures are really being driven by the twin deficits: the skills deficit, the infrastructure deficit. And the number one priority of a Rudd Labor Government is to deal with those deficits.

In narrative terms, the problem of inflation was matched with the specific causes of wage pressures, skills shortages, and infrastructure shortages and a general cause as follows:

> We are in the middle of the strongest world economy in a long time. We're in the middle of a mining boom and the government had not been putting in place the policies to head off the inflationary pressures that are building in the economy. So as a consequence we are now facing a very considerable inflationary challenge. (Swan 2007b)

The story positioned the Howard Government as the villain by dint of being inactive governors. The newly elected Rudd Government, by contrast, was framed variously as "responsible" in that they would intervene appropriately to preempt the problems above; "conservative" as economic managers, meaning that they respected market-based structures; "disciplined" in getting rid of "wasteful spending" (Swan 2007b); and "modern," usually in the sense of "redirect[ing] resources towards the productive side of the economy" away from "handouts" (Swan 2007c) and in the sense of positioning Australia as competitive within Asia and able to exploit the unique opportunity of the rises of China and India (Swan 2007a). In terms of specific measures, there were to be investments in infrastructure (notably for the resource sector, in key ports identified as bottlenecks), 450,000 new skills-training placements and the suite of measures included in the "Education Revolution," and a budget surplus of more than one per cent in the forward estimates.[1,2] In particular, the Howard Government was criticised for failing to take advantage of Australia's economic opportunities in mineral exports:

> … while the *value* of these exports is up because of sharp price increases for coal and iron ore in particular, the *volume* increase has been much more subdued. There is no doubt our export performance has been constrained by shortcomings on our roads, and our railways and ports. (Swan 2008g, emphasis in original)

While Swan does occasionally use the language of crisis, these challenges—inflation, and the "twin problems of a skills deficit and the infrastructure deficit" (Swan 2007a)—are more usually framed as being critical, but not imminent (to use the framework of 't Hart and Tindall 2009): "these pressures have been building … over the last couple of years" (Rudd in Swan with Rudd 2008) and require "long-term solutions" (Swan 2007a).[3] The important points for me are that the Government understood conservative, responsible, modern economic governance as active and vigilant, as requiring positive, preemptive action to *produce* a competitive economy and position it within the region. This is a far cry from the embrace of Keynesian management that was to appear in Rudd's *Monthly* article in the midst of the GFC (Rudd 2009), but it is also a set of articulations that differentiate the Rudd Government from its immediate predecessor.

5.2 Close Readings of Key Speeches

Speech one: Wayne Swan (17 February 2008b*) 'Government Improves Transparency of Foreign Investment Screening Process,' press release announcing the February Guidelines and the media interviews immediately following it*

While the press release announcing the Principles Guiding the Consideration of Foreign Government Relation Investment in Australia contained little text beyond the guidelines themselves—a five-line introduction from the Treasurer and a five-line background to the principles—it is nonetheless the moment of departure for the new policy. The announcement occurred soon after a suite of large-scale Chinese investments into the Australian mining sector in late 2007 and early 2008 and the dramatic "dawn raid" of Chinalco on London-listed shares of Rio Tinto (see the introduction chapter). The announcement was a considered response to a complex set of interconnected problems.

The text is mostly interesting for how little it conforms to the format of a crisis narration, which theorists like Hassan (2013) or 't Hart and Tindall (2009) might have expected. The release did not specify a problem that the Government action was resolving, a cause of the problem, or even how the elaboration on the principles produced a benefit to Australia. These elements can be read into the release—the nature of language and policy dictate that narrative elements must appear in some sense—but the guidelines were framed as only a clarification of the existing policy (Swan 2008c, d, e). The "problem" was narrowed to the extent of clarifying that the principles outlined were to be applied to investments relating to "foreign governments and their agencies (e.g. state-owned enterprises and sovereign wealth funds (SWF))" (Swan 2008b) and that "…investors with links to foreign governments may not operate solely in accordance with normal commercial considerations and may instead pursue broader political or strategic objectives that could be contrary to Australia's national interest" (Swan 2008b).

There was no reference in the announcement to China or its investors, though this did not prevent all parties outside of the Government from interpreting the release as a direct response to those events, and particularly the pending decision regarding Chinalco's purchase of Rio Tinto shares. The only justification for the release ever made was by Prime Minister Rudd on ABC Radio on the 18th of February, when he cited "legitimate interest from the community and the business community" (Rudd 2008) on how screening would occur. However, as has been noted in Chapter 3, the Guidelines did not meaningfully establish how decisions would be made by Treasurer Swan on FDI matters or bring transparency to the process. In terms of a policy narrative, the Government responding to "legitimate" calls from "the community" for transparency is not satisfactory.

In the press release, Treasurer Swan emphasised the term "national interest" and noted that decisions on proposals are made on a case-by-case basis. As I showed in Chapter 3, the catch-all term "national interest" has had tactical value in Australian FDI screening regimes for four decades, and was clearly retained by the Rudd Government. Placing the policy on a "case-by-case" basis is significant as it implied that the Government was under no obligation to respect precedents in the execution of the policy. Both elements of the policy were to appear consistently throughout its execution.

***

Speeches two and three: Wayne Swan (10 June 2008h*) 'A remarkable place at a remarkable time,' speech by Treasurer to the China–Australia Chamber* *of Commerce, Beijing; and Wayne Swan (11 June* 2008i*) 'A Modern Relationship with China,' speech by Treasurer Wayne Swan to the Central Party School, Communist Party of China*

In these two similar speeches, delivered on consecutive days while on a trip to China, Swan situated the FDI policy within the broader stories of the Australia–China economic relationship and the Rudd Government's economic agenda. They were the first scripted texts in which the Treasurer elaborated on the February guidelines. They also occurred eight and nine days after a speech in which Swan assessed the impact of the global financial crisis on Australia (Swan 2008f),[4] describing it as remote from the Australian economy, and a cross-pressure to the primary challenges of managing inflationary pressures and enabling Australia to take full advantage economically of the rises of India and China.

In the Beijing speeches, Swan charted a narrative of China's very high-growth rates of the past decade and the very high growth of Australia and China's economic interaction over the last decade. Swan stressed that the Australian economy was "open," noting that the share of trade in Australia's GDP had reached 40%. He also described the economy as balanced: while minerals was a significant component of Australia's export portfolio and economy, it only took up three per cent of Australia's total output, and only seven per cent of Australian exports.

In sections on the FDI policy, Swan was again at pains to emphasise that Australia is open and welcoming of foreign investment. He then tried to legitimise the policy by pointing out that China also screens foreign investment proposals, and that "[t]his approach has not changed with the new Government" (Swan, 10 June 2008h). Swan described the aim of Australia's screening as:

> ...to ensure that investment is consistent with our aim of maintaining a system in which investment and sales decisions are driven by market forces rather than external strategic or political considerations. (Swan 2008i)[5]

In addition to this repetition of the key metaphor of "market forces," Swan also reinvested in a second dominant theme of the policy, which was the need for China to be a "responsible stakeholder" in the global economy. This discourse was used first by Kevin Rudd, both in a speech in Washington to the Brookings Institute made six months before being elected to office and as Prime Minister,[6] but appeared in a softer form in Swan's speeches here. Instead of emphasising the need for China to subscribe to a "rules-based order," a second term that consistently appears in this theme, he made two alternative framing points. First, he argued that China's interests lie in effective regional[7] and global[8] multilateral forums:

> China's success in the global economy has in large part depended on trade, so you of course have a profound interest in a successful outcome from the current Doha Round of negotiations in the World Trade Organisation. As you become more important in the world economy, China's responsibilities to ensure it works well are steadily increasing. (Swan 2008i)

Finally, the call was framed against a series of claims placing Australia and China in the same position: two states facing the same economic and other challenges, with common interests in the strength and stability of the regional and global economies, and growing bilateral economic interaction. Furthering this point on common interests, Swan noted that

> [a]s two countries with large sovereign wealth funds, it is important for Australia and China to support global efforts to develop a set of voluntary, best-practice principles to help maintain the free flow of cross border investment. (Swan 2008h)

***

Speech four: Wayne Swan (4 July 2008j*) 'Australia, China, and This Asian Century,' speech to the Australia–China Business Council, Melbourne*

This speech was a third key instance of Swan explaining and defending the policy, but unlike the Beijing speeches, it was made to a community that Swan was aware was predominantly critical of the Government's actions. The speech contained a number of sections before arriving at the key point of interest for the audience, which was the commentary on the FDI policy, a point acknowledged by Swan explicitly in the speech. The preceding sections were on China's rise, the demands this was placing on the Australian and global economies, the meaning of this for Australia's resource and non-resource sectors, the transformations in Australia's trade relationship with China, and the ambitions of the Rudd Government to restart the FTA talks. That is, while he was aware of the interests of his audience and this speech does provide some of the clearest explanations of the policy logics, Swan was still at pains to minimise the space available for in-depth discussion of the policy.

In the section on direct investment, Swan first emphasised the "obvious but very important point" that "Australia is an open, liberal nation" and has "an open and welcoming approach to foreign investment" (Swan 2008j). He noted that Australia had one of the highest levels of foreign ownership in the world and that many other nations—China included—also apply a national interest test to foreign investment. He then repeated the line from earlier speeches that the Rudd Government's policy is in keeping with the practice of previous Australian governments, this time drawing a link to the "[p]revious governments [that] faced the same issues of resource consumers investing in resource producers in the 1970s and 1980s" (Swan 2008j).

Most importantly, the Treasurer took the opportunity to clear up some "misperceptions" regarding the policy. This section begins:

> Misperceptions will arise in this debate when participants tend to seize on individual cases as being somehow emblematic of a broader policy approach. (Swan 2008j)

A few paragraphs later, after listing the six February Guidelines, the Treasurer added to this that "[p]roposals are still examined on a case-by-case basis and the principles are not a check list" (Swan 2008j). In short: the guidelines are not rules, and precedents are not binding.

Swan acknowledged the criticisms from media and corporate actors relating to the Government's approach to Chinese investment, which he summarised as "broadly, that we have changed our policy to a more restrictive stance, and furthermore, are slowing down the processing of Chinese applications" (Swan 2008j) and countered both points. On the first, he noted that he had approved a Chinese investment once every nine days since coming into office. On the second argument, he acknowledged that while the processing of some Chinese proposals had taken longer than the norm, this was because these proposals had been large or complex. Given the "complexity and substantially increased volume of Chinese investment proposals, the approval timelines have been very reasonable" (2008j), Swan claimed, adding that all proposals are given "procedural fairness": "[t]his means taking appropriate time to consider approvals" (2008j). As a fourth justification, he cited his obligation to "the Australian people [who] rightly insist we consider the national interest carefully" (2008j). The logic on each of these is slightly fuzzy: the figure of one every nine days is not enormously meaningfully without further details, and there were already provisions in the legislation for complex proposals, which were not being respected. It is not clear how the processing of these investment proposals outside of the statutory limits could be justified by citing the Treasurer's duty to the Australian people, given that this context applied to all determinations.

Perhaps more interestingly though, Swan then explained that while the legislation allows the Government thirty days to make a determination, it does have an allowance for an extension of this deadline if it is necessary to adequately assess a proposal. He then said:

> But for commercial reasons, most proponents prefer to withdraw and resubmit, rather than having their bid become known publicly through the gazettal of a formal interim order. (Swan 2008j)

This may seem innocuous, but it undermines the claims he and other state officials subsequently made that list how few investment proposals the Government rejected or imposed conditions on. That is, if the norm is for companies to withdraw investments without public knowledge rather than it be made public that their proposals have either been rejected, or even that a proposal is being determined, then the number of unsuccessful proposals must be much higher than the count of explicitly rejected proposals. While a number of critics of the policy do argue that issues of transparency, which transmute into "sovereign risk," are likely to have deterred investments that otherwise would have been made (but do not appear as a statistic anywhere) (for example, ITS Global 2008), to my knowledge the logic used by Swan here has never been criticised.

The other points of note from this speech are the lines summarising the aims and intents of the policy. This section is worth quoting at length:

> The key is that investments are consistent with Australia's aim of maintaining a market-based system in which companies are *responsive to shareholders* and in which investment and sales decisions are *driven by market forces* rather than external strategic or political considerations.

> In particular, Australian governments–now as in the past–are particularly attentive when the proposed investor in an Australian resource is also the buyer of that resource or linked with the buyer of the resource....
>
> We usually welcome and encourage some participation by the buyer, because that offers the buyer some security of supply and the seller some stability in the market. But we need to ensure that investment is consistent with Australia's aim of ensuring that decisions continue to be *driven by commercial considerations* and that Australia remains a reliable supplier in the future to all current and potential trading partners...
>
> But it follows that as the proposed participation by a consumer of the resource increases to the point of control over pricing and production, and especially where the resource in question is already developed and forms a major part of the total resource, or where the *market disciplines* applying to public companies are absent, I will look more carefully at whether the proposal is in Australia's national interest. (Swan 2008j, my emphases)

These lines established some dominant logics that define the policy, and introduced a new element to the policy in the Government's (qualified) aversion to vertical integration. This has been criticised as being inconsistent with other policies of the government—David Uren notes that on 8 November 2007 the ACCC had found no issue with Rio Tinto's proposed takeover of the aluminium producer Alcoa despite explicitly noting the vertical integration in that industry (2012, 106; ACCC 2007). A second logic that appeared in this passage was a reinvestment in the distinction of *market forces* from *political* and *strategic* considerations. This is a foundational assumption to the liberal imaginary, and is foundational to the policy.

A third logic that appeared here was the predication of "Australia" as having an aim of remaining a reliable supplier to trading partners. That is, the role of the government was not to disinterestedly apply the rules of procedural or other fairness, but to actively guide the larger entity of Australia, combining a set of mineral producing companies, the government, and a population who have a shared interest and aim. This predication is implied constantly throughout the policy in the term "national interest." As I have noted, this element of the regime was not introduced by the Rudd Government. Usefully though, it was given more specific form here, and was laden with a presupposition that the mode of intervention that the Australian government used to pursue this aim is legitimate. It can be contrasted with the mode of intervention employed by the Chinese State, or more particularly the centralised economic agencies of the Chinese State, CISA, and the NDRC. These were, by implication, not legitimate. These interventions include the attempted organisation of China's steelmakers into a cartel capable of boycotting Australian iron ore, and the formulation of activist governmental programs bringing the financial and corporate entities together to pursue resource nationalism (see my description of the 2005 Go Out Policy in Chapter 4, Sect. 4.1 and my description of the arrangement of funding and permission for the original Chinalco Dawn Raid in the introduction chapter).

An indication of this presupposed knowledge is the use of the term "market disciplines" at the end of the long quote above. The discourse being invested in was that no market player is above the rules set by the absent-everywhere market. There is an ambiguity here worth dissecting also. While deferral of authority to the market was understood as being in the interests of the Australian miners, governments, and eventually people, the idea that the regional iron ore market was "efficient" could not really be maintained, at least using orthodox liberal economic theory. The market at this time was heavily dominated by an oligopoly of producers, as described in Chapter 4. Nonetheless, the market participants were still meaningfully constrained by conditions within an oligopolistic market. The Chinese SOEs, by contrast, were constrained by the willingness of the Chinese agencies to provide funding and organisation to allow economic actions. Again, this is a foundational logic to the policy, but almost always appears as presupposed (Ahall and Borg 2013) or organisational (Paul 2009) knowledge, and it is useful to isolate an instance of these articulations. Both of these logics will be discussed further below.

***

Speech five: Wayne Swan (26 May 2009b*) 'Resources and Recovery,' speech to Minerals Week 2009 Conference, Hyatt Hotel, Canberra*

This speech was given in a wholly different context to the previous four. The GFC had reached Australia and the Government's economic narrative as well as the Budget, handed down two weeks previously, was dominated by it. There had been a sharp fall in iron ore prices after protracted and heated annual negotiations (see Chapter 4, Sect. 4.2), and the price fall was referred to in the opening lines of Swan's speech.

The most interesting points about the speech are that the FDI policy is not mentioned, and that the FDI policy appeared to have drifted away from the Government's broader economic narrative. That is to say, the policy continued to be applied consistently with the logics outlined before the onset of the crisis in Australia in September 2008. The Government articulated a new commitment to interventionist economic governance that retained the connotations of "responsible government," now meaning one that took ameliorative action, accepted a temporary deficit, and contributed to coordinated efforts by governments across the globe to stabilise the crisis (see Swan 2009a; Rudd 2009; Laing and Tindall 2009, 216, 223).

In relation to the mining sector specifically, Swan notably did not redefine the problem being solved to the immediate deterioration of economic conditions for Australian miners. He instead retained a focus on the longer term, which had framed the Government's approach to the sector for the first seventeen months of office. The aim remained to produce "next generation" growth and opportunity in the resource sector. More specifically, Swan described the Government's aims as overcoming the "capacity constraints that hold us back" by investing in "more modern infrastructure," a "better-trained, more highly skilled workforce," and producing a more "sustainable" Budget (Swan 2009b)—all themes that appeared in the election campaign of 2007. Swan mentioned China, but only in relation to its own stimulus package and the fact that it was still expected to be the fastest growing economy that year, and would therefore support demand for Australian commodity exports.

In spite of the changed conditions, the FDI policy in relation to Chinese SOEs had been executed in accordance with the logics described above. Since the last major speech from Swan commenting on the policy (speech four, above), a number of proposals from Chinese SOEs into the Australian mining sector had been either rejected or approved with conditions with dubious reasoning provided for the decisions: first, the approval of Chinalco's bid for Rio Tinto shares up to 14.99% on 24 August 2008 came after a seventh month wait on behalf of the two companies, and could be understood as an implicit rejection of Chinalco's presumed intentions of a further cash buy-out of Rio Tinto shares (Uren 2012, 83).[9] Again, in February 2009 the Government intervened in Chinalco's second bid for an expanded ownership and collaboration with Rio Tinto by announcing its plans to pass the *FATA Amendments Act 2009*.[10] The Amendments, it was claimed, would not change the intent of the Act, but rather clarify the operation of the FDI screening regime with regard to complex investment structures. The significance of the changes to the Chinalco bid, which were to apply retrospectively, was clear.[11] A third example is the approval of Sinosteel's purchase of up to 49.99% of Murchison, when it had applied for 100% of the iron-ore producer and had been issued with an interim order before reapplying with a less ambitious proposal. These were discussed in more detail in Chapter 4. In short, the execution of the policy was unchanged by the new context.

Similarly, it should be noted that the policy remained unchanged in the face of intense media coverage and criticism of the policy and the Chinalco-Rio Tinto-BHP Billiton machinations. There had been efforts by a number of actors to return the FDI policy to the political and then policy agenda. Examples from this period at the end of 2008 include the ITS Global report in September (ITS 2008), Kirchner's Centre for Independent Studies piece in November (2008), Julie Novak's study for the Institute for Public Affairs in October (2008), and a speech by Rio Tinto Chief Executive Tom Albanese on 2 October (2008, 12), in which he tried to reopen a number of the questions that had been settled in the policy through the year:

> Australia should build stronger linkages with its most important growth markets through continually improving trade relationships. This may include being more flexible in accommodating the needs of customers, including [their] taking ownership stakes in existing and new resource producers. (Albanese 2008, 12)

Albanese also argued that this openness to investment should include permission for companies seeking to vertically integrate. As with the dog that didn't bark in the night, it is noteworthy that the Government not only refused to be flexible on any of these points, but refused to even discuss the matter despite strong pressure to do so.

***

Speech six: Patrick Colmer (24 September 2009*) Address from FIRB Executive Director Patrick Colmer to the Australia China Investment Forum, Sydney*

This speech was delivered amid a period of renewed policy activity. On 4 August 2009, Treasurer Swan had announced a set of "reforms" to the

FDI screening regime, which included replacing the four lowest thresholds with a single figure of $219 million, which was then to be pegged to inflation, as well as the abolition of the requirement for approval for certain new businesses (Swan 2009c).[12] In addition, several further contentious decisions relating to Chinese investments had been made by the Treasurer, including the conditions placed on China Nonferrous Metals (Group) Co. (CNMC) to invest in the rare-earth producer, Lynas Corporation, which eventually led to the offer of investment from CNMC being withdrawn (Lynas 2009).[13]

Colmer's speech introduced new elements of the policy narrative,[14] and garnered significant media attention in both Australia (Kirchner 2010) and China (see Uren 2012, 104). After dominating the public debate on the policy for some months, the so-called "Colmer Doctrine," which appeared in the speech was clarified not to exist by Treasurer Swan on 10 December 2009 (Swan 2009d; see below). Interestingly also, given the contentiousness of Colmer's comments, the transcript of this speech was not made public, and was only released after a Freedom of Information request was made by the commentator Stephen Kirchner (Kirchner 2010). While speech acts in the policy are often a substantive component of the policy—the lever used to signal to investors and foreign governments in order to shape their action—the fact that the Government worked hard to keep the speech of the FIRB Executive Director out of the public realm indicates that this speech cannot be read in this way.

Colmer began the speech by revisiting well-tracked points in the earlier speeches: he acknowledged the "public interest" and "controversy" that successive waves of foreign investment into Australia—"from the UK, USA, Japan, Korea, and recently China"—had generated, implying that this controversy was not, in itself, an anomaly or a problem to be managed by the Government. He briefly outlined the February Guidelines relating to "foreign government investment," noting that proposals are considered on a case-by-case basis. He then summarised the policy as not expecting "total independence" on behalf of the investor from the host government, but "[w]hat we are looking for is evidence that it is a true commercial focused investment" (Colmer 2009).

Within the three page speech, Colmer specified a number of distinct aims of the policy to which the solution was the case-by-case screening regime executed under the auspices of the February Guidelines. First it aimed to produce win-win situations, meaning that the Government aimed to attract investment into the economy. The second and third aims of the Government were to "...maintain an orderly flow of investment and help develop the Australian economic while balancing the need to maintain public support for foreign investment" (Colmer 2009). The fourth aim was "...maintaining a market-based system in Australia," including a preference for seeing "major projects maintain listings because we think the listing disciplines are important in the development of good sound businesses" (Colmer 2009). Fourthly, in relation to the resource sector particularly, where much of the Chinese investment had been focused, Colmer said the following, which is worth quoting at length due to the appearance of what came to be known unofficially as the "Colmer Doctrine":

> ...we are concerned to maintain our position as a reliable supplier of resources to all our customers. What we prefer to see is various sorts of cooperative or partnership arrangements. In the resources industries and where there is significant government ownership, our Government has expressed a preference for projects which are joint projects in various forms, and in particular we are much more comfortable when we see investments which are below 50% for greenfield projects and around 15% for major producers. (Colmer 2009)

The term "Colmer Doctrine" was not official, but appeared widely in commentaries on the policy. This preference of government-affiliated enterprises to control a maximum stake of 50% in newly established ventures and 15% in existing ones was not always adhered to by the Government. For example, Ansteel's acquisition of the existing large iron ore producer, Gindalbie Metals, in May 2009 was for 36.28% of the shares. However, many determinations did conform to it, both before and after Colmer's speech. The significance of the Colmer Doctrine is that the Government had settled, by experimentation rather than design, on a set of practices that satisfied them that Chinese SOEs would not be able to "control" commercial decision of resource firms.

Finally, a new discursive delineation appeared at the end of the speech, in the separation of policy from law:

> Another important thing I think you need to recognise is that while the foreign investment review system is enshrined in legislation, the fundamental issues at the end of the day are much more policy issues than

> legal issues. One of the problems we have also seen is where lawyers get involved and try and turn a policy argument into a legal debate. It's not effective and lawyers don't like us telling them that, but nevertheless we do try to steer people through the policy issues rather than the legal issues. (Colmer 2009)

This is an oddly ambiguous logic, and does not appear anywhere else in the policy. The main point Colmer makes is that "law" is not an appropriate framework to understand the investment screening regime. As decisions are made on a case-by-case basis, the Treasurer, who is solely empowered with decision-making power, does not have to justify his or her decisions, and there is no recourse for prospective investors to contest decisions that have been made, a framework based on rights and due process is not applicable to the policy. This is an interesting distinction given the strong emphasis that is placed on "fairness" throughout the policy, and this statement shows how narrow the use of that term is in the space, essentially being limited to non-discrimination on the basis of nationality.

***

Speech seven: Wayne Swan (10 December 2009d*) Address to the Global Foundation, Brisbane*

In Treasurer Swan's final significant speech he summarised the FDI policy of Australian governments since 1975, the Rudd Government's own FDI policy, the debate on the policy, and its future. It was "final" in that from this point on the policy was pursued according to the same structures—legislation and policy principles—that had been established to this point.

The Treasurer began the speech by acknowledging the controversy that the policy had generated, and attacked the legitimacy of a number of groups that had generated the controversy. Those who criticised the policy as being "complex and fraught with difficulty" were really lawyers aiming to convince their clients of the need to pay for legal advice, he claimed. By stirring discontent about foreign ownership, Senator Barnaby Joyce and the National Party, and later in the speech the Liberal Opposition, were irresponsible and putting potential Australian jobs at risk. Foreign investment applicants or targets providing "free advice" to the Treasurer tended "… to reflect their own commercial interests" (2009d), and dressing up sectional interests as the national interest, claimed Swan, was a source of "[m]uch of the heat and confusion in the debate" (2009d). All these actions stood in contrast to his own duty, which is "… to stay out of the cut and thrust of debate on individual applications, and to focus on the national interest" (2009d).

Swan repeated a number of claims that are by now familiar, though with some important additional elements. He explicitly refused to provide a "simple definition" of the national interest, referring vaguely to job and wealth creation as well as "*issues of our economic sovereignty*" (2009d, my emphasis). This last phrase, I will argue below, is a link to the security aspects of the policy. This is the only occasion Swan used the phrase in a scripted speech. Given the tone of the rest of the speech and the fact that the policy had now been refined for nearly two years, it is possible that Swan was able to discuss the policy in a less tightly controlled way here than he previously had.

Swan stressed the continuity of Australia's policy of welcoming foreign investment over a very long period, stretching back to the late-nineteenth century, and he noted too that the latest boom in foreign investment can be placed in a long line of similar phenomena before it. Echoing Colmer, he noted that even the controversy and "concern about foreign influence or control" was in keeping with previous iterations of the same phenomena. He described the *FATA 1975* as being applied by successive governments in "as non-intrusive a manner as possible" and being "not a roadblock" (Swan 2009d). "It keeps the Government out of the traffic," Swan expanded, "but allows the Foreign Investment Review Board to pull over more sensitive proposals" (2009d). With regard to the Rudd Government's policy, he listed the key changes as clarifying the treatment of SOEs and SWFs, changing the legislature to allow the FIRB to screen complex investment instruments, and raising the four lowest thresholds to ensure Australia remained an attractive investment destination during the GFC. These were "responses to a changing global investment environment" and "recent debate on foreign investment," and Swan framed the actions as augmenting this longstanding aim of "getting the Government out of the road of everyday transactions" (Swan 2009d).

He then downplayed the significance of Chinese investment to overall inward flows to Australia, before emphasising once again that decisions are made on a case-by-case basis and providing the clearest reasoning for this setting. In this passage, he also directly refuted the existence of the Colmer Doctrine:

> Of course, if you were concerned solely about predictability, it could be very simple to fix. You would set hard and fast rules, with capped shareholdings, and no discretion. You could publish them on a website, and simply tell non-compliant proposals not to bother.
>
> But no-one with a real interest in Australia's economy would seriously suggest this… and I have approved applications above and below the various 'caps' the Government has been said to have.
>
> Successive Australian governments have rightly decided we want to see all potential proposals, rather than have some potentially very valuable ones never leave the boardrooms of their international proponents.
>
> This is why Australian governments have rightly insisted on a case-by-case approach and the operation of a national interest test. It maximises investment flows, while protecting our core interests. (Swan 2009d)

That is, flexibility "enabled" the government to approve a set of applications that a more transparent and rule-based regime would not. Predictability was not a primary aim.

Swan noted that three "trends" had emerged from the execution of the regime over the two year period: first, that the Government carefully considered cases where a proposed investor is also a buyer of the resource and has potential control over pricing and production; second, that foreign investments in a resource company must enable Australia to remain a reliable supplier in the future; and third, that "…business transparency and shareholder discipline is important… we prefer to see major companies maintain their listing on stock exchanges" (Swan 2009d).

There are some issues with these claims. As has been noted, the concern for vertical integration did not extend beyond this very narrow issue of SOE investment: the Australian aluminium industry is highly vertically integrated and, even more specifically, several path-breaking Chinese investments into Australia in the late 1970s and 1990s into developing Australian gas resources were made with the aim of selling the gas to Chinese consumers and it was never suggested that the same issues of the investors also being the buyers were significant in those instances. In any case, and possibly more pointedly, the FIRB is not nearly as well equipped in terms of staff or technical expertise to examine issues such as influences on pricing and production decisions as other official regulatory bodies, most notably the ACCC. If the aim of the policy was to get the Government "out of the road," the ACCC overseeing commercial practices in line with other businesses seems much more appropriate, as had been noted in late 2008 by Tom Albanese (2008), among others.

***

Speech eight: Dr. Geoff Raby (28 September 2010*) 'Australia and China: An Iron Ore Partnership for the Future,' address to the 10th China International Steel and Raw Materials Conference, Dalian, Lianong Province, China*

The final speech to be examined, by the Australian Ambassador to China, Dr. Geoff Raby, occurred significantly after the other speeches when the policy settings were stabilised. It is useful to include nonetheless as it provides some access to logics aimed at maintaining this stability (see Hassan 2013). Raby stressed the significance of China as an export market of Australia, and the centrality of iron ore to that relationship, noting that it was "...hard to see a set of circumstances in the future under which China will ever be replaced as Australia's number one market" (Raby 2010, 1). He described the relationship as "... a mutually beneficial one based on long-term interests" (2010, 2). He stressed that the "... Australian Government remains firmly committed to Australia's continuing to be a long-term, stable, competitive supplier of iron ore" (2010, 4) and listed efforts being made to this goal as fostering a "strong bilateral framework in which companies can feel confident about the long-term economic relationship," providing a policy and regulatory framework to support the development of iron ore resources, investing in infrastructure to service the mining industry, and welcoming foreign investment in the Australian iron ore industry, including from China. At a number of points he re-stressed the belief that "China's demand for iron ore is likely to continue to rise for quite some time to come" (Raby 2010, 5).

Beyond the driving narrative of the speech of Australia's efforts to expand capacity and supply in the iron ore market, Raby also presented a secondary narrative with a shorter-term outlook and relating to recent changes in the iron ore market; namely the swift rises in price. Due to the swiftness of the increases in demand from China over the 2000s, the supply response had "inevitably" lagged, putting "short-term pressure on global prices." Iron ore prices, Raby emphasised, "...are fundamentally a result of global market forces, and are determined on a commercial basis between companies" (2010, 3). He urged that "despite some of the media commentary you might hear on this issue, Australia remains the most competitive supplier of iron ore to China," clarifying that this meant that Australian ore had been, over the previous ten years, "…on average about US$12 per tonne less that iron ore from Brazil and India, on a landed basis" (2010, 4). He cited a number of significant changes to China's iron ore profile, including the expansion of China's domestic production of iron ore, and its diversification to new suppliers in Brazil, India, South Africa, and Ukraine.

Finally, he turned directly to the changes of moving from an annual benchmark pricing system to a spot pricing one[15]:

> Recently, there have been changes to the pricing system which have resulted in a movement towards shorter term, market-based pricing.
>
> In my view, these changes reflect the reality that the old benchmark system was unable to respond quickly enough to changes in market conditions. Ultimately, this was not in the best interest of either the seller or buyer. A new system was needed which could respond in a more flexible way to market developments.
>
> Paradoxically perhaps, flexible pricing mechanisms lead to more stable outcomes, as frequent small adjustments in price allow demand and supply to respond more smoothly.
>
> At the end of the day, there is no reason why iron ore should be considered any different from other commodities, which are priced on a purely market basis.
>
> It is up to the companies, of course, to work through these changes together. In recent years, there have been tensions as both sides made the transition to the new arrangements. I believe this has now been done and companies have adapted to the new pricing system. (Raby 2010, 4)

This passage summarises the important points of the Government's narrative: first, the changes in pricing were leading to short-term effects, and these were distinct from the long-term dynamics described in the rest of the speech. Second, the high prices were not due to any individual actor, but to market forces. Third, market pricing was, in the longer term, in the interest of both buyer and seller of iron ore, as they lead to more stable prices. The reason for this is not given explicitly, and though the implied logic is not enormously unambiguous, the only claim to authority was that the new pricing mechanism brought the market into line with those of other commodities. Fourth, given points one and two, and the fact that the changes had occurred, the disruptive action would actually be to try to change them. Therefore, no action from the Australian Government, or anyone else, was required.

5.3 Displacements

In this section, I treat the speeches as a set and use two techniques to dislocate the articulations that occur: examining the way the discursive formations changed over time and considering the policy actions as constitutive of the social world according to the expectations of the post-structural theory examined in Chapter 2.

5.3.1 Changes Over Time

The policy was formulated largely in response to events. While Prime Minister Rudd personally requested a position paper from the Treasury soon after being elected on the scenario of a takeover bid for a major resource company from a Chinese SOE (Uren 2012, 66), this had not been written at the time of Chinalco's Dawn Raid on 31 January 2008. As a result, a framework for producing a response from the Government was demanded swiftly. It was to be produced through the National Security Committee and a cross-departmental team headed by Treasury staff, but with input from the Departments of the Prime Minister and Cabinet, Foreign Affairs and Trade, and Resources (Uren 2012, 76). Chinalco's Dawn Raid appears to have conformed very closely to what 't Hart and Tindall (2009) would call a moment of "institutional ambiguity," a concept resembling Kingdon's "policy window," but with an emphasis on the presence of crisis (see also Hassan 2013).

Given this, it is noteworthy how much effort state actors put into framing the policy as not a response to a crisis but a continuation of the existing framework and policy that the Government had inherited. This occasionally required logical stretches, as when the Treasurer listed ensuring Australia remained an attractive destination for foreign investors through the GFC as a main achievement of the policy, immediately after describing the Australian policy stretching back decades as being one designed to leave the investors as free of government intervention as possible. In the absence of positive actions to improve the attractiveness of Australia as an investment destination, the "achievement" must have been attained via the same mechanism that the policy had rested on for decades: non-interference.

A second point of interest is the lack of adaptation to the GFC. While the Government maintained a narrative of the crisis that denied its immediate significance for Australia significantly longer than the rest of the world, changing only in September 2008 (Laing and Tindall 2009), this shift did not alter the FDI policy in either its symbolic or executive components. A number of contentious decisions were made after September 2008, as well as the dramatic announcement of the intention to produce retrospectively applying legislation in the *FATA Amendment Act 2010* in order to stymie the second Rio Tinto–Chinalco deal. This all occurred after the GFC was acknowledged to have changed the overall needs of the Australian economy. This likely reflects two beliefs. First, the concern with Chinese SOE investments was of great and long-term significance and outweighed the need for immediate capital injection into the economy to foster stimulus. Second, and relatedly, it likely reflected a belief that iron ore and coal prices were likely to remain at their historically elevated levels for a very long time. This belief is stated by Ambassador Raby explicitly (2010, 5) and an expectation of rises appears multiple times in the 2008/2009 Budget Papers (see Attorney General's Department 2008, Statement 3: Economic Outlook, 2–5, 2–19). This belief was also coherent with the continued price rises in resources and particularly iron ore that defied the context of the GFC and the changes to the pricing arrangements outlined in Chapter 4. While this has not turned out to be the case, it appears to have been a widely and firmly held belief.

5.3.2 *Thinking Constitutively*

A second technique of dislocation is to imagine the subjects, objects, and articulations that occur in the policy as produced or constituted as a result of the policy, rather than imagining that a set of actors, objects, and knowledges existed a priori to the policy and then explaining the policy in terms of their interactions.

On the production of subject positions, and predictably enough for a set of official discourses, there was a strategic effort to produce a position for the Australian State. The organisational metaphor of the "national interest" is a key here. The first function of the term is tactical: alongside the refusal to conform to the legalistic practice of respecting precedents in decision-making, the refusal to define the national interest allowed the Government to justify a host of interventions that were made for a plethora of different reasons while still retaining a rhetoric of non-interventionism. This was in keeping with the dynamics of the FDI regime over the two decades preceding the Rudd Government, which combined a trend of liberalisation with increasing capacity for targeted regulation of foreign investment by a set of government agencies and an increasingly empowered Executive at the apex of government (Sadleir 2007).

A second function of the term was to predicate the Government with the Australian State, people or economy. This placed the state actors above the economic and media actors who interacted with the regime, and allowed the state actors to almost entirely ignore the opinions of non-state actors. It was enabled by there being no requirement for the Treasurer to justify individual decisions and no recourse for companies to contest decisions made. The connection of the state to the Australian people via the nebulous term "national interest" also dismantled attempts by non-state actors to produce any narrative that placed the FDI regime on the wider political agenda. The government was also differentiated from the Australian people in a complex way. On the one hand, the Foreign Investment Policy (see Chapter 3, Sect. 3.2 on the place of this document within the FDI screening regime) noted explicitly that the policy "recognises community concerns about foreign ownership" (FIRB 2009, 71) and this was used as an empowering device for the Executive. On the other, the Government aimed to "manage" public opinion on foreign investment, which was continually presumed to be opposed to foreign investment. The following lines from the speech from Patrick Colmer (2009) are instructive:

> What we are trying to achieve through the foreign investment review process is to maintain an orderly flow of investment and help develop the Australian economy while balancing the need to maintain public support for foreign investment.

The metaphor of "balance" is used to further empower the Government. It positioned the Government as uniquely having access to knowledge about what is truly in the interest of the country: neither sectional interests, the Opposition, or the public was able to speak with the authority of the state actors. Thinking constitutively, there is a dialectic here.

The Government's authority was born of its position, but the meaning of this position was constituted by the metaphors of national interest, community concerns, and balance.

Other predicative themes that appear are the description of the Government as "responsible" and "conservative." These terms were used to distinguish the Government from the Opposition, particularly in the early months of the term of office, and again in late 2009 as the Government began preparing for the 2010 election. Swan also characterised critics of the policy in the commentariat as "irresponsible" (2009d). Like national interest, "responsible" and "conservative" were used flexibly, and combined an ethos of non-intervention with an ethos of activism. The terms also justified more specific actions, such as taking longer to make decisions on key proposals—most notably the first and second Rio Tinto–Chinalco transactions—than was provided for in the FATA on the basis of "procedural fairness" (Swan 2008j).

Finally, the Australian Government was differentiated from the Chinese Government on the basis of its mode of intervention. While the speeches above make reference to the possibility of "strategic" behaviour of government-affiliated firms, the implication is that this strategy refers to the needs of the Chinese State and economy as a whole. However, the term "strategy" alone is not sufficient to explain the logic: the policy itself is constantly explained as being a structure of government intervention aimed at enhancing the "national interest" of Australia, returning "fair value" to the Australian people for resources (Swan 2008j), and maintaining the Australian mining sector as a stable supplier to all its actors demanding its produce (Raby 2010). These were also strategic goals framed in reference to the nation-state. The pre-supposed, unarticulated difference is the mode of intervention. The Australian Government intervened in economic phenomena in negative ways only and each intervention was targeted at a single transaction. The Chinese State's interventions were, by implication, illegitimate in that they were positive. The central economic agencies of the Chinese State, it was believed, aimed to *shape* strategically significant resource markets, by providing resources for outward investment from Chinese firms, by directly organising the joint financing of the Chinalco Dawn Raid, and by organising a number of attempted boycotts of Australian iron ore by Chinese steelmakers (see Chapter 4, Sect. 4.2). My point is not that this claim is sound. Indeed, even calling the Australian Government's interventions negative is problematic as a number of investment determinations involve positive and quite creative prescriptions. For example, the China Non-ferrous Metals Co Ltd purchase of Oz Minerals in March 2009 required CNMC to "maintain or increase levels of indigenous employment" (Swan 2009e) and the approval of Ansteel's acquisition of shares in Gindalbie Metals in May 2009 stipulated levels of Australian employment in Ansteel's pellet plants in China, to list the two most specific positive provisions. However, these remained interventions on the level of the individual firm. The Australian Government framed itself as active, intervening, and strategic on a national basis, but differentiated itself from the Chinese Government in terms of its mode of intervention, what Dean (1999) would call the *techne* of governance.

A second constitutive contribution to a dispositif that appeared in the policy was the delineation of normal, good, or desired economic firms from abnormal, undesired ones. The differentiation was not based on what firms did with their resources, but rather what the firms themselves were. The Government's stated concern relating to government-affiliated investors was that they might affect pricing and production decisions by operating not according to a profit principle, but to "strategic" principles. While it was suggested that a less intrusive way of managing such a situation would be regulating what firms actually *did* with their resources (Albanese 2008), the Government insisted on maintaining the regime based on intervention at the point of investment, rather than of pricing and production decision. Wilson (2011, 290) summarises the difference between Chinese SOEs and liberal firms as follows:

Recent Chinese FDI into the Australian mining industry is qualitatively unlike investment from other sources. First, it is driven primarily by demand from the Chinese steel industry for raw materials, and thus is concentrated in just two mining sectors—iron ore and coking coal. Second, these investments have largely been made by SOEs and are usually backed by governmental financial assistance. Third, they arguably originate from a state-directed agenda that aims to use FDI to influence transactions in international minerals markets.

The presupposed knowledge is that the qualitative differences were two-fold: they were located in the nature of Chinese SOEs, not their behaviour; secondly, the Chinese SOEs, while not operating in cooperation with one another, were directed by a single state-directed agenda and the response needed to be one that managed the Chinese SOE investment *as a single phenomenon*. This is the reason why the FIRB, over which the Executive had total control, was an appropriate technology for intervention, rather than the more independent regulatory bodies like the ACCC. Given that the Chinese firms certainly competed against one another and other firms, the ACCC would be unlikely to decipher any uncommercial practice[16] or examine the wave of investment as a totality.

The Government reiterated on many occasions its aim of "...maintaining a market-based system in which companies are responsive to shareholders" (Swan 2008j) on top of the points about making commercial decisions on the basis of profit. In remarkable keeping with Foucault's claims on the processes of subjectification that appear in the governmental state and the place of disciplinary technologies therein, Colmer noted a preference for seeing "major projects maintain listings because we think the listing disciplines are important in the development of good sound businesses" (2009). Seen in a governmental light, the same constitutive dialectic appears here. The Government had an explicit agenda of *producing* a set of actors within the Australian economy that were amenable to liberal-governmental governance—firms whose actions are disciplined by the market. The intervention still occurred "at a distance" on free actors, and the policy sanctions non-conforming forms rather than disallowing them. However, the essentially productive aspect of the policy is striking. Further, and again conforming to Foucault's account of the governmental state, the *ethos* of the intervention, as per the last quote from Colmer (2009), was the development of the firm for its own good.

The third constitutive element of the policy was the construction of the market a site of truth. Again, this claim is dialectical: the correct functioning of the market was both a presupposition of the policy, and also its goal. The market was presupposed as a site of truth in that market-determined prices and production decisions were constantly articulated as distinct from "strategically" determined ones, which were imposed on economic actors. On the constitutive side, the aim of "... maintaining a system in which investment and sales decisions are driven by market forces" (Swan 2008i) appeared in all the speeches annotated above, as well as the statements provided by the Treasury relating to decisions on individual investment proposals from Chinese SOEs. Market forces are preferred for their disciplining effect, as just noted, but also as they produce "stability" of prices (Raby 2010) and "flexibility" of the system in adapting to changing conditions (Raby 2010).

Perhaps the most noteworthy aspect of this logic is that the regional iron ore market, which dominated the policy, was not efficient in terms of any orthodox economic theory. As described in Chapter 4, the supply and demand sides of the market were highly unequal, as reflected in the benchmark price-setting systems. While when the system was created in the 1970s, the oligopoly of iron ore producers was matched with a small number of large Japanese steelmaking firms that acted as "champions" for the demand-side in annual benchmark price negotiations, by the late 2000s as the Japanese steelmakers were displaced by Chinese producers, the market structure was significantly changed. The Chinese steelmaking industry was highly dispersed, and the negotiations were much more dominated by the "Big Three" iron ore suppliers of Vale, Rio Tinto and BHP Billiton. This partially explains the extremity of the price rises in iron ore over the period, the (largely failed) efforts of the NDRC to organise the Chinese steelmaking industry into an organised negotiating bloc, and the eventual breakdown of the benchmarking system in the middle of 2010. The point is that the market whose integrity was being so forcefully defended by the Australian Government over this period could hardly be called efficient according to orthodox liberal economics, as beneficial as the structure was to Australian mining firms and the federal and state budgets. Nonetheless, it is clear from the speeches above that this discourse of market efficiency, fairness, stability, and flexibility was a presupposition to the policy, and the protection of market integrity in the Australian economy was a stated aim.

5.4 'Economic Sovereignty'

To my knowledge the term "economic sovereignty" appears only once in the policy, in the speech by Treasurer Swan on 10 December 2009 (2009d, speech seven above). Nonetheless, it is the central organising metaphor of the policy. The term also forms the nexus from economic to security issues in Australia's engagement with the rising regional power of China, and is worth describing in detail.

Economic sovereignty brings together the substantive, symbolic, and strategic aims of the policy. The problem the policy responded to, according to the logics found in the official speeches above, was managing the wave of investments into the Australian resource sector by Chinese SOEs. This was not materially a problem, but the fact that the Chinese firms operated according to a set of structures and behaviours discordant with the liberal market forms of the Australian economy, meant that the wave of investments, imagined as a single phenomenon was deemed to be a threat. On one level, the threat was that the firms might act in a way that was against the material interests of the Australian people and firms by affecting pricing and production decisions in the resource sector or by reshaping the structure of regional minerals markets that to counterbalance the advantages of suppliers. On another level, however, the appearance of economic firms that were heterodox to the liberal forms threatened the ability of the Australian Government to shape the behaviour of the actors and structures it was charged with governing via the technology of the market. The Government preferred firms to be listed publicly as this enabled the existing structures of discipline and intervention to occur. The meaning of economic sovereignty is the ability to unilaterally define the forms of actors that appeared in milieus of circulation in ways that made them amenable to governance.

The aim was material, but also symbolic in that the Government used the policy to communicate to Chinese investors and state agencies that it valued economic sovereignty and was willing to forego material interests to pursue it. FDI policy appeared as the optimal setting to make this statement. It was a policy instrument wholly controlled by the Australian Executive, and affected a key interest of the Chinese nation-state substantially. In Chapter 7 I will argue that FDI was an aspect of the relationship where Australia had leverage to behave as a middle power, one that "… can shape how the international system works to protect its interests… even in the face of competing objectives of a major power" (White 2009). For now, it is sufficient to note that the pursuit of economic sovereignty is coherent with, and draws together, the logics that appear in the official economic discourses of the policy that have been examined above.

5.5 Conclusion

In this chapter I have conducted close readings of eight speeches on the Rudd Government's FDI policy from state actors. Rather than treating the texts as a set, abstracting the articulations from their authors and examining emergent trends, as per a more orthodox discourse analysis, I examined the speeches with a view to the contexts in which they were delivered. I have used the theoretical devices from policymaking theories based on a central position of narratives and from a host of poststructural political theorists.

In these close readings a coherent narrative of the policy emerged. Despite the moves responding to events—a wave of Chinese SOE investments into the Australian resource sector and particularly the major investments from Chinalco in Rio Tinto—the officials' framing of the policy stressed continuity, rather than using the devices of crisis-framing to articulate the policy. These continuities rested on Australia's openness to foreign investment and the Government's preference for market discipline in the funding of firms operating in the Australian economy and in pricing and production decisions relating to minerals.

Much of the policy aimed at constituting the subject position of the Australian Government as above sectional interests and public opinion, and as different to the Chinese Government by dint of the mode of its governance. There was also an effort to delineate good economic actors from bad ones and to base this distinction on the nature of the actor, rather than its behaviour. While the policy rested on presupposed knowledge of the market as a site of truth in relation to pricing and production, and a technology that disciplined firms for their own benefit and for the benefit of the Australian markets and economy as a whole, the defence and constitution of the market as a site of truth was also a key aim and outcome of the policy.

Finally, I argued that the organisational metaphor of "economic sovereignty" formed the nexus of the economic and security issues that constituted the policy. Understanding the term is essential to explaining why the Government was willing to forego much-needed capital injections into the economy and to continue wearing criticism of the policy from domestic and international actors. This line of argument will be taken up again in Chapter 7, after the analysis of security discourses in Chapter 6.

Notes

1. The Education Revolution composed of the new skills training placements, $16.2 in infrastructure spending in primary and secondary schools (*Sydney Morning Herald* 2010), and $2.4 billion spent providing laptops to secondary schoolchildren, deploying high speed broadband to all Australian schools, and developing skills and support for the use of information and communication technologies in schools (Phillips 2016, 5).
2. 1.5% according to Rudd (Swan with Rudd 2008).
3. This is often tempered with a need to recognise the immediate pain of Australian borrowers, who had experienced six successive interest rate

rises from the RBA, and a seventh on 4 March 2008. (For example, see Swan (2008a), an interview on 4 January 2008 following National Australia Bank's [NAB] decision to raise interest rates independently of the official cash rates. NAB's rate raise was in response to a rise in the cost of borrowing as a result of early stirrings in the United States of the sub-prime mortgage meltdown.)

4. While Swan continued to downplay the impact of the crisis on the Australian economy (Laing and Tindall 2009, 223) the first policy response to the crisis occurred in June in the banking deposit guarantee.
5. The words used in the speech the previous day were almost identical.
6. Speech three in this chapter.
7. This refers to ASEAN, ASEAN + 3, the East Asia Summit and Prime Minister Rudd's newly proposed 'Asia-Pacific Community'.
8. This refers to the WTO, International Monetary Fund (IMF), Financial Stability Forum (FSF), and two UN Framework Conventions.
9. In *The Kingdom and the Quarry* Uren strengthens this claim—that the decision to allow the Chinalco bid for up to 14.99% of Rio Tinto shares included a provision that Chinalco would not attempt a complete takeover—by saying that it was actually explicitly given in private. That is the Prime Minister and Treasurer secretly met representatives of Chinalco in August 2008 to advise them that the proposed investment would be approved by the FIRB; "that if it [Chinalco] thought a bigger deal was coming, it was dreaming [and t]hird, if anyone found out that this meeting was being held, Chinalco would never do anything again" (Uren 2012, 84). Uren does not provide a reference for this information, and it does not appear in any other commentary on the policy. In any case, very soon after the supposed meeting Chinalco and Rio Tinto embarked on a new plan for expanded joint ventures and a large cash injection from the former in February 2009, as discussed in Chapter 3, Sect. 3.3.
10. This would become the *FATA Amendment Act 2010.*
11. Swan specified convertible notes as a product the Government wanted to be looked at by the FIRB. Convertible notes were a key part of the planned transaction between Rio Tinto and Chinalco, and the Treasurer's announcement that of the planned Amendment Act, which would be applied retrospectively to the announcement, occurred one hour before Rio Tinto and Chinalco were to announce the new deal (Uren 2012, 92–93).
12. The size of investment that determines whether or not a proposal is required to be submitted to the FIRB for screening.
13. The correspondence from Lynas Corporation to the Australian Security Exchange noted that "[a]s a result of additional undertakings recently

sought by the Foreign Investment Review Board ("FIRB") CNMC has terminated the CNMC Transaction" (Lynas 2009).

14. That is to say that these elements are new to these set of texts, rather than new to the execution of the policy. These are the first *public* articulations of these logics.
15. See Chapter 3, Sect. 3.2 for a description of these changes.
16. The ACCC did make ruling on one of the most controversial investments—Chinalco's second bid for a stake in Rio Tinto—and did not oppose the acquisition (ACCC 2009).

References

ACCC. (2007, November 8). *Public Competition Assessment: Rio Tinto plc—Proposed Acquisition of Alcan Inc.* ACCC (Australian Competition and Consumer Commission). Available at http://registers.accc.gov.au/content/item.phtml?itemId=803036&nodeId=664ca52c3b9c8ec4dd1b264cc6c64d-7c&fn=Rio%20Tinto%20plc%20-%20proposed%20acquisition%20of%20Alcan%20Inc%20-%208%20November%202007%20-%20bauxite,%20alumina,%20aluminium,%20.pdf. Accessed 3 Nov 2016.

ACCC. (2009, March 25). *Chinalco (Aluminium Corporation of China)—Proposed Acquisition of Interests in Rio Tinto Ltd.* Public Competition Assessment by ACCC. Available at http://registers.accc.gov.au/content/index.phtml/itemId/866064/fromItemId/751043. Accessed 30 Oct 2016.

Ahall, L., & Borg, S. (2013). Predication, Presupposition and Subject-Positioning. In L. Shepherd (Ed.), *Critical Approaches to Security: An Introduction to Theories and Methods* (pp. 196–207). London and New York: Routledge.

Albanese, T. (2008, October 2). *Consolidation and Diversity—Resources in the 21st Century.* Speech to the Melbourne Mining Club Business Lunch, Rio Tinto. Available at http://www.riotinto.com/documents/ReportsPublications/Consolidation_and_Diversity_TA_presentation_02Oct08.pdf. Accessed 3 Nov 2016.

Attorney General's Department. (2008, May 13). *Budget Strategy and Outlook: Budget Paper No. 1; 2008–09.* Commonwealth of Australia, Attorney-General's Department. Available at http://budget.gov.au/2008-09/content/bp1/download/bp1.pdf. Accessed 4 Nov 2016.

Colmer, P. (2009). *Address from Patrick Colmer to the Australia China Investment Forum.* Delivered 24 September 2009. Speech published online by Stephen Kirchner at *Institutional Economics* After an FOI Application to the Australian Government. Available at http://www.institutional-economics.com/images/uploads/colmer.pdf. Accessed 30 Oct 2016.

Dean, M. (1999). *Governmentality: Power and Rule in Modern Society.* London: Sage.

FIRB. (2009). *Annual Report 2007–2008.* Australian Government, Foreign Investment Review Board. Available at http://firb.gov.au/about/publication/annual-report-2007-2008/. Accessed 29 Oct 2016.

Hajer, M. A. (1993). Discourse Coalitions and the Institutionalisation of Practice: The Case of Acid Rain in Britain. In F. Fischer & J. Forester (Eds.), *The Argumentative Turn in Policy Analysis* (pp. 43–76). Durham and London: Duke University Press.

Hajer, M. A. (1995). *Politics of Environmental Discourse: Ecological Modernization and the Policy Process.* Oxford: Clarendon Press.

Hassan, O. (2013). *Constructing America's Freedom Agenda for the Middle East: Democracy and Domination.* London and New York: Routledge.

ITS Global. (2008, September 9). *Foreign Direct Investment in Australia—The Increasing Cost of Regulation.* ITS Global, Melbourne, Australia. Available at http://www.itsglobal.net/sites/default/files/itsglobal/Research%20Report%20on%20Foreign%20Direct%20Investment%20and%20the%20Increasing%20Cost%20of%20Regulation%20in%20Australia%20(2008).pdf. Accessed 21 Oct 2016.

Kingdon, J. (1995). *Agendas, Alternatives, and Public Policies.* New York: HarperCollins.

Kirchner, S. (2008, November 27). Foreign Investment Flows Are Damned By Political Bias. *The Centre for Independent Studies.* Available at https://www.cis.org.au/commentary/articles/foreign-investment-flows-are-damned-by-political-bias. Accessed 21 Oct 2016.

Kirchner, S. (2010, February 19). More Inscrutable Than the Chinese. *The Australian.* Available at http://www.theaustralian.com.au/opinion/more-inscrutable-than-the-chinese/story-e6frg6zo-1225831954203. Accessed 21 Oct 2016.

Laing, M., & Tindall, K. (2009). Australia: 'The Lucky Country' on a Knife Edge. In P. 't Hart & K. Tindall (Eds.), *Framing the Global Economic Downturn: Crisis Rhetoric and the Politics of Recession* (pp. 203–242). Canberra: ANU Press.

Lynas Corporation. (2009, September 24). *CNMC Transaction Update.* Lynas Corporation Ltd. Available at http://www.asx.com.au/asxpdf/20090924/pdf/31kxjlh82hdnh3.pdf. Accessed 3 Nov 2016.

Novak, J. (2008). *Australia as a Destination for Foreign Capital.* Australia's Open Investment series paper 1. Institute of Public Affairs. Available at http://www.ipa.org.au/library/publication/1226637929_document_novak_destination_for_foreign_capital.pdf. Accessed 21 Oct 2016.

Paul, K. T. (2009). Discourse Analysis: An Exploration of Methodological Issues and a Call for Methodological Courage in the Field of Policy Analysis. *Critical Policy Studies, 3*(2), 240–253.

Phillips, M. (2016). *Digital Technology, Schools and Teachers Workplace Learning: Policy, Practice and Identity*. London: Palgrave Macmillan.

Raby, G. (2010, September 28). *Australia and China: An Iron Ore Partnership for the Future*. Speech by Ambassador Dr. Geoff Raby at 10th China International Steel and Raw Materials Conference. Available at http://china.embassy.gov.au/files/bjng/100927_Ambassador%20Speech%20at%20Iron%20Ore%20Conference_Final.pdf. Accessed 4 Nov 2016.

Rudd, K. (2008, February 18). Interview with Chris Uhlmann. *AM, ABC Radio*. Available at https://pmtranscripts.dpmc.gov.au/release/transcript-15765. Accessed 21 Oct 2016.

Rudd, K. (2009, February). The Global Financial Crisis. *The Monthly*. Available at https://www.themonthly.com.au/issue/2009/february/1319602475/kevin-rudd/global-financial-crisis. Accessed 3 Nov 2016.

Sadleir, C. (2007). *On the Frontier: Australia's Policy Approach to Foreign Direct Investment 1968–2004 as a Case Study in Globalisation, National Public Policy and Public Administration*. Ph.D. thesis, submitted to the University of Canberra.

Stone, D. (2002). *The Policy Paradox: The Art of Political Decision Making* (3rd ed.). New York: W. W. Norton.

Swan, W. (2007a, December 5). *Press Conference*. Sydney, Treasury. Available at http://ministers.treasury.gov.au/DisplayDocs.aspx?doc=transcripts/2007/001.htm&pageID=011&min=wms&Year=2007&DocType=2. Accessed 2 Nov 2016.

Swan, W. (2007b, December 7). Interview with Fran Kelly. *Radio National*. Treasury. Available at http://ministers.treasury.gov.au/DisplayDocs.aspx?doc=transcripts/2007/002.htm&pageID=011&min=wms&Year=2007&DocType=2. Accessed 2 Nov 2016.

Swan, W. (2007c, 14 December). Interview with Stephen Long. *PM, ABC Radio*. Treasury. Available at http://ministers.treasury.gov.au/DisplayDocs.aspx?doc=transcripts/2007/003.htm&pageID=011&min=wms&Year=2007&DocType=2. Accessed 2 Nov 2016.

Swan, W. (2008a, January 4). Interview with Alexandra Kirk. *AM Program with Eleanor Hall*. Treasury. Available at http://ministers.treasury.gov.au/DisplayDocs.aspx?doc=transcripts/2008/001.htm&pageID=011&min=wms&Year=2008&DocType=2. Accessed 2 Nov 2016.

Swan, W. (2008b, February 17). *Government Improves Transparency of Foreign Investment Screening Process*. Treasury. Available at http://ministers.treasury.gov.au/DisplayDocs.aspx?doc=pressreleases/2008/009.htm&pageID=003&min=wms&Year=&DocType. Accessed 21 Oct 2016.

Swan, W. (2008c, February 17). *Press Conference: Waterfront Palace*. Brisbane, Treasury. Available at http://ministers.treasury.gov.au/DisplayDocs.aspx?doc=transcripts/2008/028.htm&pageID=011&min=wms&Year=2008&DocType=2. Accessed 30 Oct 2016.

Swan, W. (2008d, February 18). *Cth. Parliamentary Debates.* House of Representatives. Available at http://parlinfo.aph.gov.au/parlInfo/search/display/display.w3p;adv=yes;orderBy=customrank;page=0;query=Date%3A18%2F02%2F2008%20QUESTIONS%20WITHOUT%20NOTICE%20Foreign%20Investment;rec=0;resCount=Default. Accessed 21 Oct 2016.

Swan, W. (2008e, February 18). Interview with Marius Benson. *ABC News Radio.* Treasury. Available at http://ministers.treasury.gov.au/DisplayDocs.aspx?doc=transcripts/2008/029.htm&pageID=011&min=wms&Year=2008&DocType=2. Accessed 2 Nov 2016.

Swan, W. (2008f, June 2). *Ministerial Statement on Financial Stability.* Address to the House of Representatives. Treasury. Available at http://ministers.treasury.gov.au/DisplayDocs.aspx?doc=speeches/2008/016.htm&pageID=010&min=wms&Year=2008&DocType=1. Accessed 3 Nov 2016.

Swan, W. (2008g, June 6). *Australia in the Global Economy.* Address to the Australian Business Forum. Treasury. Available at http://ministers.treasury.gov.au/DisplayDocs.aspx?doc=speeches/2008/017.htm&pageID=010&min=wms&Year=2008&DocType=1. Accessed 2 Nov 2016.

Swan, W. (2008h, June 10). *A Remarkable Place at a Remarkable Time.* Speech to the China–Australia Chamber of Commerce, Beijing, Treasury. Available at http://ministers.treasury.gov.au/DisplayDocs.aspx?doc=speeches/2008/018.htm&pageID=010&min=wms&Year=2008&DocType=1. Accessed 2 Nov 2016.

Swan, W. (2008i, June 11). *A Modern Relationship with China.* Speech to the Central Party School, Communist Party of China, Treasury. Available at http://ministers.treasury.gov.au/DisplayDocs.aspx?doc=speeches/2008/019.htm&pageID=010&min=wms&Year=2008&DocType=1. Accessed 1 Nov 2016.

Swan, W. (2008j, July 4). *Australia, China, and This Asian Century.* Speech to the Australia–China Business Council, Melbourne, Treasury. Available at http://ministers.treasury.gov.au/DisplayDocs.aspx?doc=speeches/2008/021.htm&pageID=010&min=wms&Year=2008&DocType=1. Accessed 3 Nov 2016.

Swan, W. (2009a, January 23). *The Global Recession and Australia's Future Economy.* Address to the New York Investment Community, New York, Treasury. Available at http://ministers.treasury.gov.au/DisplayDocs.aspx?doc=speeches/2009/002.htm&pageID=005&min=wms&Year=&DocType=. Accessed 3 Nov 2016.

Swan, W. (2009b, May 26). *Resources and Recovery.* Address to Minerals Week 2009, Hyatt Hotel, Canberra, Treasury. Available at http://ministers.treasury.gov.au/DisplayDocs.aspx?doc=speeches/2009/012.htm&pageID=010&min=wms&Year=2009&DocType=1. Accessed 3 Nov 2016.

Swan, W. (2009c, August 4). *Reforming Australia's Foreign Investment Framework.* Treasury. Available at http://ministers.treasury.gov.au/DisplayDocs.aspx?doc=pressreleases/2009/089.htm&pageID=003&min=wms&Year=2009&DocType=0. Accessed 3 Nov 2016.

Swan, W. (2009d, December 10). *Address to the Global Foundation.* Brisbane, Treasury. Available at http://ministers.treasury.gov.au/DisplayDocs.aspx?doc=speeches/2009/033.htm&pageID=005&min=wms&Year=&DocType=. Accessed 21 Oct 2016.

Swan, W. (2009e, April 23). *Foreign Investment Decision (China Minmetals to Acquire Assets of OZ Minerals).* Available at http://ministers.treasury.gov.au/DisplayDocs.aspx?doc=pressreleases/2009/043.htm&pageID=003&min=wms&Year=&DocType=0. Accessed 30 Oct 2016.

Sydney Morning Herald. (2010, April 5). Abbott Demands Schools, Batts Inquiry. *Sydney Morning Herald.* Available at http://www.smh.com.au/national/abbott-demands-schools-batts-inquiry-20100405-rmqh.html. Accessed 30 Oct 2016.

't Hart, P., & Tindall, K. (Eds). (2009). Understanding Crisis Exploitation: Leadership, Rhetoric and Framing Contests in Response to the Economic Meltdown. In *Framing the Global Economic Downturn: Crisis Rhetoric and the Politics of Recession* (pp. 21–42). Canberra: ANU Press.

Uren, D. (2012). *The Kingdom and the Quarry: China, Australia, Fear and Greed.* Collingwood, VIC: Black Inc.

White, H. (2009, May 21). *The Defence White Paper.* Blake Dawson Lecture Series. Speech at the Australian National University. Available at https://www.youtube.com/watch?v=2U6sN5taOpc. Accessed 3 Nov 2016.

Wilson, J. D. (2011). Resource Nationalism or Resource Liberalism? Explaining Australia's Approach to Chinese Investment in Its Minerals Sector. *Australian Journal of International Affairs, 65* (3), 283–304.

Yanow, D. (1996). *How Does a Policy Mean? Interpreting Policy and Organisational Actions.* Washington, DC: Georgetown University Press.

CHAPTER 6

Official Discourses of Security

In this chapter I examine the speeches made by official actors in the Rudd Government that contain the logics of security according to which they understood the rise of China. I then try to see where connections from these logics to the economic logics examined in Chapter 5 might exist. I show that from these speeches we can delineate a clear policy narrative that connects the rise of China to a series of other structural changes, including globalisation and the global financial crisis. The problem these changes caused was first the obsolescence of old policymaking methods of imagining different policy areas to function distinctly, and secondly an undermining of Australian "sovereignty." The solution was an activist, middle power approach to foreign policymaking, an ambition to produce a new regional architecture that brought China and the United States together and dealt with security and economic issues at the same time, and a willingness to use new tools in foreign policymaking, including drawing on the leverage Australia gained over East Asian states by dint of its position as a provider of economically vital raw resources. In short, from the discourse set examined below, it is possible to decipher the logics of Australia's strategic response to the rise of China, and from this to articulate precisely the role of the security–economy nexus in this response.

The first section is comprised of close readings of twenty-three speeches. As with the last chapter, the speeches are taken from official actors, though I have included one speech from a non-state actor (speech twenty). The inclusion of the speech by Marius Kloppers,

© The Author(s) 2019

M. Peters, *Regulating the Rise of China*, Studies in the Political Economy of Public Policy, https://doi.org/10.1007/978-3-030-05466-3_6

the CEO of BHP-Billiton, is made on the basis that he articulates a link from the export of Australian ore to Australia's strategic engagement with China in a more explicit way than was possible for the state actors. It is treated as supplementary to the articulations of the official actors, having weight insofar as the statements made, and the logic of the policy narrative that he presents, conform to the actions and statements of the state actors and render other elements of the narrative more coherent. Twenty-one of the twenty-three speeches are from Prime Minister Rudd. This reflects his dominance in defining the security agenda of the government in relation to China (see Stuart 2010; Wesley 2012; and Chapter 8, Sect. 8.1 of this book). The number of speeches annotated is higher than in the last chapter. This is due to this set of speeches not being so tightly focused on the FDI policy. I have included speeches on the basis that they add new elements to the policy narrative being deconstructed. Again, the method of analysis is as described in Chapter 2. I employ the analytical devices from postpositivist policy studies and narrative-based discourse analysis as a toolbox of discursive formations that may assist in decoding the phenomena (see Chapter 2, Sect. 2.3). The driving aims of the analysis are to identify a policy narrative relating to the Australian Government's overall engagement with China and the place of the FDI screening regime within this.

From the close readings of official speeches, I identify a number of organisational metaphors on which the engagement with China rested: the breakdown of traditional boundaries, the need for a "rules-based order," China as a "responsible stakeholder," the need for "creative middle power diplomacy," and "political sovereignty" as an object to be protected. These form the architecture to a policy problem posed by the rise of China that was articulated by Rudd as far back as 2001. Given the clear development of the policy narrative from that point through to June 2010, I have structured the close readings of speeches into four chronological stages: the narrative's foundation, refinement, sedimentation, and use. This meta-narrative is a post hoc addition of my own, which I have included only as I think it shows clearly how the FDI screening regime was conscripted into use as a tool for managing a problem that existed long before the appearance of Chinese SOE investments in 2007. Nonetheless, methodologically speaking, this chapter mirrors the previous one: the close readings of the speeches are initially done loosely in isolation from one another, as a way of identifying important discursive linkages at the most microscopic level, before the twenty-three speeches are re-examined as a set in Sect. 6.2.

6.1 Articulations from Australian Policymakers

6.1.1 Foundation of the Discourse

There are several statements from Mr. Rudd that precede his time in office in which the roots of the strategic logics that defined his Government's engagement with China can be found.

Speech one: Kevin Rudd (2001) 'ANZUS and the 21st Century,' Australian Journal of International Affairs

In this paper, written shortly before the 2001 federal election, and before he became the shadow foreign minister in the Beazley Opposition, Rudd examined whether the "strategic assumptions that underpinned the current system of alliances" remained valid (2001, 301). In a post-Cold War world in which new challenges stemming from globalisation threatened the "sovereignty of nation-states" and the "integrity of the current international system," Rudd argued it was time to reconsider the long-term future of Australia's security framework. He noted that while the maintenance of national sovereignty had never been simply about territorial integrity, in the context of globalisation, sovereignty was "increasingly compromised" (2001, 302). This concern underpinned much of his strategic thinking, and formed the basis of a central concept to his strategic ambition, "political sovereignty." Rudd broadened the term security by adding "soft" issues such as people and narcotics trafficking and marine resource management (2001, 302). Importantly though, he drew a clear line of separation between security and economic issues. This is implied in his argument that the "maintenance of global and regional security stability underpins our international economic interests" (2001, 302). Later in the article, Rudd used a similar logic to distinguish economics from politics when noting that neo-protectionist tendencies in the Asia-Pacific region were reinforced by the Asian Financial Crisis, and argued that these had the capacity to slow regional economic growth across Asia and thereby create "political instability" (2001, 306).

While Rudd's final response to the question posed was that the ANZUS Treaty would continue to serve Australian interests for the foreseeable future, he argued there was a need to change the approach of Australia to the alliance:

> Future Australian governments should use ANZUS more proactively to shape US strategic perceptions of East Asia where, from time to time, the US is in real danger of projecting short-sighted analysis and policies, particularly in relation to China. (2001, 302)

Rudd characterised China as "not a status quo power" (2001, 307). China was pursuing a "regional foreign policy offensive primarily aimed at undermining the credibility of the principal US alliances in the region" (2001, 307) and aimed to create "an East Asian hemisphere free from American hegemonism" (2001, 307). This, in Rudd's view, would be destabilising for the region and inimical to Australia's national security. Nonetheless, he criticised President Bush's designation of China as a "strategic competitor" as a rhetorical step too far (2001, 309) and urged Australia to aim for a "positive and productive relationship with Beijing—above and beyond that which may now be possible between Washington and Beijing" (2001, 309).

The paper is, at best, a nascent version of Rudd's grand strategy for Australia in response to the rise of China. Broadening the meaning of security—which was not a dramatic leap in security studies in 2001—was noteworthy mostly in the way the conceptual shift was used by Rudd to frame the key strategic dilemma facing the nation over the long term: the rise of China. Rudd understood the dilemma Australia faced as not simply the need to ensure a continued US security presence in the region, but to engender the senior ally to engage in the region on a range of issues, which were collectively significant from a strategic point of view. The issues themselves crossed between "security," "economic," and "political" boundaries uneasily, even as Rudd left these cognitive markers essentially intact. In the 2001 article, we can also see the appearance of the values of the "Labor tradition" of foreign policy of independence and activism (see Brereton 2001) as guiding principles in the piece, and these, along with a commitment to multilateral institutions, were hallmarks of Rudd's strategy while in office.

***

Speech two: Kevin Rudd (1 October 2004) 'The Three Pillars; Our alliance with the US, Our membership of the UN, and Comprehensive engagement with Asia; A Foreign Policy Statement by the Australian Labor Party'

In October 2004, shortly before the federal election of that month, then-Shadow Foreign Minister Rudd released a comprehensive Foreign

Policy Statement outlining the Labor Party's foreign policy framework. The framework for the document was composed of the "three pillars" of commitment to the US alliance, commitment to the UN, and "comprehensive engagement with Asia." These were to remain as constants up to the Rudd Government's taking office in December 2007 (see Smith 2007) and throughout its term. The document expanded on the principles of the 2001 paper and applied them to a wider set of issues and state relationships.

The theme of activism was expanded in a number of directions. Rudd linked the pursuit of a "competitive Australia" with the economic reforms and activist trade policy of the Hawke and Keating governments (2004, 7), contrasting their approach with the "policy inertia" of the Howard Governments. Within the same theme he warned against "foreign policy drift" and "muddling through," arguing that these were not viable options for a country such as Australia, given "its relatively small population, its medium-sized economy and its unique geostrategic circumstances" (2004, 9).

The unique geostrategic circumstances referred to "major flux in the international system" that left it open to "sudden" and "unexpected" change (2004, 10). This was an expansion on the theme of the 2001 article concerning the novelty of the issues faced by Australia. Rudd further entrenched the uncertainty-vulnerability link as a major feature of the problems to be responded to in all strategic policymaking. In a period of "major flux," he argued, quoting a US National Intelligence Council address, it is necessary to take a longer-term strategic view. This was linked explicitly to China:

> The growing pressures of China may also produce a sudden, dramatic transformation that cannot be understood by linear analysis. (Hutchings 2004, quoted in Rudd 2004, 10)

The point is underlined at the end of the section in bold summary, with Rudd concluding

> A core reason why we face unprecedented international uncertainty is that we are participants in an international system in transition. (2004, 14)

These transitions were products of structural changes associated with globalisation, but also of changes in the geopolitical structure of the international system (see Rudd 2004, 11–14).

Noting that “China is likely to profoundly shape Australia’s long-term economic, foreign policy and security environment” (2004, 63), Rudd argued that

> A critical emerging factor for China’s, the region’s and Australia’s economic future is how rapidly-growing China will meet its demand for energy, metals, and other raw materials. While China will seek to satisfy as many of its resource requirements domestically as it can, the Chinese Government is developing a range of long-term strategies based on international sourcing. Central Asia, the Russian Far East, Latin America, the Middle East and Australia all feature in these plans.

Finally in this Statement, Rudd articulated the “central challenge” in relation to China’s rise as “the maintenance of a positive relationship, based on constructive engagement, between China and the US” (2004, 66). He argued that the solution to this must be “to maintain a positive bilateral relationship with Beijing and through that relationship to support China’s continued pursuit of its strategic and economic interests through multilateral engagement and effective regional dialogue” (2004, 66–67).

***

Speech three: Kevin Rudd (20 April 2007*) ‘The Rise of China and the Strategic Implications for U.S.-Australia Relations,’ Address to the Brookings Institute, Washington, DC, 20 April 2007*

By April 2007 Rudd had become Leader of the Opposition Labor Party and was preparing for an upcoming election. This speech was a significant statement of his ambitions as a prospective leader of Australia.

He began by noting that, “[f]or the last 15 years, Sino-US. relations have developed their own intrinsic momentum, and this is to the bane of strategic and economic benefit of the entire Asia-Pacific region” (2007, 4–5). This was a reinvestment in the claims about the novelty of the security situation (a point made explicitly later in the speech on page 11), and the related need for a long-term approach based on “clarity of strategic vision” (2007, 6), which have been noted in speech one and two. Rudd argued that Australia did not think that it was “in anyone’s interest for Asia to be divided into different camps on the basis of different political systems” (2007, 6) and that the investment in effective regional institutions would be needed to avoid this.

Rudd listed "resource security" as one of the five "mega challenges" being faced by the Asia-Pacific region (2007, 6) and "energy security" as one of China's top five national priorities (2007, 9–10). He also noted that China had been diplomatically "intensive" in pursuing energy security (2007, 11).

On the theme of China not being a status quo power, Rudd suggested that the ambition of "China's modernisers" was to "once again take its proper place in the comity of nations" (Rudd 2007, 8). The use of the word comity is interesting for its confluence with Rudd's overall strategy, given its connotations of mutual respect for law or custom between sovereign states. He also briefly outlined the development of (apparent) key phrases in popular political commentary in China: the movement from "*heping jueqi*" (peaceful rise) to "*heping fazhan*" (peaceful development) and then to "*hexie shijie*," (harmonious world; 2007, 9). These terms appeared often when Rudd was articulating grand strategic narratives as Prime Minister, and he often tried to connect them to the Western organising concept of the "global rules-based order." The latter appeared later in the speech, but there was no attempt to link them explicitly at this stage.

In outlining a (Western, by implication) response to the challenges posed by China's rise, Rudd argued that, "we must look beyond the somewhat simplistic debate we have seen in the past between containment on the one hand and engagement on the other" (2007, 12). Instead, the approach must be built first on "continued US strategic engagement in East Asia and the West Pacific anchored in the existing pattern of US military alliances" and second on "actively and affirmatively engag[ing] China in the maintenance of a regional and global rules-based order" (2007, 12). This is the first appearance of the term "global rules-based order," Taken from a 2005 speech by US Deputy Secretary of State Robert Zoellick, which Rudd cited explicitly in the speech, it appeared frequently throughout Rudd's statements relating to China. Taking the words from a publication from the Council on Foreign Relations Independent Task Force on China–US Relations, Rudd elaborated on the meaning of the term as: "the fabric of international regimes on security, trade, and human rights and balancing China's growing military power" (quoted in Rudd 2007, 12 with no citation).

A few lines later and again quoting Zoellick (2005), Rudd introduced the second key organising metaphor of China as a "responsible stakeholder." The connotation attached to this term, which was also taken from Zoellick, was that investment in the international order was in China's own interest:

> ...in light of China's economic success in and its rising political influence Beijing had an increasing interest, and increasing self-interest, in working with the international community to sustain and strengthen the international security order. Because China has benefitted from that order and the economic growth that has proceeded from it, China therefore, according to the logic, has an intrinsic interest in sustaining that order and contributing to its success. (Rudd 2007, 12–13)

Again, this argument would be refined slightly in the speeches Rudd made as Prime Minister. Here he urged China to invest in the existing order; as Prime Minister he would switch to China's interests being served by playing an active role in shaping a *new* order. This change would occur as the grand strategy moved from encouraging Beijing to be an active and responsible stakeholder to aiming for this alongside urging Washington to allowing Beijing to be a rule-maker in a post-hegemonic order. Rudd's comments here were partially aimed at the American policymakers (2007, 14).

The final point of note from the speech was Rudd's criticisms of the existing regional institutional framework. He made some suggestions for alleviating this—adding India as a fully fledged member of the Asia-Pacific Economic Cooperation (APEC) (2007, 19) and urging the ASEAN Regional Forum to pursue more practical security measures (2007, 19). However, these relatively undeveloped ideas are far cries from the "Asia-Pacific Community" initiative—a new regional institution bringing economic and security matters under one roof alongside "new" issues requiring collaboration, such as environmental action and transnational crime—that would be a central ambition of his period of office.

6.1.2 Refinement of the Discourse

While some of the key elements of the Rudd Government's agenda on the China relationship have appeared already in the speeches made before his taking office, there was no intention that FDI screening would play a role in this. In the next set of speeches, the way the foreign investment regime was conscripted into the security arena can be seen, as well as how the general problem and solution of this broad strategic agenda shaped the constitution of more specific policies. It is notable that the basic storyline of uncertainty and change requiring activism and pre-emption remained stable as an aesthetic of the Government's narration of its policy agenda, even as the actual issues occupying these spaces of uncertainty and change and the actions proposed as responses changed.

Speech four: Kevin Rudd (21 January 2008a*) 'Building Australia's Economic Future,' Address to the Lord Mayor's Business Breakfast, Perth*

Rudd began by once again linking the need for activism to the uncertainty of the conditions Australia faced. The uncertainty-causing elements in this iteration of the story were the unfolding US sub-prime mortgage crisis (2008a, 1),[1] and, a few sentences later to the "unfolding economic and environmental reality of climate change" (2008a, 2). These did not replace the original element—deep structural changes in the international system and globalisation—but sat alongside them. The main function of the logic, though, remained stable as a reinvestment in the need for activism in government, in this case in response to inflation. As usual the Rudd Government's activist ambitions were contrasted with the previous Howard Government's inertia. I include this speech as a clear instance of Rudd employing the framework of his security agenda narrative for this speech on the Government's economic approach. This is the first time this transition occurred so completely, and from this point on economic and security issues were intertwined in the story in a way that had not occurred before Rudd came into office.

***

Speech five, six, seven, and eight: Kevin Rudd (18 February 2008b*) Interview with Chris Uhlmann, ABC Radio, 'AM'; Kevin Rudd and Julia Gillard (18 February* 2008*) Joint Press Conference with Julia Gillard, Deputy Prime Minister, Hume, ACT; Kevin Rudd (20 February* 2008c*) Interview with Jim Middleton, Newshour, ABC Radio Canberra Australian Foreign Policy; and Patrick Colmer, as quoted in Dorling (3 March* 2011*) 'Laws 'aimed to limit' Chinese investments'*

In an interview given the day after the announcement of the February Guidelines,[2] the Prime Minister made a telling comment, which is worth quoting in full:

> Uhlmann: But you're an expert on China, Prime Minister, what's your assessment? Don't you think that these vehicles[3] would be vehicles of Chinese Government foreign policy? Doesn't that just follow?
>
> PM: My judgment, Chris, is this–and it makes no reference at all to the current manoeuvring by Chinese corporations on various stock markets–it's that, China's long term strategic interest is to secure its own resource and energy interests into the very long term future. That has been a stated part of Chinese Government policy for a long, long time.
>
> When I go to China–and I'll be going to China, I believe, in the not too far distant future–one of the matters I want to discuss with the Chinese leadership is how do we fashion this long term resource and energy relationship between our two countries.
>
> China does depend on the reliable sources of supply from Australia in a whole range of commodity areas. This will continue into the future. And what I want to talk to the Chinese leadership about is what is their long term strategy and what are this country's long term strategic interests as well. (Rudd 2008b)

This is one of only a few occasions that Rudd or any other official policymaker linked China's resource security policies to the Australian FDI regime explicitly.

A second point of note is that while the rise of China was framed as a development occurring over the long term, Rudd's argument was that there was a need for action in the present to manage the disruption of the existing order. The refinement of the narrative was that activism meant not just preparedness for unexpected changes, but immediate preventative action.

In a press conference on the same day, Rudd reiterated the placement of the FDI policy changes in a nation-based strategic setting by advising the press that he intended to:

> [s]it down with our friends in the Chinese leadership and try to think though some strategic horizons for the next 10 to 20 years on China's long-term resource and energy needs and what this country has to offer. Principally, the decision-makers in this process, of course, will be our large resource companies. I understand that. And China's corporate sector as well. But there is a role for Government in mapping out longer term strategic approaches so that we know where the Chinese Government is

> coming from, and they'll know where the Australian Government is coming from. (Rudd in Rudd and Gillard 2008)

A similar line from an interview two days later repeated the point on framing:

> The important thing is, to take our current relationship with China to a new level. I believe that the economic opportunities between us are significant. There is enormous resource in the energy relationship between our two countries and we need to have a strategic discussion about that, long term–China's interest, our national interests. (Rudd 2008c)

Finally, the point was underlined explicitly in comments made by Patrick Colmer, the Executive Member of the Foreign Investment Review Board and the head of the Treasury's Foreign Investment Division to US Embassy officers in September 2009. The comments, which were included in an embassy report and later released on Wikileaks indicated to the Embassy officers that the February Guidelines marked "a stricter policy aimed squarely at China's growing influence in Australia's resource sector" (as quoted by Dorling 2011).

***

Speech nine: Kevin Rudd (26 March 2008d*) 'Advancing Australia's Global and Regional Economic Interests,' Address to the East Asia Forum in Conjunction with the Australian National University*

This was a general account of the Government's foreign policy ambitions. The approach to China was given no special weight, and the FDI policy was not mentioned at all. Nonetheless, the speech is valuable for three reasons; first, the reappearance of the uncertainty-activism theme, and the centrality of multilateral institutions in the story. Much of the speech was devoted to the need for foreign policy activism under the principles of creative middle power diplomacy and the related need for "adequacy" in the "global and regional economic and security architecture to deal with the challenges of the future." Second, there was a reactivation of the theme of the novelty of the operating context:

> Not only are the policy challenges the nation now faces formidable, the policy environment in which the nation must now operate is increasingly complex and interconnected. There is no longer a clear distinction

> between that which was once clinically defined as "foreign" as opposed to "domestic"; "internal" as opposed to "external"; "national" as opposed to "international"; "global" as opposed to "local". (Rudd 2008d)

This argument that the old conceptual frameworks no longer applied would appear on many occasions following this point, and were an important enabling logic for the FDI regime being used as a policy lever in a strategic engagement with China.

The third reason for including the speech is Rudd's assertion that the fact that "Australia is a major supplier of energy and mineral resources to China, Japan, and the Republic of Korea" was a "not insubstantial" national asset (2008d). In the context of a discussion on Australia as a middle power, it is noteworthy that Rudd believed this position stood alongside being the "5th largest economy in East Asia" and being the "11th highest-ranked nation in the world on defence spending as a metric of capacity" (2008d) as points of strategic leverage.

***

Speech ten: Kevin Rudd (31 March 2008e*) 'The Australia–US alliance and emerging challenges in the Asia-Pacific Region,' Address to the Brookings Institution, Washington, DC*

This speech was an update to the Brookings Institute speech Rudd gave as Opposition leader a year earlier (speech three). The aims of the speech were to reflect on "the continued importance of US global leadership," "the new Australian Government's foreign policy framework" and "how we might both engage China in the future and how we might shape together China's engagement with the global and regional architecture of the future" (2008e).

The policy problem to be solved was stated more concisely: the obsolescence of the global institutional architecture of the UN, IMF, World Bank, and WTO, and the absence historically of the United States from the development of East Asian and Asia-Pacific regional architecture.

Rudd did not turn to China until the final part of the speech. Here he reiterated his preference for active engagement between Washington and Beijing "to deal with emerging challenges before they become problems," again used Zoellick's concept of China as a "responsible stakeholder," and again used the Chinese concepts of "peaceful rise," "peaceful development," and "harmonious world." More explicitly than in the earlier iteration, though, Rudd (2008e) provided the precise condition for these concepts coming together:

> It is worthwhile thinking through how we might try and draw these differing concepts of "responsible stakeholder" and a "harmonious world" together.
>
> The idea of a "harmonious world" depends on China being a participant in the world order and, along with others, acting in accordance with the rules of that order.
>
> Otherwise, "harmony" is impossible to achieve.

He concluded:

> In short, we look to China to make a strong contribution to strengthening the global and regional rules-based order.

***

Speech eleven: Kevin Rudd (7 April 2008f*) 'Australia and the UK–Global Partners in shaping the future Global Order,' Address to the London School of Economics*

In this speech Rudd developed the theme of novelty of the situation historically again and expanded the meaning of creative middle power diplomacy, linking the two themes. The overall aim of the speech was to suggest that bilateral relationships cannot be discussed in narrow terms, and must be thought of as components of order-building. On novelty, he stated:

> In today's world, we are all deeply connected to each other within an increasingly inter-connected global order. This complexity is compounded by the fact that in this age of the globalisation of security, the economy and the environment, we are also witnessing the collapse of what the international relations scholars have described as "the great divide"–between what was once clinically described as the "foreign" and the "domestic"; the "internal" and the "external"; the "national" and the "international". (Rudd 2008f)

This dual-claim—that the primary ambition of foreign policy in the new world was "order-building" and that this was itself a response to the structural changes of globalisation—was then linked a few paragraphs later to the Rudd Government's mode of operation in creative middle power diplomacy:

> In short, Australia is a full participant in globalisation and we recognise that as a beneficiary of globalisation, we also have to maintain, support and enhance the global economic order–and the political and security order that underpins it. To do so, the new Australian Government will prosecute what I call "creative middle power diplomacy". That means we will use our assets, strengths and networks and work with our partners to find solutions to global and regional challenges. (Rudd 2008f)

These challenges do not refer to the rise of China in the speech, but rather environmental and development concerns, though a large part of the speech is devoted to reforming the international financial institutions to include more voting power for the large developing countries.

A small word on the meaning of the term "middle power" is required here. The phrase has produced debate among Australian (and other) International Relations scholars, and can mean a number of things. Ungerer (2007) traces the term's influence through Australian foreign policymaking since 1945 and summarises it as being a form of the pursuit of "enlightened self-interest": it comprises an approach that favours the use of international law over the exercise of power. In the case of Labor Governments it has come to mean, according to Ungerer, an adherence to the values of (1) independence of action within alliances with great powers (2007, 550), (2) a preference for internationalist or multilateral action in the international sphere (2007, 551), and (3) activist and creative use of diplomacy (2007, 548). The reasoning is essential that in the absence of structural or material capacity to affect outcomes in international affairs, the middle power's interest is generally best served by a functioning law-based international order and the use of persuasion rather than force to effect particular outcomes. This could be termed a behaviouralist account of the middle power concept, and there is clearly resonance of these ideas in Rudd's use of the term, and indeed, his overall strategy towards China and the United States.

An alternative approach to the middle power concept is based on the state's capacity. An example of this is Hugh White's approach. According to White, a middle power is one that "can shape how the international system works to protect its interests... even in the face of competing objectives of a major power" (2009). It stands in distinction to a major power, which has the capacity to shape the international order itself, and a small power, which has no capacity to affect the international order, and whose actions are limited to those which are allowed by the major powers. Further, a middle power's "military forces can be used to achieve substantial results, not just be used in a symbolic way" (2009), and a middle power can "achieve a strategic result against the forces of a middle or major power" (2009). White clarifies that this does not mean that the middle power necessarily is able to defeat a middle or major power in battle, "…but [it] must be able to raise the costs and risks to the other power in respect to that power's interests" (2009).

In this address at LSE, Rudd's comments clearly indicate the presence of this capacity-oriented treatment of the term as well as the behaviour-oriented meaning. In a conversation with US Secretary of State in March 2009 (later leaked on Wikileaks) Rudd explicitly described Australia's planned naval build-up as "a response to China's growing ability to project force" (Flitton 2010), the clearest indication of his Government's middle power ambitions using the capacity basis.

***

6.1.3 *Sedimentation of the Discourse*

In these speeches, there is a period of sedimentation of the policy narrative. The elements appeared consistently and there was little further experimentation with the links between them. They are useful as the clearest available statements of the Rudd Government's aims in its engagement with China.

Speech twelve: Kevin Rudd (9 April 2008g*) 'A Conversation with China's Youth on the Future,' Peking University*

In this speech, delivered in Mandarin to Chinese university students, Rudd used the policy story in its developed form. China was said to be having a transformational impact on the global economy, notably that, "China's demand for resources is driving global growth"; there was a need for China to participate fully "in all the institutions of the global rules-based order"; and for China to make "active contributions to the enhancement of that order in the future" (9 April 2008g). This was again "the necessary task of responsible global citizenship" (9 April

2008g) and was again linked to the concepts of peaceful rise, peaceful development, and harmonious world. These five central terms were repeated at least once each.

***

Speech thirteen, fourteen, fifteen, sixteen, seventeen, and eighteen: Kevin Rudd (4 June 2008h*) 'It's time to build an Asia Pacific Community'; Kevin Rudd (31 July* 2008j*) Inaugural Tom Burns Memorial Lecture; Kevin Rudd (11 August* 2008k*) Speech to a Dinner Hosted by Business Groups of Seoul; Kevin Rudd (9 September* 2008l*) Address to the RSL National Congress; Kevin Rudd (3 October* 2008m*) 'The Australian Response to the Global Financial Crisis'; Kevin Rudd (20 November* 2008n*) 'Towards an Asia-Pacific Century'; Department of Defence (2009) 'Defending Australia in the Asia Pacific Century: Force 2030'*

In these speeches, the Prime Minister reiterated his argument in the settled form that it had taken by the Peking University speech, giving small inflections on different aspects of it.

In the speech of 4 June 2008, Rudd introduced the "Asia-Pacific Community" initiative. The policy problem that was articulated closely followed that of earlier speeches: the region faced a period of change that rendered the existing institutions and order inadequate. The challenges faced this time did not relate to either globalisation or the financial crisis, but instead to "climate change, questions of energy and food security, the rise of China and the rise of India" (Rudd 2008h). Later in the speech demographic changes in the economies of the region, and a rise in the region's significance to the globe both economically and in terms of security occupied this space. The solution to the problem was the Asia-Pacific Community, a "regional institution which is able to engage in the full spectrum of dialogue, cooperation, and action on economic and political matters and future challenges related to security" (Rudd 2008h). The idea rested on the same logic of Rudd's more China-focused statements, and should be read as a tactic to bring the United States and China into more frequent contact with one another. The defence of the idea in the following days centred on a line about the need to bring together "political, security, and economic matters within a single framework so that we foster over time a common sense of regional community [between] countries as diverse as the USA, China, Japan, Indonesia, and India as well as ourselves" (Rudd 2008i). While the economic, political, and security realms were treated as distinct from one another, there was a further investment in the "breaking down of traditional conceptual barriers" motif and a need for these to be treated as interrelated in the new world.

In the speech delivered in Brisbane on 31 July, Rudd delivered the argument in the form of the Peking University speech, noting its continued relevance despite the Doha trading round again breaking down several days earlier.

In a speech in Seoul he outlined the same argument, adding the need for the Asia-Pacific Community. He also defined middle power diplomacy as meaning that "we work closely with our partners around the world *to shape the international environment*" (2008k, my emphasis), the "we" referring to both Australia and South Korea.

At a keynote address on security policy on 9 September, Rudd again used all core tenets of the argument. In the speech he committed to increase the defence budget to 3% of GDP and to ring fence it from cuts ("efficiency dividends"), on the basis that, in the context of the changes to the region outlined, "[o]ur armed forces must be equipped to deal with the emerging security environment" (Rudd 2008l). As a middle power, he noted in his concluding remarks, Australia's "diplomacy must always be reinforced by a credible national defence strategy" (Rudd 2008l).

In Rudd's first speech acknowledging the severity of the global financial crisis in October 2008, he linked the discourse of China as a responsible stakeholder to the crisis. Rudd framed the crisis as a symptom of deeply ingrained issues within the financial order and urged a long-term view on the events. In particular he argued that it was right and necessary for afflicted nations to embrace Chinese injections of liquidity into US and European institutions and to embrace China acting as a stabilising force as it had done during the Asian Financial Crisis:

> It is important now for western nations to demonstrate our positive support for China as a responsible stakeholder in the global economy and in major financial institutions... It is in every nation's interest for China to strengthen its links to the global economy and to become an increasingly positive stakeholder in the global economy... On the key challenges facing the international community–the global financial crisis, the future of global trade and climate change–for China to be engaged and participating as a responsible stakeholder is strongly in the interests of China, Australia and the global community. (Rudd 2008m)

In the speech on 9 September in which the arguments of the 2009 Defence White Paper (known as *Force 2030*) were rehearsed, Rudd developed again the themes of historical novelty for the region and connected this to the need for economic and security policy to be conceptually intertwined:

> Australia's long-term national security also hinges on our long-term economic security. The Global Financial Crisis is an important reminder of the close links between economics and security. The Western Pacific will be the leading centre of global change in the 21st century. The region's economic weight is increasing rapidly. This economic growth, this economic weight is driving substantial changes in strategic weight. The challenge for all nations in the region is to cooperate effectively to manage the economic and security changes and challenges that are now unfolding. (Rudd 2008l)

The purpose of the White Paper itself was framed in relation to this new complexity:

> This document will provide a conceptual framework for dealing with the complexity, the density and the interconnectedness of the security policy challenges Australia now faces. (Rudd 2008l)

Finally, the key terms and logics outlined above were present in the 2009 Defence White Paper, forming the key planks of policy problem and solution of the document. On the problem side, the White Paper anticipated no emergence of "an alternative political and economic system to rival the network of liberal, market-based democracies that emerged after World War II" (Department of Defence, 30), but expected that globalisation would "ensure that economic interdependence links states and regions together more closely" (Department of Defence, 30). Further it anticipated "changed strategic power relativities and an increasingly 'multipolar' global order, driven by changing patterns of underlying economic power and political influence" (Department of Defence, 30). These deep structure shifts were "inevitable" as "any change in economic power relativities will affect the distribution of strategic power in Asia" (Department of Defence, 32) and as "other powers rise, and the primacy of the United States" will be "increasingly tested" (Department of Defence, 33). This point was measured, it should be noted, by a strong belief that US political, economic, and military primacy would not be challenged before 2030 (Department of Defence, 32). Nonetheless, the underlying message of the Paper was clear: Australia could no longer assume US strategic primacy in the Asia-Pacific region (White 2009).

On the solution side, there was the same commitment to institutions functioning to ensure that the major powers of the region share a commitment to stability and the continued aversion to the resolution of conflicts through the use of force (Department of Defence, 31–32). There was a return again to the organising metaphor of the "stable, rules-based global security order" (Department of Defence, 32–33).

6.1.4 Deploying the Narrative

Following the release of the Defence White Paper in April 2009, Rudd rarely discussed grand strategy and the rise of China. This was likely due to the poor reception of the White Paper from a number of quarters. While the official Chinese response was not negative, a number of Chinese political commentators and security analysts argued that the "tough stance" was a product of "Western Cold War mentality" (Guo 2009; see Reuters 2009; Zhang 2009) and aimed at signalling to Washington Canberra's undivided loyalty to the Australia–US alliance (Guo 2009).[4] In Australia there were continued criticisms of Rudd in Australia for his apparent Sinophilia on the one hand (Oakes 2009), and the unnecessary incitement of China on the other (this was by the Opposition Leader Malcolm Turnbull and [separately] ex-Prime Minister Paul Keating, cited in Tubilewicz [2010, 153]; see Tubilewicz [2010, 153–154] for a discussion of all the responses to the White Paper). In spite of this, some late speeches during the period showed an increase in the strength of Rudd's calls for China to commit to a liberal economic order. This shows the significance the Rudd Government placed on impressing this point upon the Chinese Government.

***

Speech nineteen: Kevin Rudd (20 August 2009b*) 'Joint press conference with New Zealand Prime Minister John Key'*

In a press conference not largely concerning the Australia–China relationship, Prime Minister Rudd answered a question on the state of the relationship as sharing "enormous common interests" and having "continuing differences." He followed this up with a more unusual line, which spoke to the rarely articulated logic of Australia having leverage over China:

> I'd also say that China has significant interests in Australia. China's interests in Australia go to its long term needs for resource security. China's needs and interests in Australia go to the role which we have in the wider deliberations of the Asia Pacific region. And therefore we approach–we approach this relationship mindful of our interests in China, mindful of China's interests in Australia. (Rudd 2009b)

***

Speech twenty: Marius Kloppers (18 November 2009*) 'Australia's Resources in the World,' The Annual Lowy Lecture, Sydney*

This speech was not by an official of the Rudd Government, but I include it as a clear example of how sedimented the idea of treating the Australian resource sector's relationship with China as a strategic issue was. This point seems unremarkable, but the issue could easily have stood simply as a matter of maximising the economic benefit and distributing it fairly, for example if the Australian Government did not persistently strive for middle power status. Kloppers' speech is useful in providing further delineation of how the matter was securitised, or perhaps instead strategised with the nation as the point of reference.

The foreword to the speech by the executive director of Lowy Institute, Michael Wesley, linked Australian resources to security questions clearly:

> Our resources sector has also posed some important challenges, relating to foreign investment, global warming, and non-proliferation policy. As a country with a continental abundance of resources in a world that is increasingly hungry for them, Australia's resource sector will play an increasingly central role in the strategic, economic and diplomatic challenges faced by this country into the future. (in Kloppers 2009, 1)

In the speech, Kloppers drew on a number of the themes Rudd had stressed during his time in office. He urged a long-term vision to the changes occurring in the region, and particularly to the resource needs of China out to 2030. He stressed the significance of Australian resources to the Chinese economy, noting that, "Australia provides one-third of the iron ore China is importing" (2009, 6), and devoted a section of his speech to showing that "future demand for our minerals is assured" (2009, 10–11). In the middle section of his speech, Kloppers repeated Rudd's argument in strikingly similar terms:

> It matters immensely to Australia, and specifically to Australia's resource industry that Asia should work out ways to maintain stability and harmony. And it seems obvious that this will require a strong, continuing US leadership role in Asia, a growing role for China as its power grows, and an also appropriate role for Japan which remains such an important country and economy. (2009, 13)

On the role of foreign investment, he appeared to take a line of criticism of the Government, urging openness to FDI:

> Although clearly not simple, a part of the solution [to the difficulty of funding large-scale a risky mining projects] lies in continued foreign investment, meaning that both Australia and Australian companies need to be open to this kind of investment, despite its immediate and strategic implications. (2009, 16)

Finally, in comments aimed at the consumers of Australian resources, which in the context of the speech should be understood as Chinese firms, Kloppers used Rudd's concepts precisely:

> Now is a critical time for all stakeholders to reaffirm a commitment to an open global resources market. Despite recent concerns and attempts by some nations to secure access to resources, it is important to acknowledge that the risks of supply are, at best, slight… The world's mining industry can meet growing demand for fuels and ores over coming decades, and any risks can be effectively managed by appropriate investment in spare capacity and moderate diversification of sources. (2009, 17–18)

My point in including this speech is not to suggest any form of collusion, as there is no evidence of any. Rather it is that I believe that Kloppers summarises an understanding of the logic and narrative linking the FDI policy to the Rudd Government's strategic policy clearly, possibly in a way that would not be possible for an official actor in the Government. Kloppers' understanding of the meaning of the key terms seems coherent with Rudd's use of them in the other speeches, if more detailed. In Chapter 7, I will suggest that "open global resource market" is related to Rudd's concept of a "rules-based order," both in their structural places in policy problem–solution stories, and in their common solution of the production of structures conforming to liberal theory as a method of stabilising an unstable world. The policy problem implied by the use of the term—China pursuing resource security via ownership of foreign mining interests rather than risk management via the liberal methods like diversification—seems coherent with the policy problem articulated in Rudd's speeches.

***

Speech twenty-one: Kevin Rudd (4 December 2009c*) Address to the Asia Pacific Community Conference*

In this speech, marking eighteen months since Rudd introduced the Asia-Pacific Community initiative and again arguing for its creation, Rudd provided all the elements of the strategy in its settled form, putting some stress on the claim that the days in which political, economic, and strategic questions that affect the region could be "neatly compartmentalised" were gone. This claim was the main basis of his argument that a new institution was needed that covered all these together.

***

Speech twenty-two: Rudd Kevin (23 April 2010a*) 'Australia and China in the World,' Australian National University, Canberra*

In this long speech introducing several initiatives encouraging the learning of Chinese language and the studying of China in Australia, Rudd draws on his established logics, and made some new links. He draws a line from the "awakening of Asia" at the start of the twentieth century to the era of change that the region found itself in today. He described the earlier period as an "age of openness," a phrase used by historians to describe China as a state newly freed of dynastic autocracy and colonialism, and viewed this as analogous to the openness that formed the basis of the new ascendency of China and the region today.

He used strong language in a depiction of the exploitation of China by the West historically, and framed the legitimacy of China's re-ascension to a position of power in the global order against this. From this acknowledgement he stepped to the choice facing China, in the most involved statement of the change narrative that appears the discourse set:

> The depth and breadth of China's transformation must be acknowledged. But so too must the fact that change is ongoing, and so too are its consequences. China has benefitted remarkably from its policies of domestic economic reform and global economic engagement. But there is still an ongoing debate within China itself about that reform. Will it continue to unleash the creative potential of the Chinese people? Or are the urges to re-centralise control again coming into play–as some analysts argue, citing examples of how the state is now reasserting its role in the Chinese private economy…
>
> We want to see the economic system develop in a way that brings China and the Chinese people into a globalised world economy. These facts and the question of China's future matter to us because China is now an integral part of the international system.
>
> A growing China will pursue its interests globally: that is natural. And I believe that China recognises its own fundamental interest in working with–not against–the international system that has served China so well in recent decades. Over the past 60 years or so, this system has entrenched the values, rules, conventions and foundations that have helped bring about the greatest prosperity that China has experienced in its history. As I have already noted, China has benefitted enormously from this international order. Increasingly China is also playing its part within this order. (Rudd 2010a)

That is, there was an extension of successful domestic reform in China to further integration into the existing liberal order. "What the world would welcome," Rudd claimed, "is China engaging across the board as major global stakeholder in the maintenance and enhancement of that stable, rules-based order in the future" (Rudd 2010a).

***

Speech twenty-three: Kevin Rudd (27 May 2010b*) Speech to the Opening Conference of the National Security College*

This was the last major speech on security policy that Rudd gave as Prime Minister. It came two weeks after the announcement of a \$4.3 billion "national security budget."[5] The budget reallocated funding for a strategy based on a more holistic approach than had previously been used, and provided for an enhanced as well as streamlined security community. It also committed to an increase in funding for at least a decade.

These announcements have been described as marking "the emergence of a new national security paradigm" (Dupont and Reckmeyer 2012, 34), though in light of the themes of Rudd's security strategy outlined in the speeches in this chapter, the changes seem very coherent with his approach and concerns over the entire term of office.

The speech outlined the bureaucratic changes being introduced, which will be discussed in more detail in Chapter 8, and provided an overview of the "non-traditional" threats that the new security infrastructure would be responsible for. He also listed a number of "enduring" national security interests including territorial integrity, "regional stability and a rules-based global order" and "political sovereignty" (Rudd 2010b). There was no particular emphasis put on the latter term, though it is perhaps interesting that it appeared on the list in a speech on new threats; it had not in analogous speeches previously. Rudd also offered no elaboration on the term, though included a paragraph on sovereignty later in the speech:

> As you would know, all of the systems in Australia–all of our infrastructure–cross a number of boundaries. They may cross international boundaries and call up questions of sovereignty. They almost certainly cross state boundaries in Australia and raise questions of jurisdiction. But they also cross boundaries between the public and the private. Ownership and operation of the assets that lie at the base of these systems is neither wholly private nor wholly government. The continued operation of infrastructure may rely partly on government control, and partly on industry-led standards. But it is also dependent on an effective business-government partnership. (Rudd 2010b)

This slightly opaque section situated the issue of sovereignty as relating to the theme of the breakdown of traditional conceptual barriers—here the private and public realm, but elsewhere in the speech between "foreign and domestic" and "policy and operational." As in all the speeches where sovereignty is mentioned, it was linked to the novelty of the security environment and the "rapidity of change."

In fact, the term political sovereignty is very rare in the discourse set: the only other appearance was in the Defence White Paper, where it was listed as a concern of national security, alongside but distinct from "maintaining our territorial integrity" (Department of Defence 2009, 20). Later in a point on China's growing "soft" and "economic" power, the White Paper noted that, "China will have even more interest in convincing regional countries that its rise will not diminish their sovereignty" (Department of Defence 2009, 35). More significantly, the term political sovereignty appeared in the context of major changes to the security bureaucratic infrastructure that originated in *Force 2030* (Wesley 2012, discussed in detail in Sect. 8.1).

There is however a second genealogical root for the idea in the phrase "economic sovereignty," which was used by Treasurer Wayne Swan in a speech six months earlier on 10 December 2009 (speech seven in Chapter 5). Swan used the term to summarise the changes the Government had made to the FDI policy, and listed it alongside "job creation" as the primary aim of the FDI policy.

6.2 Analysis

6.2.1 Coherence and Consistency of the Policy Narrative

This chapter has charted the articulations of key officials within the Rudd Government, almost exclusively from the Prime Minister himself. A number of points are worth noting when examining the discourse set as a whole.

First, Rudd's personal understanding of the challenge posed by the rise of China was remarkably consistent from 2001 until the end of his term as Prime Minister.[6] Instead of conflicting or replacing the old logics, the addition of new terms consistently seems to have enhanced the policy narrative by more effectively expressing the ideas that appeared in the earlier speeches. First, Zoellick's term "rules-based order" gave more precise tactical shape to Rudd's calls in 2004 for an active and creative engagement with China. Zoellick's (2005) call for China to be a "responsible stakeholder" provided the perfect vehicle for Rudd to communicate his vision for China's path for a peaceful rise and the required response needed from the United States, one of making concessions but retaining a central role in the region in a range of areas. The term political sovereignty would otherwise be unreasonably ambiguous, but given the context of the discourse set, it appears instead as a more accurate and concise way to term part of the problem as Rudd had earlier articulated it: a set of structural changes has broken down old organisational barriers; as a result nation-states face new challenges to their mode of operating; thus, states must become more creative and active in pursuing their goals. This story is captured in its most concise form in Rudd's speech of

27 May 2010 (speech twenty-three), but the elements are all present in the journal article from 2001.

Given this stability, it seems very unlikely that the overall strategy regarding China's rise—including the FDI policy—was ad hoc. It was extremely well-considered, and the arguments that the FDI policy was made on the run by a government not able to take the time to conceptualise the China problem (for example, Drysdale 2011) are not convincing. Secondly, Rudd's approach to China was a central component of his overall foreign policy ambitions, drawing together his approach to the United States, multilateral institutions, and the engagement with Asia, which is to say all of the "three pillars" of the Government's foreign policy platform. Within that, the FDI policy was a major aspect of the Australia–China relationship: the machinations of the two Chinalco bids featured heavily in the discussions between the highest level of the two governments (see Uren 2012, Chapter 5 for an extensive account), and the Chinese government tried to pressure the Australian Government to amend the FDI screening processes both immediately after the announcement of the February Guidelines (Uren 2012, 78) and during the FTA negotiations, where they demanded the same concessions American investors had been granted in the AUSFTA (Ravenhill and Jiang 2009, 41).[7] Given all this, the claim that the FDI policy was predominantly a political gesture to the Australian electorate, establishing Rudd personally as "tough on China" (for example, Wines 2009), is also not compelling.

The most interesting aspect of this point on consistency is that while the logics linking the story elements to one another are very stable, the elements that appear within those stories shift. I will leave the discussion of the significance of this to Chapter 8 and simply describe the dynamic here.[8] The source of uncertainty shifts between four options: globalisation (speeches one and eighteen); changes in the deep structure of the international system, either in the rise of China, India and Brazil (speeches two, four, thirteen, and eighteen), the rise of the Western Pacific (speech sixteen), or the move from unipolarity to multipolarity (speech eighteen); the immediate tumultuousness of the global economy caused by the GFC (speech four); and climate change (speech four, eleven, and thirteen). The "old barriers" that are broken down as a result of these changes are equally interchangeable, moving more or less freely between breakdowns between the international and the domestic (speeches nine, eleven, and twenty-four); the private and public economic spheres (speech twenty-four); "policy" and "operational" (speech twenty-four); and security and traditionally non-security (generally economic or environmental) policy areas (speeches one, sixteen, and twenty-two). Finally the nature of the order in which China must become a responsible stakeholder is fluid: it is sometimes a regional security order (speech two and then all mentions of the Asia-Pacific Community); sometimes the values of the global liberal order, which aside from all the uses of the term "rules-based order" can be non-violence (Rudd 2009a), or "values, rules, conventions, and foundations" generally (speech twenty-three); sometimes the global economy generally (speech seventeen, twenty-three); and sometimes the existing institutions of international society in the WTO or the "international regimes on security, trade, and human rights" (both in speech three).

6.2.2 Security and the FDI Policy

A third point of note is that foreign direct investment and sovereign-owned enterprises are not mentioned in relation to security in any of Rudd's speeches. The closest link is the final addition to the discourse set in "political sovereignty," which I have claimed has resonance with Treasurer Swan's use of the term "economic sovereignty" six months earlier. There is a good reason for this silence: the policy's aim was to protect a liberal assemblage of governmental technologies, and this meant that the rhetoric from official actors had to maintain the principle of non-discrimination. That is, to link the FDI policy to China explicitly would undermine the policy's coherence and the Australian Government's credibility. The fact that this term appears only twice in the discourse set (speech eighteen and speech twenty-three) does not disallow me from placing this emphasis on it. My aim in this chapter and the last one has been to read into the articulations of policymakers rather than off them. Following the instruction of Howarth and Griggs (2012), I am deconstructing the discourse sets with a view to identifying the logics on which the policy rested, and to making retroductions on the phenomena being explained (see Chapter 2, Sect. 2.2). My claims about the meaning and significance of the term "political sovereignty" rest on these two moves. In the final instance, the strength of the argument rests on my claim that my own is the most coherent account of the FDI policy that includes all the evidence and doesn't resort to accusing the Rudd Government of either economic incompetence or racism, as others have done (see Chapter 4, Sect. 4.3).

There are two legs to this argument. The first relates to the context in which the policy was introduced: I argue that certain industrial metals like iron ore, bauxite, coke, and rare earth resources were securitised by other states in the region before the Rudd Government came into office, and that Rudd and Swan understood the situation in these terms. The second leg links the FDI policy to security by using the term security to mean the prerequisite arrangement of forces that enables a particular relationship between the governor and the governed.

6.2.2.1 The Securitisation of Minerals in the Asia-Pacific

The term "comprehensive security" appeared in Japan in 1980, where, following the global energy supply issues of the 1970s, the term was used to describe Japan's vulnerability to supply shocks to vital raw resources, predominantly energy resources (Ravenhill 2013, 40). In the 2000s, a similar situation arose, though concerns about the security of supply of vital raw resources were more widely shared throughout the states of the Asia-Pacific, and these concerns were related more to metals needed for industrialisation and coal, rather than oil. This renewed relevance of the comprehensive security idea was caused predominantly by the rise of China and India as consumers of industrial metals, as well as the relatively high proportion that imports of such resources accounted for in the economies of Japan, Korea, Taiwan (Ravenhill 2013, 40) and increasingly through the 2000s, India and China. Accompanying rising prices for iron ore, aluminium, and rare earth resources, there was a perception that a global race was under way between consuming countries, each aiming to "lock up" reliable sources of supply (Ravenhill 2013, 40).[9] A number of states implemented illiberal strategies in this pursuit. The most important example of this that shaped the Rudd Government's understanding of the situation was China's 2005 Steel Policy, which provided loans for state-owned enterprises on concessional terms from state-owned banks for the SOEs to invest in iron ore mines across the globe in a strategy that was explicitly coordinated by the NDRC (see Chapter 4, Sect. 4.1). The Steel Policy was itself an iteration of the "Go Out" Policy introduced in the 1990s under President Jiang Zemin, and the programme received further funds in the midst of the GFC in 2009 and 2010, which resulted in a second wave of foreign investment in the Australian resources industry. In addition to this, there were restrictions placed on the export of rare earth resources by China.[10,11]

In short, the trade in the Asia-Pacific region in resources that featured strongly in the FDI policy were already securitised by the consumer states before the Rudd Government came into office through the logic of comprehensive security. While the Government went to great lengths to deny that the February Guidelines were in any way a response to events, let alone high-level geopolitical strategies (see Chapter 5, Sect. 5.3), this was patently the case. In any case, this is the security context in which the policy should be understood. Several decisions were made on more traditional security grounds, most notably the rejection of Minmetals' bid for OZ Minerals on the basis of proximity to the Woomera rocket testing site, but the arguments for these decisions on traditional security grounds are illogical in both cases (see Chapter 4, Sect. 4.3) and cannot be extended to the rest of the interventions on Chinese investments over the period. Instead, the security aspects of the FDI policy should be understood in the context of Chinese strategies relating to comprehensive security, and in relation to the wave of investments as a whole. This does not mean that the Government understood the problem as many small transactions leaving open the future possibility of a "global mining competitor in China [emerging] from the aggregation of all investment in Australian resources," as a private submission to the Government made by BHP in relation to the first Chinalco bid suggested (quoted in Uren 2012, 97). Rather, the security ramifications existed in relation to the present practices of Chinese investment, and the need to respond to a Chinese strategy of ensuring stability of supply in vital resources, but doing so in ways that undermined liberal norms; in short, the comprehensive security strategies of the Chinese government.

These contextual points generally only appear in the articulations in oblique ways. However, there are several explicit references, the most important being in speech five. On 18 February 2008b, Rudd referred to "China's long-term strategic interest" as its "resource and energy interests into the very long-term future," which he said had been "a stated part of Chinese Government policy for a long, long time." Given that this was in an interview defending the February Guidelines, it is clear that China's Steel Policy of 2005 and the two waves of the Go Out Policy are the events or conditions that the FDI policy was responding to. It is clear that Rudd understood China's interests as being "strategic," and that the FDI policy must be understood in kind as a strategic response. The same link is made in speeches six, seven, and eight, above.

The second reason the FDI policy can be thought of as a security or strategic policy in these terms is the use of the logic that Australia's position as a resource supplier to East Asian states provided it strategic leverage, which in turn formed a plank in the claim that Australia was a middle power. This logic appeared in its most complete form in speech eleven, but there were precursors in speech two, where Rudd noted that China had shown that it relied on external sources for key economic resources; speech three, where Rudd noted that one of China's top priorities was resource security; speech five, where Rudd noted that China relied on Australia for its supply of key mineral resources; and speech nine, where Rudd listed being "a major supplier of energy and mineral resources to China, Japan, and the Republic of Korea" as a national asset. In speech eleven, Rudd defined creative middle power diplomacy as using "assets, strengths, and networks" to achieve multilateral goals, and made this point after noting that the "great divide" between the international and domestic spheres no longer existed. The significance of this is that Rudd took a capacity approach to the middle power term as well as a behaviour approach.[12] This is given further weight in the 2009 Defence White Paper (see speeches seventeen and eighteen) and in a conversation the Prime Minister had with then-US Secretary of State, Hilary Clinton, in March 2009 which was later leaked on Wikileaks and in which Rudd explicitly described Australia's planned naval build-up as "a response to China's growing ability to project force" (Flitton, 6 December 2010).

6.2.2.2 Security of Governmental Assemblages

The second way of connecting the FDI policy to security concerns is by taking the meaning of the term security from the governmentality literature rather than the liberal one. Seen in a governmental light, the Chinese strategy of securing resource supply by using state resources to fund acquisitions in Australian mining interests was a problem because it undermined the principles on which liberal economic governance rests. Specifically, if all firms do not operate under equal conditions regarding risk, as well as their access to and the cost of credit, then the meritocratic principles of liberal economics do not hold. This is an economic issue, but is more precisely one of the integrity of a political, economic, and symbolic assemblage on which governance-at-a-distance rests. There is no settled metaphor for this type of problem in liberal political theory, but in the governmental literature, it could be termed security. The source of the term is Foucault's *Security, Territory, Population* lecture series (2007), where he uses the term to represent the mode of intervention by a governor on a substance that takes the form of placing an event within a series of probable events that can be known according to aleatory (probabilistic) rules, and acts on the population according to logics of normalisation and optimisation. In short, security is the baseline arrangement of forces that enables the modern liberal governor–governed relationship to function (see Chapter 2, Sect. 2.1). The value of using this literature is that it allows me to articulate precisely why Chinese investment was a threat. In every other account that I am aware of, the points of reference are to economics or geopolitics exclusively, and it is always taken for granted that large-scale Chinese investment with state-backing and direction is a problem, without any effort to explain why this should be so (see Chapter 4, Sect. 4.3, for my criticisms of specific accounts that are made on this basis). It should also be noted that this is a different mode of argument from my first use of the term security; the logic is imposed on the actors here by me, whereas in the first argument it was generated by the actors themselves.

There are resonances with the idea that the Chinese SOE investments threatened the integrity of Australia's governance assemblages. These appear in the logics that underpin the arguments made by Rudd and others, rather than the actors actually using the language of governmentality. The closest Rudd comes to using an exclusively governmental concept is in speech twenty-three, where he lists as one of the object being protected in the changes to Australia's security infrastructure is "political sovereignty." He goes on to define sovereignty in terms of the "infrastructure" that crosses state boundaries within Australia and the "systems" that are based on "ownership and operation of assets" that are neither wholly public nor wholly private. The concept is clearly the assemblage, the constellation of forces, beliefs, actors, and objects that enable the "systems" to function. It is remarkable that Rudd would understand this concept as "sovereignty" and have to invent the term political sovereignty to describe it. Political sovereignty traditionally has meant freedom from interference by foreign forces on the workings of the formal political system: namely voting and then the decision-making of office-holders. In the context of the speeches above, where there is no suggestion anywhere that the integrity of Australia's formal political structures was ever threatened, it seems much more likely that Rudd was concerned about the integrity of the assemblages instead. This is given weight by Treasurer Swan's use of the term "economic sovereignty" when defining the "national interest" that the FDI policy existed to protect (speech seven in Chapter 5), a term that has no orthodox meaning that I am aware of.

There is also evidence when we examine the central organising metaphors that appear in the discourse set examined in this chapter. First, the concept of the "rules-based order" is often related to security or "high political" matters by Rudd, but is also used to refer to the economic or political–economic "order" as well. In speech one, China is castigated by Rudd for undermining the US hegemony in the Asia-Pacific region that has fostered stability. Then, in speech three, the rules-based order is related to "security, trade, and human rights and balancing China's growing military power," and China is castigated for offering support to the pariah states of Iran and Sudan in exchange for "energy security and diversity of supply" (Rudd 2007, 13), which is to say, for not playing by the rules of the existing order. In the same speech, Rudd argued that it was not in anyone's interests for "Asia to be divided into different camps on the basis of different political systems" (Rudd 2007, 6, speech three), suggesting that the question of "order" was one that spanned all aspects of state-craft: the suggestion of a Cold War structure has connotations of political, economic, ideological, and geopolitical order all at the same time. This idea was expanded in *Force 2030* (speech eighteen) in the line that the Government anticipated no emergence before 2030 of "an alternative political and economic system to rival the network of liberal, market-based democracies that emerged after World War II" (Department of Defence 2009, 30). While the claim was that the event was not likely, the point is that the emergence of such a system warrants mention under a paragraph on Australia's strategic outlook.

In Marius Kloppers' speech, the idea of a rules-based order was coopted to mean an open global resource market and states (China) managing risks through "appropriate investment in spare capacity and moderate diversification of sources" (2009, 18, speech twenty). This was made on the basis that "[s]ince the 1970s, a broad consensus has emerged that commercial market mechanisms are the best way to govern economic relations between parties and to regulate economies—that the allocation of resources between consumers can be most efficiently, effectively, and peacefully determined by market prices" (Kloppers 2009, 17). Finally in the long quote from Rudd included in the annotation of speech twenty-two, it is clear that "order" referred to the economic sphere, and "rules-based" meant "market-based," and a liberal relationship between the economic actor and governor (Rudd 2010a). Domestic reform towards market-based structures is a component of integration into the global liberal economic order, claimed Rudd in the same speech.

Given this development of the connotations of the term rules-based order, we can now add (and make sense of) the economic logics that were outlined in Chapter 5. Swan's economic logics almost always relate to the relationships between the governor and the economic subject or between economic subjects: he championed the principles of "non-interference" (even while executing a policy constantly criticised for being unnecessarily interventionist and at times is defended on the basis of defending the Australian economy's ability to obtain "fair value" from its natural resources), and disinterest, meaning that as a governor he did not promote sectional interests. He opposed vertical integration, though only in the specific sense of integration that covers an entire sector and exists as a function of (Chinese) state strategy; as noted in Chapter 5, the appearance of vertical integration at the level of the individual firm was not a problem. Finally he opposed any economic actor who behaved with reference to goals outside of the economic realm: production and pricing principles must be made with reference to the profit principle only (see Chapter 5, Sect. 5.2 for the larger discussion of these points). These were the reference points of the "rules-based order" as it was relevant to the FDI policy, and when Swan speaks of "economic sovereignty" (2009, speech seven in Chapter 5), he was referring to the capacity of the Australian Government to ensure the integrity of the assemblages that maintain governor–economic subject relations to function according to these principles. This is what is meant by the security–economy nexus.

The second resonance of governmental thinking that exists in the set of speeches examined in this chapter is the repeated use of a metaphor of the breaking down of barriers that Rudd used. The trope was used in speeches one, nine, eleven, thirteen, sixteen, twenty-two, and twenty-four. In speech twenty-four, Rudd specified the breakdown of all of these barriers as the unified cause of threats to Australian "sovereignty." This repeated emphasis on the policy problems being transgressive can be read as a series of attempts to articulate the object being defended. In a governmental light, the object was the liberal economic assemblage, which is not quite the state's rights, nor the economic actors' rights, nor an economic question or a security question, nor a rule-making or execution question. It necessarily traverses the borders in exactly the way that Rudd claims. Once again, the use of this metaphor was also tactical: Rudd and Swan use the claims of the novelty of the policy context and policy problems as the justification for the changes in the FDI policy and to the security bureaucracy (discussed in Chapter 7), and the transgression of old borders is a central part of this narrative. This point is developed in Chapter 8.

6.3 Conclusion

In this chapter, I have analysed the speeches of official actors that allow me to access the logics that underpin the Rudd Government's understanding of the security-related aspects of the rise of China. I then tried to see where they might connect to the economic logics that were examined in the previous chapter. All the speeches annotated here were from Prime Minister Rudd, with additions from Defence Minister Smith, Treasurer Swan, Patrick Colmer, and the non-official actor, Marius Kloppers, only used as supplementary material. This was only a result of all the dominant logics appearing most coherently in Rudd's speeches, though it may give some weight to the idea that Prime Minister Rudd was very dominant in defining the security agenda of the government in relation to China.

The speeches show a highly coherent policy narrative, with the logics that appeared remaining remarkably consistent, even as the elements within the logics were at times changeable. The policy problem was that a series of structural changes consisting of globalisation, climate change, the global financial crisis, and the rise of China, and to a lesser extent India and Brazil, rendered old ways of formulating and executing security policymaking obsolete. This was because old conceptual barriers no longer reflected the world. These barriers included those between the domestic and international, security and non-security issues, and political, economic, and security policy areas. Importantly, these changes signified threats to the political and economic sovereignty of Australia, thought of as the ability of the Australian nation and government to assure the integrity of the liberal economic and political formations that underpin the governor–governed relationship that society is founded on. The response to these interrelated challenges was a particular form of creative middle power diplomacy: it required activist and prevention-oriented policy stances rather than a muddling through approach; it required a willingness to use whatever resources available to pursue goals, including non-traditional points of leverage like the significance of Australian raw resource supply to Asian economies; and it aimed to encourage China and the United States to embark on a new project of regional order-building, with the aim of an Asia-Pacific Society which would institutionalise a cooperative and productive US–China relationship and create one roof under which security and economic issues could be discussed.

I have argued that there are two ways to connect this narrative and the logics contained in it to the FDI policy. First, the resources that Chinese SOEs targeted in their investments in Australia from mid-2007 through to the end of the Rudd Government's term in June 2010 were already securitised within the region. Stability and security of the supply of economically vital raw resources were included in the "comprehensive security" policies of China, as well as other East Asian nations. Given the speeches annotated here, it seems clear that the Rudd Government understood this and responded to developments in the region's raw resource markets according to logics of national strategy. Secondly, if we imagine the term security as taking the governmental sense rather than the liberal one, meaning the integrity of the constellations of forces that enable a core relationship between governor and governed, then much of the meaning of the policy becomes clear. Seen in this light, the interventions on Chinese investments were intended to protect the integrity of liberal economic structures, and were used to signal to the Chinese firms and government the Australian Government's determination to protect the integrity of these structures.

This chapter sits alongside Chapter 5, and the two together used a discourse analysis to delineate the various elements of the Rudd Government's FDI policy, the place of this policy in the Government's response to the rise of China, and the exact shape of the security-territory nexus. In these analyses, I have examined the articulations of official state actors, supplementing these with statements from commentators and non-official actors where necessary, to re-state the policy in terms of the logics it rested on. I then suggested that the FDI changes must be understood in light of their symbolic components, the larger response of the Government to the rise of China as an economically significant force in the Australian economy, and the aim of protecting the assemblages that underpin neoliberal governmentality. In the next chapter, I take up these threads to provide my own account of the policy, drawing on the framework of governmentality.

Notes

1. As noted in Chapter 5, this speech stands as an exception to the usual practice of the Rudd Government of downplaying the significance of the crisis to Australia until September 2008 (see Laing and Tindall 2009).
2. These are the six principles released by the Treasurer on 18 February 2008 to clarify the Government's intentions when screening investment proposals made by foreign governments and their agencies. See Chapter 3, Sect. 3.3 for details.
3. SOEs.
4. The official Chinese response was not negative.
5. This was the first explicitly designated security budget in Australian history (Dupont and Reckmeyer 2012, 34).
6. In fact Rudd has continued to use the arguments outlined here up until the present in the exact same form. He has used his appointment as President of the Asia Society Policy Institute in New York to argue for the necessity of understanding the rise of China in the terms outlined in this chapter and the necessity of responding in the ways outlined here. He has even renewed his calls for an Asia-Pacific Society (Rudd, 29 October 2015).
7. This was eventually granted in the Australia–China FTA signed by the Abbott Government, but it should be noted that the raised thresholds for screening do not affect the requirement that all sovereign-owned or affiliated firms' investments be subject to scrutiny by the FIRB. It is unlikely that the change would have affected the execution of the Rudd Government's FDI policy.
8. In Chapter 8, I argue that we can read the changes to the FDI policy as experimentations in adapting neoliberal governmentality to new external conditions. At the same time, uncertainty and risk appear as logics that are used tactically by the Government, and they seem to have been used to enable changes to be made in certain institutional and governmental assemblages. As I will discuss, this dynamic has some precedents in neoliberal governmentality, and has also been discussed extensively in more orthodox literature on late neoliberalism as well as work on Ulrich Beck's (1999) risk society thesis.
9. Ravenhill also includes food resources in this story, linking the metals supply deficiency with the global food shortages of 2008 and 2010. This is a compelling argument, but doesn't relate to this work.
10. For a more general account, meaning one not focused exclusively on China's pursuit of stable supplies in the resources Australia has an abundance in, see Vivoda's "China challenges global capitalism" (2009), particularly pages 27–30.

11. Uren (2012, 103) reports that it was not until reading an article on the Chinese export restrictions while in Washington that Treasurer Wayne Swan decided to reverse a decision on a proposed investment by China Nonferrous Metals into the Australian Lynas Corporation that related to developing a rare earth project in Western Australia.
12. I am not taking a position on whether these two treatments of the concept are conceptually compatible. My comment is simply that Rudd used the term in both senses.

References

Beck, U. (1999). *World Risk Society*. Cambridge: Polity Press.

Brereton, L. (2001). Australian Foreign Policy—A Labor Perspective. *Australian Journal of International Relations, 55*(3), 343–349.

Department of Defence. (2009). *Defending Australia in the Asia Pacific Century: Force 2030*. Australian Department of Defence. Available at http://www.defence.gov.au/CDG/Documents/defence_white_paper_2009.pdf. Accessed 5 Nov 2016.

Dorling, P. (2011, March 3). Laws 'Aimed to Limit' Chinese Investments. *Sydney Morning Herald*. Available at http://www.smh.com.au/business/laws-aimed-to-limit-chinese-investments-20110302-1bexm.html. Accessed 25 Oct 2016.

Drysdale, P. (2011). A New Look at Chinese FDI in Australia. *China and World Economy, 19*(4), 54–73.

Dupont, A., & Reckmeyer, W. J. (2012). Australia's National Security Priorities: Addressing Strategic Risk in a Globalised World. *Australian Journal of International Affairs, 66*(1), 34–51.

Flitton, D. (2010, December 6). Rudd the Butt of WikiLeaks Exposé. *Sydney Morning Herald*. Available at http://www.smh.com.au/technology/security/rudd-the-butt-of-wikileaks-expos-20101205-18lf2.html. Accessed 5 Nov 2016.

Foucault, M. (2007). *Security, Territory, Population: Lectures at the Collège de France, 1977–78* (M. Senellart, Ed., G. Burchell, Trans.). New York: Palgrave Macmillan.

Guo, C. (2009, May 24). Playing Up the 'China Threat'. *Beijing Review*. Available at http://www.bjreview.com.cn/world/txt/2009-05/24/content_197174.htm. Accessed 25 Nov 2016.

Howarth, D., & Griggs, S. (2012). Poststructural Policy Analysis: Discourse, Hegemony, and Critical Explanation. In F. Fischer & H. Gottweis (Eds.), *The Argumentative Turn Revisited* (pp. 305–342). Durham: Duke University Press.

Hutchings, R. (2004, March 9). *Looking Over the Horizon: Assessing America's Strategic Challenges*. Address to Department of State/INR/World Affairs

Council Seminar by the Chairman of the National Intelligence Council. Washington, DC: National Intelligence Council.

Kloppers, M. (2009, November 18). *Australia's Resources in the World. The Annual Lowy Lecture*. The Lowy Institute. Available at http://www.lowy-institute.org/publications/2009-lowy-lecture-australias-resources-world. Accessed 4 Nov 2016.

Laing, M., & Tindall, K. (2009). Australia: 'The Lucky Country' on a Knife Edge. In P. 't Hart & K. Tindall (Eds.), *Framing the Global Economic Downturn: Crisis Rhetoric and the Politics of Recession* (pp. 203–242). Canberra: ANU Press.

Oakes, L. (2009, August 22). Rudd Won't Listen to the Bullies. *Daily Telegraph*. Available at http://www.dailytelegraph.com.au/news/opinion/rudd-wont-listen-to-the-bullies/story-e6frezz0-1225764945490. Accessed 25 Nov 2016.

Ravenhill, J. (2013). Resource Insecurity and International Institutions in the Asia-Pacific Region. *The Pacific Review, 26*(1), 39–64.

Ravenhill, J., & Jiang, Y. (2009). China's Move to Preferential Trading: A New Direction in China's Diplomacy. *Journal of Contemporary China, 18*(58), 27–46.

Reuters. (2009, May 5). China Rebuffs Australian Worries Over Military. *Reuters*. Available at http://uk.reuters.com/article/uk-china-australia-idUK-TRE5441P020090505. Accessed 25 Nov 2016.

Rudd, K. (2001). ANZUS and the 21st Century. *Australian Journal of International Affairs, 55*(2), 301–315.

Rudd, K. (2004, October 1). *The Three Pillars: Our Alliance with the US, Our Membership of the UN, and Comprehensive Engagement with Asia*. Foreign Policy Statement by the Australian Labor Party. Parliament of Australia. Available at http://parlinfo.aph.gov.au/parlInfo/search/display/display.w3p;query=Id%3A%22li-brary%2Fpartypol%2FZMZD6%22. Accessed 4 Nov 2016.

Rudd, K. (2007, April 20). *The Rise of China and the Strategic Implications for U.S.–Australia Relations*. Address to the Brookings Institute, Washington, DC. Available at http://www.brookings.edu/~/media/events/2007/4/20china/20070420china.pdf. Accessed 4 Nov 2016.

Rudd, K. (2008a, January 21). *Building Australia's Economic Future*. Address to the Lord Mayor's Business Breakfast, Perth. Parliament of Australia. Available at http://parlinfo.aph.gov.au/parlInfo/download/media/pressrel/F9HP6/upload_binary/f9hp62.pdf;fileType=application%2Fpdf#search=%22media/pressrel/F9HP6%22. Accessed 4 Nov 2016.

Rudd, K. (2008b, February 18). Interview with Chris Uhlmann. *AM, ABC Radio*. Available at https://pmtranscripts.dpmc.gov.au/release/tran-script-15765. Accessed 21 Oct 2016.

Rudd, K. (2008c, February 20). Interview with Jim Middleton. *Newshour, ABC Radio*. Department of the Prime Minister and Cabinet. Canberra. Available at http://pmtranscripts.dpmc.gov.au/release/transcript-15766. Accessed 4 Nov 2016.

Rudd, K. (2008d, March 26). *Advancing Australia's Global and Regional Economic Interests.* Address to the East Asia Forum in Conjunction with the Australian National University. Department of the Prime Minister and Cabinet. Available at https://pmtranscripts.dpmc.gov.au/release/transcript-15823. Accessed 4 Nov 2016.

Rudd, K. (2008e, March 31). *The Australia–US Alliance and Emerging Challenges in the Asia-Pacific Region.* Department of the Prime Minister and Cabinet. Washington, DC: The Brookings Institution. Available at https://pmtranscripts.dpmc.gov.au/release/transcript-15833. Accessed 4 Nov 2016.

Rudd, K. (2008f, April 7). *Australia and the UK—Global Partners in Shaping the Future Global Order.* Address to the London School of Economic, London. Department of the Prime Minister and Cabinet. Available at https://pmtranscripts.dpmc.gov.au/release/transcript-15847. Accessed 4 Nov 2016.

Rudd, K. (2008g, April 9). *A Conversation with China's Youth on the Future.* Department of the Prime Minister and Cabinet. Peking University, China. Available at http://pmtranscripts.dpmc.gov.au/release/transcript-15854. Accessed 4 Nov 2016.

Rudd, K. (2008h, June 4). *It's Time to Build an Asia Pacific Community.* Address to the Asia Society AustralAsia Centre, Sydney. Department of the Prime Minister and Cabinet. Available at http://pmtranscripts.dpmc.gov.au/release/transcript-15947. Accessed 4 Nov 2016.

Rudd, K. (2008i, June 5). Interview with Simon Beaumont. *Radio 6PR.* Department of the Prime Minister and Cabinet. Perth. Available at http://pmtranscripts.dpmc.gov.au/release/transcript-15949. Accessed 4 Nov 2016.

Rudd, K. (2008j, July 31). *Inaugural Tom Burns Memorial Lecture.* Department of the Prime Minister and Cabinet. Don Dunstan Foundation, Brisbane. Available at http://pmtranscripts.dpmc.gov.au/release/transcript-16040. Accessed 4 Nov 2016.

Rudd, K. (2008k, August 11). *Speech to a Dinner Hosted by Business Groups of Seoul.* Department of the Prime Minister and Cabinet. Seoul, Korea. Available at http://pmtranscripts.dpmc.gov.au/release/transcript-16059. Accessed 4 Nov 2016.

Rudd, K. (2008l, September 9). *Address to the RSL National Congress.* Department of the Prime Minister and Cabinet. Townsville. Available at http://pmtranscripts.dpmc.gov.au/release/transcript-16112. Accessed 4 Nov 2016.

Rudd, K. (2008m, October 3). *The Australian Response to the Global Financial Crisis.* Address to the Federal Labor Business Forum, Sofitel Wentworth Hotel, Sydney. Department of the Prime Minister and Cabinet. Available at http://pmtranscripts.dpmc.gov.au/release/transcript-16162. Accessed 4 Nov 2016.

Rudd, K. (2008n, November 20). *Towards an Asia-Pacific Century.* Speech to the Kokoda Foundation Australia–US Trilogy. Department of the Prime Minister and Cabinet. Available at http://pmtranscripts.dpmc.gov.au/release/transcript-16251. Accessed 4 Nov 2016.

Rudd, K. (2009a). *Managing Global and Regional Interdependence: The Future of the G20 and an Asia Pacific Community.* Paper dated 12 March 2009, developed for publication in *Foreign Affairs* but not published, posted online by *The Age*. Available at http://www.theage.com.au/ed_docs/rudd-speech-G20.pdf. Accessed 4 Nov 2016.

Rudd, K. (2009b, August 20). *Joint Press Conference with New Zealand Prime Minister John Key.* Department of the Prime Minister and Cabinet. Canberra. Available at http://pmtranscripts.dpmc.gov.au/release/transcript-16766. Accessed 4 Nov 2016.

Rudd, K. (2009c, December 4). *Address to the Asia Pacific Community Conference.* Department of the Prime Minister and Cabinet. Sydney. Available at http://pmtranscripts.dpmc.gov.au/release/transcript-16952. Accessed 4 Nov 2016.

Rudd, K. (2010a, April 23). *Australia and China in the World.* The 70th George E. Morrison Lecture, Australian National University, Canberra. Available at https://www.youtube.com/watch?v=EzLvsnWPDm0. Accessed 4 Nov 2016.

Rudd, K. (2010b, May 27). *Prime Minister Speech to the Opening Conference of the National Security College.* Australian National University, Canberra. Department of the Prime Minister and Cabinet. Available at http://pmtranscripts.dpmc.gov.au/release/transcript-17311. Accessed 4 Nov 2016.

Rudd, K. (2015, October 29). Asia Need Its Own EU More Than Ever. *Europe's World.* Available at http://europesworld.org/2015/10/29/asia-needs-eu-ever/#.VlFhc7zwxE7. Accessed 4 Nov 2016.

Rudd, K., & Gillard, J. (2008, February 18). *Joint Press Conference with Julia Gillard.* Deputy Prime Minister, Hume, ACT. Department of the Prime Minister and Cabinet. Available at http://pmtranscripts.dpmc.gov.au/release/transcript-15764. Accessed 4 Nov 2016.

Smith, S. (2007, December 3). *Speech Notes for the Annual Diplomatic Corps Christmas Party.* Department of Foreign Affairs and Trade. Available at http://foreignminister.gov.au/speeches/2007/071203.html. Accessed 4 Nov 2016.

Stuart, N. (2010). *Rudd's Way: November 2007–June 2010.* Melbourne: Scribe.

Swan, W. (2009, December 10). *Address to the Global Foundation.* Brisbane, Treasury. Available at http://ministers.treasury.gov.au/DisplayDocs.aspx?doc=speeches/2009/033.htm&pageID=005&min=wms&Year=&DocType=. Accessed 21 Oct 2016.

Tubilewicz, C. (2010). The 2009 Defence White Paper and the Rudd Government's Response to China's Rise. *Australian Journal of Political Science, 45*(1), 149–157.

Ungerer, C. (2007). The "Middle Power" Concept in Australian Foreign Policy. *Australian Journal of Politics and History, 53*(4), 538–551.

Uren, D. (2012). *The Kingdom and the Quarry: China, Australia, Fear and Greed*. Collingwood, VIC: Black Inc.

Vivoda, V. (2009). China Challenges Global Capitalism. *Australian Journal of International Affairs, 63*(1), 22–40.

Wesley, M. (2012). Australia's Foreign Policy Machinery. In J. Cotton & J. Ravenhill (Eds.), *Middle Power Dreaming: Australia in World Affair: 2006–2010* (pp. 261–272). Melbourne: Oxford University Press.

White, H. (2009, May 21). *The Defence White Paper*. Blake Dawson Lecture Series. Speech at the Australian National University. Available at https://www.youtube.com/watch?v=2U6sN5taOpc. Accessed 3 Nov 2016.

Wines, M. (2009, June 2). Australia, Nourishing China's Economic Engine, Questions Ties. *New York Times*. Available at http://www.nytimes.com/2009/06/03/world/asia/03australia.html. Accessed 2 Nov 2016.

Zhang, J. (2009, April 2). Chinese Seek to Invest, Not to Dominate. *The Australian*. Available at http://www.theaustralian.com.au/story/0,25197,25276296-5017272,00.html. Accessed 21 Oct 2016.

Zoellick, R. (2005, December). Whither China: From Membership to Responsibility? *The National Bureau of Asian Research, 16*(4), 5–14.

CHAPTER 7

A Governmental Account of the Policy

In this chapter I provide my account of the Rudd Government's FDI screening policy.

The FDI screening policy had economic, political, and geopolitical aims. It was a response to a set of structural changes in the world that required a new mode of governance from the Australian state. These included the breakdown of the great divide between the domestic and international realms, the intermingling of economic, security, and political issues, and the perceived end of US hegemony in the Asia-Pacific region. These changes, combined with the particular nature of the Chinese firm–state relations, were understood as threatening the Australian way of life. Specifically, they disrupted the governmental apparatus of market-based systems, which were a necessary component of the assemblage of forces that allowed the Australian state to use liberal methods of economic governance. The purpose of the policy was to defend the integrity of the market structures in the Australian mining sector. The functioning of markets was an end in itself, but also took on a symbolic significance as the Rudd government asserted the right to define the structures on which Australian society rested. Seen in this light, the integrity of market structures in Australia became synonymous with the sovereignty of the Australian state. They labelled this new meaning of sovereignty "economic" or "political" sovereignty. In addition, the policy had outwardly assertive geopolitical aims. The Rudd government aimed to insert Australia into the process of regional order-building as a creative middle power.

© The Author(s) 2019

M. Peters, *Regulating the Rise of China*, Studies in the Political Economy of Public Policy, https://doi.org/10.1007/978-3-030-05466-3_7

It aimed further to ensure that the order was founded on the rule of law and a respect for liberal markets as the basis of state interactions. Legal control of access to resources vital to Chinese comprehensive security appeared as an opportunity to assert meaningful leverage over the Chinese state and press these demands. In the final analysis, the FDI screening policy can be interpreted as an innovation in governmental practice that responded to the historically novel problem of an international context that was not unambiguously liberal.

This account rests on the governmental concepts of assemblages and apparatuses. An assemblage, or dispositif, is a contingently stable arrangement of forces that enable a diverse set of actors to pursue a diverse set of strategies (see Chapter 2, Sect. 2.1). It involves the production of subjects in a way that renders them governable, by themselves and by others, and a set of objects that are laden with meanings and values specific to their position within the assemblage. These are constituted in knowledge and by knowledge practices, and thus are at once political and ideological structures. The assemblage that liberal governmentality rests on requires a division of the private economic sphere from the public political sphere, autonomous firms that are both self-governing and disciplined by capital, goods, and labour markets, and a state whose actions are limited by logics of legitimacy based on the knowledge of liberal political economy. The assemblage being defended in the FDI screening policy was at once political, geopolitical, economic, and ideological in nature. The defence of this assemblage centred on its central apparatus: "market-based systems."

The chapter has three sections. I decode the economic policy narrative elements, drawing on the discourse analysis of Chapter 5. I then decode the security policy narrative elements, drawing on the discourse analysis of Chapter 6. In the final section, I explain how the two policy narratives are coherent with and complete each other, and how they centre on the protection of Australia's market-based systems and its economic and political sovereignty.

7.1 Decoding Swan's Economic Narrative

In the chapter outlining the economic discourses that founded the FDI screening policy, I argued that there were five key organisational metaphors: economic "openness," the commitment to a system "driven by market forces," "competitive neutrality," regulation on a "case-by-case" basis, and finally "economic sovereignty." Overlaying these, there were three themes of the narrative: the need for "long-term solutions," "active" economic governance, and the use of the market as a normative end in itself. In this section, I will describe these three themes, and then reconstruct the economic policy problem narrative using the five organisational metaphors.

The first theme was the need for "long-term solutions" to economic problems that had been building slowly over a number of years (see Swan with Rudd 2008; Swan 2007a). By and large, economic policy initiatives from the Rudd government did not use the crisis trope that Hassan's (2013) or 't Hart and Tindall's (2009) theories might have expected. This dynamic applied to the wave of Chinese SOE investments: the government did not frame the new investments as a crisis, and instead narrated the policy changes as continuations of existing policy structures rather than departures responding to a new issue. This choice was maintained throughout the period, extending even to the final period of swift iron ore price rises that resulted from the breakdown of the long-term benchmark price-setting mechanisms for iron ore in 2010 (described in Chapter 4, Sect. 4.2). These were, Ambassador Raby argued, a result of "short-term pressure" (2010, speech eight in Chapter 5). The move to a more market-sensitive pricing system was touted as being more "flexible," and would, it was claimed, lead to more stable outcomes in the long term.

The second theme was the need for active economic governance. The particular type of activism needed change over the course of the period, but the need itself remained as a constant solution element to the various problems that arose. At the start of the period, the need for activism was related to the problems of infrastructure and skills deficits, which were both adding inflationary pressure to the overheating economy. In the later stages it was linked to the management of the GFC. In relation to the mining sector, active management meant facilitating "next generation" growth potential by overcoming "capacity constraints" (Swan 2009a, speech five in Chapter 5). That is, activism in the present was in the service of the management of a more distant future. This indicates that the FDI screening policy was situated at a level above the immediate economic issues of the financial crisis. This theme was tempered, however, by the broad preference of the government to leave markets to function as autonomously as possible. The government FDI screening policy was designed to be "as non-intrusive as possible," "not a roadblock," and "[keeping] the Government out of the traffic" (Swan 2009b, speech seven in Chapter 5).

The third theme was the use of markets, and particularly capital markets shaped by shareholders, as a desirable end in itself. This appeared in Raby's argument for competitive markets as a foundation for *long-term* stability, as has been noted, but it was given its strongest articulation in FIRB Executive Director Patrick Colmer's speech of 24 September 2009 (speech six in Chapter 5). In this, Colmer listed the aims of the FDI screening policy as: (1) producing win-win situations between Australian firms and foreign investors; (2) maintaining an orderly flow of investment; (3) helping develop the Australian economy; (4) "maintaining public support for foreign investment;" (5) "maintaining a market-based system in Australia;" and (6) limiting foreign firms investing in the resource sector to non-controlling stakes. As an adjunct to the fifth aim, Colmer specified that the government preferred seeing "major projects maintain listings because we think the listing disciplines are important in the development of good sound businesses" (2009). The value of the market then was precisely the role it plays in disciplining firms.

The meaning of the organisational metaphors are as follows:

The first metaphor was the aim of managing an "open economy," and is, properly speaking, an adjunct to the second organising metaphor of a system driven by market forces. Openness refers to the Australian government's general and long-standing position of welcoming foreign investment. It is tempered by the (also long-standing) "… aim of maintaining a system in which investment and sales decisions are driven by market forces rather than external strategic or political considerations" (Swan 2008b, speech two in Chapter 5). The commitment to openness is doxa for liberal governance in the twenty-first century. Nonetheless, Swan stipulated the point in most speeches relating to FDI screening, occasionally with the rider that it was very obvious (for example, Swan 2008d, speech four in Chapter 5). Openness was used as a descriptor of the Australian economy and at the same time as a normative ambition for the government, an aim articulated both by official actors (for example Swan 2008b, c, speeches two and three in Chapter 5; and Colmer 2009, speech six in Chapter 5) and commentators (for example Novak 2008; Kirchner 2014). Likewise, the governing function of "market forces" and "market-based systems" was presented at once as a description of reality and a normative preference (for example Swan 2007b; Raby 2010, speech eight in Chapter 5). This conforms closely to Foucault's point on the dual role of political economics as a knowledge, as both a description of reality and the foundation of claims to legitimacy for the governmental sovereign.

Related to this point, the role of the commitment to market-based systems and openness held an important place in the justification of the Rudd government's interventions into capital flows. Openness refers to the willingness of the state to allow (or not prevent) flows of goods, people, and capital into the Australian economy. The predisposition towards openness reflected a belief that maximising flows of capital into the economy was in the interests of the Australian economy and nation. It also functioned as a limit on the intervening actions of the government. This limit was based on a logic of legitimacy, but this legitimacy was founded in the coherence of the government's actions to the realities imposed on it by the "laws" of political economy, as opposed to any sort of legitimacy founded by democratic processes and the such. At the same time, these commitments functioned as the legitimate basis for exceptional actions to the government's predisposition towards not preventing inflows of capital. That is, the government's interventions restricting the flow of capital into the Australian economy were legitimate insofar as they protected the functioning of the market systems. In the case of the FDI screening policy, the threats to market-based systems in Australia came in the form of firms that did not conform to the expectations of liberal firms. Seen in this light, state interventions oriented towards the exceptions functioned to create the reality that formed the limit on government action, the limit to which those interventions were exceptional. This conforms to the constitutive regulation dynamic of security technologies anticipated by Foucault (see Chapter 2, Sect. 2.1). The dialectic positioned political economic knowledge, claims to legitimacy on the basis of it, and governmental actions that worked on populations of investors and borrowers in relation to one another in such a way that they constituted the reality and knowledge on which it rested.

The third organisational metaphor is "competitive neutrality." This term did not appear in the discourse set, so I am really superimposing it as a metaphor of my own.[1] It stands for the logics that determined which exceptional government interventions could legitimately be made to maintain the market-based system. The reason for not using a term produced by the actors themselves is that the official actors eschewed articulating these bases so as to avoid the problems of voicing the fact that the new screening measures were targeted at Chinese investments as a class. There are three threats to competitive neutrality that appear in the discourse set. The first, from the official statements, is vertical integration. The second and third come from Wilson's (2011, 290) differentiation of Chinese investments from all other investments. He describes these as being that they were targeted overwhelmingly at the Australian mining sector, that they drew on the Chinese "governmental financial assistance," and that they were directed by a "state-directed agenda."[2] The second and third of these rendered the Chinese investments a threat to competitive neutrality between firms in Australian markets.

I have explained in Chapter 5, Sect. 5.1, my reasons for believing that vertical integration was not in itself a convincing reason for the government to move to such an interventionist stance on FDI. Despite the points made there, it is possible to fit the concern of vertical integration into the framework described here as a basis for legitimate exceptions to the government's commitment to openness. This is the only way to explain the concern without resorting to calling the Rudd government irrational or xenophobic for using this justification for FDI screening while allowing it in other parts of the economy, and indeed mining sector (see Uren 2012, 81 and 106). When Swan introduced vertical integration as an issue he used the following words:

> In particular, Australian governments–now as in the past–are particularly attentive when the proposed investor in an Australian resource is also the buyer of that resource or linked with the buyer of the resource....
>
> We usually welcome and encourage some participation by the buyer, because that offers the buyer some security of supply and the seller some stability in the market. But we need to ensure that investment is consistent with Australia's aim of ensuring that decisions continue to be driven by commercial considerations and that Australia remains a reliable supplier in the future to all current and potential trading partners...
>
> But it follows that as the proposed participation by a consumer of the resource increases to the point of control over pricing and production, and especially where the resource in question is already developed and forms a major part of the total resource, or where the market disciplines applying to public companies are absent, I will look more carefully at whether the proposal is in Australia's national interest. (Swan 2008d)

Vertical integration was a basis for intervention insofar as it constituted a threat to the functioning of market systems. This occurred when the buyer "increases to the point of control over pricing and production," or when market disciplines applying to the firm are absent.

The second issue relates to the advantage afforded to Chinese SOEs by the state-enabled preferential access to capital and discounted rates. The details of how capital from the Chinese financial system and development banks was made available to the state-owned firms investing in the Australian resource sector have been described in Chapter 4, Sect. 4.1. As a problem for the Australian government, this issue was dealt with by stipulating a preference for "major companies maintain their listing on stock exchanges" (Swan 2009b, speech seven in Chapter 5). The function of this was to enable "business transparency and shareholder discipline" (Swan 2009b). This preference was first articulated by Swan in his speech of 4 July 2008d (speech four in Chapter 5) and was later reiterated by Patrick Colmer's comment that the government preferred "major projects [to] maintain listings because we think the listing disciplines are important in the development of good sound businesses" (Colmer 2009, speech six of Chapter 5). Again, from these articulations we can see that the value of market systems was to enforce discipline on firms. The necessity of maximising profits and then returns on shares prevents firms from accepting short-term losses for the sake of market-manipulating practices as these are not endured by shareholders.

The third guiding principle for interventions was managing the "state-directed agenda" of the Chinese state. The term is from Wilson, and while it is an inference—the government always denied that the FDI policy related to China directly—it is not much of one. Swan and Rudd were not reticent about recognising the Chinese state's Iron and Steel Industry Development Policy and framing it as a problem for Australia. The wording of the original justification of the government's introduction of the February Guidelines included the line: "...investors with links to foreign governments may not operate solely in accordance with normal commercial considerations and may instead pursue broader political or strategic objectives" (Swan 2008a, speech one in Chapter 5). In the speech of 4 July 2008, in the same sentence that Swan defined companies' responsiveness to shareholders as the significant characteristic of market-based systems, he differentiated investment and sales decisions that are driven by market forces from those driven by "strategic or political interests" (2008d, speech four in Chapter 5). He made similar points in his speeches in China on the 10th and 11th of June 2008b, c (speeches two and three in Chapter 5). In Colmer's speech (speech six in Chapter 5) there is a refinement of the point to link the basis for the Australian government's interventions to the actions of a given firm in the market, rather than its ownership: the Australian government did not expect "total independence" on behalf of the investor from the host government, but "[w]hat we are looking for is evidence that it is a true commercial focused investment" (Colmer 2009).

The existence of a Chinese state-directed agenda was framed as a threat (and basis for exception) insofar as it opened the possibility of Chinese firms not functioning as price-takers in their interactions with the Australian economy as consumers of Australian exports. That is: it functioned within the narrative to the extent that it threatened the integrity of the market systems. The place of China as a security threat to Australia in the traditional sense has no meaning in the policy problem. On a similar note, I have explained elsewhere (Chapter 4, Sect. 4.3) why I am not convinced by the "China Inc." thesis, which holds that the fear of allowing excessive Chinese investments into the Australian resource sector was founded on the possibility of a future amalgamation of all these assets into a single controlling entity. Instead, the threat of the Chinese SOE investments should be understood as existing *in the present*. Given the Chinese state's extraordinary financial resources and the dominant position that Chinese steel producers held in the East Asian iron ore market (see Chapter 4, Sect. 4.1), the coordinated nature of the steel producers' investments led the Australian government to imagining them as a class of investor that aimed at recalibrating the structure of the iron ore market. This is different to a single firm using its market power in the way a China Inc. company would do, but it nonetheless relates to the issue of accepting market structures and outcomes as impersonal structures that can function as limits on actions and disciplinary apparatuses. In this sense, the threat existed on two levels: the iron ore market specifically could be undermined by having actors within it that did not operate as price-takers, and the governmental apparatus of market-based systems could be undermined as a foundation for legitimacy if the knowledge about them on which it rested ceased to be true. The investment waves of Chinese SOEs, coordinated by the Chinese state institutions, as well as the boycott actions coordinated by the China Iron and Steel Association (generally ineffective as they were; see Chapter 4, Sect. 4.1) indicated to the Australian government that the Chinese actions threatened the integrity of the Australian and regional market-based systems. In this way, state-directed agendas functioned within the narrative in the same position as access to discounted finance and vertical integration.

The fourth organising metaphor of the policy narrative was regulation on a case-by-case basis. The discussion of this metaphor will be left predominantly to the next chapter as it refers to the positioning of the Australian government in relation to other legal entities, which is discussed in more detail there. In a technical sense, the insistence on using a case-by-case approach to FDI screening provided the government with flexibility in its execution of the policy in much the same way as the central undefined term "national interest" did. It referred to the fact that firms that submitted proposals to the Australian government had no recourse to contest the decisions made, and that the government was not constrained in any way by past decisions forming precedents for the execution of the policy (see Swan 2008d, speech our in Chapter 5). However, there are two further aspects of the metaphor that need comment.

First, Patrick Colmer elaborated on the meaning of case-by-case regulation as implying that when it comes to FDI screening, "…the fundamental issues at the end of the day are much more policy issues than legal issues" (Colmer 2009). That is, it was the job of the executive government to manage this issue, not the Parliament. This relates to the positioning of the government and the need for space to be "creative" (that is, as a creative middle power). I will return to this in a moment. Second, the practice of executing the policy on a case-by-case basis was justified on the basis that it "maximises investment flows" (Swan 2009b, speech seven in Chapter 5). In this speech of 10 December 2009b, Swan contrasted a case-by-case method with "hard and fast rules" that are both predictable and rigid. He then pointed out that this would necessarily mean a number of investments would never be submitted, but which had, in the case-by-case system, been submitted and approved. That is, the case-by-case technique left space for the executive wing of the government to intervene, but it was justified on the grounds of enabling market forces to give as free expression as possible, and thus to maximise investment flows. This flies in the face of economic orthodoxy, as I have already noted, but the significant point is that, once again, the metaphor fits into a coherent narrative of minimising government intervention in economic flows.

The final organising metaphor of Swan's economic policy narrative is "economic sovereignty." In the terms of the narrative described in the last section, economic sovereignty refers to the integrity of the apparatus that is being protected and the right of the Australian government to define it and defend it in ways it sees as legitimate. Economic sovereignty implies the final positioning of the government in the policy narrative: the sole definer and protector of the apparatus of market systems in Australia. When Swan introduced the term, he delineated economic sovereignty from the material aims of the FDI screening policy:

> Let me start with the national interest. I'm not going to attempt a simple definition, but I do want to talk about the key elements–firstly about job and wealth creation, and later on about the vital issues of our economic sovereignty. (Swan 2009b)

Economic sovereignty refers to the symbolic and political good of the government having autonomy over the settings that constituted a governmental apparatus. When the term is added to Rudd's story of "political sovereignty," it takes on a geopolitical significance, on top of the economic and political meanings.

7.2 Decoding Rudd's Geopolitical Narrative

In Chapter 6, where I outlined the security discourses that founded the FDI screening policy, I argued that there were four key organisational metaphors: creative middle-power diplomacy, rules-based orders, responsible stakeholders (sometimes "responsible global citizen"; Rudd 2008f, speech twelve in Chapter 6), and finally "political sovereignty." Overlaying these, there are two themes of the narrative: a historically novel context of structural changes leading to sudden, high-risk events that demand active preventative measures from states, and the breakdown of barriers. In this section, I describe the themes, and then reconstruct the security policy problem narrative using the four organisational metaphors.

The first theme was a dynamic of long-term, slow-building problems requiring foresight and action in the present to manage. This dynamic appeared in relation to four different problems: the Asian Financial Crisis (which was then replaced by the GFC[3]), globalisation, environmental damage, and the perceived end of US regional hegemony in East Asia.

The structural changes or border-crossing challenges, like "questions of energy and food security, and demographic changes in the region" (Rudd 2008g, speech thirteen in Chapter 6) were occasionally substituted into this space in the narrative also. Such changes were structural and did not appear to pose immediate threats that needed responses, but left systems (economic, anthropological—in relation to environmental issues—or geopolitical) open to "sudden" and "unexpected" changes. This applied to China specifically, the rise of which produced a "sudden, dramatic transformation that cannot be understood by linear analysis" (Rudd 2004, 10, speech two in Chapter 6). Rudd consistently contrasted his own agenda with the practices of "muddling through" that characterised the Howard governments' foreign policy stances (Rudd 2004) and Sino–US relations for the fifteen years preceding 2007 (Rudd 2007, 4–5, speech three in Chapter 6). This theme rests on a link between uncertainty and vulnerability to change, which is to say: risk. In Rudd's words "we are participants in an international system in transition" and thus "face unprecedented international uncertainty" (2004, 14). The response required to these sorts of problems was activism in government: not just being prepared for unexpected changes, but taking immediate action to prevent unwanted events from arising.

The second theme was the breakdown of old conceptual barriers. This theme related to the "unprecedented uncertainty" states faced in the world, but had a specificity of its own. The first, and most important barrier that Rudd believed had lost its "clear distinction" was the "great divide" between the foreign and domestic, internal and external, national and international, global and local (2008d, speech nine in Chapter 6). Later, a key selling point for the Asia-Pacific Community initiative was the need to bring "political, security and economic matters within a single framework so that we foster a common sense of regional community" (Rudd 2008g, speech thirteen in Chapter 6). This didn't actually claim that these zones of activity were enmeshed in new ways, but the line was a precursor to claims in later speeches that this breakdown had occurred. On 9 September 2008i (speech sixteen in Chapter 6), Rudd developed the themes of historical novelty and the breakdown of barriers by claiming that long-term national security and strategic weight were driven by "economic security" and that the security policy challenges Australia faced were characterised by "density and interconnectedness." The 2009 Defence White Paper then insisted that globalisation would "ensure that economic interdependence links states and regions together more closely" (Department of Defence, 30, speech eighteen in Chapter 6) and that "changed strategic power relativities" and an "increasingly multipolar" global order, driven by changing patterns of underlying economic power and political influence (Department of Defence, 30). This theme was given its strongest articulations in Rudd's final speeches on foreign policy as prime minister. On the 4th of December 2009b, he claimed that the days in which political, economic, and strategic question that affect the region could be "neatly compartmentalised" were gone (speech twenty-one in Chapter 6). Then, in his final speech on the 27th of May 2010b (speech twenty-three in Chapter 6) he claimed that Australian "systems—all of our infrastructure" crossed international boundaries, and boundaries between the public and private. Later in the speech he attributed the novelty of Australia's security environment and the "rapidity of change" to breakdowns in the boundaries between "foreign and domestic" and "policy and operational."

The meaning of the organisational metaphors are as follows:

The first is the need for an activist foreign policy outlook based on the principles of creative middle power diplomacy. This sprung from the nature of the structural changes that had occurred in the region which I have just outlined, as well as shifts in the deep structure of the region and world. There were, in Rudd's words, "changed strategic power relativities" leading to an increasingly multipolar global order (Rudd 2004, speech two in Chapter 6). In response to this Rudd argued that the "old" way of muddling through in foreign policymaking was no longer viable. Instead, activism was required. Specifically, this activism should conform to the principles of "creative middle power diplomacy," meaning a commitment to multilateralism and an active and creative role in institution-building, and a strong commitment to the rule of law.

In relation to China specifically, Rudd had a clear and transparent agenda, which rested on the second and third organisational metaphors. China needed to be induced to become a "responsible stakeholder" in a new regional order. This required the United States to allow China a greater place to define the rules of the new order. It required China to respect the rules of the order, and cease founding its economic development on flouting the rules of the liberal order that had provided the conditions of its success since opening its borders. This new order would need to be rules-based for all, meaning that rule-violators would need to be punished, despite the absence of a single overwhelming power in the region. In order to bring this about, Australia would first need to act as a traditional middle power diplomat: a non-threatening, respected and responsible member of the international community that could provide technical knowledge needed to found international institutions on which the new order would be based. It would act as a mediator between the two great powers of China and the United States and in doing so protect the fundamental interest of the region as a whole in the foundation of the order in respect for rules by all. Secondly, it would require Australia acting as a middle power in the security sense of the term: a state with the capacity to impose meaningful costs on a great power in conflict, even if not to defeat them (for a discussion of this, see the annotation to speech eleven in Chapter 6). The term was explicitly relocated intact from a security setting to an economic one, or more precisely: an economic setting underpinned by a political and security order (Rudd 2008e, speech eleven in Chapter 6). In enforcing rules of the order on China, Australia's economic girth (the fifth largest in Asia) and defensive capacity (Australia then had the eleventh largest defence budget in the world) (Rudd 2008d, speech nine in Chapter 6) would be significant. More importantly, its legal control over raw resources vital to Chinese comprehensive security provided leverage in this strategic task (Rudd 2008b, speech five in Chapter 6; Rudd in Rudd and Gillard 2008, speech six in Chapter 6; Rudd 2008c, speech seven in Chapter 6; Rudd 2008d, speech nine in Chapter 6; Rudd 2009a, speech nineteen in Chapter 6). At the same time as this stick was wielded, the argument needed to be made to China that a rules-based order would be in its own interests, as it had for the previous three decades (Rudd 2007, speech three in Chapter 6; 2008h, speech fifteen in Chapter 6; 2010a, speech twenty-two in Chapter 6). The new mode of Australian statecraft would need to respect the realities of old boundaries no longer functioning (Rudd 2009b, speech twenty-one in Chapter 6).

Within this narrative, the fourth organisational metaphor, "political sovereignty," was both a new mode of operating as a state and an object to be defended, in the same way state sovereignty has always occupied this double space in fact. It described the new problems of national autonomy in the context of a world in which uncertainty-causing problems crossed state and conceptual borders, which were themselves deteriorating or no longer applied. It referred to the need for creativity in protecting the interests of the nation, including reconceptualising how the government conducts foreign policy: "[f]oreign policy, foreign economic policy and national security policy must increasingly be seen as the natural expression and extension of the nation's domestic policy interests" (Rudd 2008d, speech nine in Chapter 6). From the speech in which the term was used (2010b, speech twenty-three in Chapter 6), political sovereignty as an object that must be protected referred to the "infrastructure" owned by Australia that crosses both the boundaries of private and public ownership, and state boundaries. My contention is that a more accurate term to describe this infrastructure is apparatus, and more precisely the governmental apparatus of the market-based systems that was the centrepiece and securitised object of the economic policy narrative described in Sect. 7.1. Wayne Swan's use of the term economic sovereignty cohered with this understanding of political sovereignty: he used it to refer to the right of the Australian government to exercise autonomy over the settings that constituted the governmental apparatuses of its economy.

7.3 The Meaning of the FDI Screening Policy

This then is the meaning of the Rudd government's FDI screening policy. A set of structural changes in the world created conditions of deep uncertainty that called for activism in government, and a new creative approach to statecraft that understood the breakdown of conceptual barriers. One of these structural changes was the dissembling of the unipolar regional order and a movement to a complex multipolarity within East Asia. This did not imply an end to US military primacy in the region, but a situation where American dominance in different areas was increasingly contested. As it would be inimical to Australia's interests for conflict between the two major powers, the Government aimed to produce conditions for a peaceful transition to a new regional order, an order founded on the respect for the rule of law and underpinned by liberal markets. When the wave of Chinese SOE investments arrived in the Australian resource sector from 2007, this was perceived as a threat to the integrity of the market-based systems Australia was founded on, and also to the capacity of the Australian state to maintain this system. Interventions were made on the basis that they would contribute to the protection of these systems, or apparatuses. It was also seen as an opportunity to impart a cost on the Chinese state for facilitating practices that did not coalesce with the rules of the liberal economic order. This was done to signal to the Chinese state, as well as to other states in the region, most notably the United States, that Australia was willing to use any leverage available to it to creatively assert its right to economic and political sovereignty, and to impose a cost on China for interactions with Australia that were detrimental to this. In the tradition of Australian middle power diplomacy, this was seen as being both in Australia's and the region's interests.

The policy was both defensive and assertive. It spoke to two very large problems of order building. The first was the issue of how the new deep structure of the region would function, given the mismatch of economic, security, and political clout of the major powers, and the lack of institutional and cultural cohesion in the region. In a related way, it spoke to the need for the order to be founded in rules that were respected by all parties, not in military or economic power, and for these rules to cohere closely to liberal economic ones. Secondly, it spoke to the nature of governmentality in a changed environment. In an international context no longer founded on the overwhelming supremacy of a liberal coalition, liberal governance was no longer functional. The FDI policy was thus a form of experimentation in a new mode of governance. The primary aim was to protect the assemblages and apparatuses that make possible liberal governmentality.

Overall there is a coherent policy narrative linking a set of problems with an action that manages those problems, and assigns a set of values and subject positions within it. It resolves the issues of the existing accounts described in Chapter 4. First, it avoids the problems of explaining the FDI screening policy in overly proximate terms. In Chapter 4, I argued that defining the problem posed by Chinese SOE investment as one of vertical integration was problematic. Adding the concept of governmental assemblages as a securitised object, and situating the policy within specific ambitions of the Australian government in the relationship with China resolves these problems. Second, I argued that the existing policies were limited by their faithfulness to a liberal worldview. There is no language in liberal political theory to describe governmental assemblages. By their nature, assemblages do not exist in either the public or private spheres, and do not refer to a relationship between autonomously existing objects like the state and firms. They refer to the arrangement or dispositif of forces that are at once economic, political, and ideological. They constitute the divisions and meanings of terms like private and public, and these divisions are at the same time the content of assemblages. Thirdly, I argued that there was a disconnect between the political, economic, and geopolitical elements of the policy, which resulted in many of the existing accounts of the policy requiring the key policymakers to be irrational or pernicious. In this account, there is a clear set of policy problems to which the FDI screening practices were a coherent solution, according to the logics generated by the actors themselves.

7.4 Conclusion

In this chapter, I have provided my governmental account of the policy. It rests on the use of the analytical devices of governmental apparatuses and assemblages: arrangements or dispositifs of forces that make possible the strategic actions of different actors. Specifically, an apparatus is the technological device that functions to enable the conduct of free subjects' conducts possible; in this case, markets or "market-based systems." The assemblage is the arrangement of forces that makes the apparatus possible and keeps it functioning. I have argued that the logic of the Rudd government's FDI screening policy rested on the protection of a set assemblage that enabled liberal-governmental governance. This was both an end in itself and an activist response to a changed external context to liberal-governmentality as an entire mode of governance. Finally, it was a piece in a larger ambition of inserting Australia and Australian interests into the process of regional order-building in East Asia.

As I have noted in Chapter 2, governmentality was not produced as an explanatory theory on the level of liberalism or Marxism. There is no intrinsic property of governmental apparatuses or assemblages that induces the government to protect them, as the Rudd government did in this case. Indeed, Foucault's over-riding aim in producing the theory was to do away with the need for the state as an analytical object, and with ontology with its own intrinsic logics as a whole. Nonetheless, imagined as a set of precepts on the technologies and modalities of governance in liberal societies, the case of the Rudd government's FDI screening policy conforms remarkably with the claims made by Foucault in his work on governmental states. Even further, the policy appears as a new development in governmental practice, answering the question of how a liberal governmentality can function in a historically novel, non-liberal external context. To evaluate the policy, it must be interpreted in this light. In the next chapter, I turn to the task of evaluation and consider the significance of the policy interpreted as a development or experiment in governmental practice and in Australian statecraft.

Notes

1. The term is taken from the OECD's working group on best practices for SOEs (OECD 2008).
2. Wilson is not using the term governmental in a Foucauldian sense; he is simply referring to the particular controls the Chinese state bodies have over the Chinese financial system. For details of this, see Chapter 4.
3. Specifically, the first speech in which Rudd introduces this new element was given on 21 January 2008a, speech four in Chapter 6.

References

Colmer, P. (2009). *Address from Patrick Colmer to the Australia China Investment Forum*. Delivered 24 September 2009. Speech published online by Stephen Kirchner at *Institutional Economics* After an FOI Application to the Australian Government. Available at http://www.institutional-economics.com/images/uploads/colmer.pdf. Accessed 30 Oct 2016.

Hassan, O. (2013). *Constructing America's Freedom Agenda for the Middle East: Democracy and Domination*. London and New York: Routledge.

Kirchner, S. (2014). *Regulating Foreign Direct Investment in Australia*. Financial Services Institute of Australasia (Finsia). Available at https://www.finsia.com/docs/default-source/industry-reports-foreign-direct-investment/regulating-foreign-direct-investment-in-australia.pdf?sfvrsn=4. Accessed 21 Oct 2016.

Novak, J. (2008). *Australia as a Destination for Foreign Capital*. Australia's Open Investment series paper 1. Institute of Public Affairs. Available at http://www.ipa.org.au/library/publication/1226637929_document_novak_destination_for_foreign_capital.pdf. Accessed 21 Oct 2016.

OECD. (2008). *SOEs Operating Abroad: An Application of the OECD Guidelines on Corporate Governance of State-Owned Enterprises to the Crisis-Border Operations of SOEs*. Organisation for Economic Cooperation and Development. Available at http://www.oecd.org/daf/ca/corporategovernanceofstate-ownedenterprises/44215438.pdf. Accessed 5 Nov 2016.

Raby, G. (2010, September 28). *Australia and China: An Iron Ore Partnership for the Future*. Speech by Ambassador Dr Geoff Raby at 10th China International Steel and Raw Materials Conference. Available at http://china.embassy.gov.au/files/bjng/100927_Ambassador%20Speech%20at%20Iron%20Ore%20Conference_Final.pdf. Accessed 4 Nov 2016.

Rudd, K. (2004, October 1). *The Three Pillars: Our Alliance with the US, Our Membership of the UN, and Comprehensive Engagement with Asia*. Foreign Policy Statement by the Australian Labor Party, Parliament of Australia. Available at http://parlinfo.aph.gov.au/parlInfo/search/display/display.w3p;query=Id%3A%22library%2Fpartypol%2FZMZD6%22. Accessed 4 Nov 2016.

Rudd, K. (2007, April 20). *The Rise of China and the Strategic Implications for U.S.–Australia Relations.* Address to the Brookings Institute, Washington, DC. Available at http://www.brookings.edu/~/media/events/2007/4/20china/20070420china.pdf. Accessed 4 Nov 2016.

Rudd, K. (2008a, January 21). *Building Australia's Economic Future.* Address to the Lord Mayor's Business Breakfast, Perth, Parliament of Australia. Available at http://parlinfo.aph.gov.au/parlInfo/download/media/pressrel/F9HP6/upload_binary/f9hp62.pdf;fileType=application%2Fpdf#search=%22media/pressrel/F9HP6%22. Accessed 4 Nov 2016.

Rudd, K. (2008b, February 18). Interview with Chris Uhlmann. *AM, ABC Radio.* Available at https://pmtranscripts.dpmc.gov.au/release/transcript-15765. Accessed 21 Oct 2016.

Rudd, K. (2008c, February 20). Interview with Jim Middleton. *Newshour, ABC Radio.* Department of the Prime Minister and Cabinet. Canberra. Available at http://pmtranscripts.dpmc.gov.au/release/transcript-15766. Accessed 4 Nov 2016.

Rudd, K. (2008d, March 26). *Advancing Australia's Global and Regional Economic Interests.* Address to the East Asia Forum in Conjunction with the Australian National University. Department of the Prime Minister and Cabinet. Available at https://pmtranscripts.dpmc.gov.au/release/transcript-15823. Accessed 4 Nov 2016.

Rudd, K. (2008e, April 7). *Australia and the UK—Global Partners in Shaping the Future Global Order.* Address to the London School of Economic, London. Department of the Prime Minister and Cabinet. Available at https://pmtranscripts.dpmc.gov.au/release/transcript-15847. Accessed 4 Nov 2016.

Rudd, K. (2008f, April 9). *A Conversation with China's Youth on the Future.* Department of the Prime Minister and Cabinet. Peking University, China. Available at http://pmtranscripts.dpmc.gov.au/release/transcript-15854. Accessed 4 Nov 2016.

Rudd, K. (2008g, June 4). *It's Time to Build an Asia Pacific Community.* Address to the Asia Society AustralAsia Centre, Sydney. Department of the Prime Minister and Cabinet. Available at http://pmtranscripts.dpmc.gov.au/release/transcript-15947. Accessed 4 Nov 2016.

Rudd, K. (2008h, July 31). *Inaugural Tom Burns Memorial Lecture.* Department of the Prime Minister and Cabinet. Don Dunstan Foundation, Brisbane. Available at http://pmtranscripts.dpmc.gov.au/release/transcript-16040. Accessed 4 Nov 2016.

Rudd, K. (2008i, September 9). *Address to the RSL National Congress.* Department of the Prime Minister and Cabinet. Townsville. Available at http://pmtranscripts.dpmc.gov.au/release/transcript-16112. Accessed 4 Nov 2016.

Rudd, K. (2009a, August 20). *Joint Press Conference with New Zealand Prime Minister John Key*. Department of the Prime Minister and Cabinet. Canberra. Available at http://pmtranscripts.dpmc.gov.au/release/transcript-16766. Accessed 4 Nov 2016.

Rudd, K. (2009b, December 4). *Address to the Asia Pacific Community Conference*. Department of the Prime Minister and Cabinet. Sydney. Available at http://pmtranscripts.dpmc.gov.au/release/transcript-16952. Accessed 4 Nov 2016.

Rudd, K. (2010a, April 23). *Australia and China in the World*. The 70th George E. Morrison Lecture, Australian National University, Canberra. Available at https://www.youtube.com/watch?v=EzLvsnWPDm0. Accessed 4 Nov 2016.

Rudd, K. (2010b, May 27). *Prime Minister Speech to the Opening Conference of the National Security College*. Australian National University, Canberra. Department of the Prime Minister and Cabinet. Available at http://pmtranscripts.dpmc.gov.au/release/transcript-17311. Accessed 4 Nov 2016.

Rudd, K., & Gillard, J. (2008, February 18). *Joint Press Conference with Julia Gillard*. Deputy Prime Minister, Hume, ACT. Department of the Prime Minister and Cabinet. Available at http://pmtranscripts.dpmc.gov.au/release/transcript-15764. Accessed 4 Nov 2016.

Swan, W. (2007a, December 5). *Press Conference*. Sydney, Treasury. Available at http://ministers.treasury.gov.au/DisplayDocs.aspx?doc=transcripts/2007/001.htm&pageID=011&min=wms&Year=2007&DocType=2. Accessed 2 Nov 2016.

Swan, W. (2007b, December 7). Interview with Fran Kelly. *Radio National*. Treasury. Available at http://ministers.treasury.gov.au/DisplayDocs.aspx?doc=transcripts/2007/002.htm&pageID=011&min=wms&Year=2007&DocType=2. Accessed 2 Nov 2016.

Swan, W. (2008a, February 17). *Government Improves Transparency of Foreign Investment Screening Process*. Treasury. Available at http://ministers.treasury.gov.au/DisplayDocs.aspx?doc=pressreleases/2008/009.htm&pageID=003&min=wms&Year=&DocType. Accessed 21 Oct 2016.

Swan, W. (2008b, June 10). *A Remarkable Place at a Remarkable Time*. Speech to the China–Australia Chamber of Commerce, Beijing, Treasury. Available at http://ministers.treasury.gov.au/DisplayDocs.aspx?doc=speeches/2008/018.htm&pageID=010&min=wms&Year=2008&DocType=1. Accessed 2 Nov 2016.

Swan, W. (2008c, June 11). *A Modern Relationship with China*. Speech to the Central Party School, Communist Party of China. Treasury. Available at http://ministers.treasury.gov.au/DisplayDocs.aspx?doc=speeches/2008/019.htm&pageID=010&min=wms&Year=2008&DocType=1. Accessed 1 Nov 2016.

Swan, W. (2008d, July 4). *Australia, China, and This Asian Century.* Speech to the Australia–China Business Council, Melbourne, Treasury. Available at http://ministers.treasury.gov.au/DisplayDocs.aspx?doc=speeches/2008/021.htm&pageID=010&min=wms&Year=2008&DocType=1. Accessed 3 Nov 2016.

Swan, W. (2009a, May 26). *Resources and Recovery.* Address to Minerals Week 2009, Hyatt Hotel, Canberra, Treasury. Available at http://ministers.treasury.gov.au/DisplayDocs.aspx?doc=speeches/2009/012.htm&pageID=010&min=wms&Year=2009&DocType=1. Accessed 3 Nov 2016.

Swan, W. (2009b, December 10). *Address to the Global Foundation.* Brisbane, Treasury. Available at http://ministers.treasury.gov.au/DisplayDocs.aspx?doc=speeches/2009/033.htm&pageID=005&min=wms&Year=&DocType=. Accessed 21 Oct 2016.

Swan, W. with Rudd, K. (2008, February 5). *Joint Press Conference with the Prime Minister.* Parliament House, Canberra, Treasury. Available at http://ministers.treasury.gov.au/DisplayDocs.aspx?doc=transcripts/2008/023.htm&pageID=011&min=wms&Year=2008&DocType=2. Accessed 2 Nov 2016.

't Hart, P., & Tindall, K. (Eds). (2009). Understanding Crisis Exploitation: Leadership, Rhetoric and Framing Contests in Response to the Economic Meltdown. In *Framing the Global Economic Downturn: Crisis Rhetoric and the Politics of Recession* (pp. 21–42). Canberra: ANU Press.

Uren, D. (2012). *The Kingdom and the Quarry: China, Australia, Fear and Greed.* Collingwood, VIC: Black Inc.

Wilson, J. D. (2011). Resource Nationalism or Resource Liberalism? Explaining Australia's Approach to Chinese Investment in Its Minerals Sector. *Australian Journal of International Affairs, 65* (3), 283–304.

CHAPTER 8

Evaluating the Policy

In this chapter, I offer evaluations of the policy in a number of directions. First, I turn to the sorts of questions I think a governmental study should answer. Foucault's intention for governmentality was to produce a framework within which to conduct "reflection in… and on the practice of government" rather than to study real governmental practice (Foucault 2008, 2). My use of the approach, following Howarth and Griggs' (2012) steps for a poststructural analysis of an actual policy, has not been enormously faithful to this. Having provided my account of the policy in Chapter 7, however, I now turn to commenting on the what the policy implies about the governmentality of the Australian state, and what sorts of effects the policy had on the state of governmentality in Australia: the mental, organisational and other configurations that constitute different apparatuses or dispositifs in the state and society. I also provide an evaluation of the efficacy of the policy in terms of the degree to which the actions taken resolved the policy problem it was aimed at, and offer some suggestions for future lines of research that spring from my study.

My account of the Rudd government's FDI policy in the last chapter was that it was a response to a moment of order rupturing. This rupture had two aspects: first, East Asia was perceived to be transitioning from a US hegemony to a more complex form of multipolarity in which security, economic, and political orderings between the different states in the region were different from one another; second, China's movement to outward financial or economic force projection represented

© The Author(s) 2019

M. Peters, *Regulating the Rise of China*, Studies in the Political Economy of Public Policy, https://doi.org/10.1007/978-3-030-05466-3_8

a challenge to Australian governmental sovereignty. As a response, the Australian government coopted FDI screening into being a foreign policy tool in a way that had no precedent in the history of the regime and empowered the core executive of the government to use it with as much freedom as possible. Seen in this light, the policy stimulated some fairly profound restructuring of the Australian state, altering the relationships from the core executive to the federal bureaucracy, to the parliament, and to some extent the electorate. In this chapter, I try to use these changes as an entry point to commenting on how the mentality of governance that underpinned the FDI policy conformed and diverged from Foucault's original statements of the governmental state in *Security, Territory, Population* and the neoliberal governmental state that appeared in *Birth of Biopolitics*. I will show that while there are a number of points on which the phenomena I have described in the book conform to Foucault's formulations, there are some interesting departures also. Most notably, in the set-up of the FDI screening regime and the execution of the policy between 2007 and 2010, the Rudd Government eschewed the principle of intervention on the basis of law or formal principles. Instead, the state actors were engendered to use the policy to proactively manage risks. At first glance this appears to fit into Foucault's broad theme in *Birth of Biopolitics* that in the late stage of governmentality the state itself is coopted into taking a position very alike to that of a subject within neoliberal governmentality: to view risks as opportunities and to creatively self-actualise as an entrepreneur of an individual freedom (within highly rigorous limits). In Foucault's words, the neoliberal command to its subjects is to "live dangerously" (2008, 66). However, in the case of the Rudd Government, this imperative to creativity was interpreted as moving beyond the bounds that a neoliberal state is legitimately allowed to. The usual limitations imposed on the state's actions in neoliberal governmentality is imposed by the unknowability of the market which expresses itself in allowing interventions only on the basis of formal principles rather than planning of any sort. Instead the Rudd Government took it upon itself to intervene on economic behaviours according to its own valuations of different (state) interests and on a case-by-case basis. In my opinion, the best way of interpreting this, taking into account both these conformities with what we would expect of a neoliberal governmental state and this key divergence, is that the policy represents an instance of experimentation with liberal governmentality in the face of a new structural condition: the interaction of a liberal state with a large, illiberal other. This is unprecedented situation in the history of liberalism. Seen in this light, the task of evaluating the successes and failures of the Rudd Government's FDI screening policy takes on a much greater significance. China's role in the global economy will only grow in the coming decades, and Australia, along with many other states that are constituted as liberal governmentalities, will need to develop a framework for responding to the challenges associated with this integration over the coming years.

With regard to the efficacy of the policy, my position is that the policy was not successful in immediate terms. The main leverage that the policy was based on—the historically inflated iron ore and coal prices, which were anticipated to last well into the 2020s—proved to be temporary, and the issue of Chinese SOE investments, and their fundamental incompatibility with the liberal structures of governance that exist in Australia, was no less pertinent at the end of the period than the start. In a less proximate way, the policy can also be said not to have succeeded in the sense that it did not engender China to embrace a new role as an active and responsible stakeholder in the region in a way that included respecting liberal markets as the ultimate basis of economic interactions between states. However, we can be more nuanced in the assessment. Considered as a signalling device of the Australian government's concerns regarding and their willingness to regulate these firms to manage these concerns, the policy was a success. Thinking of the policy as a foray into "middle power economics" it seems reasonable to say that the FDI screening functioned to signal to the Chinese State and other countries that the Australian Government valued its "economic sovereignty" highly, that it understood Chinese SOE activity in the Australian economy as a threat to its sovereignty, and that it was willing to invest material and political capital to protect it. That is, in Hugh White's terms, Australia engaged with a superpower and "raise[d] the costs and risks to the other power in respect to that power's interests" (2009).

The question of whether the deepening of China's integration with the Australian economy posed threats to the Australian way of life and sovereignty was dismissed by the academic community at the time. I don't particularly feel the need to comment on whether or not it was, and, as I said in the introduction to the book, don't believe that the approach I have used empowers me to answer this question. However, I do think it is reasonable to take the position that it is a question worth asking. The policy the Australian Government produced was a deeply thought out and measured response to a complex problem, a problem that is just as pertinent today as it was then. The task of imagining new ways to structure the regional and world orders that manage the problems of the interactions of the Chinese economy with the liberal economies remains outstanding. My efforts in this book have been to provide policymakers and academics a language in which to do this.

In Sect. 8.1 of this chapter, I describe the new empowerment of the executive, showing how it was positioned relatively to the federal bureaucracy, the parliament, and the electorate. I present my argument about the empowerment of the executive relative to the federal bureaucracy as an extension of Michael Wesley's (2012) twin theses about the securitisation and presidentialisation of foreign policy that occurred over the 2000s. In Sect. 8.2, I describe the contours of the mentality of governance that were manifested in the FDI screening policy. In the third section, I expand on my evaluation of the efficacy of the policy above. Finally, in the fourth section, I offer some suggestions for further research. I suggest that understanding the "new risks" that played such an important role in the adaptation of the Australian governmentality is a valuable path for research, and that a focus on the internal and external aspects of neoliberal governmentality, which were neglected entirely by Foucault, are a second. I suggest that Jaeger's (2013) examination of the founding ordoliberal thinker, Wilhelm Röpke, is an excellent starting place for considering the international conditions of neoliberal governmentality.

8.1 The Empowerment of the Core Executive

In this section, I summarise the ways the core executive of the Australian government was empowered over the course of the FDI screening policy and situate these dynamics within larger changes that occurred within the constitution of the Australian state apparatuses.

The electorate was positioned in two ways by the policy. On the one hand, the central term "national interest" was defined in the Australian Foreign Investment Policy as an expression of the wishes of the Australian people (FIRB 2007, 68). This was diluted elsewhere in the document, however, in the line stipulating that the Policy merely "recognises community concerns about foreign ownership" (FIRB 2008, 71). There were also a number of elements in the policy that placed the Australian electorate, or "public opinion" in the opposite position: as a barrier to inward foreign investment that the government needed to manage to prevent "harmful effects". This construction occurred first in the *Foreign Takeovers Act 1972*, which tasked the government with "mitigating the harmful effects of domestic opposition to foreign investment," and the "interim arrangements" that were introduced before the legislation was passed that aimed to "assuage "intense public interest" while the legislation was being drawn up and promulgated" (Sadleir 2007, 117; see Chapter 4, Sect. 4.1 for further discussion). In this respect, the FDI screening regime has for decades been "… a mechanism for managing and defusing nationalist and protectionist sentiment in the community" (Kirchner 2014, 15). As I showed in Chapter 5, Sect. 5.3, the Rudd government continued this double positioning of public opinion, and added to it a devaluation of non-state opinions across the board by condemning non-official positions as sectional interests "dressed up as the national interest" (Swan 2009, speech seven, Chapter 5). Overall, the Treasurer gained some agency from representing the Australian people and at the same time from ignoring public opinion. Swan's moral or political basis for intervening (beyond the legal rights afforded to him) was his position as a disinterested adjudicator and possessor of a long-term vision of the national interest.

The executive was also empowered by its position relative to the legislature. I noted in the fifth chapter that there was a strange tendency for the state actors to specify that FDI screening was a matter of "policy" and not "law" (Colmer 2009, speech six in Chapter 5). Generally, this related to the insistence of the government on not treating decisions on investment proposals as precedents, that must be conformed with in the future (Swan 2008, speech four in Chapter 5). That is, it was a tactical move to allow the government greater room to execute the policy as they saw fit. It occurred in conjunction with the flouting of the statutory limits placed on how long the government could take to make a decision on a proposed foreign investment. This was also a tactical move that was made possible by the fact that a prospective investor has nothing to gain from publicly demanding that the Australian government process the matter within the time limit. Thirdly, it should be remembered that the *FATA Amendment Act 2010* was designed very clearly in relation to the second proposed deal between Chinalco and Rio Tinto. As I described in Chapter 3, the amendments ensured that the "complex financial products" that were involved in the deal—a convertible note issue—would fall under the terms of the *FATA 1975*, and the Amendment Act applied one year retrospectively, ensuring that it would apply to the Chinalco-Rio Tinto agreement. The move to produce laws in order to enable specific interventions, I will argue below, moves the mode of intervening firmly away from the neoliberal principle that laws are produced only from first principles, rather than direct "planning."

Finally, the executive was empowered by its positioning relative to the federal bureaucracy. The most obvious point here is that the key regulatory/bureaucratic body, the Foreign Investment Review Board, was hampered by a lack of autonomy, due to the institutional arrangements that I have discussed at length in Chapter 3. This was not a change introduced by the Rudd government. Interestingly though, it seems that the FIRB was also probably under-resourced. Kirchner has pointed out that in 2011–2012 the Foreign Investment and Trade Policy Division of the Treasury, which provides secretarial staff to the Board, incurred expenses of $3.9 million and employed an average staff of thirty-three (2014, 18). In that year, the FIRB considered 11,420 applications for investment approval (Kirchner 2014, 18, information from FIRB Annual Report 2011–2012 [FIRB 2013, 9–10]).

More substantially, the move to make precedents non-binding empowered the executive wing of the government relative to the bureaucracy by undermining the latter's traditional role. This is based on Weber's point about the asymmetry in the types of authority wielded by the government and the bureaucracy: the former has the authority to govern, and the latter providing expertise in the application of laws and the practice of governing (Weber 1978, Chapter 11). The bureaucracy's authority was undermined in the case of FDI screening by the move to make the application of law no longer a valid task. This was exacerbated by the move to intervening on the basis of principles that were not articulated publicly, or only articulated in a coded way, given the FIRB's institutional domination by the Treasurer. Continuing Weber's point for a moment, the expected response from the government to the "threat" of concentration of expertise in the bureaucracy is the fragmenting of the bureaucracy into smaller and smaller units and limiting the concentration of expertise. This is done in the name of "precision" in intervention, which is justified on the grounds that it allows greater openness of the domestic economy. This certainly happened in the case of FDI screening over the last three decades. As outlined in Chapter 3, and documented in much greater detail by Sadleir (2007), the FIRB existed as one of a swathe of bureaucratic regulatory and disciplinary institutions in

Australia, which the government had the capacity to select to suit a particular aim, or to use in conjunction with one another in relation to governing foreign investment. Weber's point about the justification for the breakup of the bureaucracy is repeated exactly in Swan and Raby's claims about the "efficiency" of the case by case approach (speeches seven and eight in Chapter 5).

Beyond this, though, the empowerment of the executive relative to the federal bureaucracy can be situated within broader restructurings of the Australian state that Michael Wesley (2012) has called the "presidentialisation" and "securitisation" of foreign policy. Wesley (2012, 261) argues that Australia's foreign policy machinery was transformed in the first decade of the twenty-first century more than at any time in its history, with a shift from a Department of Foreign Affairs and Trade (DFAT)-centred system in the 1990s moving to a more streamlined system centring on the Department of Prime Minister and Cabinet (PM&C). Due to a gradual slide in resourcing starting in 1996 DFAT was, by 2009, widely recognised as having diminished policy capacity. The 2009 "Blue Ribbon Panel," which Wesley draws on for many of his claims, concluded that the Department's "ability to understand our international environment, to anticipate developments affecting Australia's security and prosperity and to generate appropriate responses to them is degrading" (cited in Wesley 2012, 262). As a result of the report, DFAT received a small funding boost in the 2009–2010 budget, which reversed the trend of the previous fifteen years (Wesley 2012, 262). Causing this "hollowing out" of DFAT, Wesley claims, were forces unleashed by an interaction of the Australian domestic political cycle with "broad shifts in global politics": the overwhelming of foreign policy with a logic of national security; the expansion of the foreign policy community to include a swathe of government agencies and a consequent imperative for coordination; and the slow institutionalisation of a presidential system of foreign-policymaking, centred on the PM&C (2012, 262).

Wesley claims these dynamics began significantly before Rudd's election in late 2007. His story centres on the Howard governments, who were in power through the bursting of the bubble of optimism associated with the New World Order in the 1990s. This entailed first the movement from optimism about the positive secondary effects of global interdependence to pessimism about its problems, and second the rise of security as an issue of electoral importance (2012, 263). From 2001,

Wesley claims, Howard was able to position himself as a strong leader in the area of security, both on the issues of terrorism and asylum seekers, making the 2001 election the first in Australian history that centred on security policy. He was then able to use this platform to gain reelection in 2004. The two changes were facilitated by changes in funding and personnel for different components of the foreign policy and security bureaucracy, and the creation of a number of policy coordination bodies and positions that concentrated decision-making powers in the PM&C and Cabinet. This led to the stagnation of DFAT's budget mentioned above, and very large increases in funding for "frontline" defensive, intelligence, and policing agencies: the budget of the Department of Defence rose 62 cent over the period, Australian Secret Intelligence Service rose 437%, the Office of National Assessments rose 471% and the Australian Security Intelligence Organisation rose 562% (2012, 264). At the same time, Howard restructured the national security system to centre on the National Security Committee of Cabinet (NSCC), chaired by PM and including deputy, treasurer, attorney general, Minister for Defence and Minister for Foreign Affairs, and then other ministers as required.

When Rudd came into office, he pushed these structural changes further. Largely following the suggestions of the Smith Review, the apex of the security community had its capacities for strategic direction, policy planning, coordination, and evaluation enhanced. Waddell (2015, 26), in a similar line to Wesley's, describes the changes in the security community under Rudd as a move towards a whole of government approach, replacing the long-standing Department of Defence-centric approach. The key change, according to Waddell, was the creation of the role of national security advisor within PM&C (formally known as the PM&C Associate Secretary), which augmented the shift of the security community to the PM&C. Waddell's point about the displacement of the Department of Defence is strikingly similar to Wesley's point about the displacement of DFAT. Surprisingly, the sidelining of the relevant cabinet ministers—Joel Fitzgibbon and then Stephen Smith as Defence and Foreign Affairs Ministers—are not mentioned by either Wesley or Waddell, but these have been noted elsewhere (Stuart 2010, for example, provides a comprehensive account of Rudd's domination of the "key" issues of Australia's foreign policy).

There are three points of value in situating my story about the multiple moves that empowered the core executive of government within Wesley and Waddell's stories about the restructurings of the Australian foreign affairs and defence infrastructures. First, it suggests, that we should search for causes for the domination of FDI screening by Wayne Swan and Kevin Rudd beyond tendencies in their personalities. I have argued throughout this book that these explanations are not convincing (see Chapter 4, Sect. 4.3). Accepting my analysis in the previous chapter that FDI screening was conscripted into a new, historically novel position of significance in Australia's foreign policy, it should be analysed in conjunction to the wider changes occurring within the Australian foreign policy infrastructure. My account rests on the claim that foreign investment screening was conscripted into a new position of being a tool for positive foreign policymaking and particularly the engagement with China. Further, I claimed that its use was done on a highly securitised rationale: the need to defend a securitised objects of the integrity of Australian markets, the arrangement of forces that markets and liberal economic governance rest on, and the right of the Australian government to define the forms that appear in this arrangement.

Secondly, using my analysis of the FDI screening policy changes, it is possible to define with a little more accuracy than Wesley the structural changes that the presidentialisation and securitisation of foreign policy were a response to. Wesley (2012, 262–265) describes the changes as the rise of new risks around the turn of the century—insecurities related to globalisation such as drug trafficking, and international organised crime and, most importantly for Australia, terrorism and asylum seekers, as well as precariousness due to reliance on digital infrastructure.[1] Secondly, Wesley attributes the changes to a new place Australia occupied in the region as a "metropolitan power" from the late 1990s. In Rudd's story, described in Chapter 6, like Wesley's, the empowerment of the executive related to changes in the world that required a new mode of state strategy. These changes were the breakdown in the divide between the domestic and international, and the breakdown of the economic, political, and geopolitical arenas (see Chapter 6, Sect. 6.1). Secondly, there were new risks that appeared in the world—environmental risks associated with climate change, risks that were produced by the new ambiguity in the geopolitical structure of the region, and risks that related to globalisation. In response, Australia needed a new "creative" approach to diplomacy that used new tools to pursue foreign policy aims, and a new executive that was able to be flexible enough to draw on a range of policy tools to suit different tasks. Secondly, the executive would need to be "activist"—willing and able to anticipate these new risks and prevent them from arising, and also to innovate with them and transform them into opportunities. Rudd's account provides a clearer link from the structural changes in the world and Australia's position in it to a new mode of governing and structuring the state.

This leads to my third point, which is that the new positioning of the sovereign holds the key to the wider principles of intelligibility that underpinned the Rudd administration's mode of governance, and how they diverged from those of previous Australian governments. Writing on the history of FDI screening to 2003, Christopher Sadleir (2007) argued that successive Australian governments used restructuring the national bureaucracy as an adaptive mechanism to manage globalising pressures while retaining the ability to pursue their own political objectives. He found that the move in Australia was from "…a more administrative, closed and centralised system towards a more political, management-centred, open and decentralised system" in respect to the relations between the political executive and the bureaucracy (2007, 51, quoting Halligan 1997, 5). This, he argued involved a shift of focus or philosophy from administrative process to active managerialism, or away from concepts of due process or hierarchical control. Under the Rudd government, there appears to have been a continuation of these moves towards active managerialism and away from concepts of due process, but unlike the decades leading to 2007, the use of the bureaucracy was not towards empowerment of regulators to intervene on ever-more precise terms, but rather the empowerment of the executive to use the bureaucracy collectively as a diverse and differentiated set of policy tools. In this new state, the sovereign accesses all the resources of the state and uses them wherever possible to position the state and economy strategically in the world. In the next section, I will examine what "mentality of governance" this new positioning of the sovereign implies.

8.2 The Mentality of the Governance

I have argued throughout this book that the objects and language of liberal governmentality describe more accurately the aims and significance of the FDI screening changes. Understanding the object that was being protected as the entire arrangement of forces that made the liberal mode of life and governance in Australia possible, I have argued, allows us to understand the interplay of security and economic concerns of the Australian policymakers in a coherent way. The implication of this is obviously that the mentality of governance that underpins the policy is the liberal one that Foucault described in *Society Must be Defended* and *Security, Territory, Population* as being stable from the mid-to-late-eighteenth century. Certainly in the Rudd Government's FDI screening policy the economy appeared as a site of justice and verification, as well as an apparatus of discipline that produced subjects capable of being governed on the basis of freedom and interaction via exchange. Governance occurred "at a distance" according to logics of what Foucault calls "security" (see Chapter 2 for a detailed explanation of what the term refers to). In addition to these points, it can be seen that the mentality of governance exhibited in the Rudd Government's FDI screening policy also conformed closely to the principles Foucault ascribes to *neoliberal* governmentality in *The Birth of Biopolitics*. In this last set of lectures, the state is positioned as a *subject* of a programme of governance, within the larger project of the governmentalisation of society. The imperatives of the government are determined by the rise of "new" risks and the government feels itself obligated to interpret these risks as opportunities. Foucault's point is that this echoes the overriding command of neoliberalism to subjects within it to "live dangerously" (Foucault 2008, 66), which is now imposed on the state itself, as well as the citizens. As I have shown, Rudd's own narrative of the larger policy problems facing the Australian state in the realm of security contained a large role for new risks, which he described as non-linear and not amenable to analysis according to traditional methods (2004, speech two in Chapter 6). However, in opposition to Foucault's claims, the particular empowerment of the executive wing of government that I have described above rejected the founding imperative of the neoliberal thinkers that the governor can only intervene on the basis of a principle (see Foucault 2008, lecture seven). The significance of the policy in terms of what it implies for the mentality of governance that underpinned therefore requires further examination. To unpick the matter, we must consider the place of sovereignty, the social unity that is the foundation of law, within neoliberal theory.

The place of sovereignty within neoliberal governmentality is actually the central problematic that Foucault structures *The Birth of Biopolitics* around. He actually notes towards the end of *Security, Territory, Population* that the more he talks about security, the less he talks about the sovereign (Foucault 2007, 76). Likewise, he describes the move to the liberal governmental state in the middle of the eighteenth century as "a shift of the centre of gravity away from public law" (Foucault 2008, 39). This shift is not total, however, and the retention of technologies of sovereignty and discipline (the first two in Foucault's triptych of power modalities) remain essential to the practices of normalisation and regularisation that the liberal governmental state rests on (see Chapter 2, Sect. 2.1). This was a point fully appreciated by the ordo- and neoliberal scholars of the 1940s, 50s and 60s that Foucault turns to in *Birth of Biopolitics.* In ordo- and neoliberalism, the internal limitations placed on the state remain the "realities" of the milieu, as they were in the liberal governmental state, but are extended by additional stipulations that the government cannot intervene in the market and cannot form a screen between society and the market. Instead, it must intervene in *society* to produce and allow a general regulation of society by the market.

At first glance, this implies that the neoliberals understood law as *following* from economic reality, the rule being derived from the norm. Foucault shows in *Birth of Biopolitics* that this was not the case. The neoliberals understood law, and the unity that was implied in a system of sovereignty, as a precondition of the market. For Rougier, whose work Foucault draws on primarily for this material, economic life necessarily takes place within a juridical framework. No aspect of this framework is given in nature, as the laws of economic equilibrium are. Instead it is contingent on creations of legislation. This means that instead of distinguishing between an economic belonging to the infrastructure and a juridical-political belonging to the superstructure, we should really be speaking of an economic-juridical order. The fact that the juridical order is not thought of as emanating from the economy implies that it must be situated in history:

> … the economic must be considered as a set of regulated activities with rules of completely different levels, forms, origins, dates, and chronologies; rules which may comprise social habitus, a religious prescription, an ethics, a corporative regulation, and also a law. In any case, the economic is not a mechanical or natural process that one can separate out, except by abstraction a posteriori, by means of formalising abstraction. (Foucault 2008, 163)

The point Foucault is making here is remarkable in itself—that the starting place of the neoliberals is very close to that of Max Weber in the need for cultural and ethical preconditions of capitalism, as well as law.

The significance for me, though, is that the place of law within economic governance is the key to articulating neoliberal governmentality, as it founds the aim and limitation of action by the governor. The resolution that the neoliberals find to these discoveries is that the aim of governance must be the production of an "economic constitution." The optimal economic constitution will define the economic-institutional ensemble that can account for both the singularity of capitalism and the impasses, contradictions, difficulties, and mixtures of rationalism and irrationalism that appear in it. The injunction on the governor that derives from this is to only intervene according to the "Rule of Law," what the German ordoliberals called "*Rechstat.*" Both terms refer to the claim that the actions of public authorities will have no value if they are not framed in laws that limit them in advance, that the state may only make legal interventions in the economic order if these interventions "take the form solely of the introduction of formal principles" (Foucault 2008, 171). For Hayek, the Rule of Law simply means the opposite of a plan, which is a policy with an aim and an economic end (1944, see Chapter 6).

How then should we interpret the moves of the Rudd government in terms of its underlying mentality of governance? In Sect. 8.1 and in my analysis of the policy in the earlier chapters I argued that the executive was empowered in seven ways: the centrality of the undefined and ambiguous term "national interest" (which was, in any case, inherited by the Rudd Government); the double positioning of "public interest"; ignoring the statutory time limits the *FATA 1975* imposed on the government to reject or impose conditions on a foreign investment proposal; the use of "secret" policy guidelines in the Colmer Doctrine; the refusal to treat past decisions as precedents that the government was obligated to respect; the insistence that FDI screening was a matter of "policy" and not "law"; and the production of legislation to enable the government to intervene retrospectively on investment proposals. My point is not that the Rudd government aimed to employ an economic Hayekian "plan" in relation to the resource sector; the insistence that this is not possible and would not be in anyone's long-term interests—including the Chinese steel-producers or the economic security of the Chinese state—was the basis the of the government's argument for market-based structures throughout the policy. Nonetheless, the invocation that the government must only intervene by introducing formal principles was not respected. Interventions were made on the basis of logics produced by the core of the administration, and these were not open to verification by any realm beyond the administration.

There are two ways to interpret the Rudd government's rejection of law in this way. We can conclude that the policy was not founded on economic logics, but strategic, geopolitical ones. That is, international security[2] concerns take precedence to economic ones, and the exceptional elements to a neoliberal governmentality that appeared in the FDI screening regime can be explained by the exceptional strategic significance of the policy. In short, it is not possible to use the policy to examine the mentality of economic governance that prevailed by looking at what was, in the final conclusion, a strategic much more than an economic policy. This is not satisfying to me. First, it is not really a solution. The same questions that I have been asking here would still apply; namely: what is the mentality of governance that applies in this international security setting? Within this understanding, we would need to specify the relation of this international security governmentality to an economic governmentality. More substantially, to reproduce the divide between economy and security is a false move for two reasons. First, one of the main logics that I argued the policy rested on was a breakdown of barriers, including between the realms of economics and international security. This logic was produced by Rudd and described in detail in Chapter 6. Secondly, I don't think that the distinction of governmentalities between these realms is viable within Foucault's framework. In the next section, I will examine the problem of the absent external dimension of Foucault's neoliberal governmentality. For now it is sufficient to note that positing two heterogeneous governmentalities for different realms of statecraft is inconsistent with the rest of the framework. A governmentality produces the divisions in a social body which allow government to happen. Therefore the governmentality crosses, or rather underpins, different realms within the social at the same time, and must do so with a single set of principles that make the whole intelligible. Otherwise the analytical device has no value.

The second solution is to produce a statement of the governmentality that incorporates the economic and security logics of the policy. My answer to this, mirroring my explanation of the policy in Chapter 7, is that we must situate the empowerment of the executive within Rudd's broader narratives about the structural changes in the world, and the resulting need for activism and creativity in government. An important component of these narratives was a need for a mode of governing that respected the new reality of political, economic, and geopolitical boundaries and of the divide between the domestic and the international no longer applying. In this light, the empowerment of the core executive in this policy is not a product of a number of small innovations, but itself the large innovation that the Rudd government used to manage the new conditions. In response to the new conditions, we can see the production of a new actor and a new principle of intelligibility in the Australian mentality of governance. The actor is the technocratic sovereign, an executive that is freed from constraints previously imposed by the electorate, the bureaucracy, and law. He is flexible and creative in the use of many different types of state resources. His aim is to position the state and economy in the globe strategically. The bureaucracy is designed not just to allow ever more detailed interventions into the different milieus of circulation that appear in the population, as has been the trend in Australia for the last three decades, but also to enable the core executive to use multiple tools to position the nation and economy within multiple games—economic and geopolitical primarily—strategically. The new principles of intelligibility in this, I think, are risk and opportunity. These risks are "non-linear" and "not amenable to analysis by traditional methods," and it seems reasonable to say that the empowerment of the executive and the new central motif of risk are related: there is no oversight of a governor of risks as there cannot be. Risks abound. By their nature, risks are defined by perception.

Due to the centrality of risk and opportunity, this development can be understood as being within neoliberal governmentality. The ethos of the competition society is to "live dangerously." Taking Foucault's (2008) understanding of neoliberal governmentality as the turning of the earlier governmental project back on to the state itself, the development that the state is now enjoined by conditions of risk to turn these into opportunities seems entirely fitting with this neoliberal command. The state is positioned in relation to risks that must be understood as opportunities, as a neoliberal subject that relates to other subjects on a logic primarily of competition rather than a liberal subject that does so on the basis of exchange, and an innovating, entrepreneurial subject. The addition that I make to Foucault's statement is that due to the discursive construction of risks, the limitations imposed on the sovereign by the neoliberals is no longer functional and there is an internal contradiction.

8.3 The Efficacy of the Policy

How effective was the policy? My position is that the policy functioned as a signalling device. This may seem odd given how much time I have spent showing how misunderstood it was, however my entire account has rested on taking at face value the statements made by the policymakers themselves. In essence, I have merely restated the policy's aims using the language of governmentality, using the policymakers own words as evidence for my claims. Seen as a signalling device, the purpose of the policy was to bring to the attention of a host of actors the Australian government's concerns with the trajectory of the regional order, and to stipulate that Australia would not accept this trajectory without resistance. As a middle power, Australia did not have the capacity to impose its preferred conditions on to the order—interactions between economic actors across state borders being made in reference only via liberal markets and on the basis of profit-seeking—but it did have the resources to attempt to "shape how the international system works to protect its interests… even in the face of competing objectives of a major power" (White 2009).

The FDI policy should be seen in conjunction with the other regional order-building initiatives of the Rudd Government: the dispatching of Richard Woolcott to other states to canvass support for a new regional organisation, the Asia-Pacific Society, and the use of high-level speeches by Kevin Rudd and Wayne Swan to convince the Chinese ruling class—both in power and of the future—that China's interests lay in promotion of an order based on openness and respect for markets. These initiatives were also ineffective, but order-building is not a task that is completed in three years. It is the work of decades. If the Rudd Government is to be castigated for failure in these ambitions, this failure should also be attributed to the Australian Governments that followed Rudd's, as well as the other states whose consent and cooperation would also be required, among them the United States, the other middle powers of the Asia-Pacific region, and arguably China itself. The policy could easily be read as an exercise in agenda-setting, an attempt to define the terms for a grand bargain between China and the United States, or at least to instil upon policymakers in both states the need to proactively pursue one, and for this bargain to centre on the types of problems that the Rudd Government deemed to be most pertinent. Perhaps it is an unsatisfyingly open position to take, but I would say that if the ideas and claims of the Rudd Government's ambition for proactive management of the changes occurring in the international system were taken up anywhere—either in discussions between China and the United States (presumably following the end of the Trump Presidency) or by some consortium of middle powers in the Asia-Pacific or world—then the FDI policy would be a success. To my knowledge, they have not, so the policy is currently a failure.

8.4 Suggested Paths for Future Research

There are two clear lines of research that fall out of the reflections on the state of Australian governmentality in the second section. Firstly, the place of new risks in this form of governmentality, as the principle by which the executive is positioned and empowered, is significant. It does not really seem possible to make any more general principles about the nature of these risks beyond the comments Rudd made on them: that they traverse traditional boundaries, are not amenable to traditional analysis, and do not develop in a linear fashion (see Chapter 6). These claims seem to cohere broadly with some points about the nature of new risks that appear in Beck's (1999) risk society framework and Giddens' (1994) high modernity one, but developing these to be used in the geopolitical context as the FDI policy was goes beyond the scope of this work. Risk is not a new motif in the governmental literature: several of the first wave of governmentalists within the Anglosphere were very interested in it as a technology of governance. I am thinking primarily of Peter Miller and Nikolas Rose's 1990 paper, the chapter on risk in Mitchell Dean's seminal *Governmentality* (1999), and also the work of Pat O'Malley (2008), Aradau and Van Münster (2008), and Aradau et al. (2008). It was also one of the main early concerns of François Ewald, one of Foucault's closest colleagues (Ewald 1991). However, the rise of risk in the discourses produced by politicians, such as by Kevin Rudd here, allows a new opportunity to define the function of risk technologies in the changing governmentalities that we see in the liberal states.

Secondly, the policy can be used to develop some existing lines on the external conditions of neoliberal governmentality. This is an extension of an argument made by Hans Martin Jaeger. Jaeger (2013) points out that Foucault's statement of neoliberal governmentality was "missing" an international dimension. This is a surprising omission, given that the international elements of the earlier police and liberal governmentalities were given serious consideration in *Society Must Be Defended* and *Security, Territory, Population*. More importantly, as Jaeger argues, in these cases the international elements were central shaping factors in the development of those governmentalities in Foucault's accounts. The limitations imposed on states and statecraft from the balance of power and the globalisation of markets shaped the development of the principles of *raison d'État* and *laissez faire* as much as the internal conditions of the discourse of public right (individual sovereignty) and the truth of the market. This does not mean that the internal composition of the state can be determined by its external context. This would mean a return to some form of structural realism, which was obviously not Foucault's intent (see Foucault 2008, 68 for a direct refusal of it). Instead, the police and liberal governmentalities were "promiscuous" in relation to external contexts. Liberalism, for example, was possible within a Europe structured by the Congress of Vienna, in a Napoleonic empire project, and within the British project of globalising the European economy. In all these cases, the internal and external aspects of each particular form of governmentality are coextensive (see Foucault 2008, 51–60; Jaeger 2013, 34). Jaeger claims that the international is likely to play just as constitutive a role in neoliberal governmentality as it had for its predecessors, and that it appears to be equally promiscuous with respect to international contexts.

Jaeger's arguments are sound as far as they go, but he does not give much of an indication of what constitutive role the external might actually play in neoliberal governmentalities, either generally or in any specific cases. This is a question raised directly by the Australian FDI policy: what external conditions are neoliberal governmentality *not* compatible with? And if these conditions cannot be removed, how can we expect the entire governmentality to adapt to the new conditions? These are not a question considered by Foucault either, I might add, in relation to any of the governmentalities he examined. As I have noted, it is clear that Foucault believed there was a necessary complementarity between the domestic and international sides of a governmentality, but never considered what might occur when this complementarity ceased to exist. The reason for this is obvious: in each case—the development of the police state, the liberal state, and then the neoliberal one—Foucault examined the mentalities of states that dominated the world geopolitically and who were able to impose what might be called epistemological hegemonies on to the world. I use the word epistemologically here in the sense of a dispositif: these states had the capacity to arrange forces such that the knowledge on which each governmentality rested was true in an effective sense. By hegemony I of course don't mean that these realities were universally expressed. The parts of the world in which they were not expressed were not economically and politically powerful enough to pose a threat to the integrity of the governmentalities in question. For example, in the cases of the liberal governmentalities of France and Britain in the eighteenth and nineteenth centuries that Foucault analyses, the colonial states obviously did not respect the same state limitations or knowledge on which liberal governmentality rested, but these transgressions did not undermine the governmental arrangements in the colonial states themselves. Australia's engagement with China in the twenty-first century does not follow this format. Australia is the vastly junior partner in all ways in this relationship, and has no capacity to enforce the juridical-political conditions that make liberal market knowledge meaningful.

Despite Jaeger not considering this sort of situation, he provides a good starting point for thinking about it in the work of the neoliberal Wilhem Röpke. Röpke was an ordoliberal scholar who, almost uniquely amongst the ordo- and neoliberals, considered International Relations. (The lack of interest in international relations amongst the original German and American schools of ordo- and neoliberalism that Foucault drew on in *Birth of Biopolitics* is, I think, a second cause for Foucault's statement of neoliberal governmentality being so lacking in this department in the first place.) In keeping with the points I made in the second section on the ordo- and neoliberal treatment of law, Röpke started with the premise that it is not possible to say that the economic realm can determine the common international. This is because the economic requires a set of extra-economic social conditions to underpin it. The extra-economic social conditions according to Röpke, could be grouped into two types of social integration elements that made possible economic integration. The first is "a reliable legal order along with a generally recognised code of norms and values, which create an atmosphere of trust, security, and continuity that allows entrepreneurship to flourish" (Jaeger 2013, 40). The second is "a stable currency providing a general medium of exchange and material underpinning of economic intercourse" (Jaeger 2013, 40). The outcome of these reflections is that the economy cannot be the foundation of an international order. Successful orders must necessarily be built from the "bottom up," starting with these elements of social integration, and cannot be imposed "downwards" by either "international juridicism" or optimistic, rationalist "economism". This leads to a restatement of my point above on the relationship between epistemological hegemony and geopolitical power:

> If we want to be realistic we must recognise that every workable international order seems to require the guiding and controlling hand of a *dominant power* which, by its political force, economic weight, diplomatic experience and firmness of principles, is able to set the tone, give the example, and to assume responsibilities of the first order.[3] (Röpke 1954, 223 quoted in Jaeger 2013, 42, emphasis in Röpke's original work)

This solution here is not practically useful to the situation of Australia's response to increased economic integration with China—Jaeger actually uses the quote to criticise Röpke's position here as amounting to a defence of empire. My point, however, is that the problems being examined by Röpke in the conditions and failures of the international order are relevant to the Australian problem. Röpke provides a framework to begin thinking about the problem that was raised by Kevin Rudd and Wayne Swan, but not taken up by the academic community. As an academic community, we have remarkably little in the way of a toolbox or framework to assess the claim that increased Chinese integration into an advanced, liberal economy was itself a threat. In this book, I have suggested that the language and tools of governmentality are valuable for this. The concept of the apparatus, and the treatment of objects like the market as neither of the state or outside of it opens up a set of questions that centre on how ideology, knowledge, and rationality combine with the arrangement and interplay of forces to produce entire dispositifs and governmentalities. That is, the framework does not assume relations between these elements and is well-placed to study alternative arrangements and then the interaction of these. Here, I am suggesting that the work of the neoliberals offers similar benefits. The neoliberals were interested in the breakdown of the international monetary order in the interwar years, and the need to found a new one. Their foundational problematic of showing how an economic system is necessarily founded in a politico-ethico-cultural one, and may thus be constituted differently on some other politico-ethico-cultural order places the school much closer to the governmentalists than has been acknowledged.

The final point, I will make is that Jaeger is correct to note that the relationship between the internal and external aspects of governmentality is a valuable opening for an engagement between the governmentalists and more orthodox international relations scholars. This is predicated on two points. First, Jaeger notes that Foucault's "governmentality transcends the supposed divide of domestic and international politics, while not entirely erasing their specificity" (2013, 48). The international retains an "ontological specificity and irreducibility" (2013, 27), and Jaeger suggests that this offers a path to easier conversation between the two camps. At the same time, his point on governmental promiscuity insists on the poststructural rejection of ahistoricism as a condition for this engagement. I agree with both of these points and do not see how one could retain a governmental approach—and the benefits that fall from it—and concede either position.

8.5 Conclusion

The primary purpose of this chapter has been to open some lines of discussion on the mentality of governance that appeared in the Rudd government's FDI policy. In Sect. 8.1, I suggested that the FDI policy conformed to the broader trends that Wesley has called the presidentialisation and securitisation of foreign policy. I suggested that the press-ganging of FDI screening into the service of foreign policy and security agendas—it had never been used in this way in Australian history—extended the dynamics Wesley identified even further. By making a much broader range of government actions a part of the foreign policy toolbox a whole new swathe of government apparatuses were subject to the same processes of securitisation and presidentialisation. In Sect. 8.2, I argued that the new positioning of the executive and principle of risk as a guide for state action indicate that the mentality of governance that can be retroduced from the policy should be imagined as within a broad school of neoliberal governmentality, but with the development that the mode of government intervention is not limited to rule of law interventions. The Rudd Government's FDI policy adds weight to the idea that risk is a (arguably *the*) central technology for the modern governmental state, which is a finding which will not surprise the governmentalists of the last ten years. Finally, I suggested that there is a need to consider the external elements of neoliberal governmentality, as per Jaeger's (2013) suggestion. This is a valid aim in itself and will help augment the utility of governmental theory generally. More pertinently though, my argument speaks to the need to develop tools to answer the most important question raised by the FDI policy, which is whether the liberal way of life and governance are threatened by the rise of China, and what options are available to the Western states to adapt to the new conditions.

Notes

1. A literature born of the new place of risk in geopolitics has appeared in the last ten years. It start with a similar claim that the appearance of new risks and a shift to risk management in the operating modes of states and international organisations have lead to restructurings of states domestically as well as their modes of acting in the international. For a review see Clapton (2011).
2. I am using the term security in its orthodox International Relations sense here, not as one of Foucault's modalities of power. I will use the term "international security" to refer to the International Relations meaning to avoid confusion.
3. The first order is the extra-economic cultural and legal conditions of social integration.

References

Aradau, C., Lobo-Guerrero, L., & Van Münster, R. (2008). Security, Technologies of Risk, and the Political: Guest Editiors' Introduction. *Security Dialogue, 39*(2–3), 155–176.

Aradau, C., & Van Münster, R. (2008). Governing Terrorism Through Risk: Taking Precautions: (Un)Knowing the Future. *European Journal of International Relations, 13*(1), 89–115.

Beck, U. (1999). *World Risk Society*. Cambridge: Polity Press.

Clapton, W. (2011). Risk in International Relations. *International Relations, 25*(3), 280–295.

Colmer, P. (2009). *Address from Patrick Colmer to the Australia China Investment Forum*. Delivered 24 September 2009. Speech published online by Stephen Kirchner at *Institutional Economics* After an FOI Application to the Australian Government. Available at http://www.institutional-economics.com/images/uploads/colmer.pdf. Accessed 30 Oct 2016.

Dean, M. (1999). *Governmentality: Power and Rule in Modern Society*. London: Sage.

Ewald, F. (1991). Insurance and Risk. In G. Burchell, C. Gordon, & P. Miller (Eds.), *The Foucault Effect: Studies in Governmentality* (pp. 197–210). Chicago: University of Chicago Press.

FIRB. (2007). *Annual Report 2005–2006*. Australian Government, Foreign Investment Review Board. Available at http://firb.gov.au/about/publication/annual-report-2005-2006/. Accessed 28 Oct 2016.

FIRB. (2008). *Annual Report 2006–2007*. Australian Government, Foreign Investment Review Board. Available at http://firb.gov.au/about/publication/annual-report-2006-2007/. Accessed 29 Oct 2016.

FIRB. (2013). *Annual Report 2011–2012.* Australian Government, Foreign Investment Review Board. Available at http://firb.gov.au/about/publication/annual-report-2011-2012/. Accessed 5 Nov 2016.

Foucault, M. (2007). *Security, Territory, Population: Lectures at the Collège de France, 1977–78* (M. Senellart, Ed., & G. Burchell, Trans.). New York: Palgrave Macmillan.

Foucault, M. (2008). *The Birth of Biopolitics: Lectures at the Collège de France, 1978–79* (M. Senellart, Ed., & G. Burchell, Trans.). New York: Palgrave Macmillan.

Giddens, A. (1994). Living in a Post-traditional Society. In U. Beck, A. Giddens, & S. Lash (Eds.), *Reflexive Modernisation: Politics, Tradition and Aesthetics in the Modern Social Order* (pp. 56–109). Stanford, CA: Stanford University Press.

Halligan, J. (1997, April 5–8). *The Australian Civil Service System.* Paper presented at Civil Service Systems in Comparative Perspective, School of Public and Environmental Affairs, Indiana University.

Hayek, F. A. (1944). *The Road to Serfdom.* Chicago: University of Chicago Press.

Howarth, D., & Griggs, S. (2012). Poststructural Policy Analysis; Discourse, Hegemony, and Critical Explanation. In F. Fischer & H. Gottweis (Eds.), *The Argumentative Turn Revisited* (pp. 305–342). Durham, USA: Duke University Press.

Jaeger, H.-M. (2013). Governmentality's (Missing) International Dimension and the Promiscuity of German Neoliberalism. *Journal of International Relations and Development, 16*(1), 25–54.

Kirchner, S. (2014). *Regulating Foreign Direct Investment in Australia.* Financial Services Institute of Australasia (Finsia). Available at https://www.finsia.com/docs/default-source/industry-reports-foreign-direct-investment/regulating-foreign-direct-investment-in-australia.pdf?sfvrsn=4. Accessed 21 Oct 2016.

O'Malley, P. (2008). Governmentality and Risk. In J. O. Zinn (Ed.), *Social Theories of Risk and Uncertainty: An Introduction* (pp. 52–75). Oxford, UK: Blackwell.

Röpke, W. (1954). Economic Order and International Law. *Recueil des Cours de lAcadémie de Droit International, 86*(2), 207–271.

Rudd, K. (2004, October 1). *The Three Pillars: Our Alliance with the US, Our Membership of the UN, and Comprehensive Engagement with Asia.* Foreign Policy Statement by the Australian Labor Party, Parliament of Australia. Available at http://parlinfo.aph.gov.au/parlInfo/search/display/display.w3p;query=Id%3A%22library%2Fpartypol%2FZMZD6%22. Accessed 4 Nov 2016.

Sadleir, C. (2007). *On the Frontier: Australia's Policy Approach to Foreign Direct Investment 1968–2004 as a Case Study in Globalisation, National Public Policy and Public Administration.* Ph.D. thesis, submitted to the University of Canberra.

Stuart, N. (2010). *Rudd's Way: November 2007–June 2010.* Melbourne: Scribe.

Swan, W. (2008, July 4). *Australia, China, and This Asian Century*. Speech to the Australia–China Business Council, Melbourne, Treasury. Available at http://ministers.treasury.gov.au/DisplayDocs.aspx?doc=speeches/2008/021.htm&pageID=010&min=wms&Year=2008&DocType=1. Accessed 3 Nov 2016.

Swan, W. (2009, December 10). *Address to the Global Foundation*. Brisbane, Treasury. Available at http://ministers.treasury.gov.au/DisplayDocs.aspx?doc=speeches/2009/033.htm&pageID=005&min=wms&Year=&DocType=. Accessed 21 Oct 2016.

Waddell, A. P. (2015). Cooperation and Integration Among Australia's National Security Community. *Studies in Intelligence, 59*(3), 25–34.

Weber, M. (1978 [1921–1922]). *Economy and Society: An Outline of Interpretive Sociology* (G. Roth & C. Wittich, Eds.). Berkeley: University of California Press.

Wesley, M. (2012). Australia's Foreign Policy Machinery. In J. Cotton & J. Ravenhill (Eds.), *Middle Power Dreaming: Australia in World Affair: 2006–2010* (pp. 261–272). Melbourne: Oxford University Press.

White, H. (2009, May 21). *The Defence White Paper*. Blake Dawson Lecture Series. Speech at the Australian National University. Available at https://www.youtube.com/watch?v=2U6sN5taOpc. Accessed 3 Nov 2016.

CHAPTER 9

Conclusion

The Australian Government in early 2008 found itself, in the words of Treasurer Wayne Swan, in a remarkable place at a remarkable time (Swan 2008). The changes occurring in the region and global financial orders went beyond the transition from hegemony to multipolarity. They pertained also to the nature of the world itself, the categories and divisions in it. There was a very particular reason for this. This moment—China's move to large-scale outward foreign investment into an advanced liberal economy in the core of the global economy—was a key structural turning point for the world. The interaction of the liberal system with an illiberal other is of course not new. Capital has flowed for centuries between a more or less liberal core and a periphery composed of economies constituted in many different ways, from slave-worked plantation colonies, to complex colonial states, to various empires and kingdoms. However, up until this point, when capital moved from the periphery to core it respected the structures—ideational, organisational, and so on—of the liberal order, or was of a size so insignificant as to not threaten the integrity of markets and so their governability. China was, by the time of the Australian investments, of such size and importance that the incongruities of the two systems could not be ignored. But neither did the Australian Government have the legal power or other leverage to ban or dissuade the Chinese investment vehicles from entering and operating in the Australian economy. Nor would it have in Australia's material interest to do so.

© The Author(s) 2019

M. Peters, *Regulating the Rise of China*, Studies in the Political Economy of Public Policy, https://doi.org/10.1007/978-3-030-05466-3_9

In light of the awkwardness of the situation faced, the Government selected an economic regulatory tool over which it had a very large degree of control in FDI screening via the opaque, quasi-independent Foreign Investment Review Board. The immediate aim of the policy was to defend the integrity of the market structures in the Australian mining sector and to assert the right to define the structures on which Australian society rested. Seen in this light, the integrity of market structures in Australia became synonymous with the "economic" or "political" sovereignty of the Australian state. While the emphasis on markets was justified on the basis that they produced long-term stability and economic development, ultimately the policy can only be rendered coherent when the more fundamental aim of retaining governability is acknowledged.

My initial attraction to governmentality as an approach for this study sprang from its starting points of refusing to accept liberal ideas as given, true, or neutral. I did not begin the project as a governmentalist or Foucauldian, but rather adopted the approach as it fulfilled the needs of the study. I have noted that it is both undeveloped in crucial areas and add to that here that it is also possibly fatally difficult to reconcile with first-order claims regarding, say, economic structures or real interests. In spite of both points, however, I believe the approach has enormous value, both in general and at this precise moment in history. The general value has been stated in the previous chapters and I won't go into it again, but the particular value stems from the sorts of problem the policymakers were trying to fix. As I have shown throughout the book, there are remarkable resonances between Kevin Rudd and Wayne Swan's ideas and governmental claims. But actually, I don't think that it is so surprising that in the historical moment that the policy was formulated in—a key turning point in the development of the liberal financial system, a system-disrupting event—that an approach that counts among its strengths a strong interest in the constitution of social orders and in the processes by which seemingly 'natural' social formations are necessarily defended, perpetuated, or adjusted would perform better than approaches that take these social formations as ontic.

In addition to explaining the phenomena more convincingly, I also believe that the approaches that pay particular emphasis to constitutive processes and which connect, inextricably, the tasks of explanation with critique are better placed than the approaches that are more explanation-centric to perform a vital task of social science: imagining states of the world that do not yet exist. Part of the challenge faced by the

Rudd Government was operating in an environment that the key actors understood as changing rapidly and not being understandable using old ideas. In this, they were largely successful, despite struggling at times to convey certain ideas about the breakdown of formations of the liberal world using liberal language. A second challenge, however, was imagining a new order for the region. This, I have argued was the highest level geopolitical aim of the policy: to use Australian resources and the principles of creative middle power diplomacy to found a new regional order In this order, China's right to pursue its own unique economic system would be respected, and China would take its place as a stakeholder, both shaping the order and upholding it. At the same time, the core tenets of liberalism would remain, and the ability of the liberal powers to define *their* own economic system would also be respected, and the ability of the liberal states to govern their economic systems would be maintained. In this task, the Rudd Government was less successful. I suggest that this failure is shared by many actors, among them the scholarly community.

In the last chapter, I argued that a simplistic evaluation of this policy was difficult. Usually an evaluation would focus on the degree to which a policy brought about a desired state in the world, and the degree to which the desired state in the world was a good one. The state of the world sought in this case was a vague one: one where the United States and China took seriously the task of actively building a new order in the Asia-Pacific region, instead of muddling through, and hopefully one that accepted some of the key ideas and terms that appeared in the Australian actors' rhetoric—"responsible stakeholders," "rules-based order", and so on. I concluded that as there is little evidence that this has occurred, the policy can be called a failure. However, as tasks like order-building are pursued over decades, I pointed out, if either the US or Chinese administrations did take up this task and the particular construction of it produced by the Rudd Government, the policy would then retroactively become successful.

To this position, I will now add that the claim that the policy failed does not carry with it the implication that the Australian policymakers should have acted differently. It is not enormously useful to describe an attempt at a very ambitious task where one succeeds only partially as a failure. Further, this does not imply that the effort is not worthwhile. I think that the statements of the policy problem that appear in Chapters 5, 6, and 7 are astute and show deep understandings both of the disruptive potential of outward Chinese foreign investment and its connection to the changes we were then and still are experiencing in the region and world. Further I do not have a course of action that I believe would have been more effective, even with the benefit of hindsight. If we are to place blame on the Rudd Government for making insufficient progress on founding a new regional order that managed these issues, this blame must obviously be shared by the American and Chinese administrations that were in power or are so now, and with the other middle powers of the region.

Finally, I think blame must be accepted by the academic community for the paucity of imagination in this area. The Rudd Government's scope of ambition matched the size of the challenge faced and is to be commended. I do not believe that they ever articulated a vision of this new order which actually fulfilled the requirements listed a few paragraphs ago. The "rules-based order" that the Rudd Government envisioned seems to me to be inadequately differentiated from simply the liberal order that we have enjoyed in the region for the last seventy years, but with China as a proponent of it. This does not square the circle. However, having been tasked with such enormous challenges, both intellectual and political, I think the Australian policymakers might well be justified in asking why the scholarly community were not active in producing a debate or set of alternative visions of this new order that might have formed the basis on which the policymakers pursued their task.

It is not difficult to imagine such a debate from occurring. The liberal states and the international organisations of the financial regime are clearly ill-prepared to manage the issues arising from deepening Chinese integration. As I have tried to show in my analysis, it was not anything that the Chinese SOEs did in Australia that was deemed illegal or even objectionable. It was what they were. Their very nature placed the Australian Government in an awkward position, where all responses, including taking no special actions to regulate them at all, bore costs. At the international level, the Bretton Woods institutions and their supplementary bodies are ill-equipped to deal with these problems. They were designed to manage the frictions between liberal economies, not between liberal and illiberal ones. Nonetheless, there is little appetite within the mainstreams of IPE or IR for seriously considering the changes to the liberal order, including real concessions on behalf of the established powers, that would enable a peaceful transition to this new order.

The best prospects for the grand negotiations between the established and rising powers being made without devolving to the use of force, and the for the next stage of transformation of the liberal order being peaceful and orderly appear when scholars are able to precisely define the interests of each party and to imagine new formations that do not fit neatly into the existing categories. That is, there is a particular need to develop theories that are well-suited not just to description and explanation, but also to imagining alternatives. This is not a standard measure of the goodness of a theory. Governmentality is valuable to me because it foregrounds contingency of formations. This makes it open to the possibility of new formations, and leaves room for imagining what these might be. There are other approaches that do this well, and some of these have been drawn on in this work, particularly critical feminist IPE. Imagining what the grand bargain between China and the liberal states might be has not been a task of this book, but I believe the analysis I have laid out enables a more fruitful conversation about how Australia and other countries might accept the new reality of Chinese financial integration by founding it in the idea that markets and other governmental arrangements are very radically open to change.

Reference

Swan, W. (2008, June 10). *A Remarkable Place at a Remarkable Time*. Speech to the China–Australia Chamber of Commerce, Beijing, Treasury. Available at http://ministers.treasury.gov.au/DisplayDocs.aspx?doc=speeches/2008/018.htm&pageID=010&min=wms&Year=2008&DocType=1. Accessed 2 Nov 2016.

Bibliography

ACCC. (2000). *Submission to the Productivity Commission Review of the Prices Surveillance Act 1983.* ACCC (Australian Competition and Consumer Commission). Available at http://www.pc.gov.au/inquiries/completed/prices-surveillance-act/submissions/sub010/sub010.pdf. Accessed 28 Oct 2016.

ACCC. (2007, November 8). *Public Competition Assessment: Rio Tinto plc—Proposed Acquisition of Alcan Inc.* ACCC (Australian Competition and Consumer Commission). Available at http://registers.accc.gov.au/content/item.phtml?itemId=803036&nodeId=664ca52c3b9c8ec4dd1b264cc6c64d-7c&fn=Rio%20Tinto%20plc%20-%20proposed%20acquisition%20of%20Alcan%20Inc%20-%208%20November%202007%20-%20bauxite,%20alumina,%20aluminium,%20.pdf. Accessed 3 Nov 2016.

ACCC. (2009, March 25). *Chinalco (Aluminium Corporation of China)—Proposed Acquisition of Interests in Rio Tinto Ltd.* Public Competition Assessment by ACCC. Available at http://registers.accc.gov.au/content/index.phtml/itemId/866064/fromItemId/751043. Accessed 30 Oct 2016.

Agamben, G. (2009). What Is an Apparatus? In *What Is an Apparatus? And Other Essays.* Stanford: Stanford University Press.

Ahall, L., & Borg, S. (2013). Predication, Presupposition and Subject-Positioning. In L. Shepherd (Ed.), *Critical Approaches to Security: An Introduction to Theories and Methods* (pp. 196–207). London and New York: Routledge.

Aitken, R. (2006). Performativity, Popular Finance and Security in the Global Political Economy. In M. de Goede (Ed.), *International Political Economy and Poststructural Politics* (pp. 77–96). New York: Palgrave Macmillan.

© The Editor(s) (if applicable) and The Author(s), under exclusive license to Springer Nature Switzerland AG 2019

M. Peters, *Regulating the Rise of China*, Studies in the Political Economy of Public Policy, https://doi.org/10.1007/978-3-030-05466-3

Albanese, T. (2008, October 2). *Consolidation and Diversity—Resources in the 21st Century.* Speech to the Melbourne Mining Club Business Lunch, Rio Tinto. Available at http://www.riotinto.com/documents/ReportsPublications/Consolidation_and_Diversity_TA_presentation_02Oct08.pdf. Accessed 3 Nov 2016.

Aradau, C., Lobo-Guerrero, L., & Van Münster, R. (2008). Security, Technologies of Risk, and the Political: Guest Editiors' Introduction. *Security Dialogue, 39*(2–3), 155–176.

Aradau, C., & Van Münster, R. (2008). Governing Terrorism Through Risk: Taking Precautions: (Un)Knowing the Future. *European Journal of International Relations, 13*(1), 89–115.

Arnold, D. (2000, November 2). *Labour's Economic Policy and the Competition State: A Social Democratic Critique of the Political Economy of the Third Way.* Paper presented at A Third Way and Beyond Conference, University of Sussex.

Attorney General's Department. (2008, May 13). *Budget Strategy and Outlook: Budget Paper No. 1; 2008–09.* Commonwealth of Australia, Attorney-General's Department. Available at http://budget.gov.au/2008-09/content/bp1/download/bp1.pdf. Accessed 4 Nov 2016.

Australian Financial Review. (2010, February 23). Fed: Swan Says Approved Energy Metals Takeover by China Entity. *Australian Financial Review.* Available at http://www.afr.com/news/politics/fedswan-says-approved-energy-metals-takeover-by-china-entity-20100223-ivzbi. Accessed 30 Oct 2016.

Australian Liberal and National Party Coalition. (2012). *Foreign Investment in Australian Agricultural Land and Agribusiness.* Discussion paper by Australian Liberal and National Party Coalition. Available at http://shared.liberal.org.au/Share/Foreign_investment_discussion_paper.pdf. Accessed 2 Nov 2016.

Bach, D., Newman, A. L., & Weber, S. (2006). The International Implications of China's Fledgling Regulatory State: From Product Maker to Rule Maker. *Political Economy, 11*(4), 499–518.

Bachrach, P., & Baratz, S. M. (1962). Two Faces of Power. *American Political Science Review, 56*(4), 947–952.

Barry, A., Osborne, T., & Rose, N. (Eds.). (1996). *Foucault and Political Reason: Liberalism, Neoliberalism and Rationalities of Government.* London: UCL Press.

Baumgartner, F. R., & Jones, B. D. (1993). *Agendas and Instability in American Politics.* Chicago: University of Chicago Press.

Beck, U. (1999). *World Risk Society.* Cambridge: Polity Press.

Beeson, M., Soko, M., & Yong, W. (2011). The New Resource Politics: Can Australia and South Africa Accomodate China? *International Affairs, 87*(6), 1365–1384.

Bell, H. F. (1976). Australian Government Policy in Relation to Foreign Investment. *The Australian Quarterly, 48*(1), 44–58.

Bentham, J. (1911). *Principles of Legislation* (R. Hildreth, Trans.). London: Kegan Paul, Trench, Trubner & Company.

Berg, C. (2012, March 15). Foreign Investment and the Whims of Politicians. *The Drum*. Available at http://www.abc.net.au/news/2012-03-13/berg-foreign-investment-and-the-whims-of-politicians/3886786. Accessed 21 Oct 2016.

Best, J. (2007). Why the Economy Is Often the Exception to Politics as Usual. *Theory Culture and Society, 24*(4), 87–109.

Best, J. (2008). Ambiguity, Uncertainty and Risk: Rethinking Indeterminacy. *International Political Sociology, 2*, 355–374.

Best, J., & Paterson, M. (Eds.). (2010). *Cultural Political Economy*. London: Routledge.

Boehm, E. A. (1979). *Twentieth Century Economic Development in Australia*. Melbourne: Longman Cheshire.

Bora, B. (1995). The Implications of Globalisation for Australian Foreign Investment Policy. In *Globalisation: Issues for Australia*. Canberra: Economic Planning Advisory Council, Australian Government Publishing Services.

Boughton, J. M. (2004). *The IMF and the Force of History: Ten Events and Ten Ideas That Have Shaped the Institution* (IMF Working Paper). Washington, DC.

Bowen, C. (2008a, April 23). *Government Looks to Increase Competition Across the Economy with Changes to Foreign Investment Rules*. Treasury. Available at http://ministers.treasury.gov.au/DisplayDocs.aspx?doc=pressreleases/2008/025.htm&pageID=003&min=ceb&Year=2008&DocType=0. Accessed 29 Oct 2016.

Bowen, C. (2008b, December 18). *Rudd Government Moves to Make Administrative Changes to Foreign Investment Review Process*. Treasury. Available at http://ministers.treasury.gov.au/DisplayDocs.aspx?doc=pressreleases/2008/107.htm&pageID=003&min=ceb&Year=2008&DocType=0. Accessed 29 Oct 2016.

Bowman, M., Gilligan, G., & O'Brien, J. (2014, February 13). *Foreign Investment Law and Policy in Australia: A Critical Analysis*. Paper presented at Centre for Law, Markets and Regulation, CIFR Symposium: Financial Market Development Stream, University of New South Wales School of Law.

Bream, R., Burgess, K., Saigol, L., & Dyer, G. (2008, February 2). Dawn Raid for Rio Tinto Stuns BHP. *Financial Times*. Available at https://www.ft.com/content/a51f903e-d09f-11dc-953a-0000779fd2ac. Accessed 20 Oct 2016.

Brereton, L. (2001). Australian Foreign Policy—A Labor Perspective. *Australian Journal of International Relations, 55*(3), 343–349.

Brown, W. (2003). Neo-liberalism and the End of Liberal Democracy. *Theory and Event, 7*(1). Project MUSE. https://doi.org/10.1353/tae.2003.0020.

Cai, C. (2006). Outward Foreign Investment Protection and the Effectiveness of Chinese BIT Practice. *Journal of World Investment and Trade, 7*(5), 621–652.

Clapton, W. (2011). Risk in International Relations. *International Relations, 25*(3), 280–295.

Cohen, M. D., March, J. G., & Olsen, J. P. (1972). A Garbage Can Model of Organizational Choice. *Administrative Science Quarterly, 17*(1), 1–25.

Collier, S. J. (2009). Topologies of Power: Foucault's Analysis of Political Government Beyond 'Governmentality'. *Theory Culture Society, 26*(6), 78–108.

Colmer, P. (2009). *Address from Patrick Colmer to the Australia China Investment Forum*. Delivered 24 September 2009. Speech published online by Stephen Kirchner at *Institutional Economics* After an FOI Application to the Australian Government. Available at http://www.institutional-economics.com/images/uploads/colmer.pdf. Accessed 30 Oct 2016.

Cook, M., & Thirlwell, M. (2008). *The Changing Global Financial Environment: Implications for Foreign Investment in Australia and China* (Lowy Institute Perspectives, Outcomes Report). Sydney: Lowy Institute for International Policy.

Costello, P. (2001a, April 23). *Foreign Investment Proposal—Shell Australia Investments Limited (Shell) Acquisition of Woodside Petroleum Limited (Woodside)*. Australian Government, The Treasury, Media Release 25. Available at http://ministers.treasury.gov.au/DisplayDocs.aspx?doc=pressreleases/2001/025.htm&pageID=003&min=phc&Year=&DocType=0. Accessed 28 Oct 2016.

Costello, P. (2001b, June 4). *Foreign Investment Approval of BHP Limited-Billiton Plc Merger*. Treasury. Available at http://ministers.treasury.gov.au/DisplayDocs.aspx?doc=pressreleases/2001/040.htm&pageID=003&min=phc&Year=2001&DocType=0. Accessed 30 Oct 2016.

Costello, P. (2009, February 18). Rio Feathers Should Stay in Our Nest. *Sydney Morning Herald*. Available at http://www.smh.com.au/federal-politics/rio-feathers-should-stay-in-our-nest-20090217-8a9a.html. Accessed 28 Oct 2016.

De Goede, M. (2005). *Virtue, Fortune, and Faith: A Genealogy of Finance*. Borderlines (Vol. 24). Minneapolis and London: University of Minnesota Press.

De Saussure, F. (1966 [1916]). *Course in General Linguistics* (C. Bally, A. Sechehaye, in collaboration with A. Riedlinger, Eds., & W. Baskin, Trans.). New York, Toronto, and London: McGraw-Hill Book.

Dean, M. (1994). *Critical and Effective Histories: Foucault's Methods and Historical Sociology*. London and New York: Routledge.

Dean, M. (1999). *Governmentality: Power and Rule in Modern Society*. London: Sage.

Deleuze, G. (1988 [1986]). *Foucault* (S. Hand, Trans.). Minneapolis: University of Minnesota Press.

Department of Defence. (2009). *Defending Australia in the Asia Pacific Century: Force 2030*. Australian Department of Defence. Available at http://www.defence.gov.au/CDG/Documents/defence_white_paper_2009.pdf. Accessed 5 Nov 2016.

Department of Treasury. (1999, July 20). *Australia's Experience with the Variable Deposit Requirement*. Treasury Economic Roundup, Australian Government, The Treasury. Available at http://archive.treasury.gov.au/contentitem.asp?-ContentID=193. Accessed 28 Oct 2016.

Department of Treasury. (2000). *Implication of the Globalisation of Financial Markets*. Submission to the House of Representatives, Standing Committee on Economics, Finance and Public Administration: Inquiry into the implications of the globalisation of international financial markets for macroeconomic policy and the operation of financial markets. Commonwealth of Australia, Canberra.

Di Giorgio, F. (2011, November 9). *Speech to the 3rd China Overseas Investment Fair*. China World Trade Centre. Foreign Investment Review Board. Available at http://firb.gov.au/about/news-media/Publications/pressreleases/2011/001.asp. Accessed 13 Sept 2015.

Dorling, P. (2011a, February 15). How BHP Boss Derailed Rio's $23.9b deal. *Sydney Morning Herald*. Available at http://www.smh.com.au/business/how-bhp-boss-derailed-rios-239b-deal-20110214-1atpp.html. Accessed 25 Oct 2016.

Dorling, P. (2011b, March 3). Labor's Secret Curb on China. *The Age*. Available at http://www.smh.com.au/national/labors-secret-curb-on-china-20110302-1bex9.html. Accessed 25 Oct 2016.

Dorling, P. (2011c, March 3). Laws 'Aimed to Limit' Chinese Investments. *Sydney Morning Herald*. Available at http://www.smh.com.au/business/laws-aimed-to-limit-chinese-investments-20110302-1bexm.html. Accessed 25 Oct 2016.

Dorling, P. (2011d, March 3). Australia Worried China Buying Up Resources. *Asia Sentinel*. Available at http://www.asiasentinel.com/econ-business/australia-worried-china-buying-up-resources/#frameId=appnext_widget&height=64. Accessed 25 Oct 2016.

Doty, R. L. (1993). Foreign Policy as Social Construction: A Post-positivist Analysis of U.S. Counterinsurgency Policy in the Phillipines. *International Studies Quarterly, 37*, 297–320.

Drysdale, P. (2011). A New Look at Chinese FDI in Australia. *China and World Economy, 19*(4), 54–73.

Drysdale, P., & Findlay, C. (2009). Chinese Foreign Direct Investment in Australia: Policy Issues for the Resource Sector. *China Economic Journal, 2*(2), 133–158.

Dupont, A., & Reckmeyer, W. J. (2012). Australia's National Security Priorities: Addressing Strategic Risk in a Globalised World. *Australian Journal of International Affairs, 66*(1), 34–51.

Eastley, T. (2013, June 5). Foreign Investment Rules Discriminate Against China: Colin Barnett. *ABC*, AM with Tony Eastley. http://www.abc.net.au/am/content/2013/s3774719.htm. Accessed 2 Nov 2016.

Economics Reference Committee. (2009). *Foreign Investment by State-Owned Entities.* The Senate of the Australian Federal Parliament. Australia: Commonwealth of Australia.

Economy, E. C. (2010). The Game Changer: Coping with China's Foreign Policy Revolution. *Foreign Affairs, 89*(6), 142–152.

Epstein, C. (2008). *The Power of Words in International Relations; The Birth of an Anti-Whaling Discourse.* Cambridge, MA and London: MIT Press.

Epstein, C. (2011). Who Speaks? Discourse, the Subject and the Study of Identity in International Politics. *European Journal of International Affairs, 17*(2), 327–350.

Ewald, F. (1991). Insurance and Risk. In G. Burchell, C. Gordon, & P. Miller (Eds.), *The Foucault Effect: Studies in Governmentality* (pp. 197–210). Chicago: University of Chicago Press.

Faeth, I. (2005). *Foreign Direct Investment in Australia: Determinants and Consequences.* Ph.D. thesis, submitted to the University of Melbourne.

Financial Times. (2005, February 10). Scrap the Firb. *Financial Times.* Available at http://www.ft.com/intl/cms/s/0/e94b0012-7b0d-11d9-a3ea-00000e2511c8.html#axzz3moMpLVTv. Accessed 21 Oct 2016.

FIRB. (1977). *Report 1977.* Canberra: Australian Government Publishing Services.

FIRB. (2006). *Annual Report 2004–2005.* Australian Government, Foreign Investment Review Board. Available at http://firb.gov.au/about/publication/annual-report-2004-2005/. Accessed 1 Nov 2016.

FIRB. (2007). *Annual Report 2005–2006.* Australian Government, Foreign Investment Review Board. Available at http://firb.gov.au/about/publication/annual-report-2005-2006/. Accessed 28 Oct 2016.

FIRB. (2008). *Annual Report 2006–2007.* Australian Government, Foreign Investment Review Board. Available at http://firb.gov.au/about/publication/annual-report-2006-2007/. Accessed 29 Oct 2016.

FIRB. (2009). *Annual Report 2007–2008.* Australian Government, Foreign Investment Review Board. Available at http://firb.gov.au/about/publication/annual-report-2007-2008/. Accessed 29 Oct 2016.

FIRB. (2010). *Annual Report 2008–2009.* Australian Government, Foreign Investment Review Board. Available at http://firb.gov.au/about/publication/annual-report-2008-2009/. Accessed 1 Nov 2016.

FIRB. (2011). *Annual Report 2009–2010.* Australian Government, Foreign Investment Review Board. Available at http://firb.gov.au/about/publication/annual-report-2009-2010/. Accessed 30 Oct 2016.

FIRB. (2013). *Annual Report 2011–2012.* Australian Government, Foreign Investment Review Board. Available at http://firb.gov.au/about/publication/annual-report-2011-2012/. Accessed 5 Nov 2016.

Fischer, F. (2003). *Reframing Public Policy: Discursive Politics and Deliberative Practices.* Oxford, New York: Oxford University Press.

Fischer, F., & Forester, J. (1993). *The Argumentative Turn in Policy Analysis: Editors' Introduction.* Durham and London: Duke University Press.

Flitton, D. (2010, December 6). Rudd the Butt of WikiLeaks Exposé. *Sydney Morning Herald.* Available at http://www.smh.com.au/technology/security/rudd-the-butt-of-wikileaks-expos-20101205-18lf2.html. Accessed 5 Nov 2016.

Foroohar, R. (2018, August 12). New Investment Rules Will Squeeze US–China Flows. *Financial Times.* Available at https://www.ft.com/content/607db618-9bbe-11e8-ab77-f854c65a4465. Accessed 3 Mar 2019.

Foucault, M. (1972 [1969]). *The Archaeology of Knowledge & The Discourse on Language* (A. Sheridan, Trans.). New York: Pantheon Books.

Foucault, M. (1977 [1975]). *Discipline and Punish: The Birth of the Prison* (A. Sheridan, Trans.). London, UK: Allen Lane, republished by Penguin Books.

Foucault, M. (1978 [1976]). *The History of Sexuality; Volume I: An Introduction* (R. Hurley, Trans.). New York: Pantheon Books.

Foucault, M. (1980a). Two Lectures. In C. Gordon (Ed.), *Power/Knowledge: Selected Interviews and Other Writings 1972–1977* (C. Gordon, L. Marshall, J. Mepham, & K. Soper, Trans., pp. 78–108). New York: Pantheon Books.

Foucault, M. (1980b). Truth and Power. In C. Gordon (Ed.), *Power/Knowledge: Selected Interviews and Other Writings 1972–1977* (C. Gordon, L. Marshall, J. Mepham, & K. Soper, Trans., pp. 109–133). Brighton: Harvester Press.

Foucault, M. (1981a). Questions of Method: An Interview with Michel Foucault. *Ideology and Consciousness, 8,* 3–14.

Foucault, M. (1981b). The Order of Discourse. In R. Young (Ed.), *Untying the Text: A Poststructuralist Reader* (pp. 48–78). Boston: Routledge and Kegan Paul.

Foucault, M. (1985). *History of Sexuality, Vol. 2: The Use of Pleasure* (R. Hurley, Trans.). New York: Pantheon.

Foucault, M. (1997). *Society Must Be Defended: Lectures at the Collège de France 1975–76* (D. Macey, Trans.). London: Penguin Books.

Foucault, M. (2001 [1961]). *Madness and Civilisation: A History of Insanity in the Age of Reason* (R. Howard, Trans.). London and New York: Routledge Classics.

Foucault, M. (2002 [1966]). *The Order of Things: An Archaeology of the Human Sciences* (anonymous, Trans.). London and New York: Routledge Classics.

Foucault, M. (2003 [1963]). *The Birth of the Clinic* (A. M. Sheridan, Trans.). London and New York: Routledge Classics.

Foucault, M. (2007). *Security, Territory, Population: Lectures at the Collège de France, 1977–78* (M. Senellart, Ed., & G. Burchell, Trans.). New York: Palgrave Macmillan.

Foucault, M. (2008). *The Birth of Biopolitics: Lectures at the Collège de France, 1978–79* (M. Senellart, Ed., & G. Burchell, Trans.). New York: Palgrave Macmillan.

Freed, J. (2008, February 5). Rio Just an Investment, Chinalco Says. *Sydney Morning Herald*. Available at http://www.smh.com.au/business/rio-just-an-investment-chinalco-says-20080204-1q25.html. Accessed 21 Oct 2016.

Garnaut, J. (2008, July 26). To the Brink of War. *Sydney Morning Herald*. Available at http://www.smh.com.au/business/to-the-brink-of-war-20080725-3l0e.html. Accessed 1 Nov 2016.

Giddens, A. (1994). Living in a Post-traditional Society. In U. Beck, A. Giddens, & S. Lash (Eds.), *Reflexive Modernisation: Politics, Tradition and Aesthetics in the Modern Social Order* (pp. 56–109). Stanford, CA: Stanford University Press.

Golding, G. (2010). *Australian Regulation of Foreign Direct Investment by Sovereign Wealth Funds and State-Owned Enterprises: Are Our Rules Right?* Thompson Reuters (Professional) Ltd. Australia. Available at http://sitesdev.thomsonreuters.com.au/journals/files/2010/09/ABLR38.4_Golding_article.pdf. Accessed 28 Oct 2016.

Golding, G. (2014). Australia's Experience with FDI by State Controlled Entities: A Move Towards Xenophobia or Greater Openness? *Seattle University Law Review, 37*, 533–580.

Golding, G., & Bassil, R. (2008). Australian Regulation of Investments by Sovereign Wealth Funds and Sovereign Owned Enterprises. In R. A. Fry, W. J. MicKibbon, & J. O'Brien (Eds.), *Sovereign Wealth: The Role of State Capital in the New Financial Order* (pp. 171–187). London: Imperial College Press.

Gordon, C. (1991). Governmental Rationality: An Introduction. In G. Burchell, C. Gordon, & P. Miller (Eds.), *The Foucault Effect: Studies in Governmentality* (pp. 1–52). Chicago: The University of Chicago Press.

Gramsci, A. (1971). *Selections from the Prison Notebooks*. London: Laurence and Wishart.

Griffin, P. (2010). Gender, Governance and the Global Political Economy. *Australian Journal of International of International Affairs, 64*(1), 86–104.

Guo, C. (2009, May 24). Playing Up the 'China Threat'. *Beijing Review*. Available at http://www.bjreview.com.cn/world/txt/2009-05/24/content_197174.htm. Accessed 25 Nov 2016.

Hajer, M. A. (1993). Discourse Coalitions and the Institutionalisation of Practice: The Case of Acid Rain in Britain. In F. Fischer & J. Forester

(Eds.), *The Argumentative Turn in Policy Analysis* (pp. 43–76). Durham and London: Duke University Press.

Hajer, M. A. (1995). *Politics of Environmental Discourse: Ecological Modernization and the Policy Process*. Oxford: Clarendon Press.

Halligan, J. (1997, April 5–8). *The Australian Civil Service System*. Paper presented at Civil Service Systems in Comparative Perspective, School of Public and Environmental Affairs, Indiana University.

Hansen, L. (2006). *Security as Practice: Discourse Analysis and the Bosnian War*. London and New York: Routledge.

Harper, I. (2001). In the National Interest. *Policy, 17*(1), 59–67.

Hassan, O. (2013). *Constructing America's Freedom Agenda for the Middle East: Democracy and Domination*. London and New York: Routledge.

Hayek, F. A. (1944). *The Road to Serfdom*. Chicago: University of Chicago Press.

Hendrischke, H., & Li, W. (2013, September 27). *Chinese Direct Investment in Australia—Characteristics and Integration*. Paper presented at 7th China Goes Global Conference, Bremen Germany. Available at http://www.chinagoesglobal.org/wp-content/uploads/2013/08/Hendrischke_and_Li_CHINESE_OUTBOUND_DIRECT_INVESTMENT_IN_AUSTRALIA.pdf. Accessed 1 Nov 2016.

Hewett, J. (2008, April 25). China Told by Rudd Government to Shelve Mine Deal. *The Australian*. Available at http://www.theaustralian.com.au/business/mining-energy/china-told-to-shelve-mine-deals/story-e6frg9df-1111116159135. Accessed 21 Oct 2016.

Howarth, D. (2010). Power, Discourse, and Policy: Articulating a Hegemony Approach to Critical Policy Studies. *Critical Policy Studies, 3*(3–4), 309–335.

Howarth, D., & Griggs, S. (2012). Poststructural Policy Analysis: Discourse, Hegemony, and Critical Explanation. In F. Fischer & H. Gottweis (Eds.), *The Argumentative Turn Revisited* (pp. 305–342). Durham: Duke University Press.

Hukkinen, J., Roe, E., & Rochlin, G. I. (1990). A Salt on the Land: A Narrative Analysis of the Controversy Over Irrigation-Related Salinity and Toxicity in California's San Joaquin Valley. *Policy Sciences, 23*(4), 307–329.

Hutchings, R. (2004, March 9). *Looking Over the Horizon: Assessing America's Strategic Challenges*. Address to Department of State/INR/World Affairs Council Seminar by the Chairman of the National Intelligence Council. Washington, DC: National Intelligence Council.

ITS Global. (2008, September 9). *Foreign Direct Investment in Australia—The Increasing Cost of Regulation*. ITS Global, Melbourne, Australia. Available at http://www.itsglobal.net/sites/default/files/itsglobal/Research%20Report%20on%20Foreign%20Direct%20Investment%20and%20the%20Increasing%20Cost%20of%20Regulation%20in%20Australia%20(2008).pdf. Accessed 21 Oct 2016.

Jaeger, H.-M. (2013). Governmentality's (Missing) International Dimension and the Promiscuity of German Neoliberalism. *Journal of International Relations and Development, 16*(1), 25–54.

Jessop, B. (2007). From Micro-powers to Governmentality: Foucault's Work on Statehood, State Formation, Statecraft and State Power. *Political Geography, 26*, 34–40.

Johnson, C. (1989). *The Labor Legacy: Curtin, Chifley, Whitlam, Hawke*. Sydney: Allen and Unwin.

Joseph, J. (2010). The Limits of Governmentality: Social Theory and the International. *European Journal of International Relations, 16*(2), 223–246.

Joyce, B. (2010, February 2). *Cth. Parliamentary Debates, 'Foreign Acquisition and Takeovers Amendment Bill 2009 Second Reading'*. Senate. Available at http://parlinfo.aph.gov.au/parlInfo/search/display/display.w3p;db=CHAMBER;id=chamber%2Fhansards%2F2010-02-02%2F0125;query=Id%3A%22chamber%2Fhansards%2F2010-02-02%2F0000%22. Accessed 2 Nov 2016.

Kalfadellis, P., Gray, J., & Freeman, S. (2006). *The 'National Interest' and the Screening of Foreign Direct Investment in Australia* (Working Paper 14/06). Department of Management Working Paper Series ISSN1327-5216. Australia: Monash University.

Kelly, P. (1992). *The End of Certainty*. Sydney: Allen and Unwin.

Kelly, P. (2006). *Howard's Decade: An Australian Foreign Policy Reappraisal*. Sydney: Lowy Institute for International Policy.

Kingdon, J. (1995). *Agendas, Alternatives, and Public Policies*. New York: HarperCollins.

Kirchner, S. (2008a). Capital Xenophobia II: FDI in Australia, SWFs, and the Rise of State Capitalism. Centre for Independent Studies. *CIS Policy Monograph, 88*, 1–20.

Kirchner, S. (2008b, November 27). Foreign Investment Flows Are Damned By Political Bias. *The Centre for Independent Studies*. Available at https://www.cis.org.au/commentary/articles/foreign-investment-flows-are-damned-by-political-bias. Accessed 21 Oct 2016.

Kirchner, S. (2009a, September 30). Canberra's Investment Confusion. *Wall Street Journal*. Available at http://www.wsj.com/articles/SB10001424052748704471504574442281091477054. Accessed 21 Oct 2009.

Kirchner, S. (2009b, August 5). FDI Liberalisation Falls Short. *The Centre for Independent Studies*. Available at https://www.cis.org.au/commentary/articles/fdi-liberalisation-falls-short. Accessed 21 Oct 2016.

Kirchner, S. (2010, February 19). More Inscrutable Than the Chinese. *The Australian*. Available at http://www.theaustralian.com.au/opinion/more-inscrutable-than-the-chinese/story-e6frg6zo-1225831954203. Accessed 21 Oct 2016.

Kirchner, S. (2012). The Kingdom and the Quarry: China, Australia, Fear and Greed. *Policy, 28*(2), 58–62 (Review Essay).

Kirchner, S. (2014). *Regulating Foreign Direct Investment in Australia*. Financial Services Institute of Australasia (Finsia). Available at https://www.finsia.com/docs/default-source/industry-reports-foreign-direct-investment/regulating-foreign-direct-investment-in-australia.pdf?sfvrsn=4. Accessed 21 Oct 2016.

Kloppers, M. (2009, November 18). *Australia's Resources in the World. The Annual Lowy Lecture*. The Lowy Institute. Available at http://www.lowyinstitute.org/publications/2009-lowy-lecture-australias-resources-world. Accessed 4 Nov 2016.

Laclau, E., & Mouffe, C. (1985). *Hegemony and Socialist Strategy: Towards a Radical Democratic Politics*. London and New York: Verso.

Laing, M., & Tindall, K. (2009). Australia: 'The Lucky Country' on a Knife Edge. In P. 't Hart & K. Tindall (Eds.), *Framing the Global Economic Downturn: Crisis Rhetoric and the Politics of Recession* (pp. 203–242). Canberra: ANU Press.

Larum, J. (2011). *Chinese Perspectives on Investing in Australia*. Analyses Papers Series. Sydney: Lowy Institute.

Leaver, R., & Ungerer, C. (2010). *A Natural Power: Challenges for Australia's Resources Diplomacy in Asia*. Canberra, Australia: The Australian Strategic Policy Institute. Available at https://www.aspi.org.au/publications/a-natural-power-challenges-for-australias-resources-diplomacy-in-asia/A_natural_power.pdf. Accessed 21 Oct 2016.

Lemke, T. (2002). Foucault, Governmentality, and Critique. *Rethinking Marxism, 14*(3), 49–64.

Ludlum, S. (2010, February 2). *Cth. Parliamentary Debates, 'Foreign Acquisition and Takeovers Amendment Bill 2009 Second Reading'*. Senate. Available at http://parlinfo.aph.gov.au/parlInfo/search/display/display.w3p;db=CHAMBER;id=chamber%2Fhansards%2F2010-02-02%2F0127;query=Id%3A%22chamber%2Fhansards%2F2010-02-02%2F0000%22. Accessed 2 Nov 2016.

Lynas Corporation. (2009, September 24). *CNMC Transaction Update*. Lynas Corporation Ltd. Available at http://www.asx.com.au/asxpdf/20090924/pdf/31kxjlh82hdnh3.pdf. Accessed 3 Nov 2016.

Makin, T. (2008). *Capital Xenophobia and the National Interest*. Australia's Open Investment Series Paper 8, Institute of Public Affairs. Available at https://www.ipa.org.au/library/publication/1229298839_document_makin.pdf. Accessed 21 Oct 2016.

Marchick, D. M., & Slaughter, M. J. (2008). *Global FDI Policy: Correcting a Protectionist Drift* (CSR No. 34). Council on Foreign Relations. Available at http://www.cfr.org/foreign-direct-investment/global-fdi-policy/p16503. Accessed 28 Oct 2016.

Megalogenis, G. (2012). *The Australian Moment.* Camberwell, VA: Viking Australia.

Menadue, J. (2004). *Speaker's Notes, 1974 Whitlam Cabinet Release.* Canberra: National Archives of Australia.

Merlingen, M. (2006). Foucault and World Politics: Promises and Challenges of Extending Governmentality Theory to the European and Beyond. *Millenium: Journal of International Studies, 35*(1), 181–196.

Miller, P., & Rose, N. (1990). Governing Economic Life. *Economy and Society, 19*(1), 1–31.

Milliken, J. (1999). The Study of Discourse in International Relations: A Critique of Research and Methods. *European Journal of International Relations, 5*(2), 225–254.

Ministry of Commerce (MOFCOM). (2004, October 1). Provisions on the Examination and Approval of Investment to Run Enterprises Abroad. *Order of the Ministry of Commerce of the People's Republic of China No. 16.* Ministry of Commerce, People's Republic of China. Available at http://en.pkulaw.cn/Display.aspx?LookType=3&Lib=law&Cgid=55499&Id=3726&SearchKeyword=&SearchCKeyword=&paycode=. Accessed 1 Nov 2016.

Ministry of Commerce (MOFCOM). (2011, September 16). *2010 Statistical Bulletin of China's Outward Foreign Direct Investment.* Ministry of Commerce, People's Republic of China. Available at http://english.mofcom.gov.cn/article/statistic/foreigninvestment/201109/20110907742320.shtml. Accessed 1 Nov 2016.

Murphy, M. (2008, May 27). *Issues in Focus: China's "Going Out" Investment Policy.* Freeman Briefing, Center for Strategic and International Studies. Available at https://csis-prod.s3.amazonaws.com/s3fs-public/legacy_files/files/publication/080527_freeman_briefing.pdf. Accessed 1 Nov 2016.

Murphy, J. (2009, November 4). *Speech to the Australia–China Investment Forum.* China World Trade Centre, Treasury. Available at http://archive.treasury.gov.au/contentitem.asp?ContentID=1656. Accessed 29 Oct 2016.

National Archives of Australia. (Unknown). *The Loans Affair, 1974–75—Fact Sheet 239.* National Archives of Australia. Available at http://www.naa.gov.au/collection/fact-sheets/fs239.aspx. Accessed 28 Oct 2016.

Nesadurai, H. E. S. (2009). Economic Surveillance as a New Mode of Regional Governance: Contested Knowledge and the Politics of Risk Management in East Asia. *Australian Journal of International Affairs, 63*(3), 361–375.

Novak, J. (2008). *Australia as a Destination for Foreign Capital.* Australia's Open Investment Series Paper 1. Institute of Public Affairs. Available at http://www.ipa.org.au/library/publication/1226637929_document_novak_destination_for_foreign_capital.pdf. Accessed 21 Oct 2016.

Oakes, L. (2009, August 22). Rudd Won't Listen to the Bullies. *Daily Telegraph*. Available at http://www.dailytelegraph.com.au/news/opinion/rudd-wont-listen-to-the-bullies/story-e6frezz0-1225764945490. Accessed 25 Nov 2016.

OECD. (2008a). *OECD Investment Policy Reviews: China 2008*. Organisation for Economic Cooperation and Development. Available at http://www.oecd.org/investment/investmentfordevelopment/41734421.pdf. Accessed 1 Nov 2016.

OECD. (2008b). *SOEs Operating Abroad: An Application of the OECD Guidelines on Corporate Governance of State-Owned Enterprises to the Crisis-Border Operations of SOEs*. Organisation for Economic Cooperation and Development. Available at http://www.oecd.org/daf/ca/corporategovernanceofstate-ownedenterprises/44215438.pdf. Accessed 5 Nov 2016.

O'Malley, P. (2008). Governmentality and Risk. In J. O. Zinn (Ed.), *Social Theories of Risk and Uncertainty: An Introduction* (pp. 52–75). Oxford, UK: Blackwell.

Ostrom, E. (1986). An Agenda for the Study of Institutions. *Public Choice, 48*(1), 3–25.

Ostrom, E. (1990). *Governing the Commons*. Cambridge: Cambridge University Press.

Paul, K. T. (2009). Discourse Analysis: An Exploration of Methodological Issues and a Call for Methodological Courage in the Field of Policy Analysis. *Critical Policy Studies, 3*(2), 240–253.

Phillips, M. (2016). *Digital Technology, Schools and Teachers Workplace Learning: Policy, Practice and Identity*. London: Palgrave Macmillan.

Pokarier, C. J. (2000). *Politics of Foreign Direct Investment in Australia, 1960–96*. Ph.D. thesis, submitted to the Australian National University.

Raby, G. (2010, September 28). *Australia and China: An Iron Ore Partnership for the Future*. Speech by Ambassador Dr. Geoff Raby at 10th China International Steel and Raw Materials Conference. Available at http://china.embassy.gov.au/files/bjng/100927_Ambassador%20Speech%20at%20Iron%20Ore%20Conference_Final.pdf. Accessed 4 Nov 2016.

Rae, J. (2008). *Counting the Cost of Regulation*. Australia's Open Investment Series Paper 2, Institute of Public Affairs. Available at https://www.ipa.org.au/library/publication/1229298979_document_rae.pdf. Accessed 21 Oct 2016.

Ravenhill, J. (2013). Resource Insecurity and International Institutions in the Asia-Pacific Region. *The Pacific Review, 26*(1), 39–64.

Ravenhill, J., & Jiang, Y. (2009). China's Move to Preferential Trading: A New Direction in China's Diplomacy. *Journal of Contemporary China, 18*(58), 27–46.

Reuters. (2009, May 5). China Rebuffs Australian Worries Over Military. *Reuters*. Available at http://uk.reuters.com/article/uk-china-australia-idUKTRE5441P020090505. Accessed 25 Nov 2016.

Ring, P. S., Bigley, G. A., D'Aunno, T., & Khanna, T. (2005). Perspectives on How Governments Matter. *Academy of Management Review, 30*(2), 306–320.

Roberts, D., & Tschang, C.-C. (2008, February 6). Why Chinalco's Buying into Rio Tinto. *Bloomberg Associated Press*. Available at http://www.bloomberg.com/news/articles/2008-02-05/why-chinalcos-buying-into-rio-tintobusinessweek-business-news-stock-market-and-financial-advice. Accessed 21 Oct 2016.

Roe, E. M. (1992). Applied Narrative Analysis: The Tangency of Literary Criticism, Social Science and Policy Analysis. *New Literary History, 22*(3), 555–581.

Röpke, W. (1954). Economic Order and International Law. *Recueil des Cours de lAcadémie de Droit International, 86*(2), 207–271.

Rose, P. (1999). *Powers of Freedom: Reframing Political Thought*. Cambridge, UK: Cambridge University Press.

Rudd, K. (2001). ANZUS and the 21st Century. *Australian Journal of International Affairs, 55*(2), 301–315.

Rudd, K. (2004, October 1). *The Three Pillars: Our Alliance with the US, Our Membership of the UN, and Comprehensive Engagement with Asia*. Foreign Policy Statement by the Australian Labor Party, Parliament of Australia. Available at http://parlinfo.aph.gov.au/parlInfo/search/display/display.w3p;query=Id%3A%22library%2Fpartypol%2FZMZD6%22. Accessed 4 Nov 2016.

Rudd, K. (2007, April 20). *The Rise of China and the Strategic Implications for U.S.–Australia Relations*. Address to the Brookings Institute, Washington, DC. Available at http://www.brookings.edu/~/media/events/2007/4/20china/20070420china.pdf. Accessed 4 Nov 2016.

Rudd, K. (2008a, January 21). *Building Australia's Economic Future*. Address to the Lord Mayor's Business Breakfast, Perth, Parliament of Australia. Available at http://parlinfo.aph.gov.au/parlInfo/download/media/pressrel/F9HP6/upload_binary/f9hp62.pdf;fileType=application%2Fpdf#search=%22media/pressrel/F9HP6%22. Accessed 4 Nov 2016.

Rudd, K. (2008b, February 18). Interview with Chris Uhlmann. *AM, ABC Radio*. Available at https://pmtranscripts.dpmc.gov.au/release/transcript-15765. Accessed 21 Oct 2016.

Rudd, K. (2008c, February 20). Interview with Jim Middleton. *Newshour, ABC Radio*. Department of the Prime Minister and Cabinet. Canberra. Available at http://pmtranscripts.dpmc.gov.au/release/transcript-15766. Accessed 4 Nov 2016.

Rudd, K. (2008d, March 26). *Advancing Australia's Global and Regional Economic Interests.* Address to the East Asia Forum in Conjunction with the Australian National University. Department of the Prime Minister and Cabinet. Available at https://pmtranscripts.dpmc.gov.au/release/transcript-15823. Accessed 4 Nov 2016.

Rudd, K. (2008e, March 31). *The Australia–US Alliance and Emerging Challenges in the Asia-Pacific Region.* Department of the Prime Minister and Cabinet. The Brookings Institution, Washington, DC. Available at https://pmtranscripts.dpmc.gov.au/release/transcript-15833. Accessed 4 Nov 2016.

Rudd, K. (2008f, April 7). *Australia and the UK—Global Partners in Shaping the Future Global Order.* Address to the London School of Economic, London. Department of the Prime Minister and Cabinet. Available at https://pmtranscripts.dpmc.gov.au/release/transcript-15847. Accessed 4 Nov 2016.

Rudd, K. (2008g, April 9). *A Conversation with China's Youth on the Future.* Department of the Prime Minister and Cabinet. Peking University, China. Available at http://pmtranscripts.dpmc.gov.au/release/transcript-15854. Accessed 4 Nov 2016.

Rudd, K. (2008h, June 4). *It's Time to Build an Asia Pacific Community.* Address to the Asia Society AustralAsia Centre, Sydney. Department of the Prime Minister and Cabinet. Available at http://pmtranscripts.dpmc.gov.au/release/transcript-15947. Accessed 4 Nov 2016.

Rudd, K. (2008i, June 5). Interview with Simon Beaumont. *Radio 6PR.* Department of the Prime Minister and Cabinet. Perth. Available at http://pmtranscripts.dpmc.gov.au/release/transcript-15949. Accessed 4 Nov 2016.

Rudd, K. (2008j, July 31). *Inaugural Tom Burns Memorial Lecture.* Department of the Prime Minister and Cabinet. Don Dunstan Foundation, Brisbane. Available at http://pmtranscripts.dpmc.gov.au/release/transcript-16040. Accessed 4 Nov 2016.

Rudd, K. (2008k, August 11). *Speech to a Dinner Hosted by Business Groups of Seoul.* Department of the Prime Minister and Cabinet. Seoul, Korea. Available at http://pmtranscripts.dpmc.gov.au/release/transcript-16059. Accessed 4 Nov 2016.

Rudd, K. (2008l, September 9). *Address to the RSL National Congress.* Department of the Prime Minister and Cabinet. Townsville. Available at http://pmtranscripts.dpmc.gov.au/release/transcript-16112. Accessed 4 Nov 2016.

Rudd, K. (2008m, October 3). *The Australian Response to the Global Financial Crisis.* Address to the Federal Labor Business Forum, Sofitel Wentworth Hotel, Sydney. Department of the Prime Minister and Cabinet. Available at http://pmtranscripts.dpmc.gov.au/release/transcript-16162. Accessed 4 Nov 2016.

Rudd, K. (2008n, November 20). *Towards an Asia-Pacific Century*. Speech to the Kokoda Foundation Australia–US Trilogy. Department of the Prime Minister and Cabinet. Available at http://pmtranscripts.dpmc.gov.au/release/transcript-16251. Accessed 4 Nov 2016.

Rudd, K. (2009a, February). The Global Financial Crisis. *The Monthly*. Available at https://www.themonthly.com.au/issue/2009/february/1319602475/kevin-rudd/global-financial-crisis. Accessed 3 Nov 2016.

Rudd, K. (2009b). *Managing Global and Regional Interdependence: The Future of the G20 and an Asia Pacific Community*. Paper dated 12 March 2009, developed for publication in *Foreign Affairs* but not published, posted online by *The Age*. Available at http://www.theage.com.au/ed_docs/rudd-speech-G20.pdf. Accessed 4 Nov 2016.

Rudd, K. (2009c, August 20). *Joint Press Conference with New Zealand Prime Minister John Key*. Department of the Prime Minister and Cabinet. Canberra. Available at http://pmtranscripts.dpmc.gov.au/release/transcript-16766. Accessed 4 Nov 2016.

Rudd, K. (2009d, December 4). *Address to the Asia Pacific Community Conference*. Department of the Prime Minister and Cabinet. Sydney. Available at http://pmtranscripts.dpmc.gov.au/release/transcript-16952. Accessed 4 Nov 2016.

Rudd, K. (2010a, April 23). *Australia and China in the World*. The 70th George E. Morrison Lecture, Australian National University, Canberra. Available at https://www.youtube.com/watch?v=EzLvsnWPDm0. Accessed 4 Nov 2016.

Rudd, K. (2010b, May 27). *Prime Minister Speech to the Opening Conference of the National Security College*. Australian National University, Canberra. Department of the Prime Minister and Cabinet. Available at http://pmtranscripts.dpmc.gov.au/release/transcript-17311. Accessed 4 Nov 2016.

Rudd, K. (2015, October 29). Asia Need Its Own EU More Than Ever. *Europe's World*. Available at http://europesworld.org/2015/10/29/asia-needs-eu-ever/#.VlFhc7zwxE7. Accessed 4 Nov 2016.

Rudd, K., & Gillard, J. (2008, February 18). *Joint Press Conference with Julia Gillard*. Deputy Prime Minister, Hume, ACT. Department of the Prime Minister and Cabinet. Available at http://pmtranscripts.dpmc.gov.au/release/transcript-15764. Accessed 4 Nov 2016.

Rural and Regional Affairs and Transport References Committee. (2013). *Foreign Investment and the National Interest*. Senate: Commonwealth of Australia.

Sabatier, P. A. (1988). An Advocacy Coalition Framework of Policy Change and the Role of Policy-Oriented Learning Therein. *Policy Sciences, 21*(2), 129–168.

Sabatier, P. A. (1999). Introduction: The Need for Better Theories. In P. A. Sabatier (Ed.), *Theories of the Policy Process* (pp. 3–18). Boulder, CO: Westview Press.

Sabatier, P. A., & Jenkins-Smith, H. C. (1993). *Policy Change and Learning: An Advocacy Coalition Approach*. Boulder, CO: Westview Press.

Sadleir, C. (2007). *On the Frontier: Australia's Policy Approach to Foreign Direct Investment 1968–2004 as a Case Study in Globalisation, National Public Policy and Public Administration*. Ph.D. thesis, submitted to the University of Canberra.

Sadleir, C., & Mahoney, G. (2009). Institutional Challenges and Response in Regulating Foreign Direct Investment to Australia. *Economic Society of Australia Economic Papers Series, 28*(4), 337–345.

Salidjanova, N. (2011, March 30). *Going Out: An Overview of China's Outward Foreign Direct Investment* (USCC Research Report). U.S.–China Economic and Security Review Commission. Available at http://www.uscc.gov/sites/default/files/Research/GoingOut.pdf. Accessed 1 Nov 2016.

Sanyal, K. (no date). *Australia's Foreign Investment Policy*. Parliament of Australia. Available at http://www.aph.gov.au/About_Parliament/Parliamentary_Departments/Parliamentary_Library/pubs/BriefingBook44p/AustForeignInvest. Accessed 29 Oct 2016.

Scharpf, F. W. (1997). *Games Real Actors Play: Actor-Centered Institutionalism in Policy Research*. Boulder, CO: Westview Press.

Schattschneider, E. E. (1960). *The Semisovereign People: A Realist's View of Democracy in America*. Hinsdale, IL: The Dryden Press.

Schedvin, C. (1992). *In Reserve: Central Banking in Australia, 1945–75*. Sydney: Macmillan.

Schenk, C. R. (1998). The Origins of the Eurodollar Market in London: 1955–1963. *Explorations in Economic History, 35*(2), 221–238.

Sherry, N. (2009, October 23). *Foreign Investment Decision—Felix Resources (Yanzhou to Acquire Felix Resources)*. Treasury. Available at http://ministers.treasury.gov.au/DisplayDocs.aspx?doc=pressreleases/2009/081.htm&pageID=003&min=njsa&Year=2009&DocType=0. Accessed 30 Oct 2016.

Sherry, N. (2010, April 24). *Government Tightens Foreign Investment Rules for Residential Housing*. Treasury. Available at http://ministers.treasury.gov.au/DisplayDocs.aspx?doc=pressreleases/2010/074.htm&pageID=003&min=njsa&Year=&DocType=0. Accessed 29 Oct 2016.

Simmel, G. (1990 [1900]). *The Philosophy of Money* (T. Bottomore & D. Frisby, Trans.). New York: Routledge.

Smith, G. (1979). Minerals and Energy. In A. Patience & B. Head (Eds.), *From Whitlam to Fraser: Reform and Reaction in Australian Politics* (pp. 233–250). Melbourne: Oxford University Press.

Smith, S. (2007, December 3). *Speech Notes for the Annual Diplomatic Corps Christmas Party*. Department of Foreign Affairs and Trade. Available at http://foreignminister.gov.au/speeches/2007/071203.html. Accessed 4 Nov 2016.

Solberg, T. (2012). *Mine Your Own Business! Economic Interdependence and Sino-Australian Relations in the 2000s*. Masters thesis, submitted to Department of Political Science, Oslo University, 6 June 2012. Available at https://www.duo.uio.no/handle/10852/36979. Accessed 1 Nov 2016.

Spike Peterson, V. (2003). *A Critical Rewriting of Global Political Economy; Integrating Reproductive, Productive and Virtual Economies*. London and New York: Routledge.

Springell, S. (2012). *The Theory of Policy Alignment: An Ideational Explanation for Change*. Ph.D. thesis, submitted to UNSW.

Springer, S. (2012). Neoliberalism as Discourse: Between Foucauldian Political Economy and Marxian Poststructuralism. *Critical Discourse Studies, 9*(2), 133–147.

Steel Guru. (2008, May 16). *Iron Ore Price Negotiations—CISA to Boycott Spot Sale by Rio*. Steel Guru. Available at http://steelguru.com/steel/iron-ore-price-negotiations-8211-cisa-to-boycott-spot-sale-by-rio-/45654#tag. Accessed 1 Nov 2016.

Stevens, M. (2009, October 2). Political, Not Skin, Pigment Is the Issue. *The Australian*. Available at http://www.theaustralian.com.au/archive/business/political-not-skin-pigment-is-the-issue/story-e6frg9lx-1225781834339. Accessed 30 Oct 2016.

Stewart, F. (1975, May 22). *Cth. Parliamentary Debates, 'Foreign Takeovers Bill 1975 Second Reading'*. House of Representatives. Available at http://parlinfo.aph.gov.au/parlInfo/genpdf/hansard80/hansardr80/1975-05-22/0134/hansard_frag.pdf;fileType=application%2Fpdf. Accessed 28 Oct 2016.

Stone, D. (2002). *The Policy Paradox: The Art of Political Decision Making* (3rd ed.). New York: W. W. Norton.

Stuart, N. (2010). *Rudd's Way: November 2007–June 2010*. Melbourne: Scribe.

Sturgess, G. (1996). Virtual Government: What Will Remain Inside the Public Sector? *Australian Journal of Public Administration, 55*(3), 59–73.

Swan, W. (2007a, December 5). *Press Conference*. Sydney, Treasury. Available at http://ministers.treasury.gov.au/DisplayDocs.aspx?doc=transcripts/2007/001.htm&pageID=011&min=wms&Year=2007&DocType=2. Accessed 2 Nov 2016.

Swan, W. (2007b, December 7). Interview with Fran Kelly. *Radio National*. Treasury. Available at http://ministers.treasury.gov.au/DisplayDocs.aspx?doc=transcripts/2007/002.htm&pageID=011&min=wms&Year=2007&DocType=2. Accessed 2 Nov 2016.

Swan, W. (2007c, 14 December). Interview with Stephen Long. *PM, ABC Radio.* Treasury. Available at http://ministers.treasury.gov.au/DisplayDocs.aspx?doc=transcripts/2007/003.htm&pageID=011&min=wms&Year=2007&DocType=2. Accessed 2 Nov 2016.

Swan, W. (2008a, January 4). Interview with Alexandra Kirk. *AM Program with Eleanor Hall.* Treasury. Available at http://ministers.treasury.gov.au/DisplayDocs.aspx?doc=transcripts/2008/001.htm&pageID=011&min=wms&Year=2008&DocType=2. Accessed 2 Nov 2016.

Swan, W. with Rudd, K. (2008b, February 5). *Joint Press Conference with the Prime Minister.* Parliament House, Canberra, Treasury. Available at http://ministers.treasury.gov.au/DisplayDocs.aspx?doc=transcripts/2008/023.htm&pageID=011&min=wms&Year=2008&DocType=2. Accessed 2 Nov 2016.

Swan, W. (2008c, February 17). *Government Improves Transparency of Foreign Investment Screening Process.* Treasury. Available at http://ministers.treasury.gov.au/DisplayDocs.aspx?doc=pressreleases/2008/009.htm&pageID=003&min=wms&Year=&DocType. Accessed 21 Oct 2016.

Swan, W. (2008d, February 17). *Press Conference: Waterfront Palace.* Brisbane, Treasury. Available at http://ministers.treasury.gov.au/DisplayDocs.aspx?doc=transcripts/2008/028.htm&pageID=011&min=wms&Year=2008&DocType=2. Accessed 30 Oct 2016.

Swan, W. (2008e, February 18). *Cth. Parliamentary Debates.* House of Representatives. Available at http://parlinfo.aph.gov.au/parlInfo/search/display/display.w3p;adv=yes;orderBy=customrank;page=0;query=Date%3A18%2F02%2F2008%20QUESTIONS%20WITHOUT%20NOTICE%20Foreign%20Investment;rec=0;resCount=Default. Accessed 21 Oct 2016.

Swan, W. (2008f, February 18). Interview with Marius Benson. *ABC News Radio.* Treasury. Available at http://ministers.treasury.gov.au/DisplayDocs.aspx?doc=transcripts/2008/029.htm&pageID=011&min=wms&Year=2008&DocType=2. Accessed 2 Nov 2016.

Swan, W. (2008g, June 2). *Ministerial Statement on Financial Stability.* Address to the House of Representatives. Treasury. Available at http://ministers.treasury.gov.au/DisplayDocs.aspx?doc=speeches/2008/016.htm&pageID=010&min=wms&Year=2008&DocType=1. Accessed 3 Nov 2016.

Swan, W. (2008h, June 6). *Australia in the Global Economy.* Address to the Australian Business Forum. Treasury. Available at http://ministers.treasury.gov.au/DisplayDocs.aspx?doc=speeches/2008/017.htm&pageID=010&min=wms&Year=2008&DocType=1. Accessed 2 Nov 2016.

Swan, W. (2008i, June 10). *A Remarkable Place at a Remarkable Time.* Speech to the China–Australia Chamber of Commerce, Beijing, Treasury. Available at http://ministers.treasury.gov.au/DisplayDocs.aspx?doc=speeches/2008/018.htm&pageID=010&min=wms&Year=2008&DocType=1. Accessed 2 Nov 2016.

Swan, W. (2008j, June 11). *A Modern Relationship with China.* Speech to the Central Party School, Communist Party of China, Treasury. Available at http://ministers.treasury.gov.au/DisplayDocs.aspx?doc=speeches/2008/019.htm&pageID=010&min=wms&Year=2008&DocType=1. Accessed 1 Nov 2016.

Swan, W. (2008k, July 4). *Australia, China, and This Asian Century.* Speech to the Australia–China Business Council, Melbourne, Treasury. Available at http://ministers.treasury.gov.au/DisplayDocs.aspx?doc=speeches/2008/021.htm&pageID=010&min=wms&Year=2008&DocType=1. Accessed 3 Nov 2016.

Swan. W. (2008l, August 24). *Chinalco's Acquisition of Shares in Rio Tinto.* Treasury. Available at http://ministers.treasury.gov.au/DisplayDocs.aspx?doc=pressreleases/2008/094.htm&pageID=003&min=wms&Year=2008&DocType=0. Accessed 30 Oct 2016.

Swan, W. (2008m, September 21). *Foreign Investment Approval: Sinosteel's Interests in Murchison Metals Ltd.* Treasury. Available at http://ministers.treasury.gov.au/DisplayDocs.aspx?doc=pressreleases/2008/100.htm&pageID=003&min=wms&Year=&DocType=0. Accessed 30 Oct 2016.

Swan, W. (2009a, January 23). *The Global Recession and Australia's Future Economy.* Address to the New York Investment Community, New York, Treasury. Available at http://ministers.treasury.gov.au/DisplayDocs.aspx?doc=speeches/2009/002.htm&pageID=005&min=wms&Year=&DocType=. Accessed 3 Nov 2016.

Swan, W. (2009b, February 12). *Amendments to Foreign Acquisitions and Takeovers Act.* Treasury. Available at http://ministers.treasury.gov.au/DisplayDocs.aspx?doc=pressreleases/2009/017.htm&pageID=003&min=wms&Year=&DocType=0. Accessed 29 Oct 2016.

Swan, W. (2009c, March 27). *Foreign Investment (Rejection of China Minmetals Application to Acquire OZ Metals).* Treasury. Available at http://ministers.treasury.gov.au/DisplayDocs.aspx?doc=pressreleases/2009/029.htm&pageID=003&min=wms&Year=2009&DocType=0. Accessed 30 Oct 2016.

Swan, W. (2009d, March 31). *Foreign Investment Decision (Hunan Valin Iron and Steel Group to Acquire Shareholding in Fortescue Metals).* Treasury. Available at http://ministers.treasury.gov.au/DisplayDocs.aspx?doc=pressreleases/2009/032.htm&pageID=003&min=wms&Year=2009&DocType=0. Accessed 30 Oct 2016.

Swan, W. (2009e, April 23). *Foreign Investment Decision (China Minmetals to Acquire Assets of OZ Minerals).* Available at http://ministers.treasury.gov.au/DisplayDocs.aspx?doc=pressreleases/2009/043.htm&pageID=003&min=wms&Year=&DocType=0. Accessed 30 Oct 2016.

Swan, W. (2009f, May 8). *Foreign Investment Decision (Ansteel to Acquire Gindalbie Metals)*. Treasury. Available at http://ministers.treasury.gov.au/DisplayDocs.aspx?doc=pressreleases/2009/045.htm&pageID=003&min=wms&Year=2009&DocType=0. Accessed 30 Oct 2016.

Swan, W. (2009g, May 26). *Resources and Recovery*. Address to Minerals Week 2009, Hyatt Hotel, Canberra, Treasury. Available at http://ministers.treasury.gov.au/DisplayDocs.aspx?doc=speeches/2009/012.htm&pageID=010&min=wms&Year=2009&DocType=1. Accessed 3 Nov 2016.

Swan, W. (2009h, August 4). *Reforming Australia's Foreign Investment Framework*. Treasury. Available at http://ministers.treasury.gov.au/DisplayDocs.aspx?doc=pressreleases/2009/089.htm&pageID=003&min=wms&Year=2009&DocType=0. Accessed 3 Nov 2016.

Swan, W. (2009i, December 10). *Address to the Global Foundation*. Brisbane, Treasury. Available at http://ministers.treasury.gov.au/DisplayDocs.aspx?doc=speeches/2009/033.htm&pageID=005&min=wms&Year=&DocType=. Accessed 21 Oct 2016.

Sydney Morning Herald. (2009, September 24). China Fails in Another Bid for Resources Firm. *Sydney Morning Herald*. Available at http://www.smh.com.au/business/china-fails-in-another-bid-for-resources-firm-20090924-g4l7.html. Accessed 30 Oct 2016.

Sydney Morning Herald. (2010, April 5). Abbott Demands Schools, Batts Inquiry. *Sydney Morning Herald*. Available at http://www.smh.com.au/national/abbott-demands-schools-batts-inquiry-20100405-rmqh.html. Accessed 30 Oct 2016.

't Hart, P., & Tindall, K. (Eds). (2009). Understanding Crisis Exploitation: Leadership, Rhetoric and Framing Contests in Response to the Economic Meltdown. In *Framing the Global Economic Downturn: Crisis Rhetoric and the Politics of Recession* (pp. 21–42). Canberra: ANU Press.

Tan, R. (1999). *Foreign Direct Investments Flows to and From China* (PASCN Discussion Paper No. 99–21). Makati: PASCN.

Tellmann, U. (2007). *The Economy and the Foundation of the Modern Body Politic: Keynes and Malthus as Political Philosophers*. Ph.D. dissertation, presented to Cornell University.

Tellmann, U. (2009). Foucault and the Invisible Economy. *Foucault Studies, 6*, 5–24.

Tellmann, U. (2011). The Economic Beyond Governmentality: The Limits of Conduct. In U. Bröckling, S. Krausmann, & T. Lemke (Eds.), *Governmentality: Current Issues and Future Challenges* (pp. 285–303). New York and Oxon, UK: Routledge.

Thirlwell, M., & Shearer, A. (2008). *Is the Foreign Investment Review Board Acting Fairly?* Paper 4 in the Australia's Open Investment Future Series. Sydney: Lowy Institute for International Policy.

Thurbon, E. (2016). *Developmental Mindset: The Revival of Financial Activism in South Korea*. Ithaca and London: Cornell University Press.

Tubiliwicz, C. (2010). The 2009 Defence White Paper and the Rudd Government's Response to China's Rise. *Australian Journal of Political Science, 45*(1), 149–157.

Ungerer, C. (2007). The "Middle Power" Concept in Australian Foreign Policy. *Australian Journal of Politics and History, 53*(4), 538–551.

Uren, D. (2012). *The Kingdom and the Quarry: China, Australia, Fear and Greed*. Collingwood, VIC: Black Inc.

Vivoda, V. (2009). China Challenges Global Capitalism. *Australian Journal of International Affairs, 63*(1), 22–40.

Voss, H., Buckley, P. J., & Cross, A. R. (2009). An Assessment of the Effects of Institutional Change on Chinese Outward Direct Investment Activity. In A. Alon, J. Chang, M. Fetscherin, C. Letterman, & J. R. McIntyre (Eds.), *China Rules: Globalisation and Political Transformation* (pp. 135–165). Houndmills, Basingstoke, and Hampshire, UK: Palgrave Macmillan.

Waddell, A. P. (2015). Cooperation and Integration Among Australia's National Security Community. *Studies in Intelligence, 59*(3), 25–34.

Weber, M. (1978 [1921–1922]). *Economy and Society: An Outline of Interpretive Sociology* (G. Roth & C. Wittich, Eds.). Berkeley: University of California Press.

Weeks, D. (2011). An East Asian Security Community: Japan, Australia and Resources as 'Security'. *Australian Journal of International Affairs, 65*(1), 61–80.

Weldes, J. (1996). *Constructing National Interests: The United States and the Cuban Missile Crisis*. Minneapolis and London: University of Minnesota Press.

Wesley, M. (2012). Australia's Foreign Policy Machinery. In J. Cotton & J. Ravenhill (Eds.), *Middle Power Dreaming: Australia in World Affair: 2006–2010* (pp. 261–272). Melbourne: Oxford University Press.

White, H. (2009, May 21). *The Defence White Paper*. Blake Dawson Lecture Series. Speech at the Australian National University. Available at https://www.youtube.com/watch?v=2U6sN5taOpc. Accessed 3 Nov 2016.

Whitlam, G. (1985). *The Whitlam Government 1972–1975*. Melbourne: Penguin.

Whitwell, G. (1986). *The Treasury Line*. Sydney: Allen and Unwin.

Wilson, J. D. (2011). Resource Nationalism or Resource Liberalism? Explaining Australia's Approach to Chinese Investment in Its Minerals Sector. *Australian Journal of International Affairs, 65* (3), 283–304.

Wilson, J. D. (2012). Chinese Resource Security Policies and the Restructuring of the Asia-Pacific Iron Ore Market. *Resources Policy, 37*(3), 331–339.

Wines, M. (2009, June 2). Australia, Nourishing China's Economic Engine, Questions Ties. *New York Times*. Available at http://www.nytimes.com/2009/06/03/world/asia/03australia.html. Accessed 2 Nov 2016.

Xenaphon, N. (2010, February 2). *Cth. Parliamentary Debates, 'Foreign Acquisition and Takeovers Amendment Bill 2009 Second Reading'*. Senate. Available at http://parlinfo.aph.gov.au/parlInfo/search/display/display.w3p;db=CHAMBER;id=chamber%2Fhansards%2F2010-02-02%2F0126;query=Id%3A%22chamber%2Fhansards%2F2010-02-02%2F0000%22. Accessed 2 Nov 2016.

Yanow, D. (1996). *How Does a Policy Mean? Interpreting Policy and Organisational Actions*. Washington, DC: Georgetown University Press.

Zhang, J. (2009, April 2). Chinese Seek to Invest, Not to Dominate. *The Australian*. Available at http://www.theaustralian.com.au/story/0,25197,25276296-5017272,00.html. Accessed 21 Oct 2016.

Zhang, X. (2009, May 6). China's Military Modernisation 'No Threat'. *China Daily*. Available at http://www.chinadaily.com.cn/china/2009-05/06/content_7747203.htm. Accessed 25 Nov 2016.

Zhang, Y. (2003). *China's Emerging Global Business: Political Economy and Institutional Investigations*. Basingstoke, UK: Palgrave Macmillan.

Zoellick, R. (2005, December). Whither China: From Membership to Responsibility? *The National Bureau of Asian Research, 16*(4), 5–14.

Index

© The Editor(s) (if applicable) and The Author(s), under exclusive license to Springer Nature Switzerland AG 2019

M. Peters, *Regulating the Rise of China*, Studies in the Political Economy of Public Policy, https://doi.org/10.1007/978-3-030-05466-3

FSC
www.fsc.org
MIX
Papier | Fördert
gute Waldnutzung
FSC® C083411

Kolibri 360 GmbH
Ferdinand-Jühlke-Straße 7
99095 Erfurt, Deutschland
produktsicherheit@kolibri360.de